Kubrick's Hope

Discovering Optimism
from 2001 *to* Eyes Wide Shut

Julian Rice

The Scarecrow Press, Inc.
Lanham, Maryland • Toronto • Plymouth, UK
2008

SCARECROW PRESS, INC.

Published in the United States of America
by Scarecrow Press, Inc.
A wholly owned subsidiary of
The Rowman & Littlefield Publishing Group, Inc.
4501 Forbes Boulevard, Suite 200, Lanham, Maryland 20706
www.scarecrowpress.com

Estover Road
Plymouth PL6 7PY
United Kingdom

British Library Cataloguing in Publication Information Available

Library of Congress Cataloging-in-Publication Data

Rice, Julian, 1940–
   Kubrick's hope : discovering optimism, from 2001 to Eyes wide shut / Julian Rice.
      p. cm.
   Includes bibliographical references and index.
   ISBN-13: 978-0-8108-6206-7 (hardback : alk. paper)
   ISBN-10: 0-8108-6206-9 (hardback : alk. paper)
   eISBN-13: 978-0-8108-6224-1
   eISBN-10: 0-8108-6224-7
   1. Kubrick, Stanley—Criticism and interpretation. I. Title.
   PN1998.3.K83R53 2008
   791.4302'33092—dc22
                              2008020816

♾ ™ The paper used in this publication meets the minimum requirements of
American National Standard for Information Sciences—Permanence of
Paper for Printed Library Materials, ANSI/NISO Z39.48-1992.
Manufactured in the United States of America.

For Carol, Robyn, Noah, and Dave

Contents

~

Acknowledgments

Gene D. Phillips, S.J., a friend of Stanley Kubrick, generously conveyed personal impressions of the man and insightful perspectives on his work. My colleague, Mike Budd, educated me in film theory and encouraged me to devote my retirement to a field well known to him, and relatively new to me. Jim Rice offered a sensitive and stimulating take on *The Shining* at an early stage. At Scarecrow Press, Stephen Ryan, senior editor for Arts & Literature, and Jessica McCleary, production editor, were patient and perceptive guides. Copyeditor Sarah Soliz and proofreader Rima Weinberg thoughtfully improved my prose.

Permissions to quote from the following works have been granted by their publishers:

2001: A Space Odyssey by Arthur Clarke, copyright © 1968 by Arthur C. Clarke and Polaris Productions, Inc. Used by permission of Dutton Signet, a division of Penguin Group (USA), Inc.

A Clockwork Orange by Anthony Burgess, copyright © 1963 by W. W. Norton & Company, Inc. Used by permission of W. W. Norton & Company, Inc.

Dream Story by Arthur Schnitzler. Translated by J. M. Q. Davies. Introduction by Frederic Raphael. London: Penguin, 1999. Used by permission of Penguin Group, UK.

Kubrick: The Definitive Edition by Michel Ciment, translated by Gilbert Adair. English translation copyright © 1982 by HarperCollins Ltd. Reprinted by permission of Faber and Faber, Inc., an affiliate of Farrar, Straus and Giroux, LLC.

"Paint It, Black." Written by Mick Jagger and Keith Richards. © 1966 Renewed ABKCO Music, Ltd. www.abkco.com.

The Persecution and Assassination of Jean-Paul Marat as Performed by the Inmates of the Asylum of Charenton under the Direction of the Marquis de Sade by Peter Weiss. Translated by Geoffrey Skelton. Verse adaptation by Adrian Mitchell. New York: Atheneum, 1966. Used by permission of the Estate of Geoffrey Skelton.

"*Playboy* Interview: Stanley Kubrick," September 1968. Used by permission of *Playboy* magazine.

Film Criticism granted permission to quote parts of my essay, "Kubrick's *Barry Lyndon*: Like Father, Like Son." *Film Criticism* 1 (Summer 1976): 9–14.

CHAPTER ONE

~

Introduction

Michiko Kakutani's initial *New York Times* review of *Eyes Wide Shut* echoed two longstanding assumptions about Stanley Kubrick: that his "one great theme" was "the intrusion of irrationality upon the orderly, daylit world of logic and reason," and that the characters in his films collectively personify his "deeply cynical view of the world, his unaccommodated view of mankind as a species driven to distraction by greed and violence and its own delusions."[1] Kubrick's confidence in humanity's future may have been tentative, but he was not without hope. Beginning with *2001* his films express a consistent philosophy, a belief in the redemptive value of self-knowledge based on particular thematic sources that he recommended to his screenwriters and alluded to in the films, both verbally and visually.

Kubrick's one great theme was not irrationality but rather "Discovery," the name of the spaceship that carries humanity to transcendence at the end of *2001*. In response to an interviewer's query about how she felt "as a person and as an actor" when he demanded more takes than other directors, Nicole Kidman replied,

> I think you go through all sorts of emotions. Stanley always was waiting for something to happen. He wasn't as interested in "naturalistic" acting as he was in something that, for whatever reason, surprised him or piqued his interest. That's when he'd go . . . "Now we're onto something." He was always interested in exploring things. There was no right and wrong in relation to making a film, a performance. It wasn't about, "This is the right way and this is the wrong way to do it." It was about exploring all facets of it so that he could go

into the editing room and edit it. That's what I perceive it as. So as an actor, as long as you relaxed into the situation and said, "Okay, I'm going to go with this," then it was the most wonderful experience because you didn't ever walk away from the set feeling "Oh, I didn't get it. If only he'd let me have one more, we would've discovered something." He made sure he discovered all there was to discover in the material.[2]

Kubrick himself may never have felt that one could ever discover all there was to discover, but in any artistic endeavor it was necessary to push the limits as far as possible. This aesthetic method corresponded to his metaphysical philosophy in 2001: "I find it very exciting to have a semi-logical belief that there's a great deal to the universe we don't understand, and that there is an intelligence of an incredible magnitude outside the earth. It's something I've become more and more interested in. I find it a very exciting and satisfying hope."[3] In another interview he reflected on how the likely course of human evolution will eventually enable us to transcend our present biological and subsequent machine stages to become "pure spirit"; that this drive expressed the "yearnings of mass psychology"; and that "all myths have a kind of psychological similarity to each other, [of] the hero going somehow into the underworld, or the over-world, and encountering dangers and terrifying experiences [before] he re-emerges in some god-like form, or some greatly improved human form."[4]

Kubrick's idealistic belief in the power of myth extended to the closely related worlds of fairy tale and dream. Much of his thinking on "the hero" derived from Joseph Campbell's *The Hero with a Thousand Faces*, just as his belief in the therapeutic value of storytelling was influenced by Bruno Bettelheim's *The Uses of Enchantment*. Bettelheim emphasized that stories not only "give full recognition of difficulties" but also "suggest solutions." A story improves the individual by allowing him to elude his own worst instincts and can have a collective effect by suggesting "what the next steps in the development toward a higher humanity might be."[5] Kubrick's agreement with Bettelheim was highlighted when his cowriter on *The Shining*, Diane Johnson, suggested that the five-year-old protagonist should die at the end. She reported that Kubrick immediately replied, "Oh, no, impossible."[6] Danny's survival implies the wisdom to be gained from fairy tale terror, both for him and for the spectator. After *Dr. Strangelove* and beginning with *2001*, each Kubrick film leaves its audience with new possibilities for self-reflection and growth. Though Alex (*A Clockwork Orange*) and Barry (*Barry Lyndon*) ultimately fail, Danny, Joker (*Full Metal Jacket*), and Alice (*Eyes Wide Shut*) recall *2001*'s Star Child and embody Kubrick's hope.

The use of color to express complexity of mind and to affirmatively coun-terpoint brutality also distinguishes the post-*Strangelove* films. As Sergei Eisenstein (an early theoretical influence on Kubrick) predicted, color in se-rious cinema would become integral to meaning.[7] But unlike some of Eisen-stein's ideological descendants, Kubrick did not consider beauty to be a var-nish for social injustice. Regardless of the regressive tendencies he forthrightly depicted, the aesthetic beauty of the frame, the sound, and the pacing always provided a holistic vision that critics like Kakutani missed. Kubrick's films include ugliness, but the films themselves are never ugly. As his friend and cowriter on *Full Metal Jacket*, Michael Herr, put it, "You could always count on Stanley every time to vote for Beauty over Content, since he didn't think of them as two separate things."[8] An elaborated version of this feeling was put forth in an early *Sight & Sound* piece on *2001* by Don Daniels:

> Kubrick's film is a study of various capacities for consciousness, an attempt to suggest through spectacle the possibilities and limitations of the powers of Mind for perception, intellection, and feeling. As a spectacle, the film appeals to the sensuous, emotional, non-rational appetites of the mind with an imme-diacy and power that argue for the potential value of such faculties, an argu-ment proposed even as human powers for perception come to seem finite in-deed in the spectacle's rendering of the immensity of space.[9]

Pauline Kael attempted to turn the beautiful surface of *Barry Lyndon* against its director, "the Kubrick message [is] that people are disgusting, but things are lovely,"[10] but Kubrick had established the merging of his aesthetic and philosophical intent in *2001*, and he sustained that belief in every sub-sequent film over a twenty-year period. In response to critics who felt that *2001* needed more words, he replied,

> There are only 46 minutes of dialogue scenes in the film, and 113 of non-dialogue. There are certain areas of feeling and reality—or unreality or inner-most yearning, whatever you want to call it—which are notably inaccessible to words. Music can get into these areas. Painting can get into them. Non-verbal forms of expression can. But words are a terrible straitjacket. It's interesting how many prisoners of that straitjacket resent its being loosened or taken off. There's a side to the human personality that somehow senses that wherever the cosmic truth may lie, it doesn't lie in A, B, C, D. It lies somewhere in the mys-terious, unknowable aspects of thought and life and experience. Man has al-ways responded to it. Religion, mythology, allegories—it's always been one of the most responsive chords in man.[11]

However, in another post-2001 interview, Kubrick seemed to regret giving the impression that he had slighted language and admitted that "the crucial things that generally come out of a film are still word-delivered. There's emotion backing them up, you've got the actors generating feeling, etc. It's basically word communication."[12] Herr reflected on how "language was one of the most striking things about his films," from the "crushingly banal" dialogue of *Lolita*, to the "manic bursts of frantic satire" in *Strangelove*, to the "yarblocko nadsat" of *A Clockwork Orange*, to the "brutal locutions of the eighteenth century" in *Barry Lyndon*, to the "vicious comedy" of *Full Metal Jacket*: "He was highly sensitive to literary mise-en-scene, completely susceptible to it . . . he was drawn to his projects as much by the writing of the source material as by anything else. . . . He was always looking for the visual equivalents of what he'd first responded to when he'd read the book, and in that way paying real respect to it."[13]

The kind of thoughtful skepticism toward language that Kubrick expressed could only come from someone who immersed himself in books. Many of his friends and associates were awestruck by the breadth of his knowledge and the catholicity of his taste. In an extensive *New York Times* postmortem of memories and tributes, Keir Dullea recalled dinners at Kubrick's home where he invited people "from all walks of life and different disciplines—art historians, authors and intellectuals. And he was as informed as anybody about their disciplines. He was like an onion—every layer you peeled off there were two new ones to be exposed."[14] And responding to the query—what books did he like?—on an Internet Kubrick news group, his daughter, Katharina Kubrick Hobbs, replied, "My immediate reaction was, is he kidding? But not to be unfair; war, history, film, science fiction, science fact, art, photography, novels, biography, thrillers, scandal, espionage, dictionaries in every language, politics, natural history, birds, dogs, cats, not to mention every periodical printed I reckon. etc. etc. etc."[15]

Herr wittily capsulized innumerable similar reports by observing that "Stanley never went to college; he was only a stunningly accomplished autodidact, one of those people we may hear about but rarely meet, the almost but not quite legendary Man On Whom Nothing Is Lost."[16] And Kubrick's enthusiastically urgent response to his reading helps to explain why his received ideas were inseparable from the spectator's emotional reception of his films. Herr reported on how Kubrick sent an unabridged twelve-volume set of *The Golden Bough* to John Calley, an executive at Warner Bros., in the early 1970s. He "bugged him every couple of weeks for a year about reading it." Calley finally begged off as politely as he could: "Stanley, I've got a studio to run. I don't have time to read mythology." "It isn't mythology, John," Stanley said. "It's your life."[17]

Considering the seriousness that Kubrick accorded to ideas, Kubrick criticism would benefit by delving into his thematic sources more deeply. Like any storyteller, Kubrick understood the world by synthesizing thoughts and feelings from other narrators he admired. Some presented acknowledged myth, while others created narratives viewed variously as probable or proven fact, or as imaginative fiction, depending on the readers who received them. These forebears in turn acknowledged the ones who impressed them, and by following up a few biographical clues we can develop a sense of Kubrick's thinking before and after *2001*.

In an interview appended to the DVD version of *Eyes Wide Shut*, Steven Spielberg said that each film was different in genre, period, and artistic "risk," and that Kubrick "never made the same picture twice."[18] Nevertheless, in the work of any great storyteller we can expect to find persistent themes that comprise a narrative vision. Certainly, film directors are not exclusively influenced by cinema, and thematic inspirations are often (if not usually) absorbed from written works. If we know that Kubrick read works by Robert Ardrey and Joseph Campbell while he was filming *2001: A Space Odyssey*, or that he read Freud and Bettelheim while working on *The Shining*, we ought to take a look at those sources in trying to understand the films. In *The Shining*, the Bettelheim connection is manifest in references to classical fairy tales, such as "Hansel and Gretel," "The Three Little Pigs," and "Snow White," and to contemporary children's mythology from Snoopy and Mickey Mouse to Bugs Bunny and the Road Runner. In *Eyes Wide Shut* allusions are made to Ovid, Greek myth, and *The Nutcracker*. Considering Kubrick's reputation for detail, it is helpful to consider why he chose certain allusions, even particular cartoon figures, from so many well-known alternatives.

The best currently published information on Kubrick's source material is *The Encyclopedia of Stanley Kubrick* by Gene D. Phillips and Rodney Hill. It is indispensable for anyone reflecting seriously on a Kubrick film. For example, if you suspect that the *2001* anthem, *Also Sprach Zarathustra* by Richard Strauss, has thematic importance, Phillips and Hill quote the composer explaining why he took his title from Nietzsche's most well-known book: "I mean to convey in music an idea of the evolution of the human from its origin through the various phases of development, religious, as well as scientific, up to Nietzsche's idea of the Ubermensch." Strauss's statement provides dimension for anyone considering a theme central not only to *2001* but to all of Kubrick's work. The authors then add an interesting perception of their own when they write that the composer's "vacillation" between the major and minor keys "suggests man's perplexity at the sublime mysteries of nature."[19] As encyclopedists, Phillips and Hill do not integrate their entries into extensive studies of particular films, but they have provided invaluable information that will ensure the vitality of Kubrick scholarship for decades to come.

My book draws upon Phillips and Hill and supplements their contribution by offering additional contexts that they did not. My overall point of view coincides with their "attempt to combat the negative perception" that Kubrick despaired over the biological atavism and cultural "desensitizing" that currently threatens humanity.[20] Unlike them, however, I am not providing a reference book for other critics so much as interpretations of my own based on close readings of the films. My comments are linked to cinematic details that can be seen and heard by anyone with access to the DVDs, giving readers an opportunity to re-view specific scenes, notice things they may have missed, and think about them in a new way, whether or not they agree with me. Those wishing to refresh their memory of a film's whole story will find detailed synopses just before the bibliography.

Kubrick told Eric Nordern that he did not have a specific moral message in *Dr. Strangelove*, because "the only real immorality is that which endangers the species, and the only absolute evil [is] that which threatens its annihilation."[21] His films, as John Hofsess sums them up, express the "constant struggle between creative and destructive impulses, between people who build and people who destroy."[22] Kubrick's relativism is consistent with postmodern thought, and several book-length studies have cast him as a postmodernist par excellence. In his study of *Eyes Wide Shut*, Michel Chion eschews assertions of meaning in favor of detailed descriptions of symmetry, shooting, sound, and dialogue. Accordingly, he believes that Kubrick too rejected conscious themes and chose instead to present "signifiers without anything signified." Still, he does venture to say that the film is about a paranoid relationship to the world and that it is "just like life."[23]

Sometimes Chion goes to absurd lengths to safely describe rather than dogmatically interpret. For example, he notes that when a prostitute gives Bill the shocking news that the woman he almost had sex with has AIDS, her blank facial expression proves a key point: that Kubrick uses words strictly to unfold plot and that visual "images become what does not reveal."[24] Since everyone knows that film images and words are often at odds, and that separate viewers may read different emotions into a facial expression, Chion's excessive generality seems an overly strenuous attempt to remind his readers that he has been well schooled in the manners of deconstruction.

However, like many another postmodern critic, Chion goes on to offer personal interpretations after initially announcing that he will not. In a previous book, *Kubrick's Cinema Odyssey*, he offers a solution to *Eyes Wide Shut's* cryptically concluding line where Alice says that in an uncertain world all she and her husband can do is lovingly "fuck." This, he avers, deliberately evokes *2001's* Star Child because a male child will surely come from their union. Moreover, the whole film has been shot from that child's point of view: the "camera takes the position [of the Star Child] waiting to be embodied, who is floating in the air and roving through life on earth," where he "witnesses multiple possibilities of union and birth, and finds [himself] catapulted into a cosmic space full of matrices." Chion acknowledges the source of this maternal space as *The Tibetan Book of the Dead*, which explicitly influences the film when Bill sees his party mask on Alice's pillow. The mask foreshadows the "magical child," who wishes to replace him, because "an unborn male child is always jealous of the man who impregnates his mother."[25]

In spite of his stated refusal to interpret, Chion defensively supports this interpretation by citing the camera's tracking past a baby stroller in the toy store and connecting it to Alice's last "declaration."[26] In his *Eyes Wide Shut* book, published one year later, Chion may have been advised to fend off the charge of sexism by not forecasting the unborn child as a boy: "For this hypothetical new human being life will project itself as a new adventure, a path of light always drawing us on, even beyond our awakened vision, to another infinite country."[27] Again, almost recklessly venturing toward conviction, he refers back to Victor Ziegler's party where Bill met some models who introduced the theme of cosmic adventure by inviting Bill to follow them to the "rainbow's end."

Chion seems to deliberately ignore the identity of the speakers, the context of the line, and the connotations of the words. For Gayle and Nuala the rainbow's end is the ecstasy of a threesome rather than a spiritual transformation, and the proverbial end of the rainbow is a nonexistent pot of gold. Perhaps Chion indulges in wild flights of speculation to show contempt for traditionally argued criticism. He seems to be saying: "Film texts can't be understood because our reactions are too subjective, so let's really be subjective and spin our own fictions, making them as far removed as possible from the text, so we can't be accused of limiting its ambiguity to our private experience." And so the postmodern pendulum swings from one extreme to the other—from no interpretation to an interpretation that leaves the story behind, setting up the critic as a storyteller inspired by another story, rather than an interpreter of that story.

In another highly influential book, *Kubrick: Inside a Film Artist's Maze*, Thomas Allen Nelson uses postmodern terminology to describe a "cinema of contingency . . . erected on the epistemologically shifting sands of total probability and zero signification." Such works result "whenever there is a loss of faith in teleological explanations, in the inviolability of institutionalized meaning, in the rational structures of nature, or the signifying power of mind and language."[28] For Nelson, the catastrophic end of *Dr. Strangelove*, and the greatest danger to humanity, comes not from atavistic drives but from "fictional constructs" that refuse to acknowledge humanity's subjection to chance and the illusions of language. He implies that Kubrick himself realizes that even his own films are such constructs, and that therefore they have little or no curative power: "All that a film aesthetic based on a recognition of contingency can do is speculate" about planetary destruction and "in the absence of a total belief system be true to itself in the act of creation."[29] Having displayed his allegiance to postmodern doctrine, Nelson feels free to apply the same ideal of subjective integrity to his own prose and proceeds to offer thoughtful and intricate readings of individual films and particular scenes in the old style of New Critical explication.

Though many of these tour de force interpretations justify the definition of criticism as an art equal to the arts it treats, most are short on context. In his introduction Nelson veers briefly from the "zero-signification" line to state that Kubrick drew upon the ideas of Carl Jung and Joseph Campbell in order to "explore the universal (i.e., generic) myths and archetypes of both our shared cultural experience and our collective unconscious."[30] The parenthetical use of "generic" is apparently offered to absolve him from subscribing to anything "universal," but the statement is ultimately irrelevant since the rest of his book makes no reference to Campbell and only one to Jung (when he writes that Joker of *Full Metal Jacket* "resembles Jung's negative archetype of the Trickster," all reason and no feeling).[31]

Here and there, however, Nelson offers enriching contextual insights, such as the following comment on *Barry Lyndon*:

> In a brief satirical episode in which Barry bribes an unnamed nobleman by purchasing works from his art collection at exorbitant prices, he fatuously admires [a] painting . . . by one "Ludovico Corday, a disciple of Alexandro Allori, [that] shows 'The Adoration of the Magi.'" Kubrick, I suspect, creates an inside joke here. . . . No such painter as "Ludovico Corday" ever existed [but] the first name, of course, recalls *Clockwork*'s Ludovico Technique (which, then, de-

codes as an imitative and mechanical art). Alexandro Allori (1535–1607) was known for his mediocre anatomical drawings; he was an imitator of the Florentine school, which means that the fictional "Ludovico" is an imitator of an imitator. Moreover the Adoration of the Magi has to be one of the most hackneyed and overdone subjects in the history of art.[32]

Nelson's "decoding" violates postmodern practice, but the passage demonstrates the kind of creative interpretation that generates further interpretation and keeps a work alive. For example, Nelson's note might suggest that the scene reflects Barry's attempt to ape the nobility, an analogy Nelson does not make, or even further, that it exposes the primitive stupidity of the society he aspires to join.

While Nelson (despite the requisite disclaimers) concentrates primarily on theme and character, Luis M. García Mainar, author of *Narrative and Stylistic Patterns in the Films of Stanley Kubrick*, seems to emancipate himself from deconstruction by reinventing the wheel, as if the new criticism he proposes had not already been born over a half a century ago: "The liberation from the constraints of the paradigmatic theoretical systems of poststructuralism might open the door to a new criticism that would focus on the details of the text rather than on a complex theoretical world disconnected from the experience of viewing."[33] But Mainar then tries to please every manner of reader by throwing these details into a stew of deconstructive and Marxist clichés.

Calling attention to his seemingly neutral point of view as a Spanish scholar, Mainar feels obligated to inform his European readers about "American" culture, especially in regard to *Full Metal Jacket*. In several cases he seems to be as uninformed about America, especially during the Vietnam era, as a newly arrived alien might be about life on earth. For example, the opening music of the film "emphasizes the popular [!] nature of the Vietnam War, singing about the common experience for every [!] American boy in those days of being called up";[34] the word "heartbreakers" (Cowboy's name for his platoon) is "typical of American pop songs [that] associate love with violence and competition among teenage boys";[35] and the Mickey Mouse song at the end represents Joker's individuality being "engulfed by the cultural background of the United States, which has led the country to the war in the first place."[36]

Mainar ventures onto even shakier ground when he finds that Joker's execution of the sniper "reconciles the act of killing with America's constant justification for its presence in Vietnam."[37] The statement seems to confuse "America's" motive with that of Kubrick and Herr. Did the writers have Joker perform a mercy killing to justify the war? Certainly, they gave Joker no lines to that effect. In a still more strenuous attempt to simultaneously please both postmodernists and historicists, Mainar asserts that *2001* concludes in the alien room because it is making a political statement: "The final scene destroys [conventional] subjectivity by laying bare the system of formal design necessary to create it. The last scene is, therefore, revealed to be ideologically subversive"[38] because its "artificiality of narration" breaks "the ideological illusion" that sustains the status quo.[39]

Mainar pushes the postmodernist envelope even further when he observes that Kubrick's inclusion of double-time marches in the basic training sequence of *Full Metal Jacket* has an anti-elitist purpose because they "reject subjectivity, since they show us a group from which it is difficult to isolate individuals." The audience therefore receives the beneficial opportunity to identify with a group rather than an individual, allowing them "a panoramic point of view from which we perceive the various ideologies without committing ourselves to any of them."[40] At the end of that film Mainar finds a way to combine advocacies in a final bon mot: "The discovery that the enemy is feminine suggests the identification of Joker with the woman, but the act of killing her means the victory of American masculinity over Vietnamese femininity."[41]

However much he bends and stretches to hew to a postmodernist line, Mainar at least attempts to augment his readings with general ideas about history, psychology, and culture. Randy Rasmussen's book, *Stanley Kubrick: Seven Films Analyzed*, consists almost entirely of detailed interpretations devoid of context. Occasionally this isolated form of reading results in naive oblivion to satire. When Joker delivers his zinger, "It's a Jungian thing," to an officer who is as lacking in erudition as Buck Turgidson is in *Dr. Strangelove*, Rasmussen seems to miss the joke: "Joker tries in vain to justify his mixed symbolism ["Born to Kill" *and* the peace symbol] with a reference to the psychological theories of Carl Jung" only to discover that the colonel "imposes his own preferred metaphors on the debate."[42] Commenting later on a TV interview that highlights Joker's sarcastic wit, Rasmussen solemnly infers that Joker removed his helmet but retained his peace button because he is "pandering to his own civilian sensibilities by concealing his more aggressive urges."[43] Sometimes Rasmussen assigns conscious thoughts to characters that they could not possibly have had. When Joker shoots the sniper and another marine says "Hardcore, man. Fucking hardcore," Rasmussen comments, "In marine-speak, astonishment and admiration can be expressed in language commonly associated with pornography. Most of Joker's comrades realize that he has faced and overcome one of the most obscene challenges of combat."[44]

Rasmussen's jump from associating "hardcore" with pornography to the grunts' incredibly sensitive realization that killing is obscene may seem a stretch, but it can't hold a candle to the critical leaps that Geoffrey Cocks takes in his book, *The Wolf at the Door: Stanley Kubrick, History, and the Holocaust.* Cocks conveys a fascinating account of the impact of the Holocaust on American consciousness, but then constructs an obsessed Kubrick persona based on a generalized assumption of Jewish paranoia. As a historian rather than a critic, Cocks extrapolates a context he believes Kubrick shares, but his application of this context to the film is often strained. The opening paragraph of his book is worth quoting:

> Stanley Kubrick's last film, *Eyes Wide Shut* (1999), contains a scene in which actor Tom Cruise is elbowed off the sidewalk by a group of college boys. In a block packed with parked cars, the one Cruise falls against is a blue Mercedes-Benz. The choice of car against which Cruise stumbles—surely unnoticed by almost everyone who has seen the film—is anything but an idle one. As we shall see, a Mercedes the color of blue is a carefully chosen reference to the Austrian novella on which *Eyes Wide Shut* is based. And, like many details small and large in Kubrick's films, it is an example of the way in which Kubrick communicates meaning. And that it is a Mercedes is, moreover, a typically tiny clue to Kubrickian passions and concerns directly related, though most often indirectly expressed, about the problematic nature of human existence in general and the dangerous history of the modern world in particular.[45]

For Cocks the fact that the Mercedes is German and that the main character "stumbles" against it is a eureka moment. That it is blue has an even more bizarre connection to his notion that the color blue in *The Shining* augments the horror of that film because bodies retrieved from the gas chambers had turned blue.[46] *The Shining*'s Holocaust referent is enhanced, Cocks believes, by the use of the color yellow because the Germans forced Jews to wear yellow stars, and because they associated yellow with typhus, a disease they believed to be rampant among Jews.[47] Moreover, since the most notorious of concentration camps, Auschwitz, was in Poland, the bat Wendy wields when she knocks Jack down the stairs bears the signature of a Polish American baseball player:

> Since the Holocaust was the greatest horror of our or perhaps any time, it is buried [everywhere in the modern psyche and in Kubrick's films where] the deepest . . . traces of it are especially rare, odd, and difficult to detect. . . . If one looks closely, one can see that the baseball bat with which Wendy slugs Jack bears the signature of Carl Yastrzemski. . . . It is likely that Yastrzemski was

chosen since he was the only baseball star in the 1970s of Polish extraction. This connects his repeatedly displayed name with the musical references to Poland [the score by the Polish composer Penderecki] as the geographical location of the Nazi Final Solution.[48]

Many of Cocks's interpretations are supported by his assumption that Kubrick betrays his obsession most by unconsciously concealing it. One of the more interesting of these subliminal adaptations concerns Jack Nicholson's recital from "The Three Little Pigs" as he breaks down the bathroom door to chop up his wife and son with an ax: "Little pigs, little pigs, / Let me come in. / Not by the hair on your chinny chin chin. / Then I'll huff and I'll puff, / And I'll blow your house in." Cocks believes that Kubrick adapted these words from Disney's version of the story because he consciously or unconsciously remembered that Disney's original drawings of the wolf portrayed him as a Jewish peddler:[49]

> The wolf disguises himself as a "Fuller Brush Man" trying to work his way through college in order to trick the pigs into letting him in. The character in question is a caricature of a Jewish peddler as well as of the more recent American upward educational mobility of Jews. The only human being portrayed in "Three Little Pigs" thus gave the young Kubrick a short primer in contemporary American anti-Semitism. The wolf wears a disguise comprised of a long nose, black beard, small round glasses with green lenses, a small, flat, round cap, and a long coat. On the soundtrack is Yiddish fiddle music. In the original version, the wolf speaks in a "Jewish" voice and accent.[50]

Of course, this would make the Jewish wolf the perpetrator rather than the victim, but Cocks wants to say that Kubrick is associating all horror with some variant of anti-Semitism and that anti-Semitism is the basis not only of his concept of horror in *The Shining* but of an all-encompassing paranoia that is the major feature of his films.

The most interesting thing about Cocks's book is his attention to a pre- and post-Holocaust context of horrific hatred that has strongly impacted the consciousness of Jew and Gentile alike, most probably Kubrick as an artist, and most obviously Cocks as a thoughtful human being and historian. But his attempt to reduce every detail of Kubrick's art to this single obsession has resulted in the interpretive absurdities just quoted. Cocks is so fixated on Jewish paranoia, per se, that he misses the power of humor in Kubrick's overall response to the presence of evil in the world. You don't have to be Jewish to appreciate one of Kubrick's favorite jokes, and madness in great literature and film is, unfortunately, not limited to any particular group of haters in any particular time and place. Michael Herr recalled how much Kubrick enjoyed William Burroughs's line, "'A paranoid-schizophrenic is a guy who just found out what's going on' . . . 'Wait a minute wait a minute . . . I've gotta write that down. . . . What is it they say, Michael: What one has thought so often, but never said so well?'"[51] Kubrick deliberately employed humor to portray humanity's flaws and foibles, not simply as an educated person aware of man's inhumanity to man before and after the Holocaust, and not simply to show that being open-minded is a safer way to proceed than the coherent "totalizations" postmoderns deplore.

As part of their reluctance to offer strong interpretations, postmodern critics often refrain from examining contexts or sources that might structure meaning. Cocks goes to the opposite extreme by piling up more speculative history and psychology than the films can bear. An alternative approach might allude to a stated rather than an unconscious source. In Kubrick's 1962 version of the *Dr. Strangelove* script, written before cowriter Terry Southern signed on, the title was preceded by "Nardac Blefuscu Presents" and followed by "A Macro-Galaxy-Meteor Picture."[52] In the first book of Jonathan Swift's *Gulliver's Travels*, the shipwrecked narrator is held captive by a race of mini-people who have created absurd divisions among themselves, and between themselves and a neighboring nation. The Lilliputian emperor has banished all who break their eggs on the big end to "Blefuscu," because he is of the faction that breaks their eggs on the small end. In an effort to win his freedom Gulliver attaches threads to each ship of an invading Blefuscuian fleet and ends the war by drawing them in to Lilliput. For saving his country, the emperor bestows the coveted title "Nardac" upon Gulliver, though still refusing to set him free. Later, jealous courtiers plot Gulliver's death, whereupon he escapes to Blefuscu, whose king, grateful that Gulliver did not agree to reduce his nation to a Lilliputian colony, harbors him until he can arrange an escape by sea that eventually returns him to England.[53]

Kubrick's juxtaposition of the Lilliputian title "Nardac" to "Blefuscu," Lilliput's enemy, suggests political neutrality. The end of the working title, "A Macro-Galaxy-Meteor Picture," probably meant that the film (like its source novel, Peter George's *Red Alert*) would be narrated by a perplexed alien imagining how the earth's most advanced species had managed to cremate every living thing on their planet. The other explicit Swift reference in the script is "Laputa," the name of the Russian ICBM complex, Major Kong's initial target. In Book III of the *Travels*, Gulliver finds himself on a flying island populated by brilliant scientists, mathematicians, and astronomers. Wrapped up in the pleasures of their intellectual pursuits and at the same time filled with anxiety over unlikely problems their inventions will solve, the Laputans maintain practical necessities by exploiting and intimidating Balnibarbi, the land over which they perpetually hover. The King of Laputa has several options for quelling potential revolts: He can let Laputa remain motionless above Balnibarbi to starve and sicken the inhabitants by depriving them of sun and rain; he can destroy large numbers of people and buildings by hurling down huge stones; and, finally (going nuclear), he can drop his whole island on top of them to achieve total destruction.

This option, however, would be a last resort. By destroying Balnibarbi altogether, Laputa would suffer economically from no longer being able to exploit its property interests there and, most tellingly, because they might annihilate themselves: "If [the target city] abound in high Spires or Pillars of Stone, a sudden Fall might endanger the Bottom or under Surface of [Laputa], which, although it consists as I have said, of one entire Adamant two hundred Yards thick, might happen to crack by too great a shock, or burst by approaching too near the Fires from the Houses below."[54] Since Laputa's power depends on its superior technology, and the word is also the Spanish word for "whore," Kubrick uses the reference to underscore the film's ironic disparity between the complexity of human intellect and its persistently primitive use.

According to Herr, Kubrick "dug Swift,"[55] and the director's statement of satiric purpose in *Strangelove* reflects that of the Anglican dean: "A satirist is someone who has a very skeptical, pessimistic view of human nature, but who still has the optimism to make some sort of joke out of it. However brutal the joke might be."[56] In *The Mysterious Stranger*, set in 1590, Mark Twain had his under-terrestrial persona, Satan, produce a hologram of human history evincing the "progress" of arms: "Cain did his murder with a club; the Hebrews did their murders with javelins and swords; the Greeks and Romans added protective armor . . . and the Christian has added guns." His fictive audience, less prepared to be cynical than that of *Dr. Strangelove* and *2001*, is horrified by futuristic images of "slaughters more terrible in their destruction of life, more devastating in their engines of war, than any we had seen." Then Satan adds prophetically that from Cain on, killing has been "the chiefest ambition of the human race. . . . Two or three centuries from now it will be recognized that all the competent killers are Christians; then the pagan world will go to school to the Christian—not to acquire his religion, but his guns."[57]

The antidote, Twain advises, is for human beings to cultivate their sense of humor. At present most human beings are only susceptible to "broad incongruities, grotesqueries, absurdities," and the "ten thousand high grade comicalities which exist in the world are sealed from their vision." Human beings are adept at finding new ways to destroy themselves, but they might be saved by a comedic version of the Manhattan Project. Though power, money, and negotiation might be able to weaken suicidal stupidity "a little, century by century . . . only laughter can blow it to rags and atoms at a blast. Against the assault of laughter, nothing can stand."[58]

Kubrick must have been thinking along these lines when he defended *Dr. Strangelove* shortly after its release:

> Why should the bomb be approached with reverence? Reverence can be a paralyzing state of mind. For me the comic sense is the most eminently human reaction to the mysteries and the paradoxes of life. I just hope some of them are illuminated by the exaggerations and the style of the film. And I don't see why an artist has to do any more than produce an artistic experience that reflects his thinking.[59]

In the current critical climate, however, the idea that Kubrick's films express "thinking" at all has come under attack. Jason Sperb, author of *The Kubrick Facade*, believes that Kubrick was seriously concerned with refuting emphatic thought. Taking the assumptions of postmodernism to the nth degree, Sperb rhapsodizes over Kubrick's power to drive his viewers out of their minds: "Kubrick's films . . . force us to fear the consequences of thought . . . and think outside the mind . . . the films may push us . . . to an unthought realm where mutual experience and interaction exists. But how can we think in a way that tentatively attempts to unthink these films?"[60] He goes on to warn that a refusal to unthink could be catastrophic: *Dr. Strangelove* expresses "an aggressive clashing of conflicting narrative constructions" in a world reduced to a grid of "preemption, aggression, and patriotism."[61] And the end of Arthur C. Clarke's novelization of *2001* (unlike Kubrick's film) betrays elitism when the newborn Star Child speeds toward earth to blow it up: "The Star Child is interested only in himself, not in communicating or evolving with others."[62]

For postmodern believers like Sperb, literary authorship and cinematic auteurism are on a continuum with evil because they separate the isolated self-aggrandizing individual from the cooperative group. But because he likes Kubrick and wants to write about him on a computer in a private space, he must find ingenious ways of disassociating Kubrick from auteurism and himself from assertion. Therefore, Sperb repeatedly reminds us that he does not "think" about the films but more justifiably "senses" them, so that the experience of the film is never tyrannically explicit. For example, he "gets the sense" that the "inaudible voices" that accompany the appearance of the monolith in *2001* were put there to replace "the neat and clean order of voiceover narration" that Clarke and Kubrick had originally planned.

Although Sperb finally does admit to a thought—that the ending of *2001* is pessimistic because it leaves David Bowman in the alien room trapped in his own subjectivity—he is immensely grateful to Kubrick for freeing him from the same fate:

> Ultimately, like *Dr. Strangelove*, I feel *2001* tells the story of a human race refusing to move beyond its own self-interests, its own reassuring addiction to words and artificial barriers, and assumed narratives of shallow politeness, so much so, in fact, that humanity ends up producing a machine, in HAL, capable of reproducing its creators' own egotistical selfishness and denial of its own fallibility and subjective instability, even to the point of murder. Yet for a while, *2001* privileges the breakdown of the magic of words over the story world. Consequently, the film implicitly creates in me the need for social interaction—the intensely, multiply, intersubjective (and thus nonsubjective) affective sense of experience—over the isolated, asocial human mind and its singular destructive attempts at meaning and understanding.[63]

Sperb and others confirm their refusal to find meaning in Kubrick's films by selectively quoting him where it serves their purpose. The director's refusal to publicly interpret his films is well known. As he told Joseph Gelmis in 1970, ambiguity is both unavoidable "on a nonverbal level," and desirable because it allows the audience to "fill in the visual experience themselves."[64] However, in 1960 before he had become experienced in giving interviews where his comments could have been reductive, Kubrick was quite clear about wanting to express ideas and about his respect for critical attempts to articulate them: "The point of view [a film] is conveying . . . has to be got across through a subtle injection [of] ideas which are valid and truthful,"[65] and

> the intellectual is capable of understanding what is intended and gets a certain amount of pleasure from that, whereas the mass audience may not. . . . I believe Bergman, De Sica, and Fellini . . . don't just sit and wait for a good story to come along and then make it. They have a point of view which is expressed over and over and over again in their films, and they themselves write or have original material written for them.[66]

The last statement conveys the young Kubrick's fulfilled ambition to be an "auteur" whose personal vision predetermines the content and effect of his films. He wrote the screenplays for *A Clockwork Orange* and *Barry Lyndon* by himself and cowrote the screenplays for all the other films except *Spartacus*. Though he gave Vladimir Nabokov the writing credit for *Lolita*, he did so much rewriting that the finished version was essentially his. Kubrick did not conceive of himself as a postmodern voice, arising spontaneously from the "matrix" of a particular time and place. His vision transcended contemporary political issues, and he never subscribed to Walter Benjamin's dictum that "Truth Is the Death of Intention."[67] Though human beings are clearly subject to the vagaries of chance in an externally "contingent" universe, the individual person is capable of self-knowledge and purposeful communication.

Diane Johnson recalled his emphasis on structure and verbal precision. He taught her that "words on screen have three or four times more force than they do on the page" and that it "was pointless to write dialogue" until they had decided "what was logical and illogical" and how similar events impinged upon opposing characters. After interviewer Michel Ciment commented on Kubrick's "pronounced taste for language," Johnson replied, "Speaking with him was like speaking with another writer. Much more so than other directors I've worked with." Other directors "represented things visually, but had little interest in narrative elements and the way they functioned. And during the writing stage he wasn't really thinking about visual effects. In this sense he was very compartmentalized. He thought like a writer, which I found quite unique."[68]

Kubrick frequently changed lines, scenes, and even final outcomes in the course of production, but with the rare exception of Peter Sellers, he never kept spontaneous improvisations in the final cut. Although he told Malcolm McDowell (Alex in *A Clockwork Orange*) to sing during the rape scene, the choreographed version of "Singin' in the Rain" took a long time to perfect: "Everyone who worked with him will tell you that he knew what he didn't want but was slow to learn what he really wanted. The big scenes in *A Clockwork Orange* were the result of improvisation, although we didn't improvise the film. There was a script and we followed it, but when it didn't work, he knew it, and we had to keep rehearsing endlessly."[69] Jack Nicholson (Jack Torrance in *The Shining*) recalled that although Kubrick allowed him to add "The Three Little Pigs" and "Honey, I'm home," he always reshot from a new written script each time a change was made. Each updated version was typed on different colored paper and distributed to the actors a day in advance. Like Diane Johnson, Nicholson was impressed by Kubrick's verbal precision. "He wanted each word to count. Once we had the text he wanted, we had to follow it faithfully, because he was meticulous about it, as he was with everything. We rehearsed each scene the day we were supposed to shoot it."[70]

Twenty-five years later this same process made Sydney Pollack (Victor Ziegler in *Eyes Wide Shut*) feel that Kubrick expected his actors to be screen-writers. The actors' additions had to be written into the script, and as with *The Shining*, each version was written in a different color until the available colors were exhausted, at which point the sequence would start all over again. Kubrick's literary control is also evident in his insistence that Pollack exaggerate his acting, rather than try to be "truthful" in his scenes with Tom Cruise. Pollack found it fascinating when Kubrick would come up with a spontaneous interjection on the set such as Cruise's line: "The girl at the orgy, was she the same girl we saw earlier?" They would spend hours discussing what the character would and wouldn't know, what words they would say and who would say them: "I frequently tried to condense my dialogue: Stanley, this is like an aria, a grand, stately, majestic finale for the film. And Stanley replied: 'Oh no, you're perfect!' He was a great manipulator."[71]

In his 2005 book *Full Metal Jacket Diary*, Matthew Modine wrote of how his emotions on the set swung from admiring devotion to frustration and rage. Kubrick was not happy with the written ending and continually tried to tap the actor's instinct for an idea, but Modine obliviously put him off, saying he thought the ending was fine the way it was. Eventually Kubrick made Modine furiously jealous by inviting him to a meeting with actors playing the other marines, in order to get their input on the ending. Soon after that, Kubrick dismissed him from the set for not knowing his lines. When he cooled off and returned, having assured himself that his public humiliation was only Kubrick's attempt to stoke emotion for the scene, Kubrick ignored his attempt at a joke, and regarding him coldly, once more challenged him to provide an ending. Shocked and hurt, Modine blurted out exactly what Kubrick wanted: Joker should live and remember for the rest of his life the deaths of Pyle and Hartman, how Cowboy, his only friend, died in his arms, and how he took lives in a stupid war he didn't understand: "Stanley's eyes seem blacker. He looks really focused. 'That's the ending.'"[72] Kubrick's Zen-like response revealed his respect for intuition, his reliance on a gifted actor to provide it, and his own ability to recognize it when it was right.

That may well be the same ending Kubrick envisioned for an enlightened humanity. Several months after the film's release, the director telephoned Modine for the last time: "We end our conversation and he says something that stays with me. 'The longest line is never outside the best restaurant.' I think about this and its implication. The comment reminds me of something I read, 'Don't give them what they want. Give them what they don't know they want yet.'"[73] Modine was probably remembering Gene Youngblood's memorable line: "Entertainment gives us what we want; art gives us what we don't know we want. To confront a work of art is to confront oneself—but aspects of oneself previously unrecognized."[74]

For Kubrick, confronting oneself did not boil down to simply admitting that the self cannot know. Even noted critic James Naremore in his 2007 British Film Institute study, *On Kubrick*, excises "big important ideas" from the films in favor of aesthetic description and immediate response. Like Cocks, he discovers Kubrick through what he takes to be a motivating fear, "his anxious fascination with the human body." Using this fear as a creative spur, Kubrick ceaselessly explored the expressive potential of "the grotesque," a genre that displayed the "deformed and disgusting" and that he depicted cinematically with masks, makeup, wide-angle close-ups, and actors made to seem "grossly fat, emaciated, or ugly."[75]

Above all, Kubrick's films fit the genre because their "blackly humorous moments" leave the spectator with confused emotions rather than limiting ideas. Still, Naremore has to admit that "viewers can react differently" and that "the grotesque is always to some extent in the eye of the beholder."[76] When he conceives of Kubrick as endlessly tweaking his mix of "laughter, fear, and disgust" to achieve a grotesquerie of style and subject, he seems to conflate the director's purpose with his own. It is unlikely that an artist who addressed profoundly serious problems, from aggressive atavism to spiritual yearning to sexual obsession, would have concerned himself about whether or not he left his audience teetering between the "sportive grotesque" and the "ludicrous grotesque."[77]

Naremore's attempt to align Kubrick consistently with expressionists like George Grosz or Diane Arbus ignores the consensus, expressed admiringly (Michael Herr) or adversarially (Pauline Kael), that for Kubrick beauty and content were one and the same. The obvious distortions that Naremore observes, such as *Clockwork*'s Alex bludgeoning the Cat Lady with a ceramic penis or Sir Charles Lyndon fatally convulsing in a paroxysm of jealous rage, do not dominate their films so much as they are encompassed by larger elements of visual and aural beauty. When Naremore insists that Kubrick fears the physical body as a "source of a horror that can be held in check only with a kind of radical, derisive humor," he ignores the sensitive faces and beautiful bodies of actors like Ryan O'Neal, Matthew Modine, or Nicole Kidman that counterpoint the disturbing images their films portray.[78]

Kubrick's portrayal of psychological ugliness is particularly powerful in *Full Metal Jacket*, but Naremore's effort to impose the grid of the grotesque on particular scenes often detracts from the credibility of his readings. In the opening scene he makes much of what he takes to be confusion between the "scary" and "funny" effects of drill sergeant Hartman's tirade, in line with the

contradictory effects of the "grotesque." He attempts to underscore the presence of the genre by pointing to "Hartman's intense preoccupation with bodily secretions, especially shit, which is the prime source of his grotesque verbal humor." Naremore then adds appreciatively, "Everything the Drill
Instructor says is outrageously offensive, but delivered with such theatrical
flair and poetic talent for disgusting metaphors that it invites laughter."

In pressing this thesis Naremore ignores the obvious—that exaggeration is
part of satire, especially the type of Swiftian satire that Kubrick emulated in
Strangelove. Rather than feeling discombobulated, many spectators will find
themselves entertained and delighted by a line like "I want [the latrine] so
sanitary and spotless and sparkling that the Virgin Mary herself would be
proud to go in there and take a dump." When Naremore asks rhetorically—
"Is this the way Marine sergeants really behave, or are we in the realm of
satiric stylization, a la *Dr. Strangelove?*"[79]—the answer seems obvious rather
than confusing. This is the way a drill sergeant behaves when he is written
and directed by Stanley Kubrick.

In other scenes during the opening sequence, however, Hartman's behavior is not funny or mixed with comedy but repulsively sadistic. There is not
likely to be confusion on the part of any spectator when he nearly strangles
one of the recruits for what he takes to be disrespect. Here is Naremore's description of the encounter:

> The more insulting Hartman becomes, the more difficult it is for Pyle to stop
> grinning. "Do you think I'm cute, Private Pyle?" Hartman asks in hysterical
> rage. "Do you think I'm funny?" Pyle says no, and Hartman yells: "Then wipe
> that disgusting grin off your face!" Pyle struggles to keep his composure. "I'm
> going to give you three seconds, exactly three seconds, to wipe that stupid
> looking grin off your face," Hartman screams, "or I will gouge out your eyeballs
> and skullfuck you!" The image of Hartman having intercourse with a skull is
> so horrible yet so ridiculous that Pyle cannot control himself and he begins to
> exhibit a kind of panicked amusement. "Get on your knees, scumbag!" Hold-
> ing his hand at waist level, Hartman commands Pyle to lean forward, place his
> neck in Hartman's palm and be choked. "Are you through grinning?" he asks
> as he squeezes the recruit's windpipe. Pyle's grin disappears and his face changes
> color. "Yes, sir," he gasps. "Bullshit!" Hartman replies. "I can't hear you. Sound
> off like you got a pair!" When Pyle manages to say "yes" a second time, Hart-
> man releases him.[80]

In this passage Naremore's attempt to replace interpretation with reaction
fails because he implies that his idiosyncratic response is universal. Many
viewers might not see Pyle's grin as amusement but as nervous fear or the nat-

ural configuration of his face, and how many will agree with Naremore that Pyle is conjuring a vivid image of Hartman sticking his penis into an actual skull after hearing the word "skullfuck"? To attribute such imagining to Pyle, in particular, distorts everything we come to know of this Lennie-like innocent as the film develops. In attempting to recall his and presumably others' immediate response to particular images and lines, Naremore seems to forget that criticism ideally expresses reflections distilled from repeated viewings rather than subjective efforts to universalize the visceral response of a group.

Naremore sums up Kubrick's oeuvre as a "unified" attempt to exhibit the "paradoxical and potentially disturbing truth" that "there is always something potentially comic about horror and horrible about comedy."[81] Shakespeare, too, mixed hornpipes and funerals, but few would say that such inclusiveness constituted his artistic purpose. Do artists of the first rank focus primarily on forms and effects rather than content? Asked to sum up what she had learned in her three years on *Eyes Wide Shut*, Nicole Kidman put it this way: "The great storytellers of our past, and now, are so important to our future, and I think that Stanley gave me a belief in that again; he was one of the great storytellers of all time, and he used film to do that, and it was beautiful."[82]

Recently, a highly regarded cinematic artist frankly dismissed narrative: "I equate this work with painting more than I do theater or literature. Stories don't interest me. Basically I'm more interested in behavior. I don't direct, I watch."[83] Kubrick also watched, but for him neither form nor behavior was an end in itself. Both were subordinated to a polished story that served a consistent purpose. Stories show us our limitations and our possibilities, and now considering technology's contrary potential, Stanley Kubrick's grand narrative has become nothing less than a matter of life and death.

Notes

1. Michiko Kakutani, "A Connoisseur of Cool Tries to Raise the Temperature," *New York Times*, July 18, 1999.

2. Nicole Kidman, interview by Paul Joyce, "Remembering . . . Stanley Kubrick, Kidman . . . on Kubrick," July 12, 1999, in "Special Features," *Eyes Wide Shut*, DVD, directed by Stanley Kubrick (1999; Burbank, Calif.: Warner Bros. Home Video, 2001).

3. Stanley Kubrick, interview by Craig McGregor, "Nice Boy from the Bronx," *New York Times*, January 30, 1972.

4. Stanley Kubrick, interview by William Kloman, "In 2001, Will Love Be a Seven-Letter Word," *New York Times*, April 14, 1968.

5. Bruno Bettelheim, *The Uses of Enchantment* (New York: Vintage, Random House, 1989), 26.

6. Diane Johnson, interview by Donald Williams, "An Interview with Diane Johnson," *C. J. Jung Page Film Review*, www.cgjungpage.org/index2.php?option= content&do_pdf=1&id=490.

7. Sergei Eisenstein, "On Color," in *Selected Works*, vol. 2, ed. Michael Glenny and Richard Taylor, trans. Michael Glenny (London: British Film Institute, 1991), 263.

8. Michael Herr, *Kubrick* (New York: Grove Press, 2000), 92.

9. Don Daniels, "A Skeleton Key to *2001*," *Sight & Sound*, Winter 1970–1971, 29.

10. Pauline Kael, *When the Lights Go Down* (New York: Holt, Rinehart, and Winston, 1980), 105.

11. William Kloman, "In 2001, Will Love Be a Seven-Letter Word," *New York Times*, April 14, 1968.

12. Stanley Kubrick, interview by Maurice Rapf, "A Talk with Stanley Kubrick about *2001*," *Action*, January/February 1969; repr. in *Stanley Kubrick: Interviews*, ed. Gene D. Phillips (Jackson: University Press of Mississippi, 2001), 78.

13. Herr, *Kubrick*, 45–46.

14. Keir Dullea in Peter Bogdanovich, "What They Say about Stanley Kubrick," *New York Times Magazine*, July 25, 1999.

15. Katharina Hobbs, e-mail to Kubrick News Group, www.alt.movies.Kubrick .com, October 29, 1999.

16. Herr, *Kubrick*, 9.

17. Herr, *Kubrick*, 10.

18. Steven Spielberg, interview by Paul Joyce, "Remembering . . . Stanley Kubrick . . . Spielberg on Kubrick," July 22, 1999, in "Special Features," *Eyes Wide Shut*, DVD, directed by Stanley Kubrick (1999; Burbank, Calif.: Warner Bros. Home Video, 2001).

19. Richard Strauss, quoted in "*Also Sprach Zarathustra*," in *The Encyclopedia of Stanley Kubrick*, by Gene D. Phillips and Rodney Hill (New York: Checkmark Books, 2002), 12.

20. James M. Welsh, preface to *The Encyclopedia of Stanley Kubrick*, by Gene D. Phillips and Rodney Hill (New York: Checkmark Books, 2002), x.

21. Kubrick, interview by Eric Nordern, *Playboy*, September 1968; repr. in Phillips, ed., *Stanley Kubrick: Interviews*, 68.

22. John Hofsess, "Mind's Eye: *A Clockwork Orange*," *Take One*, May/June 1971; repr. in Phillips, ed., *Stanley Kubrick: Interviews*, 107.

23. Michel Chion, *Eyes Wide Shut* (London: British Film Institute, 2002), 41, 44.

24. Chion, *Eyes Wide Shut*, 70.

25. Michel Chion, *Kubrick's Cinema Odyssey* (London: British Film Institute, 2001), 169.

26. Chion, *Kubrick's Cinema Odyssey*, 171.

27. Chion, *Eyes Wide Shut*, 88.

28. Thomas Allen Nelson, *Kubrick: Inside a Film Artist's Maze*, 2nd ed. (Bloomington: Indiana University Press, 2000), 15, 16.

29. Nelson, *Kubrick*, 88.

30. Nelson, *Kubrick*, 5.

31. Nelson, *Kubrick*, 245.

32. Nelson, *Kubrick*, 186n.

33. Luis M. García Mainar, *Narrative and Stylistic Patterns in the Films of Stanley Kubrick* (Rochester, N.Y.: Camden House, 1999), 6.

34. Mainar, *Narrative and Stylistic Patterns*, 55.

35. Mainar, *Narrative and Stylistic Patterns*, 202.

36. Mainar, *Narrative and Stylistic Patterns*, 219.

37. Mainar, *Narrative and Stylistic Patterns*, 231.

38. Mainar, *Narrative and Stylistic Patterns*, 143.

39. Mainar, *Narrative and Stylistic Patterns*, 143.

40. Mainar, *Narrative and Stylistic Patterns*, 212.

41. Mainar, *Narrative and Stylistic Patterns*, 232.

42. Randy Rasmussen, *Stanley Kubrick: Seven Films Analyzed* (Jefferson, N.C.: McFarland, 2001), 316.

43. Rasmussen, *Stanley Kubrick*, 321.

44. Rasmussen, *Stanley Kubrick*, 328.

45. Geoffrey Cocks, *The Wolf at the Door: Stanley Kubrick, History, and the Holocaust* (New York: Peter Lang, 2004), 1.

46. Cocks, *The Wolf at the Door*, 238.

47. Cocks, *The Wolf at the Door*, 244.

48. Cocks, *The Wolf at the Door*, 251.

49. Jack Nicholson told Michel Ciment that "we," presumably he and Kubrick, improvised "The Three Little Pigs" during the shoot; see Michel Ciment, *Kubrick: The Definitive Edition* (New York: Faber & Faber, 2001), 298.

50. Cocks, *The Wolf at the Door*, 37–38.

51. Herr, *Kubrick*, 55.

52. See David Hughes, *The Complete Kubrick* (London: Virgin, 2000), 109, and the entire script at www.scifiscripts.com/scripts/strangelove.txt.

53. Jonathan Swift, *Gulliver's Travels* (1726), 1.7, December 10, 2005, www.jaffebros.com/lee/gulliver/bk1/chap1-7.html.

54. Swift, *Gulliver's Travels*, 3.3, www.jaffebros.com/lee/gulliver/bk3/chap3-3.html.

55. Herr, *Kubrick*, 13.

56. Stanley Kubrick, quoted in 1971 by Hofsess, in Phillips, ed., *Stanley Kubrick: Interviews*, 107.

57. Mark Twain, "The Mysterious Stranger," in *Great Short Works of Mark Twain*, ed. Justin Kaplan (1916; New York: Harper & Row, 1967), 347.

58. Twain, "The Mysterious Stranger," 360.

59. Stanley Kubrick, quoted by Loudon Wainright, "The View from Here: The Strange Case of *Strangelove*," *Life*, March 13, 1964, 15.

60. Jason Sperb, *The Kubrick Facade: Faces and Voices in the Films of Stanley Kubrick* (Lanham, Md.: Scarecrow Press, 2006), 4–5.

61. Sperb, *The Kubrick Facade*, 64.

62. Sperb, *The Kubrick Facade*, 88.

63. Sperb, *The Kubrick Facade*, 95–96.

64. Stanley Kubrick, interview by Joseph Gelmis, "The Film Director as Superstar: Stanley Kubrick," in *The Film Director as Superstar* (Garden City, N.Y.: Doubleday, 1970); repr. in Phillips, ed., *Stanley Kubrick: Interviews*, 91.

65. Stanley Kubrick, "Words and Movies," *Sight & Sound*, Winter 1961, 14.

66. Stanley Kubrick, interview by Robert Ginna, "The Odyssey Begins," *Horizon*, 1960; repr. in *Entertainment Weekly*, April 9, 1999, 16–17.

67. Walter Benjamin, *The Origin of German Tragic Drama*, trans. John Osborne (London: New Left Books, 1977), 36.

68. Diane Johnson, interview by Ciment, *Kubrick*, 295.

69. Malcolm McDowell, interview by Ciment, *Kubrick*, 285.

70. Jack Nicholson, interview by Ciment, *Kubrick*, 298; on the different colored script versions, see Vivian Kubrick, "The Making of *The Shining*," in "Special Features," *The Shining*, DVD, directed by Stanley Kubrick (1980; Burbank, Calif.: Warner Bros. Home Video, 2001).

71. Sydney Pollack, interview by Michael Henry, "What Stanley Wanted," *Positif*, September 1999, 18; in French, my translation.

72. Matthew Modine, *Full Metal Jacket Diary* (New York: Rugged Land, 2005), 205–206.

73. Modine, *Full Metal Jacket Diary*, 287.

74. Gene Youngblood, *Expanded Cinema* (New York: Dutton, 1970), 60.

75. James Naremore, *On Kubrick* (London: British Film Institute, 2007), 27–28.

76. Naremore, *On Kubrick*, 27.

77. Naremore, *On Kubrick*, 26.

78. Naremore, *On Kubrick*, 35.

79. Naremore, *On Kubrick*, 36.

80. Naremore, *On Kubrick*, 38–39.

81. Naremore, *On Kubrick*, 41.

82. Kidman, "Remembering . . . Stanley Kubrick, Kidman . . . on Kubrick."

83. Robert Altman, voice-over to clips from his films upon winning an honorary Oscar at the 2006 Academy Awards, March 5, 2006.

CHAPTER TWO

~

Shaping the Future
2001: A Space Odyssey

If we did not know that *2001* and *A Clockwork Orange* were both Stanley Kubrick films, they might appear at first to be an argument between dueling directors. For Steven Spielberg, the Star Child at the end of *2001* is "the greatest moment of optimism and hope for mankind that has ever been offered by a modern filmmaker."[1] And in 1968 shortly after its release, a National Catholic Award offered high praise: "By the scope of its imaginative vision of man—his origins, his creative encounter with the universe, and his unfathomed potential for the future—[*2001*] immerses the eye, the ear, and the intuitive responses of the viewer in a uniquely stimulating human experience."[2] *A Clockwork Orange*, on the other hand, is usually seen as anything but an affirmation of humanity's future, even by eminent critics with extensive personal access to the director. Michel Ciment uses the film to demonstrate that "man is for Kubrick, as for any other disciple of Hobbes, a wolf to his fellow man. He does not change." To bolster this view he offers a statement that Kubrick made about the film: "Man isn't a noble savage. He is irrational, brutal, weak, unable to be objective about anything where his interests are involved."[3]

Further reflection on the larger scope of Kubrick's many interviews can contextualize this statement, but after *Clockwork* and ever since, the pessimistic stereotype has flourished. Richard Schickel of *Time* felt that Kubrick's view of human nature was so bleak that it was "fairly miraculous [that] in this day and age [he could] pursue the kind of career he pursued in making these uncompromising movies."[4] Pauline Kael's legendary animus against Kubrick was fueled by her perception of his "chortling over madness" without indicating "any possibilities for sanity."[5]

Although Kubrick stated that he did not believe in "any of earth's monotheistic religions," he did believe that self-knowledge could initiate redemption.[6] He diagnosed the hysterically negative reactions to the portrayal of violence in Clockwork as pathological denial: "There is the basic psychological, unconscious identification with Alex . . . as a creature of the id. He is within all of us. In most cases, this recognition seems to bring a kind of empathy from the audience, but it makes some people very angry and uncomfortable."[7] After a pompous officer in Full Metal Jacket demands to know why the central character wears a peace symbol when his helmet displays the words "Born to Kill," Private Joker replies, "It's a Jungian thing." Kubrick's collaborating writer on Full Metal Jacket, Michael Herr, reported that they spent many hours considering how to portray Jung's concept of "the shadow," the dark side of human nature, in cinematic terms.[8]

Kubrick followed Jung in rejecting political solutions in favor of philosophical and psychological recognitions:

> I think that when Rousseau transferred the concept of original sin from man to society, he was responsible for a lot of misguided social thinking which followed. I don't think that man is what he is because of an imperfectly structured society, but rather that society is imperfectly structured because of the nature of man. No philosophy based on an incorrect view of the nature of man is likely to produce social good.[9]

Jung's grim understanding of the Cold War as pathological differs only in tone from Kubrick's hilarious satire in Dr. Strangelove: "In theory, it lies within the power of reason to desist from experiments of such hellish scope as nuclear fission, if only because of their dangerousness. But fear of the evil which one does not see in one's own bosom but always in somebody else's checks reason every time, although one knows that the use of this weapon means the certain end of our present human world."[10]

In 1964, the year Dr. Strangelove was released, Kubrick and Arthur C. Clarke began part II of the 2001 screenplay with a scene that did not appear in the final cut. A shot from space reveals five nuclear bombs two hundred miles above the earth, bearing the insignias of Russia, the United States, France, Germany, and China. Each nation had placed hundreds of thousand-megaton bombs "capable of incinerating the entire Earth's surface from an altitude of 100 miles" in "perpetual orbit." With the exception of Germany the prediction has come true, but the original voice-over includes another over-the-top prediction that recent events have proved less than paranoid: "Matters were further complicated by the presence of twenty-seven nations in the nuclear club. There had been no deliberate or accidental use of nuclear weapons since World War II, and some people felt secure in this knowledge. But to others, the situation seemed comparable to an airline with a perfect safety record; it showed admirable care and skill, but no one expected it to last forever."[11]

Today, the term "nuclear club" has become common coin for four of the previously named states, plus England, India, Pakistan, Israel, and North Korea. Though the list still falls far short of twenty-seven, the following nations have begun and abandoned nuclear weapons research since World War II: Argentina, Australia, Brazil, Egypt, Iraq, Libya, Romania, South Korea, Yugoslavia, Taiwan, and amazingly, Sweden and Switzerland. Shortly before the orbiting bombs appear in the 2001 screenplay, the three-million-year-old human ancestor, Moonwatcher, sees his future in the crystal cube that would eventually become the opaque black monolith of the finished film. Just as the Star Child may be a hopeful present-day vision, the cubic screen showed pre-humans a marvelous vista of prosperity and power. But Clarke's voice-over reminds us that the future from here on is far from secure: "Moonwatcher feels the first faint twinges of a new and potent emotion—the urge to kill. He had taken his first step towards humanity."[12]

On his first day on the set, Dan Richter, the actor who played Moonwatcher, was informed by Clarke that the ideas of Robert Ardrey were "central to 2001," and that his 1961 book, *African Genesis*, "caused quite a stir" over its assertion that "we evolved from our ape ancestors because we learned to kill."[13] Ardrey, in turn, acknowledged his admiration for Raymond Dart, the South African anatomist who discovered a skull belonging to a creature halfway between ape and human that he named *Australopithecus africanus*. During their initial meeting, Kubrick asked Richter if he had read Dart and immediately gave him copies of his books and papers. Dart had concluded from studying the teeth of his four-foot-tall specimen that *Australopithecus* had been a carnivore and a hunter, and that baboon skulls near the sites had characteristic indentations suggesting that the victims had been killed by an antelope humerus used as a weapon. Ardrey was especially struck by a particular skull in Dart's collection—the broken, toothless jawbone of a twelve-year-old australopithecine with a dented jaw where the boy had apparently been struck a mortal blow.

Ardrey had been a playwright before devoting himself to popular anthropology, and with a characteristic flourish he wondered, "What if a weapon had done this deed? What if I held in my hands the evidence of an antique murder committed with a deadly weapon a quarter of a million years before the time of man?" In the rest of his book he went on to elaborate his thesis that "human history has turned on the development of superior weapons" from genetic necessity: "We design and compete with our weapons as birds build nests."[14]

Ardrey was vigorously condemned by the countercultural romanticism of the sixties and seventies for advancing a fascist doctrine of original sin that justified totalitarian rule. Though he and Dart were initially criticized for their science by more optimistic counterparts, they advanced an idea that (like "unproved" global warming) still demands attention: "A world dedicated to the manufacture of explosive playthings can scarcely afford the luxury of neglect." Ardrey felt a personal responsibility to disseminate Dart's conviction that "the predatory transition and the weapons fixation explained man's bloody history" and that humanity "must listen when man at last possessed weapons capable of sterilizing the earth." He explained further that "if the verdict of a hundred authorities had been other than what it was, then I doubt that a dramatist would now feel impelled to review the findings of a scientist's revolution."[15]

Kubrick conveyed the same message but kept it within the symbolic confines of his art. He was quite explicit, however, in 1968 when he told Eric Nordern: "In Strangelove I was dealing with the inherent irrationality in man that threatens to destroy him; that irrationality is with us as strongly today, and must be conquered. But a recognition of insanity doesn't imply a celebration of it—nor a sense of despair and futility about the possibility of curing it."[16] The statement reveals an idealistic resolve to sustain the good fight in a Manichaean world. In Dr. Strangelove, 2001, and every film thereafter, he took his cue from Ardrey. In a 1972 letter to the New York Times defending Clockwork, Kubrick cited Ardrey's view as ultimately optimistic, because it posits a more hopeful future than an Edenic expulsion that "leaves man a monster who has gone steadily away from his nobility." He then quoted Ardrey directly:

> We were born of risen apes, not fallen angels, and the apes were armed killers besides. And so what shall we wonder at? Our murders and massacres and missiles and our irreconcilable regiments? Or our treaties, whatever they may be worth; our symphonies, however seldom they may be played; our peaceful acres, however frequently they may be converted into battlefields; our dreams, however rarely they may be accomplished. The miracle of man is not how far he has sunk but how magnificently he has risen. We are known among the stars by our poems, not our corpses.[17]

It is noteworthy that Kubrick gave Clarke a copy of Joseph Campbell's *The Hero with a Thousand Faces* at the same time they were reading Ardrey, since the two writers are philosophical opposites.[18] Where Ardrey concentrated on the persistence of aggression, Campbell focused on the spiritual evolution of an internal hero, potentially realized in the individual person as a unique variation on a pattern of universal growth that he called the "Monomyth":

> The hero . . . is the man or woman who has been able to battle past his personal and historical limitations to the generally valid, normally human forms. Such a one's visions, ideas, and inspirations come pristine from the primary springs of human life and thought. . . . The hero has died as modern man; but as eternal man—perfected, unspecific, universal man—he has been reborn. His . . . solemn task . . . is to return then to us, transfigured, and teach the lesson he has learned of life renewed.[19]

In *2001* Kubrick and Clarke transmitted their own sense of this spiritual journey. Commenting on the film's final scene in a 1970 interview with Joseph Gelmis, Kubrick spoke of the monolith "sweeping" David Bowman through present human limits as "a journey through inner and outer space."[20] As he enters Jupiter space, Bowman shakes and appears to be afraid. Campbell warns that an individual's recognition of himself as a universal being appears at first to be a horrific "danger," threatening one's psychological existence and the family relationships based on that limited self. But although self-knowledge can destroy the world of the present, it will lead to "a bolder,

Figure 2.1.   Bowman trembles as he enters Jupiter space. He will die as an individual before becoming the "hero with a thousand faces," the film's retrospective image of itself. *Courtesy of MGM/Photofest © MGM.*

Figure 2.2. **In the hero's form as Star Child, a light-suffused face and large eyes promise freedom from biological compulsion and psychological fear.** *Courtesy of MGM/ Photofest © MGM.*

cleaner, more spacious and fully human life."[21] At the end of *2001* the audience is drawn into the blackness of the monolith, which then opens out (or in) upon a vast starry expanse just before the Star Child with his larger than human eyes appears.

Vincent LoBrutto notes that *2001* "from the outset" was "inspired by Homer's *Odyssey*."[22] In a 1965 interview, Kubrick told Jeremy Bernstein that *Journey beyond the Stars* (the film's original title) would be a new kind of science-fiction film with no monsters or sex:

> About the best we've been able to come up with is a space odyssey—comparable in some ways to the Homeric *Odyssey*. It occurred to us [Kubrick and Arthur C. Clarke] that for the Greeks the vast stretches of the sea must have had the same sort of mystery and remoteness that space has for our generation, and that the far-flung islands Homer's wonderful characters visited were no less remote to them than the planets our spacemen will soon be landing on are to us. *Journey* also shares with *The Odyssey* a concern for wandering, exploration, and adventure.[23]

In Clarke's post-film novel, Poole sleeps while Bowman explores the ship's "in-exhaustible electronic library." He had become fascinated by the great explorations of the past. He would "cruise with Pythias out through the Pillars of Hercules, along the coast of a Europe barely emerging from the Stone Age," or sail with Anson, Cook, or Magellan, "and he began to read *The Odyssey*, which of all books spoke to him most vividly across the gulfs of time."[24]

Ardrey's hope that self-awareness might prevent "evolutionary disaster" finds a precedent in the microcosmic evolution of Odysseus.[25] During his sojourn among the Phaeacians, their king introduced the first narrative of Troy to an audience that associated art with social dominance: "I invite you that are sceptred kings to my palace with a view to entertaining our visitor indoors. . . . And let our glorious bard, Demodocus, be summoned. For no other singer has his heavenly gift of delighting our ears with whatever theme he chooses for his song."[26] When the time-scarred Odysseus hears how he had emerged from the wooden horse, "looking like Ares himself," he cannot rejoice over the widows he has made: "He wept as a woman weeps when she throws her arms round the body of her beloved husband, fallen in battle before his city and his comrades, fighting to save his hometown and his children from disaster."[27]

The Odyssey portrays the best man as an explorer, a creator, and a flawed human being. He is decidedly not a savior, and he cannot prevent lesser men from destroying themselves. Near the beginning of the story, while the suitors listen to their "admirable" bard sing of how the Greeks suffered during their return from Troy, Odysseus's wife, Penelope, asks for a ballad that is not so sad. Her son, Telemachus, who has inherited his father's innate intelligence (personified by their mutual helper, Athena), replies that poets are not responsible for the events they sing about. After all, new stories can only tell old tales: "You must be brave and nerve yourself to listen, for Odysseus is not the only one who has not returned from Troy."[28]

Only "depressing" stories enable happy endings, not for the world at large, but for the few who survive long enough to become their best selves. Odysseus's devotion to his wife, son, and country finds its counterpart in Kubrick's concern for humanity's future. Kubrick told Nordern that man "must have something to care about, something that is more important than himself." Though he rejected religion, per se, his creative drive arose from the same faith that buoyed Homer: "You don't stop being concerned with man because you recognize his essential absurdities and frailties and pretensions. . . . In the deepest sense I believe in man's potential and in his capacity for progress."[29]

Jung felt that the evolution of individual consciousness, assisted by concomitant individual contributions to "culture," could replace the religious striving for an immortality that modern people no longer consider plausible: "All great religions hold out the promise of a life beyond, [but] . . . for the man of today the idea of life after death seems to him questionable or beyond belief."[30] For Jung the death of the ego and its limited concerns would bring about the birth of a collective identity that extended beyond an individual's death. Having discovered the universal forms or "archetypes" within himself, the vulnerable, anxious person would become "transfigured," as Joseph Campbell put it, into "eternal man—perfected, unspecific . . . reborn."[31] Kubrick used the same term emphatically in an interview with Gene D. Phillips:

> Somebody said that man is the missing link between primitive apes and civilized human beings. You might say that the idea is inherent in the story of 2001 too. We are semi-civilized, capable of cooperation and affection, but needing some sort of transfiguration into a higher form of life. Since the means to obliterate life on earth exists, it will take more than just careful planning and reasonable cooperation to avoid some eventual catastrophe. The problem exists as long as the potential exists, and the problem is essentially a moral and spiritual one.[32]

Kubrick felt that transfiguration would be delayed by the "mind-paralyzing" fear of mortality that "gnawed away at [man's] ego and his sense of purpose." He noted that with the decline of the world's religions, "man has no crutch on which to lean," and the "terrifying" indifference of the universe has made it necessary to create personal affirmations: "However vast the darkness, we must supply our own light."[33] In 2001 Kubrick endeavored to fill the Jungian gap. He substituted a belief in the quasi-scientific evolution of the species for what Jung had termed the "supramundane goal" of Christianity. Passing into a "timeless state," David Bowman is "reborn, an enhanced being, a star child, an angel, a superman, if you like, and returns to earth prepared for the next leap forward of man's evolutionary destiny." Kubrick's purpose was not to create a new doctrine but to "stimulate, however inchoately, [the spectator's] mythological and religious yearnings and impulses."[34]

Kubrick's A.I. collaborator, Brian Aldiss, said that 2001 was the first work of science fiction "that depicts the future as unknowable."[35] And in the film the relatively unimaginative chief scientist and NASA spokesman, Heywood Floyd, terms the "four-million-year-old black monolith . . . completely inert, its origin and purpose still a total mystery." Kubrick told Joseph Gelmis why he and Clarke did not present an alien life-form: "You cannot imagine the unimaginable. All you can do is try to represent it in an artistic manner that will convey something of its quality. That's why we settled on the black monolith—which is, of course, . . . something of a Jungian archetype."[36] The indefiniteness of the monolith reflects Jung's distinction between a symbol and a sign. A sign refers to something limited and universally understood, the Cross or the Crescent in a religious sense, the elephant or the donkey in American politics. A symbol implies something vague or hidden: "A word or an image is symbolic when it implies something more than its obvious and immediate meaning. It has a wider 'unconscious' aspect that is never precisely defined or fully explained. . . . As the mind explores the symbol, it is led to ideas that lie beyond the grasp of reason."[37]

While signs define and limit, symbols connote and open up:

> A symbol always stands for something more than its obvious and immediate meaning. Symbols, moreover, are natural and spontaneous products. No genius has ever sat down with a pen or a brush in his hand and said: "Now I am going to invent a symbol." . . . No matter what fantastic trappings one may put upon an idea of this kind, it will still remain a sign that hints at something not yet known.[38]

The monolith is a "true symbol" in that it is "suprapersonal," and its "content" can only be understood intuitively. The individual artist stands outside his work "as though he were a second person," who has "fallen within the magic circle of an alien will."[39]

However, as a psychologist rather than an artist, Jung did not emphasize that magic requires craft. In the arts, as in ritualized religion, miracles don't just happen, and the space where creation occurs must be rigorously cleared. While spontaneity is the quality most prized by method actors, those directed by Stanislavski had to perfect every line and movement in rehearsal and to systematically map their characters' "objectives" and "super objectives" (immediate and overall motivations). Careful preparation enabled inspired variations during the elevated intensity of performance. Such moments were often precipitated by something that inadvertently upset the rehearsed routine: "A chair falls over, an actress drops her handkerchief and it must be picked up, or the business is suddenly altered. . . . These real actions can put life into stereotyped acting. . . . On the other hand, we cannot leave things to chance. It is important for an actor to know how to proceed under ordinary circumstances."[40]

James B. Harris, Kubrick's first producer, recalled how Kubrick advised him to read Stanislavski's works and that he particularly valued the idea in *Stanislavski Directs* that it is the director's responsibility to correct scenes that are not working: "The essential thing—which no one else could do for you—was to exercise your judgment and your taste."[41] Kubrick's "method" of eliciting the strongest possible performances from his actors resembled Stanislavski's, except that Kubrick often went further than most directors in breaking down the walls to the unconscious. Like most artists (or spiritual adepts in yoga and Zen), he realized that the energy of creative expression would dissipate if it were not strongly contained. Within the limits of that containment (the actor's technique and the written script), inspiration could operate at a peak level of intensity. The legendary number of takes on single scenes arose from the sense that in order to transcend control, one had to first be in complete control.

Kubrick told Matthew Modine (Joker in *Full Metal Jacket*) that extra takes occurred when actors didn't "do their homework," but descriptions of the process indicate that he was always pushing his actors toward those special moments that Stanislavski's actors were systematically trained to achieve:

> I once asked him why he so often did a lot of takes. He said it was because actors didn't know their lines. And he talked about Jack Nicholson: Jack would come in during the blocking and he kind of fumbled through the lines. He'd be learning them while he was there. And then you'd start shooting and after take 3 or take 4 or take 5 you'd get the Jack Nicholson that everybody knows and most directors would be happy with. And then you'd go up to 10 or 15 and he'd be really awful and then he'd start to understand what the lines were, what the lines meant, and then he'd become unconscious about what he was saying. So by take 30 or take 40 the lines became something else.[42]

Biographer Vincent LoBrutto quoted Nicholson's later reflection on the process in John Boorman's *The Emerald Forest Diary*: Kubrick "was trying to get performances that came out of extremity, exhaustion."[43] Tom Cruise described a similar experience during the first bedroom scene in *Eyes Wide Shut*. As he and Nicole Kidman completed take after take he began to feel that the scene had reached an "acceptable" and "interesting level." Exasperated, he asked Kubrick, "What do you want?" Kubrick replied, "I want the magic." Cruise said that then they would keep working until they got stale and the scene didn't work at all: "Then suddenly [the scene would] break into a place that none of us had really thought of before."[44] Kubrick applied the same artistic principle of spontaneity within a space of orderly and pure containment to cinematography. Douglas Milsome, the lighting cameraman on *Full Metal Jacket*, noted that the symmetry of Kubrick's frame was offset by a potentiality for last-minute changes conferred by the wide-angle lens:

> Stanley's composition is very stylized. . . . You'll never find a Kubrick set-up where the actor's feet are cut off—every shot is either from the waist up or full length. Every one of his movies has that look: very square, very level and symmetrical. Things are placed exactly right every time. . . . The use of extreme wide angle lenses is distinctive, too, and allows us a great area in which to manipulate the action. We used a lot of wide angles to compose interesting shots, as well as a lot of very close angles on the same shots, and then Stanley would cut from one extreme to the other.[45]

Careful preparation of his cinematic tools allowed the director to improvise as spontaneously as the actors. Ciment asked Kubrick if he had planned to order the first three sequences of *A Clockwork Orange* in the same way— "zoom pull-back shots, starting from a close-up and ending on the whole set." Kubrick replied that he frequently changed his plans intuitively during the editing process, but only when the actors had learned their lines, were dressed in the right clothes, and after he had the benefit of knowing what he already had on film: "It's important to save your cinematic ideas until you have rehearsed the scene in the actual place you're going to film it. The first thing to do is to rehearse the scene until something happens that is worth putting on film."[46]

This faith in inspiration appears in *2001* when Dave tries to retrieve Poole after HAL has cut him adrift. HAL's fearsome efficiency accentuates Dave's danger. As soon as Dave learns that HAL knew of the astronauts' intent to destroy him, he knows that he must fight for his life. Playing by rules he understands, HAL expects Dave to echo Poole's abject "I resign" after HAL "killed" him at chess. He thinks he has defeated Dave within the rules he knows, and he delivers the coup de grâce as a farewell:

> *Dave:* I'll go in through the emergency lock.
>
> *HAL:* Without your space helmet, Dave, you're going to find that rather difficult.
>
> *Dave:* HAL, I won't argue with you anymore. Open the doors.
>
> *HAL:* Dave, this conversation can serve no purpose anymore. Good-bye.[47]

Resembling the eyes of the ape leader in his cave as he listens to the leopard's growls, Dave's eyes now shift warily back and forth in his pod as he considers his options. He steers the pod directly up to the ship's airlock, opens it, and, using the pod's "explosive bolts," ejects himself inside. It is an act of daring that neither the bolts' engineers nor Dave's trainers could have foreseen. (As Alex will say later in A Clockwork Orange, "thinking [is] for the gloopy ones . . . the oomny ones [use] like inspiration and what Bog sends.")[48]

In 2001 (unlike A.I.) biological man, rather than the computer he creates, survives to perpetuate his evolutionary line. Dave's inherited instinct to risk violence now becomes the shot that saves his life. However, instead of using a bone or bullet to extend the force of his body, Dave's body itself closes the technological circle and becomes the bullet. In the fastest physical movement in the film to this point, Dave hurtles through the red-orange airlock as if he had been shot from a cannon. After bouncing back from the inner door, he remains focused enough to stop himself by grabbing the frame around the "emergency hatch-close," so that he can turn the handle and resume breathing. The spectacular ejection has occurred in total silence. When the hatch door finally comes down, its sounding crash is Dave's victory cry.[49]

As in artistic creation or the martial arts, personal and collective evolution is a progress from planned to spontaneous action. The monolith and Bowman himself herald that change. In the alien room the mature Bowman is dressed entirely in black from his slippers to the pajama shirt that barely shows under a shoulder-padded robe. As he advances toward the "aperture" of the bathroom door, he holds his arms straight down at his sides. The resulting vertical, rectangular shape of his body, accentuated by the heavy shoulder pads, suggests that he is the monolith, as Kubrick himself had implied when he told Gelmis that Bowman's journey entered "inner space."[50]

Jung described black as being an inchoate "germinal phase of all processes."[51] Symbolically, black is the antithesis of the most common abstract meaning of the rectangle, "of all geometric forms, the most rational, the most secure and regular, in all times and in all places . . . the shape favored by man when preparing any space or object for immediate use [such as] a house, room, table, or bed."[52] (Kubrick's awareness of the psychological impact of shapes determined the design of the war room in Dr. Strangelove, according to production designer Ken Adam: "When I came up with the sort of triangular solution, he said he felt the triangle was the strongest geometric form. And so combat developed at this circular table; playing for the fate of the world would be like a poker game.")[53]

To the extent that Bowman is trained, prepared, and knowledgeable as a scientist, he is "rectangular," the monolith's outer form. But in the film's decisive action, he is impelled by hidden forces in his "black" inner depths, dark in the sense that he becomes a killer, and dark in that a creative potential has not yet assumed color. Anticipating Bowman's final appearance as the incarnation of humanity's rational phase, the lead ape becomes a black rectangle when he stands upright for the first time after discovering the bone.[54] At this point humanity becomes separate from the curved and irregular formations of the animal body and terrain: prior to the discovery of the bone tool, the apes hunch into individual balls while eating, or, seen from a distance, they cluster into a single black ball with no individuality. Even in movement their bodies are stooped and curved. After they stand erect their shoulders become square, and seen from the rear, they have assumed the general configuration of the monolith.

Figure 2.3. After discovering the bone tool, the ape leader's erect black torso resembles the monolith, his guiding source. *Courtesy of MGM/Photofest © MGM.*

Figure 2.4. In the alien room, Bowman in his square-shouldered black robe embodies the monolith in its final phase. *Courtesy of MGM/Photofest © MGM.*

Jung provided a spatial metaphor that corresponds to the monolith's upright stance. Knowledge of the external world is "horizontal," while psychological knowledge is "vertical." As a source of all knowledge the monolith stands vertically, but as a storytelling device, signaling both transition and transmission, Kubrick makes extraordinary use of the horizontal black screen. The monolith as a symbol of vertical insight into human nature is a black screen, a device that demarcates and advances the story, initiating the spectator into new possibilities whenever it is used:

> When the spiritual catastrophe of the Reformation put an end to the Gothic Age with its impetuous yearning for the heights, its geographical confinement, and its restricted view of the world, the vertical outlook of the European mind was forthwith intersected by the horizontal outlook of modern times. Consciousness ceased to grow upward, and grew instead in breadth of view, as well as in knowledge of the terrestrial globe. This was the period of the great voyages, and of the widening of man's ideas of the world by empirical discoveries. Belief in the substantiality of the spirit yielded more and more to the obtrusive conviction that material things alone have substance, till at last, after nearly four hundred years, the leading European thinkers and investigators came to regard the mind as wholly dependent on matter and material causation . . . the irresistible tendency to account for everything on physical grounds corresponds to the horizontal development of consciousness in the last four centuries, and this horizontal perspective is a reaction against the exclusively vertical perspective of the Gothic Age.[55]

Jung goes on to indicate the need for recovery of vertical exploration but reverses its direction, downward into the psyche rather than upward toward the stars. In *2001* the monolith appears in a crater beneath the surface of the moon as well as "above" the earth as it beckons Bowman onward. The monolith's locations suggest that explorations of outer space are actually unconscious ways of exploring ourselves. Jung expressed the same perspective on the perceived external world as a mirror when he said, "Today the psyche does not build itself a body, but on the contrary, matter, [according to the prevailing scientific view] by chemical action, produces the psyche. This reversal of outlook would be ludicrous if it were not one of the outstanding features of the spirit of the age."[56] In *2001* the vertical, black monolith may be the infinite inner space within the collective human form, or the depths from which ideas spring within the artist, or the ambiguity of a great work of art that continually elicits new interpretations.

When the apes first touch the monolith shortly after it initially appears, its black body reflects their black bodies and its gray edge reflects the gray of their hands. It rises out of a deep indentation in the ground, foreshadowing its second appearance in the crater on the moon, but the bodies of the apes have not yet attained the vertical stature of Floyd and the space scientists who approach the monolith for the second time.[57] This second approach was the first live shot of the film's production,[58] and it suggests that Kubrick had already conceived of the monolith as a mirror and of the screen frame as a larger monolith.

The parallels between the apes ending and beginning a major expansion and present-day humans coming to the limits of physically based science are expressed in visual echoes. The scientists approach the monolith single file down an incline that recalls the apes approaching the water hole, especially when the leader turns back as if to make sure the others are following. Just as each ape carried a bone club, each scientist is equipped with a rectangular black backpack, and the back of each helmet has a rectangular black opening. As they approach, the lights and boxes on tripods evoke a movie set while another astronaut aims a camera at the men and the audience, snapping pictures that attempt to confine the experience within a frame that is absurdly small.

As Floyd approaches the monolith, he raises his left hand. The center of the monolith's edge is now brightly white between its silver top and bottom, reflecting Floyd's black-gloved hand like a mirror. As he moves his hand upward, his fingers in the reflection lighten until they are momentarily flesh colored, the spidery shadow just below them recalling the hairy wrist of the ape. Then just after he begins to move his hand downward, the scene cuts to a side close-up of his black extended thumb and fingers firmly "grasping" a narrow vertical shaft of white light that echoes the bone. The hand contracts and pulls away, and once again we see Floyd standing where he was, facing the silver edge. This is the limit of his ability to penetrate the mystery that Bowman will enter at the end when he passes directly through the monolith's wide face.

2001 begins and ends with an extended black screen that suggests evolutionary transition. The spectator must enter into darkness, both in the sense of destructive tendencies in human nature and in the sense of an unknown future. Before new differentiations of vision can be perceived, present expectations must be suspended. The strange music that introduces the apes to the monolith echoes the strange music already heard during the three-minute "Overture" that plays under the opening black screen, the horizontal monolith that the spectator is about to enter. After the MGM logo appears, the screen remains black for eight seconds before the ascending *Zarathustra* triad begins and continues to be black for nine more seconds before the moon and sun become visible rising over the curve of the blue-black earth. After another forty-seven seconds, "2001: A Space Odyssey" appears with the sun fully visible. Twenty seconds later, the black screen returns for eight seconds before the first shot appears with the frame divided between the horizontal black land at the bottom of the screen and the brightening orange sky above—light and energy created out of "nothing." Then the screen remains horizontally divided between darkness and light in six landscape shots for forty seconds before full daylight appears. Symmetrically, at the end of the film the white-lettered credits are followed by a completely black screen that holds for four and a half minutes, while *The Blue Danube* waltz continues to play.

Black screens as conventional transitions are repeatedly used in "The Dawn of Man" to subliminally identify the monolith with evolutionary transition, and with the unfolding of a story within the black screen that was established during the prolonged "Overture." There are black screens lasting several seconds after the leopard attack, the first water hole confrontation, and the scene in the cave immediately before the monolith actually appears.[59] Then, shortly after the leap to twenty-first-century space, the black screen takes on ingenious forms.[60] A black screen appears for a moment before the camera backs away to reveal the horizontally rectangular black opening of the space station ready to receive Floyd's space shuttle. A shot from inside the shuttle reveals the two wheels of the space station whirling on their axis until the black space between them enlarges to fill the screen, just before Floyd enters a sliding rectangular door into a lounge that contains a pink-suited flight attendant. Another black screen, signaling new spaces and stages, appears after Floyd leaves the Russian scientists and before he is shown on board the craft taking him to the moon.

In transit we pass through the monolith long before the dying Bowman passes through it in the last scene. From the time the ape hurls the bone, the stars are either invisible or barely seen on our journey through space, so that once again outer space, inner space, and the film itself reflexively merge. Then, within Floyd's shuttle, various smaller black rectangles repeatedly absorb or offset people and objects.[61] The blackness of space seen repeatedly through the horizontally rectangular windows and during the vertical descent into the black landing pad speaks to explorations and discoveries in every dimension, recalling Jung's distinction between the prevailing breadth of external knowledge (the space program as such) and the relatively shallow penetration of inner space (the psychological naïveté that enables destruction).

The disproportion between breadth and depth of knowledge is especially prominent in Floyd's briefing to the assembled scientists on Clavius,[62] a scene that emphasizes social confinement before Floyd touches the monolith and the film embarks upon "The Jupiter Mission." The black roof of the rectangular conference room is low, and the three visible walls (seen from the fourth wall) are rectangular white screens. The table forms a rectangular U shape with the opening at the speaker's end, while the chairs are all blue squares. The scene implicitly contrasts the film's cosmic vision to that of those still trapped within the room.

Here, as later in the crater scene, constant picture-taking alerts the audience to the visual motif. Floyd emphasizes the need to contain the public in a smaller frame: "I'm sure you're all aware of the extremely grave potential for cultural shock and social disorientation contained in this present situation if the facts were suddenly made public without adequate preparation and conditioning." Ironically, he keeps the scientists themselves in a smaller frame by not mentioning the political motive for the "cover story" of "an epidemic" that was first implied during his verbal sparring with the Russian scientists. As he speaks, the black corner of the room directly to his right looks like a solid black rectangle. It holds "within it" a standing American flag that accentuates the satire of political motivation as a "cover story" for psychological and anthropological ignorance and "epidemic" as a continuing primitive drive toward group rivalry and dominance.

On both sides of the black corners, large, horizontal white "projection screens" form the three walls of the room. They suggest the blank page of perception and self-knowledge that characterizes the assembled group, a state prior to the awareness of "black depths" that the film itself explores. Floyd's lectern is a white "screen" that exposes the shadows of his legs behind it, extending the idea of the vertical rectangle as a symbol of an unfilled outline of consciousness, a space of potential awareness that in the case of "advanced" technology has barely begun to be filled. In a Jungian sense Floyd's "shadow" appears during a territorial assertion of power crudely disguised by a polite speech of social control. Accordingly, the flag in the vertical black monolith seen on Floyd's right presides over the scene on and off for about forty seconds.

Floyd is then seen from the back of the room over a man looming large in the foreground. His square-shouldered black suit visually rhymes with Bowman's robe in the alien room, reiterating the theme of man-as-monolith. The image holds for twenty seconds before, during, and after the man's question: "Doctor Floyd, have you any idea how much longer this cover story will have to be maintained?" The question corresponds to the surrounding visual

blanks: how much longer before human beings advance enough to understand their common heritage and destiny, before they outgrow primate hierarchies and rival bands that attempt to extend *their* flag into space. The Russian scientists' complaint that their cosmonauts were endangered after being
denied a landing on Clavius suggests that the territorial imperative still
reigns in politically managed research.

Unlike Floyd, Kubrick did not work from a preset hypothesis or blueprint.
He had said that "the God-concept is at the heart of *2001*" but that he did
not believe in a monotheistic God. According to Alexander Walker, Kubrick
saw intelligence as "a sort of God."[63] For Jung, God is the transcendent intelligence of the Self, the integrated ego and unconscious. Part of the Self is
finite, the ego or rectangular shape of the monolith, and part is infinite, its
black color. In the creative process the ego plans, but in the "shooting stage"
the unconscious may alter that plan: "I do a tremendous amount of planning
and try to anticipate everything that is humanly possible to imagine prior to
shooting the scene, but when the moment actually comes, it is always different. . . . It is always tempting to think of how you're going to film something
before you know what it is you're going to film, but it's almost always a waste
of time."[64]

In an early stage of prewriting, Kubrick and Clarke planned to have the
monolith implement an alien blueprint by turning its surface into a vertical
screen that displayed a literal future. In the Clarke novel the lead ape sees
images of a well-fed family group "with sleek and glossy pelts" in contrast to
his own protruding ribs. When he awakens he has no memory of what he has
seen, but "discontent had come into his soul, and he had taken one small
step toward humanity" (a phrase later echoed by Neil Armstrong, the first
astronaut on the moon, as "one small step for man, one giant leap for
mankind").[65] As a teaching device in Clarke's novel, the monolith commu-
nicates precisely according to a plan in order to produce a particular result,
quite unlike Kubrick's stated way of working. It also has other limited functions that are never spelled out in the film: it is a cosmic alarm on the moon
to alert the aliens to human advancement and a "star gate" to bring Bowman
to the end of man qua man and the Star Child.[66]

At some point in conceiving the project, Kubrick changed the monolith
from a teaching device to a mirror of human potential. In making the monolith ambiguous, Kubrick followed Jung: "Psychologically the God-concept
includes every idea of the ultimate, of the first or last, of the highest or lowest. The name makes no difference."[67] Accordingly, Kubrick felt free to mod-
ify each facet of his archetypal plan, much to the annoyance of Frederick I.

Ordway III, the film's special consultant from the U.S. Space and Rocket Center:

> Suddenly, he asked me what my reaction would be if he were to substitute Saturn for Jupiter as the target of the spaceship Discovery expedition. I said something like, "Isn't it a bit late to make such a change?" He persisted, pointing out the beauty of the Saturnian ring system and the spectacular visual effect of the Discovery's traveling near or even through it. Would I do some investigation and prepare a memo outlining the latest knowledge of Saturn, its rings, and its moons, he asked? And would I focus on anything that seemed out of the ordinary, something intriguing and unexplainable that Arthur Clarke might weave into a revised screenplay?[68]

Kubrick's irregular shifts undercut Ordway's scientific priority of working logically from a preconceived idea, and he complained that "many design aspects of the vehicles in the film change regularly so that it becomes impossible at times to finalize anything." On the set he sought to confirm his disapproval by consulting unnamed "film experts," who told him that *2001* was more "unorthodox and difficult" than necessary. Ordway's discomfort with the process extended to his response to the finished film. His scientific orientation made him unable to appreciate Kubrick's removal of the explanatory voice-over that originally accompanied the opening scenes, because the audience "has a right to know" that "we are concerned with nothing less than racial extinction, the end of a line that eventually evolved into man." He also castigated Kubrick for cutting the "indispensable dialogue" between Bowman and Poole that revealed HAL's knowledge of the mission's purpose and his subsequent breakdown because he was not programmed to lie: "In an age of super science, of incredible information-processing and display devices, of computer-assisted thinking and delicately tuned responses, nothing less than total understanding can be tolerated. We are now on the Discovery midway between Earth and Jupiter. And the audience must know why. Fuzzy thinking, incomplete explanations, lost coupling scenes, missing bits of essential information have no place in *2001*."[69]

Kubrick asserted the right to think rather than the right to know. In his foreword to Krzysztof Kieslowski and Krzysztof Piesiewicz's published screenplay of *Decalogue: The Ten Commandments*, he praised the authors for "allowing the audience to discover what's really going on rather than being told" and for doing this "with such dazzling skill [that] you never see the ideas coming and don't realize until much later how profoundly they have reached your heart."[70] For Kubrick, discovery was paramount and pervasive.

By experimenting with every aspect of his craft, he often amazed "film experts" like Larry Smith, his cinematographer on *Eyes Wide Shut*:

> If there was a new tool out there, he knew all about it, even though he didn't necessarily have hands-on experience with it. For that reason, he had no preconceptions about what a piece of equipment could do. He'd simply say, "Well, let's get it and try this or that with it." During all of this research and testing Stanley would gradually get an overall picture of what he wanted to do, how he wanted to do it, and where he wanted to do it. He had a great deal of foresight, and he didn't restrict himself to a particular mode of working. He created a new style every time he did a movie, and along the way, he invariably came up with some incredible ideas.[71]

When Dave initially looks into the alien room through the pod bay door, the frame is dominated by the large white diamonds of the room's floor tiles.[72] As Dave scans the space, its decor and furniture appear to be a virtual parody of the "Enlightenment," the structured complacence of eighteenth-century Reason that the Romantics shattered. Then the walls and lines of the tiles unnaturally begin to curve, foreshadowing the shift from the monolith to the Star Child's globe. Paraphrasing Jung, Cirlot observes that "the square, representing the lowest of the composite and factorial numbers, symbolizes the pluralist state of man who has not achieved inner unity," while "the circle corresponds to an ultimate state of oneness."[73]

A symmetrical shot from the inside of the slate blue door opening presents a striking image. In the center of the frame-within-a-frame a gray-haired man in a black robe, seen from behind, is seated in a gray-green chair at a table covered with a gray-green cloth. When the man in the chair turns slowly toward his right to face him, Dave sees a version of himself that is now at least twenty years older than he was inside his space suit and forty years older than he was in the pod. Next to the man, on his right side, we see a wheelchair, but the man rises to walk unaided toward the camera. The wheelchair evokes material achievements, the discoveries of the bone tool, of fire, and the invention of the wheel pictured in the turning space station in DVD chapter 4 (and on the cover of the DVD). But the elderly Bowman rises to walk without it, suggesting that we will eventually outgrow our dependence on technology.

Kubrick spoke of this liberation in the 1968 Nordern interview:

> When you think of the giant technological strides that man has made in a few millennia—less than a microsecond in the chronology of the universe—can you imagine the evolutionary development that much older life forms have

taken? They may have progressed from biological species, which are fragile shells for the mind at best, into immortal machine entities—and then, over innumerable eons, they could emerge from the chrysalis of matter transformed into beings of pure energy and spirit.[74]

The old man's demeanor is dignified, and adjacent tones of blue in the background are pleasing to the eye. Still, his continuing to chew as he walks reminds us of his animal origin. But if the senses are limited, they are also the basis of the best human beings have conceived. The pace of the film invites appreciation of the aesthetic range that we can presently hear and see. Bowman begins to eat slowly, relishing the food and wine, but within a few seconds, he accidentally sweeps the wine glass onto the white floor where it shatters. The glass is a final symbol of containing form, and since it holds wine, critics have likened it to a "last supper." After the wine glass shatters, Bowman looks down at the fragments of the aesthetic past before he lifts his head and slowly turns to his right, just as he turned to his right when we first saw him from behind.

Squinting, he narrows his eyes to black slits resembling the obscured eyes of the apes. Following this variant of darkness preceding light, the camera tracks left to its first image of a still older Bowman lying on his deathbed. But the bed is beautiful. For the first time in the film green appears in a shade of summer vibrancy, on a velvet headboard that is framed within a white oval ornamented with scrolled flowers. The bedspread has modulated from the yellow-green of death to become the yellow-orange of the desert in "The Dawn of Man." In a 1968 interview Kubrick said that we are unique among animals in being able to conceptualize our own end and that "man's physical shell is his only buffer" against the "mind-paralyzing realization that only a few years of existence separate birth from death."[75] The final images of *2001* picture the mortality of both the individual and the species as a graceful transition.

Bald, as if to accentuate the loss of his shell, his orange fire now cooled to the pale gold of the blanket, an ancient Bowman lies in right profile on light green sheets. He raises his head a few inches and extends his right hand. A high-angle shot from the back of his head reveals the monolith standing ceiling high at the foot of the bed. In that the mind may come to function in ways that no longer depend on the senses, Bowman, unlike the ape leader and Floyd, does not physically touch the monolith. Not touching it prepares the way for the viewer to experience the surprise of passing through its apparently solid wall. Then the Star Child, in his womblike globe, appears in right profile, replacing Bowman on the bed.[76] The most striking quality of humanity's successor is an implicitly enhanced ability to "see." The Star Child's enormous eyes are deep blue, and their scope of vision will be larger than ours.

The last time we see the monolith in a low-angle shot, all its edges are visible, just before the camera advances into it. Its vertical shape expands to fill the horizontal screen for a moment, just before Jupiter appears slightly below center surrounded by dim stars. The film's vision is about to end so that ours may begin. To the ascending triad of *Also Sprach Zarathustra*, the monolith advances toward the camera until its blackness fills the screen. The monolith then absorbs us, not into a black hole of death, but into a vision of the blue earth's continuing life. A minute later we see that instead of disappearing into a void of cessation, we and our planetary home are still alive. We see the lower right curve of the earth on the left side of the frame and the Star Child's profile facing the earth in his blue globe on the right. The globe then fills the screen, and the Star Child begins to slowly turn toward the right, as Bowman had done twice previously in his black robe. In the film's final image, as the music sounds the end, the Star Child's face is gentle and serene.

Most importantly, perhaps, the Star Child's turn conveys a new kind of vision. Up until the last few seconds we have seen the Star Child only in profile, just as our first views of the monolith showed only its narrow edge. Earlier in the film, profile shots of the astronauts and images of HAL's single eye expressed limitations of consciousness and perception. At the end, both eyes of the Star Child look lovingly back at us within a circular "lens" that we have seen before. However, the aperture of HAL's eye and the opening of Dave's pod were relatively small circles in relation to the surrounding darkness. Here the curve of the Star Child's globe extends beyond the border of the frame. A small area of black space appears to his right, but on his left the projected light of our vision cannot contain the Star Child's sphere.

Notes

1. Steven Spielberg, foreword to *Stanley Kubrick: A Life in Pictures*, by Christiane Kubrick (Boston, New York, London: Little, Brown, 2002), 10.

2. National Catholic Award, written by Gene D. Phillips, S.J., read by Tom Cruise, in *Stanley Kubrick: A Life in Pictures*, DVD, directed by Jan Harlan (1999; Burbank, Calif.: Warner Bros. Home Video, 2001).

3. Stanley Kubrick, interview by Michel Ciment, *Kubrick: The Definitive Edition* (New York: Faber & Faber, 2001), 122.

4. Richard Schickel, in *Stanley Kubrick: A Life in Pictures*, DVD.

5. Pauline Kael, review of *Doctor Strangelove*, in *Kiss Kiss Bang Bang*, by Pauline Kael (New York: Little, Brown, 1968); quoted by Gene D. Phillips, "Stop the World: Stanley Kubrick," in *Stanley Kubrick: Interviews*, ed. Gene D. Phillips (Jackson: University Press of Mississippi, 2001), 150–151.

6. Stanley Kubrick, interview by Eric Nordern, *Playboy*, September 1968; repr. in Phillips, ed., *Stanley Kubrick: Interviews*, 49.

7. Stanley Kubrick, interview by Philip Strick and Penelope Houston, "Modern Times: An Interview with Stanley Kubrick," *Sight & Sound*, Spring 1972; repr. in Phillips, ed., *Stanley Kubrick: Interviews*, 129.

8. Michael Herr, foreword to *Full Metal Jacket*, by Stanley Kubrick, Michael Herr, and Gustav Hasford (New York: Alfred A. Knopf, 1987), v.

9. Kubrick, interview by Ciment, 163.

10. Carl G. Jung in Carl G. Jung, M.-L. von Franz, Joseph Henderson, Jolande Jacobi, and Aniela Jaffe, *Man and His Symbols* (Garden City, N.Y.: Doubleday, 1964), 112–113.

11. Stanley Kubrick and Arthur C. Clarke, *2001: A Space Odyssey Screenplay* (England: Hawk Films, Ltd., 1965); repr. on the Kubrick Site, www.visual-memory.co.uk/amk/doc/0057.html.

12. Kubrick and Clarke, *2001: A Space Odyssey Screenplay*, the Kubrick Site.

13. Dan Richter, *Moonwatcher's Memoir: A Diary of 2001: A Space Odyssey* (New York: Carroll and Graf, 2002), 18.

14. Robert Ardrey, *African Genesis* (New York: Atheneum, 1961), 30.

15. Ardrey, *African Genesis*, 31.

16. Kubrick, interview by Nordern, in Phillips, ed., *Stanley Kubrick: Interviews*, 68.

17. Ardrey, *African Genesis*, 348; Kubrick's letter to the *New York Times*, February 27, 1972.

18. Clarke called Campbell's book "very stimulating" in a diary entry of September 26, 1964, in *Lost Worlds of 2001* (1972; Boston: Gregg Press, 1979), 34; see also Vincent LoBrutto, *Stanley Kubrick: A Biography* (New York: Donald I. Fine, 1997), 266.

19. Joseph Campbell, *The Hero with a Thousand Faces*, 2nd ed. (Princeton, N.J.: Princeton University Press, 1968), 20.

20. Stanley Kubrick, interview by Joseph Gelmis, "The Film Director as Superstar: Stanley Kubrick," in *The Film Director as Superstar* (Garden City, N.Y.: Doubleday, 1970); repr. in Phillips, ed., *Stanley Kubrick: Interviews*, 91.

21. Campbell, *The Hero with a Thousand Faces*, 8.

22. LoBrutto, *Stanley Kubrick*, 270.

23. Stanley Kubrick, quoted in Jeremy Bernstein, "Beyond the Stars," *New Yorker*, April 24, 1965; repr. in Phillips, ed., *Stanley Kubrick: Interviews*, 18.

24. Arthur C. Clarke, *2001: A Space Odyssey* (1968; New York: New American Library, 2000), 126–127.

25. Ardrey, *African Genesis*, 318.

26. Homer, *The Odyssey*, trans. E. V. Rieu (Baltimore: Penguin, 1946), 123.

27. Homer, *The Odyssey*, 124.

28. Homer, *The Odyssey*, 34.

29. Kubrick, interview by Nordern, in Phillips, ed., *Stanley Kubrick: Interviews*, 68.

30. C. G. Jung, "The Stages of Life," in *The Portable Jung*, ed. Joseph Campbell, trans. R. F. C. Hull (1930; New York: Viking, 1971), 19.

31. Campbell, *The Hero with a Thousand Faces*, 20.

32. Stanley Kubrick to Gene D. Phillips, in *The Movie Makers: Artists in an Industry*, by Gene D. Phillips (Chicago: Nelson-Hall, 1973); repr. in Phillips, ed., *Stanley Kubrick: Interviews*, 152.

33. Kubrick, interview by Nordern, in Phillips, ed., *Stanley Kubrick: Interviews*, 73.

34. Kubrick, interview by Gelmis, in Phillips, ed., *Stanley Kubrick: Interviews*, 91, 92.

35. Brian Aldiss, in *Stanley Kubrick: A Life in Pictures*, DVD.

36. Kubrick, interview by Gelmis in Phillips, ed., *Stanley Kubrick: Interviews*, 93.

37. Jung, *Man and His Symbols*, 4.

38. Jung, *Man and His Symbols*, 41.

39. C. G. Jung, "On the Relation of Analytical Psychology to Poetry," in *The Portable Jung*, ed. Joseph Campbell, trans. R. F. C. Hull (1930; New York: Viking, 1971), 311.

40. Constantin Stanislavski, *An Actor Prepares*, trans. Elizabeth Reynolds Hapgood (New York: Theater Arts Books, Robert M. MacGregor, 1952), 133.

41. James B. Harris, interview by Michel Ciment, *Kubrick: The Definitive Edition* (New York: Faber & Faber, 2001), 202.

42. Matthew Modine in Peter Bogdanovich, "What They Say about Stanley Kubrick," *New York Times Magazine*, July 25, 1999.

43. John Boorman, *The Emerald Forest Diary: A Filmmaker's Odyssey* (New York: Farrar, Straus, and Giroux, 1985); quoted in LoBrutto, *Stanley Kubrick*, 431.

44. *Stanley Kubrick: A Life in Pictures*, DVD.

45. Douglas Milsome, quoted by Ron Magid, "*Full Metal Jacket*: Cynic's Choice," *American Cinematographer*, September 1987, 77; quoted by LoBrutto, *Stanley Kubrick*, 473.

46. Kubrick, interview by Ciment, 152.

47. *2001: A Space Odyssey*, DVD, directed by Stanley Kubrick (1968; Burbank, Calif.: Warner Bros. Home Video, 2001), chapter 24.

48. *A Clockwork Orange*, DVD, directed by Stanley Kubrick (1999; Burbank, Calif.: Warner Bros. Home Video, 2001), chapter 13.

49. *2001: A Space Odyssey*, DVD, chapter 25.

50. Kubrick, interview by Gelmis, in Phillips, ed., *Stanley Kubrick: Interviews*, 91.

51. C. G. Jung, quoted in J. E. Cirlot, *A Dictionary of Symbols*, trans. Jack Sage (New York: Philosophical Library, 1962), 55.

52. Cirlot, *A Dictionary of Symbols*, 260.

53. Ken Adam, in Bogdanovich, "What They Say About Stanley Kubrick."

54. *2001: A Space Odyssey*, DVD, chapter 3.

55. C. G. Jung, "The Basic Postulates of Analytical Psychology," C. G. Jung Page website, www.cgjungpage.org/content/view/5/15/1/.

56. Jung, "The Basic Postulates of Analytical Psychology," C. G. Jung Page website.

57. *2001: A Space Odyssey*, DVD, chapter 11.

58. See David Hughes, *The Complete Kubrick* (London: Virgin, 2000), 137–138.

59. *2001: A Space Odyssey*, DVD, chapter 3.

60. *2001: A Space Odyssey*, DVD, chapter 4.

61. *2001: A Space Odyssey*, DVD, chapter 8.

62. *2001: A Space Odyssey*, DVD, chapter 9.

63. Alexander Walker, Sybil Taylor, and Ulrich Ruchti, *Stanley Kubrick, Director: A Visual Analysis* (New York: W. W. Norton, 1999), 193.

64. Stanley Kubrick, interview by Penelope Houston, "Kubrick Country," *Saturday Review*, December 25, 1971; repr. in Phillips, ed., *Stanley Kubrick: Interviews*, 114.

65. Clarke, *2001: A Space Odyssey*, 18, 19.

66. Walker, Taylor, and Ruchti, *Stanley Kubrick*, 181.

67. C. G. Jung, "Answer to Job," in *The Portable Jung*, ed. Joseph Campbell, trans. R. F. C. Hull (1930; New York: Viking, 1971), 631n.

68. Frederick I. Ordway III, "Part B: *2001: A Space Odyssey* in Retrospect," in *Science Fiction and Space Futures: Past and Present*, ed. Eugene M. Emme, American Astronautical Society History Series 5 (San Diego, Calif.: Univelt, 1982), 65; repr. on the Kubrick Site, www.visual-memory.co.uk/amk/doc/0075.html.

69. Ordway, "Part B: *2001*," 66.

70. Stanley Kubrick, foreword to *Decalogue: The Ten Commandments*, by Krzysztof Kieslowski and Krzysztof Piesiewicz (London: Faber & Faber, 1991), 1.

71. Larry Smith, interview by Stephen Pizzello, "A Sword in the Bed: Cinematographer Larry Smith Helps Stanley Kubrick Craft a Unique Look for *Eyes Wide Shut*, a Dreamlike Coda to the Director's Brilliant Career," *American Cinematographer*, October 1999, www.theasc.com/magazine/oct99/sword/.

72. *2001: A Space Odyssey*, DVD, chapter 30.

73. Cirlot, *A Dictionary of Symbols*, 45.

74. Kubrick, interview by Nordern, in Phillips, ed., *Stanley Kubrick: Interviews*, 50.

75. Kubrick, interview by Nordern, in Phillips, ed., *Stanley Kubrick: Interviews*, 72.

76. *2001: A Space Odyssey*, DVD, chapter 31.

~

CHAPTER THREE

Leading the Way

A Clockwork Orange

Michel Chion has observed that three "central pieces" of ascending music establish *2001*'s "optimistic character": the arpeggio of Richard Strauss's *Also Sprach Zarathustra* at the beginning and the end, Johann Strauss's *The Blue Danube* "on the perfect major chord" after the four-million-year jump cut, and the "Kyrie" from György Ligeti's *Requiem* during the first three appearances of the monolith.[1] The opening of *A Clockwork Orange* brings the Star Child's vision back to earth. A tolling drumbeat accompanies a descending electronic drone that precedes the introduction of the primary musical theme, Walter Carlos's synthesized version of Henry Purcell's seventeenth-century *Elegy on the Death of Queen Mary*. This plays under a blank, brown-bordered orange screen for thirty-four seconds until the white-lettered words "Warner Bros. Presents" appear, followed by the dramatic contrast of a royal blue card with the white-lettered words "A Stanley Kubrick Production," followed by a third and final orange card with the title, "A Clockwork Orange." The assertive sound and bold colors contrast sharply with the soft orange and blue tints that concluded *2001*.

In the first shot after the titles, the ape leader's shadowed sockets have brightened into Alex's predatory stare. Both are ultimate alpha males, and both have dual possibilities. Though Alex can be the moving force of life-as-a-horror-film, he is also the source of its energy, passion, and beauty. Though his actions can be monstrous, he is the child that the film defends against proponents of utopia. Without his indomitable will to full expression, the Star Child would be impossible. *A Clockwork Orange* asserts the value of natural aggression in its sublimated form as art, and in making the thuggish Alex attractive, Kubrick did not mean to glorify violence:

> We can identify with Alex on the unconscious level . . . you find much the same psychological phenomenon at work in Shakespeare's Richard III. You should feel nothing but dislike towards Richard, and yet when the role is well played, with a bit of humor and charm, you find yourself gradually making a similar kind of identification with him. Not because you sympathize with Richard's ambition or his actions, or that you like him or think people should behave like him, but as you watch the play, because he gradually works himself into your unconscious, and recognition occurs in the recesses of the mind.[2]

Kubrick shared Freud's faith in redemptive self-knowledge. For Freud the id was the original psychic reality and the origin of physical and psychological motivation. The id seeks only pleasure and even when successfully repressed, it seeks and occasionally breaks through to express itself in selfish or antisocial acts, or at the very least in fantasies and dreams. Kubrick called Alex "a creature of the id" and understood the anger of some critics and audience members as inadmissible empathy: "They are unable to accept this view of themselves and, therefore, they become angry at the film."[3]

But while Kubrick apparently accepted Freud's basic concept of the psyche's structure, he opposed Freud's social philosophy. Freud believed that the major purpose of society was effective repression, and he thought that the arts were useful primarily as a means of controlling rather than sublimating nature. He believed that strengthening the superego (the internalized voice of social order or "conscience") was the "most precious asset in the psychological field. Those in whom it has taken place are turned from being opponents of civilization into being its vehicles."[4] To assist this long-range progress the arts are (as Dr. Brodsky also says later in *Clockwork*) merely "a useful heightener" of social loyalty: "When those creations picture the achievements of his particular culture and bring to his mind its ideals in an impressive manner, they also minister to his narcissistic satisfaction."[5] Civilization was rightfully imposed on the majority by the powerful in order to control nature and to use its resources to satisfy human needs.[6]

Freud asserted the welfare of the group over the anarchic id-driven desires of the individual:

> Human life in common is only made possible when a majority comes together which is stronger than any separate individual and which remains united against all separate individuals. . . . The power of this community is then set up as "right" in opposition to the power of the individual, which is condemned

as "brute force." This replacement of the power of the individual by the power of the community constitutes the decisive step of civilization.[7]

Kubrick implicitly agreed with Freud that an individual lacking social control would vent his aggression on his neighbor, "use him sexually without his consent, seize his possessions, humiliate him, cause him pain, torture and kill him. *Homo homini lupus.*"[8] But while Freud resigned himself to a degree of failure, since a "certain percentage of mankind (owing to a pathological disposition or an excess of instinctual strength) will always remain asocial," Kubrick found evolutionary hope in these very individuals.[9]

Since 2001's *Zarathustra* arpeggio and evolutionary theme have an obvious connection to Nietzsche, the philosopher's views of the relationship between the individual and the state may well have provided the two-part premise of *A Clockwork Orange*: (1) that the nation-state is the enemy of nonconformity, self-realization, and the "single one's" transfiguration, and (2) that moral progress may just be emasculation—"To be moral is to overcome one's impulses; if one does not have any impulses, one is not therefore moral. . . . There is more hope for the man of strong impulses than for a man of no impulses."[10] In the novel, Burgess has his villain, Dr. Brodsky, defend the Ludovico conditioning treatment against Alex's complaint that morality may kill the passion that makes music beautiful: "Delimitation is always difficult. The world is one, life is one. The sweetest and most heavenly of activities partake in some measure of violence—the act of love, for instance; music, for instance. You must take your chance, boy. The choice has been all yours."[11]

But Alex had no choice because he did not realize that freedom from prison would result in psychological enslavement. The film means to warn the viewer that spiritual survival requires the craft of Odysseus, that is, assuming the semblance of a socially reduced self while refusing to surrender one's spirit. As a retrospective narrator in the novel, the mature Alex intuits that society's attempts to discover and root out the causes of evil are crudely destructive because they are psychologically naive. Since evil is an inextricable part of every individual, the "cure" for evil is the death of the self: "The not-self cannot have the bad, meaning they of the government and the judges and the schools cannot allow the bad because they cannot allow the self. And is not our modern history, my brothers, the story of brave malenky [tiny] selves fighting these machines?"[12]

Contra Freud, Jung saw the ultimate triumph of the superego as "crushing out the insight and reflection" of the individual. The Soviet bloc and Western democracy both threatened spiritual genocide since they shared the tendency to conglomerate their citizens in a mass pursuit of material gain. Since the individual is "the supreme and only real object of investigation," Jung rejected any universal psychology that would reduce people to statistical units that might just as well be designated by letters of the alphabet (humorously represented by Alex's parents, Pee and Em, and by the symbolic doubling and shrinkage of Alex's prison name, 6554321): "The State . . . is turned into a quasi-animate personality from whom everything is expected. In reality it is only a camouflage for those individuals who know how to manipulate it."[13]

In a post-*Clockwork* interview, Kubrick was quite explicit about these themes:

> The film explores the difficulties of reconciling the conflict between individual freedom and social order. Alex exercises his freedom to be a vicious thug until the State turns him into a harmless zombie no longer able to choose between good and evil. One of the conclusions of the film is, of course, that there are limits to which society should go in maintaining law and order. Society should not do the wrong thing for the right reason, even though it frequently does the right thing for the wrong reason.[14]

But Kubrick also understood that political power was not the only threat to sentience. As in *The Odyssey*, drugs and distraction could be as deadly as political intimidation or war. Far from advocating the fascism that some saw in his film, Kubrick stated that his film was a warning against "the new psychedelic fascism—the eye-popping, multimedia, quadrasonic, drug-oriented conditioning of human beings by other beings—which many believe will usher in the forfeiture of human citizenship and the beginning of zombiedom."[15]

Kubrick's belief that conformity and addiction threatened evolutionary advance is implicit throughout his oeuvre and explicit in interviews. The workings of intellect and inspiration depend on maintaining the integrity of the self:

> The illusion of oneness with the universe . . . and the pervasive aura of peace and contentment is not the ideal state for an artist. It tranquillizes the creative personality, which thrives on conflict and on the clash and ferment of ideas. The artist's transcendence must be within his own work; he should not impose any artificial barriers between himself and the mainspring of his subconscious. People on LSD cannot distinguish between things that are really interesting and things that appear to be under the influence of the trip. They seem to completely lose their critical faculties and disengage themselves from some of the

stimulating areas of life. Perhaps when everything is beautiful, nothing is beautiful.[16]

Burgess opens his novel with a similar rejection of the oceanic feeling when Alex says that using an LSD-like drug to lose "your name and body" just to "get in touch with God" is cowardly: "That sort of thing could sap all the strength and goodness out of a chelloveck."[17] Waking up from the effects of a recreational drug has the same effect that social "correction" has on Alex later in the film when he wants to "snuff it." Though he feels "real horror-show, like in heaven," while high on the drug, or while he enjoys the afflu-ent comforts of the Ludovico center in contrast to prison, he eventually wakes up in suicidal despair.

In a letter to the *New York Times* Kubrick rejected "Rousseau's romantic fallacy that it is society which corrupts man, not man who corrupts society" as a "self-inflating illusion leading to despair."[18] Humanity would be doomed if Dave had not retained the killer instinct that allowed him to overcome the technological perfection of HAL, or if Odysseus had killed and invented only to serve the martial perfection his society professed. Jean-Jacques Rousseau's *The Social Contract* (1762) advocated a type of communism that was the nat-ural human state before civilization produced tyrants. His assertion that kings rule by the will of the people rather than by God fired the zeal of the French Revolution, but his belief that babies are born good and that primi-tive people were innately moral seemed ludicrous after the Enlightenment produced the guillotine and the Napoleonic wars. Nietzsche considered Rousseau's "natural man" to be pernicious, because the idea obscured the danger that could be unleashed when all that repressed "goodness" was al-lowed to return. For him, mature individuals were antirevolutionary because they sublimated their aggressive energies into philosophy and art and because they focused on absorbing "the riches of the world" into their souls rather than their societies.[19]

Robert Ardrey emphasized that recognizing natural aggression through the study of animal evolution was the most valuable knowledge humanity could absorb, since planetary survival depends on redirection while destruc-tion will result from denial. After three billion years of evolving life on the planet, humans are still "a supreme experiment" rather than finished beings that need only reclaim their original state. He observed that innate aggres-sion enabled two primary drives: territoriality and dominance, and he dis-missed the Darwinian assumption that male animals compete to possess females. In reality females compete for the strongest males, while rivalry for rule consumes males within and between groups.[20] At the time of *A*

Clockwork Orange, English gangs (teddy boys, mods, and rockers) could not fight for turf they did not control, but dominance for its own sake moved them to bash peaceful citizens and each other. Billy Boy's militarily garbed knife squad gleefully abandons their ritualized rape to spill from the proscenium arch of the casino into a melee with Alex and his droogs. Burgess had commented on the motiveless violence of the fifties gangs: "These young people seemed to love aggression for its own sake. They were expressing the Manichean principle of the universe, opposition as an end in itself, yin versus yang, X against Y."[21] The droogs are indifferent to money until they dimly realize that having money defines strength in their society. Even so, they rebel against Alex only because he abuses them rather than because they reject anarchy.

The French Revolution established just enough "equality" to redirect the killer instinct from beheading the local aristocracy to conquering all the nations of Europe. Alex's former subjects as grown-up police officers find the same outlets that they found as droogs. Ardrey observed that economic concerns became paramount only in times of starvation and that economic motives do not explain the individual's compulsion to seek dominance in a particular sphere or group, or the mass fascination with weapons, crime, and wealth enjoyed directly by the few and vicariously by the many.[22]

Kubrick's fascination with the eighteenth century may stem from the period's stark contrasts: its excessive formality in art, clothing, and manners versus its orgiastic delight in bloody wars and duels. The alien room at the end of *2001* is decorated in the height of prerevolutionary French style, as if to signal the demise of an enlightened rationality, foreshadowed by the death of HAL. Patrick Magee, who played Frank Alexander in *Clockwork,* also starred in Peter Brook's acclaimed theater and film productions of Peter Weiss's 1964 play, *Marat/Sade,* set in an insane asylum in postrevolutionary France. Another character in that play, Jacques Roux, "a former priest and radical socialist," expresses the inadequacy of political solutions to problems that are fundamentally psychological and spiritual: "And you came one day to the Revolution because you saw the most important vision, that our circumstances must be changed fundamentally and without these changes everything we try to do must fail."[23]

One of Sade's speeches foreshadows the "Modern Age," Frank Alexander's term for the world of *Clockwork Orange:* "Now I see where this revolution is leading: To the withering of the individual man and a slow merging into uniformity, to the death of choice, to self denial, to deadly weakness in a state which has no contact with individuals, but which is impregnable."[24] From Ardrey's point of view the overmanaged security of the modern state both impels violence and threatens something worse. His ironic alternative to natural determinism appears in the film as the "horrorshow" Ludovico treatment:

> When a predatory species [evolved] its inherent talent for disorder, natural selection favored as a factor in human survival that sublimating, inhibiting, super-territorial institution which we call loosely, civilization. . . . Its grayness is appalling . . . its foundations are shallow . . . [yet] man beset by anarchy, banditry, chaos and extinction must at last resort turn to that chamber of horrors. . . . The masters of a universal society with the aid of a captive science might just possibly succeed in producing, over a long period, a lasting answer to the problem of our animal nature: a universal human slave inherently obedient to other people's reason.[25]

Kubrick's films suggest alternative extinctions—in the fire of Strangelovian apocalypse or the ice of "Enlightened" rigor mortis. Both become more likely as technology threatens to control its inventors, while self-knowledge stalls or declines. Either way, political and social events consistently express the ongoing stupidity of blindly pursuing dominance. In the madhouse of the world, *Marat/Sade*'s inmates chant on a treadmill of futility: "Now the Prussians retreat [1806], Russia faces defeat [1807] / All the world bends its knee to Napoleon and his family. Fight on land and on sea [1808] / All men want to be free / If they don't, never mind, we'll abolish all mankind / Fifteen glorious years . . . each year greater than the one before . . . we're marching on behind Napoleon."[26]

Kubrick's fascination with Napoleon has become legendary. He had hoped to make a Napoleonic epic immediately after *2001* but failed to get studio backing and had to postpone the project. After completing *A Clockwork Orange*, Kubrick planned to base the film on a novel he proposed to Burgess. Burgess completed *Napoleon Symphony: A Novel in Four Movements* (1974), but Kubrick never found a practical means to film the novel or the script he had written himself in 1969.[27] The negative references to Rousseau in his post-*Clockwork* letters and interviews reflected his prior immersion in the Napoleon project. In the screenplay that he wrote himself (based on Felix Markham's biography), Napoleon's address to his dinner guests echoes both Ardrey and *Marat/Sade*:

> Napoleon [*addressing his dinner guests*]: The Revolution failed because the foundation of its political philosophy was in error. Its central dogma was the transference of original sin from man to society. It had the rosy vision that by nature man is good, and that he is only corrupted by an incorrectly organized

society. Destroy the offending social institutions, tinker with the machine a bit, and you have Utopia—presto!—natural man back in all his goodness [*laughter at the table*]. . . . They had the whole thing backwards. Society is corrupt because man is corrupt—because he is weak, selfish, hypocritical, and greedy. And he is not made this way by society, he is born this way—you can see it even in the youngest children. It's no good trying to build a better society on false assumptions—authority's main job is to keep man from being at his worst, and thus, make life tolerable, for the greater number of people.[28]

But Kubrick was interested even more in the man than in his social philosophy. Napoleon was the ultimate alpha male, and though he was responsible for innumerable deaths, he was driven more by a creative impulse to push his limits than to conquer. The contradictions of genius became an enduring Kubrick theme. Alex's aesthetic sensibilities and inspired strategies for mayhem might have made him another Napoleon had the circumstances of his life allowed. Alex and Joker both narrate their tales, and the implication is that in their evolution from killer to storyteller their alpha energy has not been diminished. But the behavioral psychology that Kubrick associates with addictive media in the Ludovico treatment shares its ultimate goal with Freud's vision of the superego triumphant. If the id-driven individual is extinguished in the interest of social order, the soul will not evolve, and the entropy epitomized by Alex's parents will become universal.

In contrast to B. F. Skinner who saw "no virtue in accident or in the chaos from which somehow we have reached our present position,"[29] Ardrey retained a fervent faith in "the pure wild gene, in natural selection as opposed to human, and in the strength and balance of our natural endowment as sufficient" for evolutionary advance.[30] For Ardrey and Kubrick, human survival depends on the extraordinary individual rather than the utopian society. Kubrick saw Napoleon as more of an artist than a ruler, not quite an Odysseus, but certainly not an Agamemnon or Menelaus. His films express concern for the future of alpha individuals who excel in thought, feeling, and imagination rather than governing. Dominance can lead to tyranny, but dominance per se is not evil. It is, according to Ardrey, "a force at least as old and as deep as territory . . . among social animals it is universal, and among our primate family the source of society's most mysterious subtleties; among all animal sources of human behavior, the instinct for status may in the end prove the most important."[31] A gifted individual can consciously or unconsciously transform the character of society. Ardrey cites an experiment involving a rhesus monkey in which "that all powerful natural accident, conception, had placed in [his] genes . . . such resources of strength, of energy, of courage, and of assurance that he had become a giant of dominance." Despite the general rule that rhesus monkeys are content to maintain a territory, this monkey's group "acquired the capacity as a society to dominate its neighbors." When the master monkey was removed from the master society, "the troop immediately fell back to its own territory."[32]

Of course, hierarchies are not limited to political or social entities but are found in every subculture of complex societies. Celebrity worship of every ilk has now metastasized into the creation of instant celebrities to be vicariously worshipped for their willingness to bare their souls on reality TV or expose their shortcomings on ubiquitous talent shows. Recent animal studies have confirmed Ardrey's thesis that dominance is more compelling than greed. Market research has recently drawn upon primate research to confirm its long-standing conviction that celebrity sells. Field observers report that wild "social primates spend a lot of time just keeping track of the highest ranking troop member," and laboratory studies show that monkeys "will give up a considerable quantity of [task-reward] fruit juice for the chance just to look at a picture of a higher-ranking individual."[33] Judging by this data, France's post-Terror aggression was fired more by the charisma of its leader than by an abstract zeal for liberty. Marat/Sade implies that the only freedom achieved by individual soldiers under their beloved dictator was the liberation of their killer instincts. As a field commander, however, Napoleon was a consummate artist. His technique consisted of seeking a weak point in the enemy's line, but he depended on inspiration to determine the precise moment of attack. The invariable result was a routed enemy and the confirmation of the French army's unqualified devotion to their leader. Napoleon's own devotion was to himself. The willingness of the French nation as a whole to surrender their freedom and their lives for a worshipped leader recalls Ardrey's rhesus monkey troop that uncharacteristically attacked and occupied neighboring territories under its "giant of dominance." The Duke of Wellington recalled that he "used to say of [Napoleon] that his presence on the field made the difference of forty thousand men."[34]

But Napoleon was a bit more complicated than his rhesus cousin. On his Egyptian expedition, the enlightened killer brought a team of scholars who translated the Rosetta Stone, an achievement that initiated the deciphering of hieroglyphics. His general cast of thought was that of a skeptical philosopher rather than a grandiose patriot—"If I had to choose a religion, the sun as the universal giver of life would be my god"—and his political sentiments were anything but democratic: "In a great nation, the majority are incapable of judging wisely of things," and "the public spirit is in the hands of the man who knows how to make use of it." Though his outlook was cynical, he had an artist's faith in intuition. "Take time to deliberate, but when the time for action has arrived, stop thinking and go."[35] Kubrick described Napoleon's life as "an epic poem of action" and called him "one of those rare men" who "mold the destiny of their own times and of generations to come."[36]

Kubrick's research into all things Napoleon included reading hundreds of books, from nineteenth-century English and French accounts to modern biographies. He must therefore have known that Napoleon avidly studied the campaigns of great generals and that he had a particular favorite: "If I had not been born Napoleon, I would have liked to have been born Alexander."[37] One of his favorite paintings was Albrecht Altdorfer's *Battle of Alexander at Issus*.[38] Anthony Burgess also thought highly of Alexander, or at least of the symbolic value of his name. In his memoir, *1985*, he explained that *Clockwork*'s "hero needed a noble name, nicely met by Alexander ('leader of men') the Great." He added that "Alex is a rich and noble name, and I intended its possessor to be sympathetic, pitiable, and insidiously identifiable with 'us,' as opposed to 'them.'"[39]

Burgess and Kubrick wanted to give the culturally deprived Alex the same innate energy and sensibility as the great world conqueror. Alexander's father had been an invincible general, but as a Macedonian he was relatively rough around the edges in comparison to the Greeks he had conquered. He decided to remedy the situation by having his son personally tutored by Aristotle, from whom he acquired a keen interest in botany, biology, geography, and distant cultures. His mother taught him that Achilles was his ancestor, and he was so imbued with *The Iliad* that he carried it on all his campaigns.

In the first year of his spectacular eleven-year conquest of most of the known world, Alexander visited Troy where he made offerings to Athena, donned the armor of Achilles, and brandished his shield. The company of scholars that Napoleon took on his Egyptian expedition echoed the brigade of artists, geographers, historians, botanists, and geologists that accompanied Alexander on his campaigns. And, of course, both men led their troops to the exultant slaughter of hundreds of thousands of people. At Thebes, Tyre, and Persepolis Alexander killed and enslaved entire populations. He was often the first man over the wall of a besieged city and suffered many wounds. His flair for the dramatic included physically leading his troops into battle astride Bucephalus, an untamable horse that only he could ride, and improvising events that became legendary.[40]

In Kubrick's script Alex has two names: Alexander de Large and Alex Burgess. In the novel "Alexander de Large" is used only once, when the narrator alludes to his phallic size after the ménage à trois, but in the film

Kubrick emphasizes the contrast between the pre- and post-Ludovico Alex by having him repeat it twice just before the prison guards officially reduce him to "6554321." Near the end of the film the other name appears in a montage of news articles that presage the hero's return: "Brainwashing techniques were responsible for the suicide bid of Alex Burgess, the 'wonder-cure' boy murderer" and "Doctors last night blamed secret laboratory experiments on criminals for causing Alex Burgess, the 'Cat-Woman killer,' to attempt suicide."[41]

Burgess groused that "the cinema gets away with inconsistencies that no copy editor would stomach in a novel,"[42] but Kubrick may have conflated the names of the world conqueror and the scintillating writer to underscore the likeness between Alex and Ludwig van Beethoven, an analogy that Burgess did not make. In the novel there is no poster of Beethoven in Alex's room, while in the film it is an intense, presiding presence. For Kubrick, Beethoven was the supreme ideal of man's evolution from killer to explorer. He had heard that Burgess was planning to structure "a Jane Austen parody" in the four-movement pattern of a Mozart symphony. Seizing an opportunity to recruit Burgess's remarkable talent for his long-cherished project, Kubrick suggested a different novel based on a different symphony: "He meant Beethoven's symphony no. 3 in E flat, the Eroica, which began by being about Napoleon. . . . The first movement was clearly about struggle and victory, the second about a great public funeral, and in the third and fourth the hero was raised to the level of myth—a specific myth, that of Prometheus."[43]

In the heady atmosphere of individual freedom that the revolution had promised to all of Europe, Beethoven himself became a Promethean myth. His initial admiration for Napoleon was personal as well as political, since both men had to overcome their status as social underdogs. Beethoven's paternal ancestors were singers in the choir of the archbishop of Cologne, but the family declined into poverty when his father became an alcoholic. Napoleon's family had questionable aristocratic credentials but managed to get him admitted to a royal military school. Both grew up in provincial towns, and both were unimpressively short, Napoleon standing five feet two, and Beethoven five feet four.[44]

But Beethoven fiercely asserted his will to resist social or physical humiliation. When his patron, Prince Lichnowsky, tried to make him play to entertain some visiting French officers, Beethoven walked out and upon returning home, sent the prince a note: "Prince, what you are you are by accident of birth; what I am I am through myself. There have been and still will be thousands of princes; there is only one Beethoven." After he had dedicated his Ninth Symphony to Frederick William III of Prussia, and the king sent him a ring with a cheap stone in return, a friend told him to keep it because at least it came from a king. Beethoven retorted, "I too am a king!"[45] Beethoven was the first major European composer to support himself, free of church, royal, or aristocratic patronage. (After losing control over *Spartacus* and having to accede to the censorship of *Lolita*, Kubrick achieved independence from the studio system with the success of *Dr. Strangelove*. From then on he exercised complete artistic and financial control over his films.)

But Beethoven became truly Promethean when he refused to bow to a crushing affliction. In his early thirties his hearing began to deteriorate, the ultimate musician's nightmare. As the condition worsened he had suicidal moments but characteristically recovered and defied despair: "It seemed unthinkable for me to leave the world forever before I had produced all that I felt called upon to produce."[46] As Kubrick strongly suggests, that untamable will to create sublimated a basic alpha drive. Rejecting religious resignation as forcefully as he had scorned kings, Beethoven wrote, "I will seize fate by the throat!"[47] During the last ten years of his life he wrote brilliantly and even conducted while he was totally deaf.

A noted philosopher of aesthetics, Morse Peckham, has observed that the highest critical acclaim "is reserved for artists, like Michelangelo and Beethoven, who continued to grow until they died, that is, continued to exhibit a steady and sometimes an increasing rate of stylistic dynamism throughout their entire careers."[48] In a statement appended to the *Eyes Wide Shut* DVD, Steven Spielberg admired Kubrick for experimenting with a different genre in every film and taking a different artistic risk. He observed that Kubrick told stories in a way that was "sometimes antithetical to the way we are accustomed to receiving stories" and added that *2001* changed the form of cinematic narrative.[49]

Like *2001*, Beethoven's Ninth Symphony, his last and most legendary, was a turning point in the history of his art, "not only for its novel inclusion of chorus and vocal soloists in the last movement and the extraordinarily variegated sonata form of that movement—incorporating a Turkish march, double exposition, double fugues, strophic (stanzaic) variations—but for the scope of the whole."[50] Claude Debussy offered an encomium that set the general tone for subsequent acclaim:

> It is the most triumphant example of the molding of an idea to the preconceived form; at each leap forward there is a new delight, without either effort or appearance of repetition; the magical blossoming, so to speak, of a tree whose leaves burst forth simultaneously. Nothing is superfluous in this stupendous work. . . . Beethoven had already written eight symphonies and the figure

nine seems to have had for him an almost mystic significance. He determined to surpass himself. I can scarcely see how his success can be questioned.[51]

In Kubrick's *Clockwork* the piece is a symbol of *pothos*, the pushing of personal limits that drove Alexander and Napoleon. In Burgess's novel, Alex selects the "glorious Ninth of Ludwig van" for sexual stimulation when he beds the teenyboppers and as a first choice to play on his new stereo after he promises to cooperate with the government minister.[52] Otherwise, Burgess puts no particular emphasis on Beethoven. In the novel Beethoven's picture does not appear in Alex's bedroom, and Alex achieves masturbatory "bliss" as he imagines himself creating havoc to the "lovely sounds" of Bach, Mozart, and "Geoffrey Plautus."[53] In the film the second movement of the Ninth transports Alex as he conjures up "lovely pictures" of B movie disasters.[54] In the novel the opera singer in the Korova Milk Bar sings a few bars "from an opera by Friedrich Gitterfenster called Das Bettzeug," while in the film she "suddenly came with a burst of singing" from the Ninth's concluding "Ode to Joy."[55] In the novel Alex cries "Stop!" when he hears the last movement of Beethoven's Fifth during the Ludovico treatment—"It's a sin . . . using Ludwig van like that"—while in the film it is the fourth movement of the Ninth.[56] In the novel Alex tells Dr. Brodsky that he feels sick when he hears "lovely Ludwig van, G. F. Handel and others."[57] In Kubrick's script Alex tells Frank Alexander's associates that only one piece of music has that effect, and the dialogue emphatically repeats the reference:

Alex: No, missus, you see, it's not all music. It's just the Ninth.

Rubinstein: You mean, Beethoven's Ninth Symphony?

Alex: That's right. I can't listen to the Ninth anymore at all. When I hear the Ninth, I get like this funny feeling.[58]

Kubrick hated Skinnerian conditioning because it threatened to quell the aggressive energy that makes art innovative and dynamic, while Burgess hated it because it removed a person's ability to make a moral choice. He was unhappy with the American version of his novel because the publisher, W. W. Norton, cut a final chapter that presented a tamed and civilized Alex, "a hooligan hero who is now growing up, falling in love, proposing a decent bourgeois life with a wife and family, and consoling us with the doctrine that aggression is an aspect of adolescence which maturity rejects."[59] In the introduction to his 1987 stage version of the story, he condemned Kubrick's film for truncating "a genuine novel (whose main characteristic must always be a demonstration of the capacity of human nature to change)" to a mere "fable." But he was especially upset by what he saw as the perversion of his message: "I had tried to write . . . a sort of allegory of Christian free will. If [man] chooses good, he must have the possibility of choosing evil instead: evil is a theological necessity. I was also saying that it is more acceptable for us to perform evil acts than to be conditioned artificially into an ability only to perform what is socially acceptable."[60]

Although Kubrick defensively repeated the free will theme in postfilm letters and interviews, the film's Alex acts on instinct rather than choice, and he has no inkling of what the Ludovico treatment will do. Ardrey had written that *West Side Story* emphasized the "amity/ enmity complex," that is, the loyalty of gang members to each other and their hatred toward members of a rival group. Kubrick was less interested in free will or group rivalry than in dominance and evolution. Rather than individual choice he concerned himself with freedom from "animal bondage" (as Ardrey put it), and from social restraint.[61] Courage and "deviance" are prerequisites of the artist, and both Kubrick and Ardrey share "the pitiless ridicule" of the delinquent toward "those who would see his soul as sick."[62] Violent youths express healthy, natural instincts that they are unable to socially channel, either because they are individually incapable of doing so, or because they are free of the economic comforts or religious restraints that might tame them, or because they lack the education that might express dominance in an acceptable way. Ardrey and Kubrick fiercely resisted social controls that could dissipate violent energy to the point that nothing would be left to sublimate.

After a 1971 pre-*Clockwork* interview, Kubrick revised an answer for postfilm publication. In response to a question as to whether or not he sympathized with Alex and supported "his point of view," Kubrick defined the responsibility of the artist. First he quoted the advice to the poet in Cocteau's *Orphée*, "Astonish me." Then he paraphrased Samuel Johnson's statement "that a work of art must make life more enjoyable or more endurable" and added, "Another quality, which I think forms part of the definition, that a work of art is always exhilarating and never depressing, whatever its subject matter may be."[63]

Clockwork begins with satiric images that counterpoint aggression by making it ridiculous. It is a way of refusing despair in light of the horror that will inevitably come. Macho posturing may or may not precede bloodshed, but it is always dumb. Alex is flanked by an archetypal army of murderous goons. Their outfits combine the codpieces of Elizabethan swashbucklers with the collarless shirts of gunslingers, and they lean against a back wall like the James gang in a saloon. At the same time the derby hats of Alex, Georgie, and Dim, combined with Pete's beret, suggest stereotypes of civilized veneer from theoretically less violent times that ironically parallel the present.[64]

As the camera tracks backward, the widening perspective alerts and excites with bizarre imagery that keynotes the film's first fifteen minutes. The tables on either side of the aisle are female figures with their legs spread inviting "use," and the hair colors of the ones on the right alternate in orange and in purple, the royal color associated with dominance in subsequent scenes. Both ends of the aisle are overseen by white-clad bouncers to represent the enforced peace that Alex and his gang are about to elude. But in the next scene, freedom from social restraint does not bring freedom from genetic compulsion, when the boys cane the old drunk under the culvert with the savage delight of Moonwatcher's band.

Alex pointedly hates the drunk for singing the "filthy songs of his fathers and going blerp, blerp in between as it might be a filthy old orchestra in his stinking rotten guts." He seems to sense that his spirit is as threatened by sentimentality as his body is by the drunk's decay. In the ballad of "Molly Malone," and in his complaints about the decline of law and order, the old man laments his lost youth and approaching death. Though he conflates personal and general decline by complaining about astronauts spinning around a lawless earth, he faces up to his tormentors with a fighting spirit that time has not killed in him or in the species: "Oh, dear land I fought for thee and brought . . ." as if to say that he too was a killer in his time and that only circumstance has turned the tables.[65] His song celebrates having "brought" the patriotically sanctioned violence that the next scene satirizes as war with a rival gang.

The drunk's fearless, wholehearted groans rhythmically alternate with the blows he is dealt, and the whole scene is theatrical and stylized. The next scene begins on a symbolic stage of the world where similar actions are endlessly repeated, as if they were rituals of nature. Just as the beating of the drunk occurs below the urban surface, so Billy Boy's gang is raping a girl below a pretty painting of faded rococo flowers confined to a vase above the stage. While the drunk's groans segue into the girl's screams, the camera moves down past a golden-faced Zeus (both lawgiver and rapist) and then back to frame the small figures of the gang intermingled with grotesque heads used as props in a previous "show." One of the heads is a black-faced clown, evoking other victims of dominance run amock. The gang wears military camouflage jackets to suggest the universal soldier.[66]

Alex and his gang initially appear as shadows, just as they had in the culvert (perhaps to suggest Jung's archetypal "shadow," a nonsexualized version of the id), but in the blatant cinematic parody that follows they amalgamate a Gene Autry posse with Robin Hood's merry men. First, Alex issues an ornate challenge: "Ho, ho, ho. Well, if it isn't fat, stinking Billygoat Billyboy in poison. Come and get one in the yarbles [balls], if you have any yarbles, you eunuch jelly thou." Billy Boy's gum-chewing baby face is framed by unkempt long hair, topped by a Nazi cap, and set off by an iron cross. In response to Alex's primate chest thump, he smiles moronically, clicks open his *Blackboard Jungle* switchblade, and loutishly spits like a saloon bully, "Let's get 'em boys."

The alacrity with which both groups exultantly prefer battle to sex echoes Ardrey's assertion, contra Freud, that dominance is more compelling than sex,[67] and as they spill off the stage into the seeming freedom of a larger space, their actions are both leashed and unleashed by biology. The fight generally echoes the cowboy precedent with bodies flying through window frames, but the breaking glass is more than a cinematic cliché: it represents the unabated ritual of civilized war. Alex's droogs are the good guys in that they are dressed in white and distinguishable as individuals, while Billy's gang could be any projected enemy. But the droogs' white outfits are topped by black hats, as if to relativize any concept of good and evil once a war has begun, and as the scene ends their fallen foes suffer the blows of animal-bone canes.

Alex had theatricalized the drunk by applauding his song and by eliciting his tour de force display of nostalgic rage. And he had delighted in verbally slapping Billy Boy before springing to attack. In the escapade that follows the fight, Alex takes the droogs and the audience on a mind blower of a ride called "Hogs of the Road," in which he is the star and director. He drives the stolen "Durango '95," while his wild bunch gleefully play their typecast roles. Dim holds his hat like a rodeo rider and yells like Slim Pickens. Georgie sits on the top of the convertible's backseat and yells too, but braces his hand on top of the windshield. And Pete, sitting in the front passenger seat beside Alex, looks slightly scared before he scrunches down behind the "screen" of the windshield.

Pete reflects the film's anticipated audience, especially the "teens" of the time. He isn't sure what to expect, but as the ride continues he starts screaming like the others. He is Alex's follower and fan, and like an Elvis or James Dean clone he apes his hero. He is the only droog besides Alex to wear a fake eyelash, but while Alex wears his on the right eye, Pete mirrors him by wearing his on the left. As a "director," Alex raises the adrenaline of his beholders just enough to secure their adherence, and as a "writer" his narration reveals the self-fulfilling flair that distinguished Napoleon and Alexander. Within the story he lives, Alex acts, but retrospectively for *Clockwork*'s audience, he writes, and his voice-over sublimates his physical energy into vibrant and evocative poetry delivered in McDowell's fine, classic style. The car verbally "purrs" for the audience, even as it physically does for its riders. They feel a "warm vibraty feeling all through [their] guttiwuts" until they find them-selves among "trees and dark . . . with real country dark."[68] This is Alex's way of saying that the story is now about to return to nature in the worst possible way.

The first rape scene does nothing to prepare the audience for the trauma of the second. The casino fight is essentially a decoy, an invitation to be tit-illated and entertained. The "surprise visit," on the other hand, transforms fantasy to nightmare. In a postrelease letter to the *New York Times* that de-fended *Clockwork* against charges of fascism and gratuitous violence, Kubrick referred to political idealism as an "alibi" that began with the opening sen-tence of Rousseau's 1762 novel, *Emile*: "Nature made me happy and good, and if I am otherwise, it is society's fault."[69] Rousseau's "novel" is more of a primer than a story. It instructs mothers to protect their children's innate ra-tionality by relieving their childish fears with a form of behavioral escalation. In an example that seems to impinge directly on the "surprise visit," Rousseau advises a loving mother to cure her son's fear of masks by donning increasingly ugly ones while laughingly coaxing her child to try them on. She should then have other people try on the masks until the child loses his fear and wants to try them on himself. The same progressive education applies to other fears like the sound of a gunshot. The guide should detonate louder and louder bangs until a great big one doesn't matter.

Instead of strengthening *Clockwork*'s audience to withstand the real hor-ror of the home invasion, the scenes of beating the drunk and brawling with Billy Boy are feints to provide an expectation of bizarre fun. Rousseau had condemned fables that might encourage a child to speak and behave fool-ishly. In *A Clockwork Orange* and *The Shining*, Kubrick implies that only the grimmest of fairy tales can protect a child from adversity and from himself. In Burgess's novel the comical masks that the droogs wear in their surprise visit represent varied forms of timeless dominance: Alex is Disraeli, Pete is Elvis Presley, Georgie is Henry VIII, and Dim is Percy Bysshe Shelley.[70] In the film the masks of the three droogs are generically bestial, but the mask that Alex wears is simultaneously a Freudian joke and a psychotic horror. It serves his attempt to intimidate and the film's intent to teach.

As he points his grotesque phallic nose down into the trapped face of the liberal writer, he taunts the audience for being unable to deny his view of hu-man nature. His sadistic version of "Singin' in the Rain" parodies the ro-mantic mendacity of popular art, and the line, "Viddy well, little brother, viddy well," precedes a rape that horrifies because it violates the psychological innocence of forties cinema and the political idealism of sixties society. As a child of Freud, Alex lives out an Oedipal fantasy, and as a child of Ardrey, he trumpets the return of the killer ape. The Rossini overture to *The Thieving Magpie* that plays throughout the casino fight and the car sequence connotes delightful entertainment, but it stops as soon as the gang climbs the landscaped rocks that lead past a reflecting pool to the Alexander home.[71] In an explicit rhyme with the attack on the water hole in *2001*, Alex turns and beckons his cane-carrying band toward a feral assault.

As the Rossini softens and disappears, the sound of Frank Alexander's typewriter precedes a Beethoven's Fifth doorbell. The extremity of the scene that follows conforms to Freud's idea that sublimation works best for intellectuals like Alexander, not at all for untamed apes like Dim, and only in relatively crude forms for the average filmgoer: "The feeling of happiness derived from the satisfaction of a wild instinctual impulse untamed by the ego is incomparably more intense than that derived from sating an instinct that has been tamed."[72] The film entices filmgoers into the voyeuristic excitement of witnessing the near rape of a voluptuous victim on the casino stage, and then hurls them into a mirror not only of their own repressed violence but of the cultural hypocrisy that gives the lie to enlightened prosperity. The scene crosses evolutionary borders but moves backward from imperfect sublimation to perfect brutality. Alex's theatricality no longer provides delight. We see him savagely amusing himself with verbal and balletic satire, but he is also the personification of dominance. The strong take what they want as the spoils of victory, from the bodies of conquered women to the riches of modern nations.

The film offers the audience a second "surprise visit" when it follows the gang to their watering hole immediately following the rape.[73] In the scene's opening voice-over Alex has returned to his poetic mode with the scintillating parallelism, alliteration, and mockingly civilized understatement that resemble Richard III's in wit as well as wickedness: "We were all feeling a bit shagged and fagged and fashed, it having been an evening of some small energy expenditure. . . . So we stopped off at the Korova for a nightcap." In a Shakespearean contrast of kings and clowns, Dim tells the naked babe milk dispenser that he has had "a busy day at work" in baby-talk cockney. His name is not only an obvious eponym but a measure of status from "A" individuals at the top, to "D's" like Dim and the parole officer Deltoid, to lower downs like Pete, and, finally, to Alex's parents, Pee and Em. As mentioned, Alex reaches bottom in prison when his appellation becomes a diminishing number, "6554321."[74]

The scene in the Korova emphasizes parallel forms of dominance. The underlying music once again is the Purcell elegy dedicated to royalty, and Alex's bearing, language, and superior taste establish him as a king. He sits just behind a purple-wigged table-girl as he listens ecstatically to the female opera singer who "suddenly came with a burst of singing" from the last movement of Beethoven's Ninth. The orgasm joke makes the obvious connection between the carnal and the ethereal, but the attraction between Alex and the woman is a kinship of spirit rather than sex. She too sits with four sycophantic droogs, and her golden stage makeup suggests a queenly persona. As Alex compels her gaze, his large blue eyes mirror hers and connect him to a form of expression he yearns for but cannot achieve.

Lacking social pretension, Alex reveres the music because it transcends "the wicked world" and resembles an angelic visitation: "It was like for a moment, O my brothers, some great bird had flown into the milk bar and I felt . . . the shivers crawling up like slow malenky lizards and then down again. Because I knew what she sang. It was a bit from the glorious Ninth by Ludwig van." Dim's raspberry triggers the same rage that Alex felt on viewing the drunk. Because both represent infantile regression and animal indignity, they clash with his alpha instinct to survive by expanding knowledge and power. Even in the "high" arts this need is amoral and innately selective. With a lightning shot Alex canes Dim's thighs without even looking and, continuing to smile, lifts his glass with the aplomb of an Edwardian gentleman pursuing an actress.

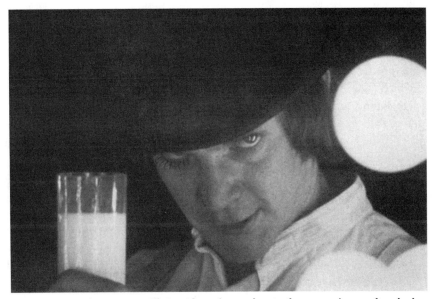

Figure 3.1. **In the Korova Milk Bar Alex raises a glass to the opera singer, after she has made him "shiver" by launching an impromptu "bit from the glorious Ninth."** *Courtesy of Warner Bros./Photofest © Warner Bros.*

Dim's outrage at having blows delivered to him "reasonless" is comical because he tries to oppose Enlightenment morality to a force of nature: "It stands to reason I won't have it." Though he is much larger physically, he begs off a fight with the "reasonable" excuse that they are irritated from fatigue. By adjusting "reason" to save his skin, Dim escapes the consequences of his appeal for justice. The scene suggests that democracy allows the masses to believe that the social order is rational by granting them an illusion of influence, even though alpha leaders still rule the roost. Subsequent scenes, however, demonstrate that in the modern world only those alpha leaders with a Machiavellian gift for deception can fool the masses into thinking that they are ruled individually by reason and socially by law. The fate of alphas lacking this gift is abdication or death. It is a rare "king" (as Beethoven called himself) who can sublimate his drives into art, a gift that Freud observed was not applicable generally and is accessible only to the few.[75]

The bedroom that Alex retires to after he leaves the Korova offers hope for humanity in contrast to the events of the "night." Alexander and Napoleon were imaginative killers, and Alex has the soul of a king, but he also has the sensibility of an artist. The color scheme of his sanctuary combines a purple rug with the orange and gold squares of his quilted bedspread. A small orange typewriter resembles that of Frank Alexander. These colors are offset by the deep blue of the bedsheets, the same contrast that represented perfect balance in 2001. Altogether, Alex's room is an ironic Eden where violence is innocently natural and where a love for color, proportion, and music is equally natural. Upon entering, Alex sheds his dominant social role by removing his false eyelash. Just below the mirror an elaborate stereo system sits on a narrow, cassette-covered counter over shelves stocked with albums.

Stripping away his persona and its trappings of status, Alex puts away his stolen cash in a drawer full of watches. From the drawer on the other side of the bed he liberates his pet snake and places it on a mounted tree branch over his bed. Directly behind the branch a woman in a painting blissfully spreads her vagina to admit the snake.[76] The painting reverses Alex's role in the rape scene as he prepares to be ravished by a more powerful soul. Jung emphasized that the biblical serpent was a symbol of gnosis or emerging consciousness.[77] In Genesis Adam and Eve's awareness of their naked vulnerability accompanies the knowledge of good and evil. After the Fall, human beings agonize over moral opposites because they think that choosing the right one will make them safe. They call the one that distances suffering "good" and the one that threatens mortality "evil."

But Alex is innocently indifferent to this collective obsession. Just before he inserts the gold tape of the Ninth that plays throughout the scene, he removes an orange one with the name Gogol clearly visible on the label. Later in the record store one of the girls Alex beds asks him if he is a Goggly Gogol fan, so the presence of the tape in his room suggests that Alex's musical tastes are transitional and that part of him remains a normally primitive teenager. More importantly, the Russian author Nikolay Gogol (1809–1852) wrote *Dead Souls*, the story of a man who buys the names of dead serfs before they are removed from the census and then sells them as if they were alive. Given Kubrick's aversion to any form of "zombification" (from drugs to media to psychology), the name "Gogol" is particularly apt.

Kubrick aspired to produce an art that was "exhilarating and never depressing." As the Ninth thrillingly infuses the room, a draft from the open window breathes life into the portrait of Beethoven on the shade. The composer's riveting stare offsets the closed eyes of the woman and the naive rapture of Alex. The portrait's eyes are those of the film, and along with the firmly set mouth, they register a will to reconceive the world. Kubrick pictures the religious "decline" that he addressed in *2001* in the four Christ figures directly below the derriere of the woman in the painting. The mockery of their bizarre dance affirms the liberating effect of satire. Fragmented shots of their bodies reveal an awkward, off-balance stance; small, impotently raised fists; and sad, pale blue eyes. They are the antithesis of the Nietzschean vitality that surges through the music, and their promise of consolation appeals to the defeated, who see their suffering redundantly nailed into red-stained wrists.

The saviors stand on the pale orange shelf, and the matching paleness of their orange hair and beards does not enliven their alabaster bodies. Their replication suggests religious efforts to tame the individual, a method that the Ludovico treatment supplants. In the novel Alex says that "the judges and the schools" fear the "self." The specific detail of their orange pubic hair echoes that of the writer's wife and links them as eternal victims. Their power to live has been diminished or destroyed by the deeper orange of biologically determined aggression, a force that is as predictably "clockwork" as knee-jerk conditioning. Later when Alex is strip-searched in prison, his orange pubic hair suggests that only circumstance separates victims and perpetrators, and that the Ludovico treatment will now crucify him.

Music, on the other hand, offers Alex a communion of spirit that is an exalting experience rather than a depressing creed. The existence of a "creator" does not have to be argued. It is there for Alex as Kubrick intended it to be for agnostic viewers of *2001*: "Oh, bliss . . . bliss and heaven. Oh, it was gorgeousness and gorgeosity made flesh. It was a bird of rarest spun heaven metal, or like silvery wine flowing in a space ship, gravity all nonsense now."

In contrast to the highly developed aural sensibility evident in the poetry of these lines, the "lovely pictures" Alex sees while listening are horrifically absurd: a delighted vampire, a bride falling through a trapdoor to be hung, huge falling rocks about to crush cavemen, crosscut by fiery explosions. The same paradox is apparent in a portrait directly over Alex and next to the Beethoven shade. The subject's mustached face and hairstyle have a nineteenth-century look, and his shadowed head and shoulders surmount a musical score. The portrait's recessive darkness contrasts sharply to the shade's sunlit force, and the man's expression reflects Alex's self-effacing submission to his god. The angle of the man's head suggests that he is supine, and his upwardly rolled eyes conceal the iris, as if to show that, like Alex, he feels but does not see.

Just after the portrait appears, Alex's mother interrupts his dream. Wearing a purple wig, black jumper, and brown shoes, she represents the adult subjugation that her rebel child instinctively rejects.[78] Their exchange alternates between the cramped brown corridor where she stands and Alex's light-filled orange and blue cave. His retreat's mirror-enhanced size and square shape convey his expanding scope, before the cut to the small, garish breakfast nook where his clueless parents wonder where their boy "goes to work of evenings." After Pee and Em have gone off to "a nice day at the factory," Alex emerges to find his bizarre probation officer sitting on his parents' bed. At the conclusion of a threatening harangue, Mr. Deltoid realizes that the glass of water he just drank contained dentures. His groan of recognition cues an immediate cut from the sickly mauve bedroom to the sparkling scene in the music store.[79]

The background score of that scene is Carlos's electronic version of the sprightly march from the last movement of the Ninth, while the visual music is a pastiche of primary colors and bright reflections that recalls the Star Gate. Released from the aesthetic hell of the parental bedroom, the spectator sees a pretty girl sucking a popsicle and facing a stack of top ten titles vibrantly illuminated in primary colors: red, blue, and green with gold at the top and purple at the bottom. Alex enters a corridor of sensory delights decked out in a long purple coat with eighteenth-century lace trim.

The corridor's direction, like the film's opening, suggests a backward flow from Jupiter space. Mirrors on either side of the corridor project variegated flashes of brilliant color, but the "dominant" pattern is purple and gold. Alex is Kubrick's version of the "natural man" contra Rousseau. He has the swagger of an aristocrat, and when he raps his cane at the circular counter, the salesman immediately responds with an officious smile. Alex takes his descent from Moonwatcher, as suggested by an album of the 2001 score that appears in a purple sleeve in the center of the frame. In another "Dawn of Man" echo, a large circular light fixture above the counter has zebra stripes, and its light makes Alex's hair look orange. In the human journey from the water hole to the stars, Alex's superior energy and aesthetic sensibility potentially prefigure the Star Child. The album also implies that Kubrick made *Clockwork* into a visual symphony just as he had done with *2001*, and as he had hoped to do with *Napoleon*.

The girls to whom Alex will transmit his dominant genes have their own hierarchy. The prettiest one wears a purple sweater and jumper that match Alex's coat, and she has dark, dynamically curled hair. When she smiles she is a knockout. She is immediately taken by the narrator-hero's wordplay, and when she accepts his advance, her drabber droog understands that she too may finally look up and smile. The speeded up, fast-motion orgy occurs in Alex's sanctuary, where impressively multiple deeds are done under the Beethoven shade to a frenetic *William Tell* overture.[80] This time, however, the bright sun shining in from outside erases Beethoven's eyes and mouth and reduces the spectrum of evolved consciousness to the pure energy of light. In addition to being an operatic entertainment, like the Rossini overture that played under the casino fight, the *William Tell* would be immediately associated in 1972 with *The Lone Ranger* radio and TV program, and given the gender ratio of the scene, Alex is certainly that.

Figure 3.2. Alex invites the girls in the record store to play their favorites on his stereo: "Hear angel trumpets and devil trombones. You are invited." *Courtesy of Warner Bros./Photofest © Warner Bros.*

The mood becomes serious in the next scene when the droogs attempt a coup. Dim is angry because Alex has taken on the enemy role of parental authority, "giving orders and discipline and such," and Georgie's resentment suggests that political revolutions have Freudian overtones: the authority to be overthrown is a subconscious surrogate of the parent the child fears. Georgie tells Alex that equality must now be the order the day, "No more picking on Dim, brother. That's part of the new way." His motivation is ostensibly economic; Alex's leadership is not producing "big money," but the adjective suggests that economic equality is really about the illusion of adult status. Alex answers that they need not measure themselves in money, since all their needs are satisfied: "If you need a motor car, you pluck it from the trees. If you need pretty polly [money], you take it." But Dim wants to pull off a "man-size" burglary, and Georgie accuses Alex of "talking like a little child."[81]

The demonstration of dominance in the opera singer incident has diminished the droogs' self-esteem by making their role painfully plain, and they need the democratic illusion that status is based on a shared wealth that will make them all "big." Alex is childlike in the sense that an artist is free of competitive anxiety. His criminal acts are his art, and possessions are easily obtained necessities that have little to do with the explorative exhilaration he needs to live. His mental space exists before and after civilization. For him the physical world serves to feed the spirit, and he confidently lives off the land.

In this scene, however, he senses that the droogs are *his* children and that on the surface at least he will have to play to their level. They are the tools of his technique and serve his expression in the same way that emperors (or film directors) "use" large numbers of people whose needs and goals are not their own. But Alex lacks the guile to channel his alpha impulse when he vanquishes Georgie and Dim at the flat-block marina.[82] Kubrick again merges the primitive and the advanced by having "lovely music" from a nearby stereo impel the tour de force attack. Its suddenness recalls the trust that Alexander and Napoleon had in themselves when they intuitively seized the moment to break the enemy's line. But as Alex balletically wields his weapon-tool, his demonic face resembles Moonwatcher's after the world's first murder.

The droogs finally vanquish their primal father as he attempts to escape after unintentionally killing the Cat Lady.[83] He has not realized that the "new way" is the way of the modern world and that his droogs belong to a larger society that saves face by associating power with the will of the people. The Cat Lady, however, is a throwback. She is more outraged at the insult to her rank by a "wretched, slummy, bedbug" than in fear for her life, and she shows the combative spirit that has impelled her to fight physical decay on her health farm by knocking Alex down with a small bust of Beethoven. In her space "Ludwig van" has been reduced to a trivial object, dwarfed by a spurious avant-garde. In the novel the woman is a Victorian relic, and her art consists of premodern portraits of aristocratic women and crucifixion scenes.[84] In the film the woman is a rich bohemian, and her art is the high culture version of the Korova's obscenity.

In a postfilm interview Kubrick commented that "the erotic décor in the film suggests a slightly futuristic period for the story. The assumption being that erotic art will eventually become popular art, and just as you now buy African wildlife paintings in Woolworth's, you may one day buy erotica."[85] He saw this as part of a general trend toward making money by addicting zombies to momentary jolts: "There is an accelerating erosion of any kind of mystique which authority may have once had, and an over-awareness of the romantic concept of rebellion."[86] Ironically, the huge, disembodied penis that Alex uses as a weapon stands for the triumph of the superego that it purports to resist, the capitalist absorption of rebellious art from Picasso to The Rolling Stones.

After Alex kills the Cat Lady he becomes a victim rather than a perpetrator of violence, and his role is increasingly sympathetic. Kubrick was repeatedly asked to explain the contradiction. When asked if he considered violence a growing problem, he replied that *Clockwork* was not "a topical, social story" and that Alex represents universal dualities: "He does things which one knows are wrong, and yet you find yourself being taken in by him and accepting his frame of reference. As in a dream, the film demands a suspension of moral judgment."[87]

However, the film does make an aesthetic judgment about the deterioration of popular art in the modern world. The camera's attention to details in the first view of the Cat Lady's room tells us who she is and what she represents, just as Alex's room had done. It sets up a conflict of taste, or as Kubrick put it, "the giant white phallus is pitted against the bust of Beethoven."[88] Though the Cat Lady's paintings and objets d'art conform to the sexual revolution, their defiance is infantile, lacking in intelligence and skill. Georgie had described the health farm as "full up with like gold and silver, and like jewels." But the first image of the victim in her mansion reveals a topsy-turvy world. The modern art subsidized by upper-class wealth provides a symbol of dominance that is as primitive as Moonwatcher's club.

In fact, the club has become the penis and buttocks sculpture, so "important" a work of art in the Cat Lady's eyes that she risks her life to defend it, and so impotent a weapon in Alex's hands that he destroys himself by wielding it. Everything in the room suggests the erasure of complexity and wholeness that serious art has sought to express. The reversal is shown visually by the Cat Lady's upside-down position and color scheme. The dyed red hair on the top of her head rests on the red carpet at the bottom of the frame, and her green leotard matches the green ceiling that her upturned legs seem to touch. White feline companions lounge on the carpet to her left and right, and two large paintings on the side walls depict naked women presenting their asses to be mounted, much as Moonwatcher's females would have done.

The two paintings that face the audience to the Cat Lady's left and right show masturbating women. The one at frame left continues the ass-upward motif with the woman resting one arm on her pillow, while the other reaches around her back to fondle herself. The red, white, and blue one at frame right immediately draws the eye as the brightest object in the room. In it a smiling, naked woman reclines on her back and masturbates with her left hand while reaching up to touch the leg of a spread-eagled spaceman flying directly over her head. But while the woman reaches up to touch the spaceman, the spaceman's left hand reaches down to touch the nipple of an udderlike breast that emerges from the blue sky below the white-rayed clouds.

In *2001* prehumans received spiritual inspiration from outer space. Here the alien presence excites in order to turn its viewers back to the helpless hedonism of infancy. Kubrick's target here is the making and marketing of fashionable modern art. After the Cat Lady turns Alex away at the door and goes to the telephone to call the police, a painting to her left shows a woman licking a celluloid breast that encloses a real breast, as if to suggest the vicarious satisfaction of pornography. To the right of the telephone another painting depicts a woman whose mouth is covered and whose black and white leotard has a circular opening that exposes one breast. The image echoes the stripping and gagging of the writer's wife just before Alex raped her.

Alex had masturbated to Beethoven and to "lovely pictures" from bad movies. His fantasized images of film violence correspond to the Cat Lady's pornographic stimulation, but his Beethoven portrait speaks to a potential in Alex that he feels but is not yet evolved enough to see. The black and white Beethoven portrait is balanced by the black and white painting on the other side of the bed in which the woman opens her vagina to admit the snake. Her eyes are closed and her expression is blissful in contrast to Beethoven's brooding, all-seeing gaze.[89]

The painting of the woman is the most prominent object in Alex's room just after he enters it. It hangs to the immediate right of his bed and expresses his experience in the scene. After removing his eyelash, Alex falls backward on the bed with his legs straight up in the air next to the woman whose legs are also up. The painting's black and white color scheme matches Alex's white pants and black boots, and the spherical light behind him corresponds to the round shape of the woman's body. Her eyes are small black spots that form a symmetrical pattern with her nipples and fingernails, as if to indicate that she can receive pleasure but cannot understand or create. As he masturbates to Beethoven, Alex cannot understand the difference between the evolved sounds he hears and the backward images he sees.

When the Cat Lady first appears, her legs are also straight up in the air before they spread to the sides and curl backward, turning her into a grotesque pretzel.[90] She opens herself to misshapen paintings that disproportion sexuality, and unlike Alex, her atrocious taste in one art is not balanced by sensitivity to another. The room's combination of pornographic paintings and exercise machines conveys a division of soul and body, and though the Cat Lady is athletically toned, she lacks taste and grace. For her, Beethoven is only a sign of social rank, and she uses his bust against Alex as if it were a proto-human club. Until the fight with the Cat Lady, Alex had epitomized primitive potency. After the Cat Lady strikes him with the bust, he commits an unintentional murder and loses control of his life. As he drives the giant phallus into the Cat Lady's face, it becomes a painting of concentric screaming mouths that resemble toothed vaginas. In effect, Alex is raped by the Cat Lady and castrated by society.

Initially, Kubrick stages rape as a Freudian nightmare and a theatrical display. Alex jabs the old drunk with his cane before applauding his song. Billy Boy's gang strips the girl on the casino stage, and in the Alexander home the phallic, masked Alex produces rubber balls from his codpiece to stuff the mouths of his victims before he forces himself into their bodies and minds. He straddles Dim's thighs to quash his complaints and canes Georgie in the balls to reassert control at the marina. The roles are reversed after Alex involuntarily kills the Cat Woman and is blinded by Dim's milk bottle. He then becomes the victim in a series of Freudian humiliations. These are foreshadowed by the earlier scene where Deltoid watches Alex urinate and then comically puts his arm around him before punching him in the balls, which Alex anticipates but cannot prevent. In prison Alex is stripped and made to bend over for an anal inspection, and in the chapel homosexual prisoners blow him kisses.

In conceiving *The Shining*, Kubrick and Diane Johnson discussed Freud's "The Uncanny," where Freud connects fears of blindness and castration.[91] Kubrick may have had the essay in mind for *Clockwork* as well. After being beaned by Dim's milk bottle as he exits the Cat Lady's mansion, Alex is reduced to the same infantile helplessness to which he had reduced his victims. He cries out helplessly, "I'm blind, you bastards! I'm blind!!! I'm blind, you bastards!!! I can't see! Oh, you bastards!!! I'm blind!" His helplessness is accentuated in the next scene where the camera angles accentuate the power of the sadistic officers looming over him, as he lies literally cornered on the floor of a small room in the police station. Alex tries to fight back by grabbing an officer's balls after his injured nose is pressed, but he is beaten and kicked. The rape motif concludes the scene when his parole officer, Deltoid, to whom he pathetically appeals, spits in his face. There had been a homoerotic element in the scene where Deltoid first appeared when he grabbed Alex by the balls. Now he revels in the oral satisfaction of "You are now a murderer, little Alex," just before ejaculating his scorn.[92]

Kubrick portrays a telling association between rape, castration, and blindness in the Ludovico theater where the second film depicts the gang rape of a naked pink-haired woman by white-suited droogs wearing military hats of various eras.[93] The Latin root of "rape" means to seize and carry away by force. Kubrick uses the rape metaphor to connote the capture and possession of the spectator through cinema's power to compel the eye. The addicted viewer is unaware that his mind and feelings are being neutered. As the woman's vagina is repeatedly rammed, Alex's eyes are forcibly held open and assaulted by Dr. Brodsky's sadistic cure.

In "The Uncanny," Freud summarizes "The Sandman" by E. T. A. Hoffman to show that "the uncanny" provokes a fear of castration that is the equivalent of being reduced to an automaton, doll, or machine. The protagonist, Nathaniel, is terrified by his nurse's story of the Sandman who "comes when children won't go to bed, and throws handfuls of sand in their eyes so that [the eyes] jump out of their heads, all bleeding. Then he puts the eyes in a sack and carries them off to the half-moon to feed his children." Hoffman suggests that children are conditioned in childhood to stay symbolically asleep to suppress discontent with the social roles they are forced to play.

Later as a college student, Nathaniel encounters a strange, itinerant optician selling spectacles that he calls "fine eyes." Nathaniel has an uncomfortable feeling of déjà vu, but he does buy a small telescope. By repeatedly using it to look through his window at a beautiful girl in a neighboring house, he becomes addicted to a masturbatory image that makes him forget about his fiancée. The object of his obsession is actually an "automaton," a doll named Olympia, belonging to her "father" and his mentor, Professor Spalanzani. While visiting him, Nathaniel discovers Spalanzani violently arguing with Coppola, the supplier of Olympia's eyes. During the quarrel Coppola rips out the eyes of the doll whereupon Spalanzani accuses him of stealing them from Nathaniel.

Nathaniel then becomes delirious and tries to strangle Spalanzani. If Olympia's eyes and Nathaniel's are one and the same, then both Spalanzani and Coppola have inflicted an artificial vision that threatens to turn him into a robot, just as Brodsky threatens Alex, and as pornographic images threaten Bill Harford in *Eyes Wide Shut*. By the end of their films Bill and Alex are still alive, but Nathaniel is not so lucky. After seeming to have recovered, he returns to his fiancée, and on an afternoon walk they ascend the tower of the town hall to enjoy the view. When Nathaniel looks through the spyglass, he sees Coppola, its Sandman maker, on the street below. As before, his vision is possessed, and after trying unsuccessfully to throw his fiancée off the tower, he screams "Yes! fine eyes—fine eyes!" just before leaping to his death.[94]

Near the end of *Clockwork* Alex tries to "snuff it" by jumping from a third-floor window after suffering the effects of the Ludovico treatment. Before that, near the beginning of the treatment, he had appreciatively commented that a bloody cinematic scene was more satisfying than if it had been real: "It's funny how the colors of the real world only seem really real when you viddy them on the screen." In 1964 Marshall McLuhan theorized that a replication of oneself in a media image is so excessively exciting that it results in "a self amputation [that produces] a generalized numbness or shock that . . . forbids self-recognition."[95] Kubrick ironically connects Alex's loss of self to Bowman's transformation in the alien room of *2001* through the bizarre music that plays during Alex's first voice-over in the Ludovico theater. The backlit, haloed scientists at the rear of the auditorium have the cold aura of aliens in conventional science fiction, and the light from the projector at the rear forms a large pulsating star from which a single ray beelines over the tops of the empty seats straight into Alex's skull.[96] As an experimental subject he is clearly an object of malevolent manipulation, unlike Bowman whose guides seem to be benign. His predicament is pictured in the first film image where a man falls backward down a fire escape before he is beaten to a pulp by a group of droogs wearing military hats. Alex praises the film's bloody realism as "very good like it was done in Hollywood" but begins to feel sick from the drugs injected by the scientists to create a Skinnerian association between violence and nausea.

Kubrick's satire is twofold. People sickened by violence have been conditioned out of a natural propensity for it. Violent films decrease these impulses through vicarious release, thus making society more secure but the individual less alive. Alex, the man falling down the stairs, and spectators of popular film are merged in their passivity. While they are entertained, they are being destroyed. In Kubrick's 1972 letter to the *New York Times* he warned against the multimedia "fascism" that could turn human beings into "zombies." Dr. Brodsky quotes an earlier test subject describing the effect of the Ludovico drugs as "being like death, a sense of drowning or stifling." When Alex is strapped into his seat in the Ludovico theater, he becomes Ludovico director Brodsky's version of Spalanzani's doll. His eyelids are held open so that he cannot blink, and the wires that seem to be coming out of his head resemble the crown of thorns seen on the Christ figures in his bedroom and in the Hollywood parody he fantasizes as he reads the Bible in prison.

While the Ludovico treatment dehumanizes with enforced morality, the films Alex watches equate Hollywood violence with addictive pornography. Both forms of "sinny" (the pun becomes apparent) rape helpless spectators and take possession of their minds. And both resemble fascism in their reduction of spectators to a massive entity subject to predictable response. The concept corresponds perfectly to the clip from Leni Riefenstahl's *Triumph of the Will* where Hitler stages himself striding through symmetrical walls of

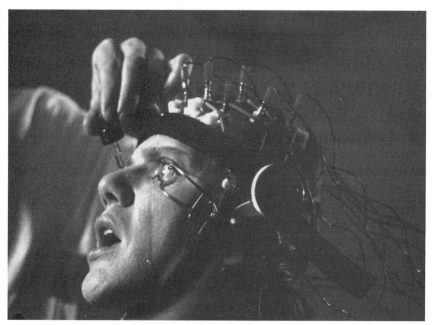

Figure 3.3. During the Ludovico treatment, Alex wears a wired crown of thorns, resembling those of the Christ carvings in his bedroom and the movie Christ he imagines from the prison Bible. *Courtesy of Warner Bros./Photofest © Warner Bros.*

fused humanity.[97] The sprightly accompanying march from the second movement of Beethoven's Ninth echoes Alex's entrance through the corridor of
the record store just before his costume and his patter help him seduce the
two girls. In that scene his charm, bolstered by music and color, can seduce
the audience as well, in spite of what they have just seen him do. Hitler was
a failed painter, but with the aid of the microphone he mastered the "art" of
spectacle and oratory. Using that tool, he turned adoring crowds into a
McLuhanesque extension of his own voice. His speeches in Riefenstahl's film
show him modulating crowd response as if he were turning a dial. Rather
than eradicating instinct, he manipulated aggressive energy through controlled containment and release, cuing and silencing the thundering voice of
the attending masses like a conductor directing a vast orchestra composed of
only one instrument.

The spectacularly unsuccessful hellfire sermon given earlier by the prison
chaplain represents an obsolete attempt to standardize behavior.[98] Kubrick's
comic emphasis on the chaplain's failed persuasiveness undercuts any wholehearted endorsement of free will. Burgess, on the other hand, genuinely believed in free will: "The French and Italian terms for free will were close to
St Augustine's *liberum arbitrium,* and to speak of *libre arbitre* or *libero arbitrio*
was automatically to invoke theology. *A Clockwork Orange* whatever Protes-
tant Britain might say, was theologically sound." However, he qualified his
position somewhat when he added that the right choices could only be made
after testosterone-fueled teenage mania had been ratcheted down to post-
twenty-one equanimity. (The number of his intended last chapter was "21.")
Though Burgess believed that "the artificial extirpation of free will through
scientific conditioning" would be "a greater evil than the free choice of evil,"
he admitted that "youthful free will having the choice of good and evil"
would "generally choose evil."[99] In the film Alex spontaneously thinks and
acts without ever stopping to choose. Pre-Ludovico he acts on instinct. Post-
Ludovico his conditioning prevails.

Kubrick's treatment of free will is largely ironic since its strongest advo-
cates are the anachronistic chaplain and the satanic Dr. Brodsky. When
Alex pleads that "it's not fair" to deprive him of Beethoven, Brodsky offers
him legal logic in a HAL-like tone: "You must take your chance, boy. The
choice has all been yours."[100] Kubrick further qualifies the statement with
an immediate close-up of Dr. Branom, Brodsky's female colleague whose
face betrays misgivings. Alex then pathetically tries to show that he should
be rewarded for espousing enlightened ethics. His desperate claim that he is
cured, because he has learned that everyone has "the right to live and be

happy without being tolchocked and knifed," reflects Freud's belief that people only forgo aggression out of self-interest and fear.

The prison chaplain had warned Alex that the Ludovico treatment could not "really make a man good" because "goodness is chosen." Speaking as Burgess's mouthpiece, the chaplain adds, "When a man cannot choose, he ceases to be a man." Conversely, B. F. Skinner believed that moral choice was a delusion: "The bad do bad because the bad is rewarded. The good do good because the good is rewarded. There is no true freedom or dignity." Skinner's book, *Beyond Freedom and Dignity* (1971), was much in the news at the time *A Clockwork Orange* was filmed. Burgess objected to Skinner because he felt that conditioning was a greater evil than choosing evil. But the book was probably less repulsive to Kubrick for its denial of free will than for its praise of predictability. In his autobiography Skinner had written, "I see no virtue in accident or in the chaos from which somehow we have reached our present position. I believe that we must now plan our own future and that we must take every advantage of a science of behavior in solving the problems which will necessarily arise."[101]

Like Ardrey, who believed that evolution could best be accomplished by "the free wild gene," Kubrick believed that an individual person, like a work of art, needed to diverge from any preconceived blueprint. In 1972 he told Andrew Bailey of *Rolling Stone*: "Skinner is wrong, and that what is sinister is that this philosophy may serve as the intellectual basis for some sort of scientifically oriented repressive government. . . . I like to believe that there are certain aspects of the human personality which are essentially unique and mysterious."[102] Skinner's philosophy could not account for artistic genius any more than it could explain or allow the parapsychology portrayed in *The Shining*. Kubrick was inspired by exploration, in sources like *The Odyssey* and by "the magic" that he patiently awaited on his sets. For him, as for Jung, inspiration was the purpose of technique. Skinner sought outcomes that conformed to a plan. Kubrick planned only to lay the groundwork for exceeding the plan. Skinner assumed that absolute values existed to be imposed. Kubrick believed that insight and expression changed and grew in an ongoing process of discovery.

Though many postmodern artists denigrate the idea of beauty because it masks social injustice, Kubrick believed that an immersion in beauty might help to achieve "some sort of transfiguration into a higher form of life." Even in films that depict people at their ugliest, the cinematography and the music offer a counterpoint that offers immediate hope. Innovative fusions of form reflect expansions of soul. Alex's artistic sensibility is highlighted when his room becomes that of Joe, the lodger. Alex's perfectly made bed, unruffled even when he slept in it, is now messily unmade. Its deep blue sheets are now grayish white, and the unusual orange and gold quilt is now a blue linen bedspread. The stereo system has devolved into a small radio; barbells and a school binder have replaced the records and books; magazine clippings of soccer stars have supplanted the paintings; and a tacky floral pattern has ousted Beethoven from the shade.[103]

The synesthesia that Kubrick initiated in *2001* extends into *Clockwork* through the emphasis on Beethoven's eyes. The portrait asks, what was the source of Beethoven's power and what does Beethoven's music "see"? *A Clockwork Orange* sees that the violent energy of the "glorious Ninth" is inseparable from its beauty, and though Kubrick stated that "man is the most remorseless killer who ever stalked the earth," he channels his own killer instinct into the kinetic vitality and satiric verve of the film.[104] The black screen transition that Kubrick used repeatedly in *2001* occurs only once in *Clockwork*, for four seconds just after Alex attempts suicide. When he reappears he is breathing deeply and wrapped like a mummy, as if to suggest the indefinite survival of all he has been: "I jumped, O my brothers, and I fell hard, but I did not snuff it. If I had snuffed it, I would not be here to tell what I have told. I came back to life, after a long black, black gap of what might have been a million years."[105]

Retrospectively, *Clockwork*'s final line—"I was cured, all right"—offers a larger ambivalence than simple irony. The energy of "evil" is the dynamic factor in evolution. If we can't harness it, we will die. If we kill it, we will die. No Napoleon—no Beethoven. No Alex—no Star Child.

Notes

1. Michel Chion, *Kubrick's Cinema Odyssey* (London: British Film Institute, 2001), 94–95.

2. Stanley Kubrick, interview by Michel Ciment, *Kubrick: The Definitive Edition* (New York: Faber & Faber, 2001), 158.

3. Stanley Kubrick, interview by Philip Strick and Penelope Houston, "Modern Times: An Interview with Stanley Kubrick," *Sight & Sound*, Spring 1972; repr. in *Stanley Kubrick: Interviews*, ed. Gene D. Phillips (Jackson: University Press of Mississippi), 129.

4. Sigmund Freud, *The Future of an Illusion*, ed. James Strachey, trans. W. D. Robson-Scott (1927; Garden City, N.Y.: Doubleday, 1961), 13.

5. Sigmund Freud, *Civilization and Its Discontents*, ed. and trans. James Strachey (1930; New York: W. W. Norton, 1962), 18.

6. Freud, *The Future of an Illusion*, 2–3.

7. Freud, *Civilization and Its Discontents*, 42.

8. Freud, *Civilization and Its Discontents*, 58.

9. Freud, *The Future of an Illusion*, 8.

10. See Walter Kaufmann, *Nietzsche: Philosopher, Psychologist, Antichrist* (Cleveland and New York: World, 1956), 144, 194.

11. Anthony Burgess, *A Clockwork Orange* (1962; New York: W. W. Norton, 1987), 116.

12. Burgess, *A Clockwork Orange*, 43.

13. See Carl G. Jung, *The Undiscovered Self* (New York: New American Library, 1957), 13, 18–19, 26.

14. Kubrick, interview by Ciment, 163.

15. Stanley Kubrick, letter to the editor, *New York Times*, February 27, 1972.

16. Stanley Kubrick, interview by Eric Nordern, *Playboy*, September 1968; repr. in Phillips, ed., *Stanley Kubrick: Interviews*, 66.

17. Burgess, *A Clockwork Orange*, 12.

18. Kubrick, letter to the editor.

19. See Kaufmann, *Nietzsche*, 143.

20. Robert Ardrey, *African Genesis* (New York: Atheneum, 1961), 10, 17, 18, 38.

21. Anthony Burgess, *You've Had Your Time: The Second Part of the Confessions* (New York: Grove Press, 1991), 26.

22. Ardrey, *African Genesis*, 157, 159–160.

23. Peter Weiss, *Marat/Sade, or The Persecution and Assassination of Jean-Paul Marat as Performed by the Inmates of the Asylum at Charenton under the Direction of the Marquis de Sade*, trans. Geoffrey Skelton, verse adaptation Adrian Mitchell (New York: Atheneum, 1966), 70.

24. Weiss, *Marat/Sade*, 49.

25. Ardrey, *African Genesis*, 333, 338, 352–353.

26. Weiss, *Marat/Sade*, 98.

27. See Vincent LoBrutto, *Stanley Kubrick: A Biography* (New York: Donald I. Fine, 1997), 321–333; and Gene D. Phillips and Rodney Hill, *The Encyclopedia of Stanley Kubrick* (New York: Checkmark Books, 2002), 261–264.

28. "Napoleon" (unproduced screenplay, September 29, 1969); quoted in Phillips and Hill, *The Encyclopedia of Stanley Kubrick*, 262.

29. B. F. Skinner, "B. F. Skinner: An Autobiography," in *A History of Psychology in Autobiography*, vol. 5, ed. E. G. Boring and G. Lindzey (New York: Appleton Century-Crofts, 1967), http://ww2.lafayette.edu/~allanr/scientst.html.

30. Ardrey, *African Genesis*, 338.

31. Ardrey, *African Genesis*, 90.

32. Ardrey, *African Genesis*, 107–108.

33. Jerry Adler, "Mind Reading," *Newsweek*, July 5, 2004, 44.

34. Napoleon guide website, www.napoleonguide.com/leaders_napoleon.htm.

35. Napoleon guide website.

36. Stanley Kubrick, interview by Joseph Gelmis, "The Film Director as Superstar: Stanley Kubrick," in *The Film Director as Superstar* (Garden City, N.Y.: Doubleday, 1970); repr. in Phillips, ed., *Stanley Kubrick: Interviews*, 84.

37. Napoleon guide website.

38. Betty Radice, *Who's Who in the Ancient World* (Baltimore: Penguin, 1973), 56.

39. Anthony Burgess, *1985* (London: Hutchinson, 1978); quoted in Phillips and Hill, *The Encyclopedia of Stanley Kubrick*, 63.

40. See Edwyn Robert Bevan, "Alexander the Great," *Encyclopædia Britannica*, vol. 1, 11th ed. (1910), 545–550; and Ellis L. Knox, "Alexander the Great," August 19, 1996, history.boisestate.edu/westciv/alexander/03.htm.

41. *A Clockwork Orange*, DVD, directed by Stanley Kubrick (1971; Burbank, Calif.: Warner Bros. Home Video, 2001), chapter 32.

42. Burgess, *You've Had Your Time*, 253.

43. Burgess, *You've Had Your Time*, 247; eventually, Burgess did write *Napoleon Symphony: A Novel in Four Movements* (New York: Alfred A. Knopf, 1974).

44. See Christopher T. George, "The *Eroica* Riddle: Did Napoleon Remain Beethoven's 'Hero'?" Napoleon series website, www.napoleonseries.com/articles/misc _art/eroica.cfm.

45. "The Tempestuous Ludwig van Beethoven," BBC website, www.bbc.co.uk/ music/classicaltv/eroica/beethoven/napoleon.html.

46. Ludwig van Beethoven, "The Heiligenstadt Testament," a letter to his brothers, Carl and Johann, dated October 6, 1802, and discovered in March 1827 after Beethoven's death by Anton Schindler and Stephan von Breuning, who had it published the following October. See en.wikipedia.org/wiki/Heiligenstadt _Testament.

47. Ludwig van Beethoven, letter to Franz Wegeler, 1802, in "Ludwig van Beethoven," *Encyclopædia Britannica Online*, 1997, www.swil.ocdsb.edu.on.ca/ ModWest/Enlightenment/music/bthoven.html.

48. Morse Peckham, *Man's Rage for Chaos: Biology, Behavior, and the Arts* (New York: Schocken, 1967), 35.

49. Steven Spielberg, interview by Paul Joyce, "Remembering . . . Stanley Kubrick . . . Spielberg on Kubrick," July 22, 1999, in "Special Features," *Eyes Wide Shut*, DVD, directed by Stanley Kubrick (1999; Burbank, Calif.: Warner Bros. Home Video, 2001).

50. "Ludwig van Beethoven," *Encyclopædia Britannica Online*, 1997, www.swil .ocdsb.edu.on.ca/ModWest/Enlightenment/music/bthoven.html.

51. Elizabeth Schwarm Glesner, "Ludwig van Beethoven—Symphony no. 9, Opus 125, 'Choral,'" Classical Music Pages website, w3.rz-berlin.mpg.de/cmp/ beethoven_sym9.html.

52. Burgess, *A Clockwork Orange*, 48, 174.

53. Burgess, *A Clockwork Orange*, 36.

54. *A Clockwork Orange*, DVD, chapter 8.

55. Burgess, *A Clockwork Orange*, 32; *A Clockwork Orange*, DVD, chapter 7.

56. Burgess, *A Clockwork Orange*, 114; *A Clockwork Orange*, DVD, chapter 22.

57. Burgess, *A Clockwork Orange*, 116.

58. *A Clockwork Orange*, DVD, chapter 31.

59. Burgess, introduction to *A Clockwork Orange: A Play with Music* (London: Century Hutchinson, 1987); repr. on home.wlv.ac.uk/~fa1871/burgess.html.

60. Burgess, introduction to *A Clockwork Orange: A Play with Music*.

61. Ardrey, *African Genesis*, 330–331.

62. Ardrey, *African Genesis*, 331.

63. Kubrick, interview by Strick and Houston, in Phillips, ed., *Stanley Kubrick: Interviews*, 131.

64. *A Clockwork Orange*, DVD, chapter 2.

65. *A Clockwork Orange*, DVD, chapter 3.

66. *A Clockwork Orange*, DVD, chapter 4.

67. Ardrey, *African Genesis*, 162.

68. *A Clockwork Orange*, DVD, chapter 5.

69. Kubrick, letter to the editor; the opening sentence of *Emile* in French reads, "Tout est bien, sortant des mains de l'auteur des choses: tout dégénère entre les mains de l'homme." The standard English translation identifies the auteur as God rather than Nature: "God makes all things good; man meddles with them and they become evil"; see Jean-Jacques Rousseau, *Emile*, trans. Barbara Foxley (London: J. M. Dent & Sons, 1966); repr. on www.gutenberg.org/dirs/etext04/emile10.txt.

70. Burgess, *A Clockwork Orange*, 16.

71. *A Clockwork Orange*, DVD, chapter 6.

72. Freud, *Civilization and Its Discontents*, 26.

73. *A Clockwork Orange*, DVD, chapter 7.

74. *A Clockwork Orange*, DVD, chapter 16.

75. Freud, *Civilization and Its Discontents*, 27.

76. *A Clockwork Orange*, DVD, chapter 8.

77. See Edward F. Edinger, *Ego and Archetype* (Baltimore: Penguin, 1973), 18.

78. *A Clockwork Orange*, DVD, chapter 9.

79. *A Clockwork Orange*, DVD, chapter 10.

80. *A Clockwork Orange*, DVD, chapter 11.

81. *A Clockwork Orange*, DVD, chapter 12.

82. *A Clockwork Orange*, DVD, chapter 13.

83. *A Clockwork Orange*, DVD, chapter 14.

84. Burgess, *A Clockwork Orange*, 61.

85. Kubrick, interview by Ciment, 162.

86. John Hofsess, "Mind's Eye: *A Clockwork Orange*," *Take One*, May/June 1971; repr. in Phillips, ed., *Stanley Kubrick: Interviews*, 107.

87. Stanley Kubrick, quoted by Hofsess, in Phillips, ed., *Stanley Kubrick: Interviews*, 107.

88. Stanley Kubrick, interview by Penelope Houston, "Kubrick Country," *Saturday Review*, December 25, 1971; repr. in Phillips, ed., *Stanley Kubrick: Interviews*, 111.

89. *A Clockwork Orange*, DVD, chapter 8.

90. *A Clockwork Orange*, DVD, chapter 14.

91. On the use of "The Uncanny" by Kubrick and Diane Johnson in preparing the script, see Dennis Bingham, "The Displaced Auteur: A Reception History of *The Shining*," in *Perspectives on Stanley Kubrick*, ed. Mario Falsetto (New York: G. K. Hall, 1996), 290.

92. *A Clockwork Orange*, DVD, chapter 15.

93. *A Clockwork Orange*, DVD, chapter 21.

94. Sigmund Freud, "The Uncanny," in *The Standard Edition of the Complete Psychological Works of Sigmund Freud*, ed. James Strachey, Anna Freud, Alix Strachey, and Alan Tyson, trans. James Strachey, vol. 17 (1919; London: Hogarth Press, 1955), 219–252.

95. Marshall McLuhan, *Understanding Media: The Extensions of Man*, 2nd ed. (New York: New American Library, 1964), 51–52.

96. *A Clockwork Orange*, DVD, chapter 21.

97. *A Clockwork Orange*, DVD, chapter 22.

98. *A Clockwork Orange*, DVD, chapter 18.

99. Burgess, *You've Had Your Time*, 27.

100. *A Clockwork Orange*, DVD, chapter 22.

101. Skinner, "B. F. Skinner: An Autobiography," ww2.lafayette.edu/~allanr/scientst.html.

102. Stanley Kubrick, quoted by Andrew Bailey, "A Clockwork Utopia: Semi-Scrutable Stanley Kubrick Discusses His New Film," *Rolling Stone*, January 1972, 20–22.

103. *A Clockwork Orange*, DVD, chapter 26.

104. Paul D. Zimmerman, "Kubrick Tells What Makes *Clockwork Orange* Tick," *Newsweek*, April 1, 1972, 29.

105. *A Clockwork Orange*, DVD, chapter 32.

~

CHAPTER FOUR

Painting It White

Barry Lyndon

The evolutionary philosophy that underlies Kubrick's films is musically suggested by *2001*'s signature theme. In *Thus Spake Zarathustra* Nietzsche's concept of evolution had nothing to do with Darwinian struggle but rather with
the attempt of all living creatures to "enhance themselves, to grow and to
generate more life."[1] As with the Star Child's birth from the dying Bowman,
the evolved person will not be a radical departure from his less-developed
self, but a being that will incorporate and transcend all previous stages, not
"after-one-another," but only "into-one-another."[2] Nietzsche was initially
confident that the attempt to sublimate characterized the human species,
since the drive to enhance being was "the very way of nature."[3] But by the
time of *Zarathustra*, late in his career, he addressed himself only to the perceptive few: "Not to the people let Zarathustra speak, but to companions.
. . . To lure many away from the herd, therefore I came."[4] Kubrick could see
creative possibilities in Alex de Large and Barry Lyndon, though as characters they are ultimately stuck in the past along with Jack Torrance and Animal Mother. But in Joker and Alice Harford of *Eyes Wide Shut*, he presented
extraordinary individuals who are clearly apart from "the herd."

In *Barry Lyndon* Kubrick urges individual spectators to adopt insights derived from Ardrey and Freud, and thereby accomplish what the film's characters cannot. According to Freud, the violent, jealous ruler of the "primal
horde" drove his sons away because he wanted all the females for himself.
One day a band of expelled brothers slew the father and after devouring him,
they each acquired a part of his strength.[5] But the father had been loved as

well as feared, and the ambivalent feelings of the primal murderers led to an endless alternation of war and peace:

> After their hatred had been satisfied by their act of aggression, their love came to the fore in their remorse for the deed. It set up the superego by identification with the father; it gave that agency the father's power, as though as a punishment for the deed of aggression they had carried out against him, and it created a repetition of the deed. And since the inclination to aggressiveness against the father was repeated in the following generations, the sense of guilt, too, persisted, and it was reinforced once more by every piece of aggressiveness that was suppressed and carried to the superego. Now, I think, we can at last grasp two things perfectly clearly: the part played by love in the origin of conscience and the fatal inevitability of the sense of guilt.[6]

The residual remorse the brothers felt had vast repercussions. Freud felt it was the origin of society, morality, and religion, and Kubrick extends the concept beyond Redmond Barry's personal story to the history of nation-states from his time to ours. For the screenplay that he wrote himself, Kubrick invented several scenes that do not appear in Thackeray's *The Luck of Barry Lyndon*: the opening scene of Redmond and Nora playing cards, the confrontation with Feeney, both battle scenes of Redmond carrying off the wounded "fathers," Grogan and Potzdorf, the meal with Lischen, the climactic duel with Bullingdon, the resultant amputation of Barry's leg, and the scene of Lady Lyndon and Bullingdon paying bills at the end—all to maintain the unifying vision of Oedipal conflict as a central, drama-engendering ritual.[7]

The Oedipal theme is introduced immediately in the film's opening sequence. The narrator tells us that Barry's father was killed in a duel. We see the image (repeated in the film) of duelists pointing their pistols, then a muffled shot, followed instantly by one man being driven into the ground. Next we see Redmond as a tall adolescent with his mother on their farm. The widowed Mrs. Barry had rejected all suitors and "lived for her son only, and the memory of her departed saint."[8] In the next scene Barry and his cousin Nora are playing cards. Between Barry on the left and Nora on the right, in the middle background behind the card table, a statue of a plump infant vaguely resembles Barry in its baby-fat sleekness. The narrator slyly remarks that "first love" makes a great difference in a man, and the love symbolically expressed is the son's love for his mother. When the game ends, Nora tells Redmond to shut his eyes; she then says that she has hidden a favor somewhere on her person and that she "will think very little of him if he does not find it." After several modest failures and repeated coaxing, Barry finally withdraws the ribbon from her bosom with a look of exquisite pleasure. Nora's obvious contempt—"Why are you trembling?"—reveals that she does not regard Redmond as a male powerful enough to merit further favors.[9]

Barry's first primal father is the comical Captain John Quin. Against a natural background of green mountains, the disciplined marching of Quin's regiment represents the structured sense of order that allows power-preserving fathers to maintain their position against invading sons. Captain Quin has raised a regiment to repel a rumored landing by the French, but instead he will have to deal as a father with Barry, the archetypically invading son. We see Barry standing with Nora and watching the marchers, while the narrator relates that the soldiers' "scarlet coats and swaggering airs filled Barry with envy." Nora and Quin then dance a formal jig of alternate display, where each dances alone while the other looks on. The repeated crosscuts to Barry show that his Oedipal "envy" has found a focus in Quin.

His rage ignites in the next scene, when Nora consolingly tells him not to fret because "Captain Quin is a man and you're only a boy." In a subsequent confrontation between the three of them, Captain Quin angrily denounces Nora after Redmond returns her ribbon, saying, "It is not the English way for ladies to have two lovers." But the film implies that a woman having two lovers, a husband and a son, is the universally human way. Barry's challenge, subsequently delivered at the Bradys' dinner, disrupts the civilized order of the occasion. The bewildered Uncle Brady poses a question that in the Freudian context is delightfully rhetorical: "In heaven's name, what did the row mean?"[10]

The row finds its ritual culmination in an absurd duel where Redmond shoots the captain with a globe of wax that Nora's brothers have put in his pistol, in order to protect and appropriate Quin's "five hundred a year." Thematically, Barry's rigged expulsion (presumably to save him from arrest) preserves society by preventing the son from overcoming the father and forcing him to embark upon a search for a surrogate mother. On this journey, however, he will face other threatening fathers and competing sons. The first of these is the highwayman, Captain Feeney. He relieves Redmond of his purse, his pistols, and his horse in a symbolic castration that the ineffectual Quin had been unable to perform. The feared and loved ambivalence of the father appears in Feeney, who, accompanied by his own son, treats Redmond courteously but with implacable firmness.[11]

Having been subdued by Feeney, Redmond joins the army (a collective image of disinherited sons), where he soon has the opportunity to redeem his manhood in ritual combat with another comically threatening father. While sitting at an outdoor meal with his regiment, Redmond asks the mess boy for

Figure 4.1.   Redmond is unmanned by the paternal Captain Feeney. The camera makes the highwayman's son boyishly small, but he holds a pistol to highlight the potency Redmond has lost. *Courtesy of Warner Bros./Photofest © Warner Bros.*

a new beaker, "This one is full of grease." A brutal veteran named Toole then mocks him by quaffing his soup with an exaggerated leer, suggesting sexual contempt for an uninitiated adolescent. Oedipal tension intensifies when Redmond accuses Toole of fearing his wife, "Mr. Toole, why did you hide so when she came to visit you. Were you afraid of havin' your ears boxed?" A reverse castration follows in the form of a boxing match in which Redmond is bloodily victorious.[12]

After decisively achieving his manhood in the subjugation of Toole, Redmond swings from filial hatred to an equally natural filial love directed toward the conveniently arrived Captain Grogan, his second in the duel with Quin. Grogan paternally tells Redmond that he will write to his mother and that she "won't care a pin" about Redmond's losing his father's (phallic) pistols, for which the young man expresses a shamefaced remorse. Grogan then tells Redmond that if he needs cash, he may draw on him and that "as long as Jack Grogan lives," Redmond "shall never want."[13]

The duel that Barry's father lost, and the two ritual combats that Barry has won, precede our viewing of skirmishes in the collective combat of the Seven Years' War. Kubrick suggests that the Oedipal feelings that motivate personal battles also account for the mass manhood trials of war. The narrator introduces us to the European battlefields with a disclaimer that the film reflexively answers, "It would take a great philosopher and historian to determine the causes of the Seven Years' War" (1756–1763).[14] Ostensibly, it stemmed from a conflict between Britain and France for territory in America and India, and its shifting alliances imply its absurdity: Prussia and France broke a long-standing bond; England and Prussia became allies; and in 1762 Russia enabled Prussia to win by switching sides because Peter III was "a fanatical admirer of Frederick the Great." Given this respite Frederick recovered, even though Britain withdrew before the end of hostilities because the war was too expensive, and Russia withdrew because Peter's throne was usurped by his wife, Catherine II, after Peter had held the throne for only one year.[15]

In the film's psychological context, however, these emotions and events play out only on the surface. On the Freudian battlefield another conflict is taking place. At the same time that the hated father is attacked in the ritually formed rows of enemy troops, the loved father, Grogan, is shot. Around his prone body, the other soldiers march indifferently as if driven by an impersonal collective will, while Redmond lifts Grogan on his back and bears him through the smoke into a muddy ravine. His "father" then bids him farewell, and as he dies, Redmond kisses him passionately on the lips and then weeps like a baby. As Freud formulates the theory, the son's love for the father, and the paradoxical guilt he feels for hating him, cause the child to transpose his fear of castration into a voluntary surrender of maleness, and a subsequent wish to be a mother to the father—thus the erotic quality of Redmond's kissing Grogan.[16]

In an ironic transition from the loved father, Grogan, to Redmond's next threatening father, Captain Potzdorf, Barry wins a "mother" in the person of the German farm girl Lischen. Her husband has been gone in the war for a long time, and while she is seated at dinner with Barry and obviously distracted by his charms, she forgets to feed her son. The infant cries as Barry kisses her hand, and as they embrace, the child looks up at them with large, solemn eyes.[17] The image echoes Barry's impotent witness to Quin's theft of Nora and suggests a Freudian version of the Fall of Man. The Edenic bliss of unrivaled possession is irrecoverable, and attempts at compensation can only result in endless failure. Like the hollow victories of the film's forgotten wars, Barry's temporary triumph in supplanting the child's father is soon followed by another subjugation.

Detected as a deserter by the shrewd Captain Potzdorf, Redmond is impressed into the Prussian army. A key thematic scene depicts a minor violator of discipline, helpless and stripped to the waist, walking a gauntlet where more highly ranked males strike him with phallic canes. The narrator adds that every officer had the right to inflict punishment and that more serious crimes were punished by the symbolic castrations of "mutilation or death." The hated father becomes an image of the loved father when Barry rescues Captain Potzdorf from a burning building in the midst of a battle sequence.[18] The shot of Redmond bearing Potzdorf on his back through the smoke and flames echoes the earlier one of Redmond carrying Grogan, and the repetition evokes an archetypal icon, Aeneas bearing Anchises from the flames of Troy. However, Barry's loved father turns out not to be the man he rescues, but, as the multiplication of fathers continues, the Chevalier de Balibari, a gambler he has been sent to spy upon by Potzdorf.

In the novel the chevalier, named "Ballybarry" after an Irish village, turns out to be Redmond's uncle, so that Barry betrays Potzdorf out of family loyalty and a longing to hear his native tongue. In the film the chevalier is emphatically not Barry's uncle, so that Redmond's affection for him is psychological rather than familial. Continuing the film's alternation between Oedipal aggression and remorse, the narrator precedes Barry's tearful confession of espionage to Balibari with "There's many a man who will not understand the cause of the burst of feeling that was now about to take place."[19]

Under the tutelage of the chevalier, Barry becomes a successful gambler. Psychologically, he has begun a "winning streak," where the loved father has been secured and the hated father is repeatedly subdued. When one of the losing noblemen refuses to pay, Barry displays his superb swordsmanship by whipping the deadbeat in a duel.[20] The narrator adds that opportunities to humiliate high-ranking males were not infrequent, but as time passed, these small victories failed to confer satisfaction in "a wandering and disconnected life." Having completed his apprenticeship as a rebellious son, Barry is ready to become a father himself.

The next father he must subdue in order to win the sexual and financial security that civilized "fatherhood" confers is Sir Charles Lyndon, a man already subdued by time and disease. His condition graphically reinforces the ritual nature of the film's major actions. The battle against the fathers is, in a deeper sense, a battle against time. At Spa, the resort in Belgium where they meet, Sir Charles mocks Barry for wanting to "step into his shoes," to which Redmond replies, "Let those laugh that win." (The same line was spoken by Othello when Iago caused him to misinterpret Cassio's laughter as contempt for Desdemona as a whore and himself as a cuckold, *Othello* IV.i.124.) Within one minute of screen time Sir Charles is dead, and the intermission that immediately follows marks the end of Barry's minority. In the next scene the triumphant hero marries Lady Lyndon.[21]

But predictably true to the Oedipal pattern, Barry's brief day in the sun will end when his stepson does him in. To Lord Bullingdon, Barry is the castrating father and possessor of his beloved mother. His hatred becomes obsessive after Barry twice canes him on the buttocks, especially since the second beating occurs when he is well past puberty.[22] (The two canings echo the film's first, the feminizing ritual of the Prussian gauntlet.) Barry's matching hatred stems from two simultaneous threats: on the one hand, Bullingdon is the father who blocks his path to a title that in eighteenth-century terms would have confirmed manhood, and on the other, he is the son "much attached to his mother," who wishes to step into Redmond's shoes.

At a formal concert meant to further Barry's social ambitions, Lord Bullingdon interrupts a Bach harpsichord concerto with a brilliantly staged drama. It begins with the scraping sound of his own shoes on the much too small feet of his younger half brother, whom he leads in to play a secondary role. His monologue includes a passionate declaration of love for his mother, and an eloquent attack on Barry's desire to have his own son inherit the family fortune. The "play" succeeds beyond Bullingdon's wildest dreams when Barry loses control and launches a brutal physical attack in front of the horrified guests.[23]

This display of ferocity confirms Bullingdon's merciless denunciation. In the scene just prior to his being caned for the second time, Bullingdon had been intent on his studies. In at least two instances Kubrick suggests that he had read *Hamlet*. Here his identification with the prince's Oedipal rage and social disinheritance enables him to put his education to use. Several years earlier when he had refused to kiss Barry, the exchange with his mother echoed the play:

Lady Lyndon: Lord Bullingdon, you have insulted your father.

Bullingdon: Mother, *you* have insulted my father.

The exchange in *Hamlet* occurs in Gertrude's room:

Queen: Hamlet, thou hast they father much offended.

Hamlet: Mother, *you* have my father much offended. (*Hamlet* III.iv.10)

Later at the play that Hamlet has commissioned to see if his stepfather betrays guilt, he focuses just as emotionally on his mother's response, "Madam, how do you like this play?" (*Hamlet* III.ii.235). Bullingdon begins his own play by bowing like an actor to the musicians before he begins. His assault and tone are skillfully theatrical: "Don't you think he fits my shoes very well, your ladyship?" He then kneels to Bryan and turns toward the onscreen audience and the camera: "Dear child, what a pity it is that I am not dead for your sake." After praising the "illustrious blood of the Barrys of Barrydom" as more worthy than his own, Bullingdon provokes his mother into a speaking role.

Protectively holding Bryan's shoulders, she angrily tells the still kneeling Bullingdon that her maternal affections had been equal until now and turns to shepherd Bryan from the room. Bullingdon rises and stunningly captures her attention and that of everyone in the room with a speech that has the motivation and tone of his Shakespearean model: "Madam! I have borne as long as mortal could endure the ill treatment of the insolent Irish upstart whom you have taken into your bed." She breaks into tears as he concludes, "And as I cannot personally chastise this low bred ruffian, and as I cannot bear to witness his treatment of you, and loathe his horrible society as if it were the plague, I have decided to leave my home and never return, at least during his detested life or during my own." As she hurries from the room an ironic image of two boys, an older leading a younger, appears in a Renaissance painting to the left of the door. At this point Barry springs at Bullingdon and knocks him down by hitting him in the buttocks, echoing the earlier scenes and confirming an Oedipal hatred strong enough to evoke an involuntary response. But Bullingdon's attack is ultimately the stronger of the two, lethal in its social impact, and adumbrating the symbolic castration Barry suffers after the concluding duel.

In the film's second half Barry's greed and ambition are mitigated by the unstinting love he holds for his own son, Bryan, a devotion he had previously given to only two other males, the surrogate fathers, Grogan and the chevalier. Bryan's fatal attempt to master a horse that is too large for him resembles Barry's attempt to achieve a position of unassailable paternal security, only to be overthrown by the mutability of existence itself. The film's striking images of gamblers with heavily painted faces resolve variations of individual personality into a collective ritual of trying to beat the odds against those very frailties of disease and age that the paint so ineffectively conceals. In this game, of course, everyone eventually loses. Although he is, from one point of view, only a petty social climber, the film's hero also represents a Sisyphus-like climbing toward permanent "manhood" that belongs in the end only to the impersonal god of change itself.

The narrative voice-over offers an alternative to the blindly driven actions of the characters. Kubrick told Michel Ciment that the voice-over "works as an ironic counterpoint to what you see portrayed by the actors" and that in lessening "surprise," it creates a sense of "inevitability." He felt that the story was about universal and timeless patterns of behavior, that "what is important is not what is going to happen, but how it will happen."[24] But he also implies that the spectator, from a perspective even larger than that of the narrator, may be freed from destructive impulses that motivate personal relations and historical events.

As contributions to the long-term evolution of the species, Kubrick's films reverse the usual moral priorities of actions over words and engagement over observation. *Barry Lyndon*'s opening scene of the duel where Barry's father was killed contains aesthetic and comic elements that are apparent only to the spectators, privileged at least for the moment to gaze down like angels at the follies of human beings. The scene's timelessness echoes *2001*. Both films begin at dawn to the sound of cawing crows. Within the scenically gorgeous frame the descendants of Moonwatcher continue to vaunt their power to kill, though here the contrast between the narrator's genteel tone and the abrupt keel-over of Barry's father conveys more absurdity than horror.

The long shot of honorable men primed to kill in a dispute "over the purchase of some horses" foreshadows in miniature the epically stupid carnage of the Seven Years' War. The duel is an icon of destructive blindness, and the frame's composition helps to separate the spectators from the characters' compelled actions. The curve between two gray mountains in the background matches that of a gray rock wall in the foreground that curves away from us toward the right of the frame. Two trees at either end of the wall— one near, one far—form the side borders. Separated by the wall, the spectators see five tiny human figures in the distance. The adversaries point their guns toward each other at the right and left center, while two seconds and a referee in the exact center mirror the audience.[25]

While the small figures see only their targets and the witnesses focus on the action, the spectator's mood is immediately calmed by the harmony of composition and color. The grass in the bottom foreground is lush and green, suggesting the surviving life and energy of the earth, while the dark gray clouds augur a storm that will maintain that green, even as storms traditionally suggest a future threat. That the still unknown protagonist's father dies may conventionally be tragic, but the reason that he dies, the argument over horses, is comic. Additional irony is supplied in that "like many a son of a genteel family," Barry's father had been "bred to the profession of the law." Though duels are currently obsolete, the laws of genteel nations have never prevented their citizens from slaughtering each other in wars, such as those the film graphically depicts.

In this scene the squaring off of killer apes in a primitive setting is a natural phenomenon. The art of storytelling is just as natural, redirecting fear and violence away from the physical world and into the imagination.

However, fictions that further awareness are often less entertaining than those that simply plunge beholders into a vicarious experience they are predisposed to feel. *Barry Lyndon* repeatedly employs comic elements to prevent the audience from sentimentalizing the characters. The wall separating awareness from involvement continues to be present in the next scene where Barry and his mother first appear.

A small fragment of rock wall stands in the foreground of a pastoral scene where the two characters walk decorously in front of their cottage and barn. As they turn left at the right of the screen, a high stone wall appears extending toward the back of the frame. These walls imply the attempt to provide shelter, but the wall in the foreground is broken down, symbolically allowing the spectator to see through the psychological illusions that impel mother and child to place security in money and rank. Walls appear subsequently along a mountain road where Barry, thinking he has safely escaped the war, meets Captain Potzdorf and along the road where a servant gallops to fetch a doctor after Bryan falls from his horse.[26] In these cases neither guile nor love can secure the future.

The opening duel scene pictures death and prefigures war beneath thunderclouds. Though the idyllic second scene tranquilly unfolds in bright sunlight, the twitter of birds and the predominance of gray connect it to the first. In war or peace human beings strive to recover the security and omnipotence of infancy. The narrator's ironic tone comically mitigates sympathy for the undying devotion of Barry's mother to her "dear departed saint," while Barry himself is posed, mannequin-like in his gray waistcoat and pantaloons, untested in the world and as yet unknown to the audience.

Barry's gray outfit and his mother's gray and white striped dress, along with the gray rock walls of the cottage and barn, suggest unknown potentialities, though the initial narration misleadingly suggests an infinite vista of pastoral content. Instead, Mrs. Barry will temporarily become a grotesque harridan, fiercely bent on keeping the fortune her son temporarily secured before circumstance returns her in the final scene to a more conventional form of devotion. While gray and white suggest the unknown joys and sorrows that any human future contains, the deep green grass in the foreground, carried over from the duel scene, affirms the certainty of growth elsewhere on the earth and elsewhere in human nature. The visual continuity thematically unifies cycles of war and peace into a single process.

The walls in both scenes secure nothing but may serve to divide spectators impelled toward vision from those who worship power. Even before they learned to wield weapons, the apes of *2001* understood dominance. Though they had no weapons, they could at least display superior energy to drive rival bands from their water hole. Through Redmond's mother the film shows that the satisfaction inherent in power is not a male prerogative. In the next scene Barry's cousin, Nora, wields that power.[27] The two are seen playing cards, a form of competitive ritual that in the eighteenth century barely sublimated primitive aggression. In subsequent scenes the Prince of Tübingen and Lord Ludd resort to physical challenge rather than accept their losses at cards.[28] This scene purports to express "first love," as the narrator puts it, but the Oedipal metaphor mocks this, and the thunderstorm outside the window that Nora turns to face reiterates the idea that peace may be short-lived. Moreover, the "first love" Barry feels is purely one sided, and the blue of the outdoor backdrop seen through the structure of the diamond-patterned window is as cold as Nora's heart.

In the film's larger context, winning the "game" symbolizes a triumph over death and vulnerability, and when Nora declares victory by saying "Killarney," it is as if the rules give the victor license to discard them. She then initiates a new game that erotically intoxicates Barry but carries a darker excitement for her. When she asks him to withdraw the ribbon from the bosom of her gown, Nora stands above his chair contemptuously mocking his arousal as he fumbles to find the "favor" she deigns to offer. Her expression throughout the game is tense, as if she is testing her own self-control, while attacking his and mocking his shyness. After she guides his hand to the ribbon and he withdraws it, she asks, "Why are you trembling?" and when he says, "At the pleasure of finding the ribbon," she mocks his chivalry as naive, "You're a liar." As she bends down from a height that the camera exaggerates, Barry's rapture makes him oblivious to the fact that he has been humiliated, almost raped, rather than lovingly initiated into pleasure.

Though the scene is ostensibly erotic, Nora's face during the seduction remains the same as it had been during the game: determined, almost grim, extending her dominance from cards to complete sexual control. Rather than stirring maternal affection, Barry's adolescent awe disqualifies him as Nora's choice. Her quest to find a dominant male turns out comically because she perceives that dominance in the oafishly pretentious Captain Quin, simply because he wears a uniform, is an Englishman, and is worth five hundred pounds a year. Though Barry stares in envy as Nora dances with Quin, the audience cannot sympathize with either cousin's misplaced infatuation.

The scene creates further distance with a variation of the film's opening image—a long shot of tiny figures suicidally preparing for an ordered game that will kill some of them, against a background of mountains looming over rectangular fields, unsubdued nature over nature seemingly controlled.[29] The yokels stand facing the soldiers with their backs to the audience in the opening shot, mirroring again the difference between the limited view of those involved in the action as opposed to the spectators' comprehensive view. Subsequent "arena" scenes maintain this distance, reminding us of our Star Child vantage: When Barry's regiment marches toward its first engagement in Europe, we see them coming at a distance from behind the backs of an outfit of French defenders; Lord Ludd plays the simpering dandy to adoring female companions on either side as he attempts to remain gracefully casual while the chevalier and Barry trounce him at cards; a Prussian soldier, walking a gauntlet between officers with canes, reacts in increasing agony for the satisfaction of the participant-observers; and much later Barry and the chevalier observe the initial entrance of the Lyndon family in a scene distanced by Barry's having become a cold-blooded predator, intent on seeking (like Nora before him) a marriage that will place him in the highest possible social rank.

The film alienates us most when it portrays social ambition and war and involves us most when Barry expresses a dazzling grace that fulfills itself in action, a kind of art for art's sake. His boxing match with Toole occurs in a rectangular ring formed by the soldiers, and a handheld camera takes us directly into the action where we root for Barry as he cuts down a fairy tale giant. Here and in the scene where his superior swordsmanship makes an honest man of Lord Ludd, Barry is at his best. His technique is precise, and his moves are a tour de force combination of unexpected strokes that only pure talent could produce. Like Alex at the flat-block marina, Barry is an artist of violence.

Beginning with 2001 Kubrick refuses to present characters that permit complete identification. In Barry Lyndon he employs a unique but characteristic pattern of colors to portray everyman's circular journey from birth to death and, simultaneously, his spiraling ascent toward the light. In the three opening scenes gray and white are the colors of potentiality: the gray and white sky of the opening scene with its black wall, the gray clothing of Barry and his mother in front of their gray cottage, and the beige suit and white dress that Barry and Nora, respectively, wear during the card game. Just as black was the color of beginnings, endings, and transitions in 2001, white fulfills that function in Barry Lyndon. Its most specific thematic expression is spoken by the magician at the celebration of Bryan's eighth birthday.[30]

On a glorious sunny day, Bryan and the magician stand on a stage with a painted backdrop of blue sky and white clouds. The magician performs two tricks involving color, as if Kubrick is underscoring its symbolic significance. In the first the magician holds up a bright blue hat with a white border and proclaims, "I shall show you the knot that never was." Then he has Bryan look inside the hat and asks him to reach in to feel if anything is there. Miraculously, the child pulls out a long tied string of "wonderful, wonderful" white, yellow, blue, orange, green, and purple silk handkerchiefs. Next, the magician manifests a new array of color: "I want you to wave your hand over my green silk handkerchief and see if we can produce a magic flower." The handkerchief that produces the flower is green, like the bright green grass in the duel, cottage, and marching scenes, perhaps because it represents the life process. Beauty is a mystery without purpose and, like the magic show and the film, delightful while it lasts. The handkerchief now becomes a second bouquet of cloth, this time an array of ribbons in pink, yellow, green, blue, white, and black.

The transition to the magician's finale uses white to reiterate the ex nihilo theme: "[With the ribbons] we have the colors of the rainbow, there they are; the colors of the rainbow produce but one color, Bryan (*showing Bryan the open drawer of a small brown box with a green interior*)—nothing in my magic cabinet—they produce the color white. And (*reaching into the drawer*) there is your very own beautiful white rabbit." Correspondingly, Bryan is his father's prize, and his coming into the world miraculously humanizes Barry by restoring some of the sensitivity he lost during his years in the military and with the chevalier. But like the rabbit, Barry's joys and triumphs will vanish as inexplicably as they appear.

Here, especially, Thackeray's title applies: *The Luck of Barry Lyndon*. The withdrawal of the ribbons recalls the fulfillment of Barry's adolescent fantasy when he received Nora's "favor," but just as that ecstasy was short-lived and deceptive, so will his "magic flower" wither when Bryan unexpectedly dies a year later. Kubrick's use of white to suggest certain transience and uncertain fate is evident throughout the film. Philosophically, its symbolism corresponds to Newton's discovery that colors have no absolute reality but are only illusions produced by white light passed through a prism. The idea had become common knowledge by the mid-eighteenth century, and it provided a metaphysical basis for the most significant single symbol in American literature.

At the same time Thackeray began *The Luck of Barry Lyndon*, Melville was writing *Moby-Dick*. In chapter 42, "The Whiteness of the Whale," Ishmael expresses "despair" over putting "into comprehensive form" a mystery that "above all things appalled" him:

> Is it that in essence whiteness is not so much a color as the visible absence of color, and at the same time the concrete of all colors. . . . And when we consider that other theory of the natural philosophers, [especially Newton] that all

other earthly hues—every stately or lovely emblazoning—the sweet tinges of sunset skies and woods; yea, and the gilded velvets of butterflies, and the butterfly cheeks of young girls; all these are but subtle deceits, not actually inherent in substances but only laid on from without so that all deified Nature absolutely paints like the harlot, whose allurements cover nothing but the charnel house within; and when we proceed further and consider that mystical cosmetic which produces every one of her hues, the great principle of light, for ever remains white or colorless in itself, and if operating without medium upon matter, would touch all objects, even tulips and roses, with its own blank tinge. . . . And of all these things the Albino whale was the symbol. Wonder ye then at the fiery hunt?[31]

By the mid-twentieth century the absence of divine presence and purpose was no longer appalling, but color could still retain its significance for every new variety of ancient skepticism from Camus to Lévi-Strauss to Derrida. Kubrick's use of white as the blank origin of color and experience may also be influenced by the Void of Eastern religion, considering his explicit use of the *Bhagavad Gita* in *Full Metal Jacket* and *Eyes Wide Shut*. But the fear of "annihilation" has never become obsolete, and throughout *Barry Lyndon* the metaphor of painting "the charnel house within" is strikingly present in the face paint worn by those gambling against their mortality. This is especially apparent in the heavily made-up face of Sir Charles Lyndon as he dies of an apparent heart attack on screen immediately after boasting that it will be a long time before Barry can step into "his shoes."

Not a single one of the characters in the film faces the fact that the game they struggle to win is ultimately one of musical shoes. After the magician produces the rabbit, the camera goes to a medium close-up of Barry's beaming mother, one of the story's most determined schemers. Of course, her "beautiful white rabbit" is Barry, the son that has come from her. All of the spectators behind her in this shot are children. At this point the film seems to say that to believe that one's efforts will assure good fortune is as childish as to believe that a rabbit can be drawn from a drawer. Here the white rabbit is a comic version of the white whale, and Barry's quest is as single-minded, misguided, and ultimately self-destructive as Ahab's.

The wisdom of Ishmael is in the story he unfolds, not in its ending or in any extrapolated meaning. The magician at the birthday party is Kubrick's archetypal artist. Like a storyteller he creates magical illusions that redirect attention and delight to the present moment, the passing show. The white rabbit may be the grand finale, but the show's interlude is a transient rainbow, an illusion of light valuable for itself rather than for untying "the knot

that never was." Repeated cuts to the onscreen audience during the show reveal uniform delight, except for Lord Bullingdon who can see nothing but his
jealousy and hatred of Barry. Just as the eye serves as a prism to create light,
so the light thrown by a story can only shine through a mind not rendered
opaque by self-concern.

To the sprightly sounds of Schubert's *German March*, Bryan next appears
joyously shaking a wand with the rainbow ribbons attached as he rides by
himself in a canopied, white-plumed carriage drawn by white sheep. Lady
Lyndon walks with her hand on the carriage, while Barry leads the sheep. All
around children beat drums, gambol, and cheer. Their joy is wholehearted
and of the moment, but the spectators' experience is of a different order. We
have seen enough ugliness and suffering in previous scenes to prevent us from
thinking that the complete happiness shown here can last. The keynote is
appreciation of the process—manifestation, full expression, disappearance.
Accordingly, the brightest objects in the picture are six exceptionally tall
white plumes, two attached to the heads of the sheep and four at each
corner of the coach's canopy. Along with the off-white tones of the sheep,
the spokes of the wheels, and the canopy itself, the white of the plumes signals the beginning and the end, and the necessity of replacing striving with
celebration.

The film celebrates all phases of experience including the darkness that
appears in the next frame. This time the repeated transitional shot of Castle
Hackton across the lake is entirely black except for the afterglow of sunset il-
luminating just enough indigo sky to reveal the location. The shot is a variation of the black screen transitions used in *2001* to indicate a change of
scene within the story and the introduction of further recognitions for the
audience.

The next cut shows a candlelit scene of Bryan in bed wearing a white
nightshirt, holding a white stuffed sheep, and lying on a huge white pillow,
all illuminated by white light from a candelabra to his right. Barry sits on the
bed looking lovingly down on his son, seconded by his mother who sits just
behind him. We are seeing three generations of the Barry family, with Bryan
symbolizing the fulfillment of their dreams and the immortality of their
achievement. The visual picture suggests the ultimate human hope: peace,
health, and prosperity beyond the foreseeable future, but Barry's bedtime
story grotesquely undercuts this dream.

> We crept up on their fort and I jumped over the wall first. My fellows jumped
> after me. Oh, you should have seen the look on the Frenchmen's faces when

twenty-three rampaging he-devils, sword and pistol, cut and thrust, pell-mell came tumbling into their fort. In three minutes' time we left as many artillery men's heads as there were cannonballs. Later that day we were visited by our noble Prince Henry: "Who is the man that has done this?" I stepped forward. "How many heads was it ye cut off?" "Nineteen," says I, "besides wounded several." When he heard, I'll be blessed if he didn't burst into tears: "Noble, noble fellow," he said. "Here is nineteen golden guineas for you, one for each head that you cut off." Now, what do you think of that?[32]

For Bryan the story functions as a fairy tale, but for the spectator it ironically refers back to Barry having grudgingly received a much smaller sum, two Frederick d'Or for rescuing Captain Potzdorf after being scorned as a reprobate.[33] Like General Broulard in *Paths of Glory*, Prince Henry oversees the deaths of others from a safe vantage, rewarding their bloody deeds with ridiculous prizes, especially considering what would have happened to them if they had refused to follow orders. (Barry unintentionally parodies British military glory by naming his "prince" after Henry V, Britain's greatest soldier-king.) When Bryan asks, "Were you allowed to keep the heads?" Barry voices the recurring theme of dominance: "No, the heads always become the property of the king." And when Bryan asks Barry if he will play cards with him tomorrow, the boy expresses the universal compulsion to compete: his fatal

Figure 4.2.   In an ironic image of love and hope, Barry tells Bryan how he led "twenty-three rampaging he-devils" over the wall of a French fort where he single-handedly beheaded nineteen men. *Courtesy of Warner Bros./Photofest © Warner Bros.*

fall from a horse in a subsequent scene is spurred by jealousy of another boy's having a full-size mount in comparison to his small one.

Though Barry's unstinting love is apparent, he will be as unable to protect Bryan from random circumstance as he is to secure his own "luck." When Bryan asks if he can sleep with the candles lit because he is afraid of the dark, the spectator understands the subtext to be inner darkness in light of Barry's tale, the larger frame of the film, and the still larger frame of history. On this level Bryan's fear is legitimate. His grandmother's gentle reproach that "big boys don't sleep with the candles lit," because "there's nothing to be afraid of," is both hilarious in light of Barry's tale and tragically prescient in light of what befalls Bryan within eight minutes of screen time.

Just before his deathbed scene, the colors of death and rebirth suffuse the transitional shot of Castle Hackton across the lake, seen this time at dawn under a gray sky reflected in the water with a thin, bright, horizontal line of white mist cleanly dividing the frame. Irregular lines of black weeds and black trees flank the white line at top and bottom. The image remains as the narrator reflects, "The doctors were called, but what does a doctor avail in a contest with the grim invincible enemy?"[34] The lines recall the fort story from the previous bedroom scene, accentuating the game motif: all competitive acts symbolically attempt to overcome death, suggesting that the "realities" of personal struggle and collective war are involuntary paroxysms rather than evidence of human rationality or cosmic design.

The gray, black, and white nature image and the sound of crows evoke the film's first scene where Bryan's grandfather was killed. Barry's male forebear and his only male heir die surrounded by the colors of transition. The cut to a close-up of Bryan's hand in Barry's presents a poignant image of inevitable loss, and the reverse zoom reveals the child in his canopied bed in a puffy white gown with the top of his head and forehead swathed in a white bandage, angelically bathed in bright light with his anguished parents in relative darkness on either side. A close-up of his pale face makes the whiteness even more emphatic as he asks if he is going to die because, except for his hands, his whole body is numb.

In that all the colors of the rainbow produce only white, and in light of Melville's reflections on the color's threatening quality, the conventional white of Bryan's innocence is qualified by the color's darker meaning. The exaggerated melodrama of the scene maintains enough distance to keep the spectators aware of its ironies. At its tear-jerking peak, Bryan makes his parents promise "never to quarrel so, and to love each other, so that we may meet again in heaven, where Bullingdon and such people will never go." The exclusion of Bullingdon undercuts the speech's Christian sanctity, since

Bullingdon has earlier been shown as a victim of circumstance and of humiliating canings by Barry. It satirizes the facility with which Christians forgive their enemies selectively and comes just before Bryan's last request, "Papa, will you tell me the story about the fort?"

Through his tears Barry repeats the tale, word for word, including the reference to his comrades as "twenty-three rampaging he-devils," before breaking down just before the first version's vaunt that "in three minutes' time" they had chopped off "as many artillery men's heads as there were cannonballs." Barry's duality here epitomizes Kubrick's central interior drama: killer ape versus loving preserver. Accordingly, the ambivalence of gray suffuses the room: the curtains under the bed canopy, the bedspread, the back of Barry's chair, and the line of trees outside the window. Lady Lyndon wears a gray dress, and Barry's gray coat matches his hair, previously seen as light brown or red orange depending on the mood and energy of the scene. Even his eyes are gray. As he tells Bryan the fort story, his right shoulder and the right side of his head look white, while most of the screen surrounding him is black, except for the white vertical windows over his right shoulder.

In the immediate cut to Bryan's funeral procession, the central object is his white casket in the same white and gold carriage seen at his birthday party, but in the brightest part of the frame the large white plumes appear in the foreground attached to the heads of the sheep that we do not see. As the camera slowly zooms back we see the gold birthday canopy topped, as before, with four white plumes. On either side two children dressed entirely in black, except for the white trim of their cuffs and collars and the borders of their three-cornered hats, accompany the carriage. A third child leads the sheep. Directly behind walks the always pale Reverend Runt, clad in a pure white surplice with a narrow black sash over his shoulders extending to the ground. Directly behind him Barry, Lady Lyndon, and Mrs. Barry lead the other mourners all uniformly dressed in black, except for Barry's white lace scarf and cuffs and the narrow gold band on the upper edge of his hat.

In addition to these stark black and white symbols of transition, the rest of the scene has the same combination in softer tones: bathed in light mist the lake and sky are white, while the nearby trees are black, and the distant ones are a darker shade of gray than the wall of the church that appears as the scene ends. As in the opening scene where Barry's father dies, a swath of green grass between the path and the lake affirms the continuity of life and beauty, though that can be no immediate consolation to the bereft. Nor can the reverend's mellifluous reading: "I am the Resurrection and the Life, sayeth the Lord. . . . And whosoever believeth in me, though he were dead shall never die. . . . We brought nothing into this world and it is certain we can carry nothing out. The Lord gave and the Lord has taken away. Blessed be the name of the Lord."

For the spectator, however, the film's skepticism about providential justice does not interfere with the calming distance of its take on mutability. The body may be taken at any time regardless of virtue or desert, but the circular journey of physical existence is offset by the spiraling expansion of vision in the ideal spectator. Kubrick places his faith in the soul's growth here and now rather than in the hereafter. The immediate unconscious experience of the spectator, as the film unfolds, reflects the implicit hope of all great story-tellers: that beyond the three hours' traffic of the screen the beholders may, like Telemachus, discover courage in the face of suffering and death. After 2001 each Kubrick film has a wholeness best imagined from the Star Child's sphere.

The partial, smaller story concerns the fate of an individual. After the duel with Bullingdon, Barry is taken to an inn. Its exterior colors suggest the reduction of his story to its beginning. Seen under a white early morning sky, the inn's roof is black; its walls are white with black vertical strips of wood; and its doorframes and windowpanes are dark gray. The black coach bearing Redmond arrives at the inn door as a rooster greets a new day, affirming continuity and new growth elsewhere on the earth. Though he is younger than Shakespeare's "seventh age," the next interior scene suggests "second childishness and mere oblivion," the end of his adult identity.

In the next shot we see the surgeon standing at the foot of the bed probing Barry's wound. The sound of a dog barking outside replaces the rooster's crow and subtly invokes Barry's return to a humble condition. The circularity is further suggested by the surgeon's appearance and manner. With his glasses lowered on his nose and his gentle but cold courtesy, he resembles Captain Feeney. Like the highwayman, he is about to perform a symbolic castration that will reduce the hero to a helpless child, who can barely stifle a sob when he learns that his leg must be amputated below the knee.[35]

The surgeon's gray coat, hair, and eyes mirror the hopelessness of Barry's case, and in their indefiniteness the fragility of "luck." When Barry asks why he must lose his leg, the surgeon replies that amputation and survival have become one: "The ball has completely shattered the bone below the knee and severed the artery; unless I amputate there's no way I can further repair the artery and prevent further hemorrhaging." The initial low-angle shot of the surgeon, seen from Barry's point of view, suggests in its grayness an inexorable diminishing toward death.

But the next shot, paradoxically but consistently for Kubrick, places Barry's defeat in one of the film's most beautiful frames. Seen from the side of the bed Barry lies supine with the surgeon in profile now, still standing at the foot, and his two seconds facing the camera on the opposite side of the bed. The shadows, light, and composition resemble a Vermeer. The back window and the one behind Barry's head are blue and white like the magician's painted backdrop at Bryan's birthday, and the light they admit creates a beautiful horizontal pattern of white highlights across the frame: from the top of Barry's head at the right, to the white cravat of the second standing at his shoulder, to the towel held by the second at his knee, to the white pillow that supports Barry's feet, to the white cuffs of the surgeon at his feet.

The extraordinary visual quality here is the reintroduction of color into a previous display of blank hopelessness. The second standing at Barry's knee is unnamed, but his violet coat, centered in the frame, immediately draws the eye. It is offset by the shadow on his right shoulder and the black wall to his left. In the duel scene he appeared only as a small gray figure in the background. He continues to be anonymous here, but the beauty of the color he wears contains an affirmation that counterpoints Barry's defeat. Beneath him the light gives Barry's gray breeches a blue tone, and, instead of lying on pure white sheets, as Bryan did before he died, Barry lies on a bedspread patterned in a plaid of maroon, blue, pink, and white. Here, instead of dominating the scene as a tragic end, white is only one phase of the larger life process. In the same way it had been just one of the many colors that the "magician" tied to the "wonderful, wonderful" string of silk handkerchiefs on Bryan's birthday. Barry, like Bryan, and each member of the audience will vanish (relatively) soon, but the film reminds us that though it is about to end, its colors will remain.

The window Barry turns toward as the scene ends has the same diamond pattern as the window centered in the scene where he and Nora played cards. At the end he is just as powerless as he was then, and accordingly the next cut shows Bullingdon's coach racing through bright green hills on a cloudless day. He may be in the ascendant now, but the natural scenes throughout have the effect of saying that while men rise and fall, the earth remains. Crows are cawing as they did when Barry's father and Bryan died, while Bullingdon calmly plots Barry's doom. He tells the family servant, Graham, that upon their arrival he is to tell Mrs. Barry of the duel and her son's wound, knowing that she will immediately go to him, never to return.

As his instructions end, Barry's erasure is accented by a twelve-second shot of Reverend Runt under a black hat with his pale face matching a small white collar that points down stiffly in an inverted V over his black cassock.

His satisfaction over having won his own contest with Mrs. Barry—she had fired him earlier—is apparent on his usually expressionless face, but in this brief interval between Barry's last two scenes his black clothes and pasty face resemble a comic version of Death. The colors associated with him establish an elegiac tone for the following scene between Barry and his mother. Just before it begins, the passage of time is shown by a cut to the carriage arriving at the castle in the afterglow of sunset. There is a narrow slash of orange against an indigo sky, while the bottom third of the screen is a transitional black, announcing the end of Barry's "day."

The transition adds poignancy to Barry's helplessness in his last scene. It opens with a medium shot of Mrs. Barry gazing down at her boy with sad but loving devotion.[36] Her dress is gray, as it had been in her first appearance, with white lace trim. In her right hand she holds a white fan, while her left holds a hand of white-backed cards. But the colorlessness of her accoutrements is offset by the effect of the light coming in from the window over her right shoulder. It gives her face a pink warmth and the arras behind her a rich brown cast with golden highlights on either side.

As the Handel Sarabande plays softly, sadly, and mournfully rather than with its usual confidence, the camera pulls back to a view of Barry propped up in bed with a pained expression, listlessly going through the motions of playing his cards. Here, as in the first scene with Nora, he has become a child in the hands of a strong woman, though this time she is protectively maternal rather than harshly dominant. Like Bryan on his deathbed, he wears a white nightshirt, and the white bandage covering his amputation is prominent in the center of the frame.

Once again the diminution expressed by the white and gray of the actors' clothing is offset by the beauty of the frame: it is partly a Vermeer with its clear natural light shining in from the diamond-shaped windows, and partly a Rembrandt in the dark richness of its velvet backdrop. The light shines on the hidden side of Barry's face, giving his profile a golden outline, while the white light from the window behind him creates a halo effect. Color harmony is achieved by the soft violet and pink tones of his sheets and bare leg, balancing the brown backdrop.

This painterly scene disappears when Mrs. Barry turns to answer a knock at the door. Just before she opens it the image prepares us to witness Bullingdon's coup de grâce. The external light has become dull. Mrs. Barry's dress seen from behind is a slightly lighter shade of gray than the walls and the door, while the arras to the right, covering almost half the screen, is now black balanced by a black upright desk on the left. The door then opens to reveal the family servant clad in a dark brown, almost black coat and breeches offset by stark white stockings covering his thin legs below the knee.

Graham is clearly uncomfortable at having to deliver Barry's death sentence—that in return for a small annuity he must leave England, never to return upon penalty of going to jail. When Graham asks Barry how he feels, his sympathy is genuine. Barry in turn replies gently, "I'm feeling much better, thank you, Graham." In another echo of Bryan the light on the right side of his face and the top of his head gives him an angelic look. The cards neatly laid out on the shadowed sheet to his right along with the single white card in his hand sadly recall the "lad" Captain Grogan had affectionately praised as more "game" than any he had seen in "all me life."

Just before Graham begins to speak a church bell tolls eight times. Though Barry has been humbled and is as a little child again, there is no redemption in his story. But if salvation holds no charm for Kubrick, his film reveals admiration for the continuity of love and courage in humanity, and the continuity of creation in nature and in art. The beauty of the scenes in Barry's room at the inn exemplifies this affirmation with their evocations of Rembrandt and Vermeer. Similar uses of light and shadow for interior scenes occur in a long shot of the Brady family at the table where Quin announces his engagement to Nora, and the scene at the table in Mrs. Barry's cottage where Barry's cousin persuades Barry to escape to Dublin after the duel. Still another "Vermeer" appears in a long shot of Barry's family seated at the dinner table, just before Bryan learns that Barry has bought him a horse for his birthday. Here, light streaming in from a large window at frame right creates the effect.[37]

In our last view of him, Barry emerges from the inn into a dull morning light that reveals an "utterly baffled and beaten" man, his left leg now a stump, still wearing the gray hat and suit he wore in the duel.[38] Barry and his mother initially appear as tiny figures, and though the camera slowly zooms in, it reaches its closest point only when Barry has passed, showing his back just before he enters the coach. In the freeze frame at 2:58:09, the largest figure is Mrs. Barry, also seen from behind as she exits the story. Since she is Barry's first and last shelter in his circular journey, the story seems to imply that its everyman hero has lived a vain and futile life. As Reverend Runt says at Bryan's funeral: "We brought nothing into this world, and it is certain we can carry nothing out."

Nevertheless, there is much to admire in the final frames if one considers aesthetic and emotional experience to be more valuable than possessions and power. All through the scene of Barry's final exit, feelings of sadness or cynicism are mitigated by the loveliness of the Lady Lyndon theme, Schubert's

Piano Trio. Its continuity through the film's second half, as well as that of the assertively masculine Barry theme, Handel's Sarabande near the beginning and end, affirms human existence in general even as individuals conquer or fail, suffer or rejoice. Barry's future may be hopeless, but humanity's is not. The beauty of the music, the grace of the prose, and the gentle intelligence of the narrator are timeless and universal.

And above all, *Barry Lyndon*, like every Kubrick film, celebrates the experience of the eye. Immediately after Barry enters the coach and the narrator says, "He never saw Lady Lyndon again," the final frames deliver forms of vision that cannot disappear. First the camera cuts to a last view of Castle Hackton.[39] This time, however, we are closer to the lake's edge, so that the reeds in the foreground are as large as the castle on the opposite shore. Once again the insignificance of the individual is set against the beauty of nature that can be witnessed and shared. The reeds, the trees, and the sky put the castle in perspective, a small part of the harmonious scene. Instead of expressing a driven aspiration to transcend nature, the castle's dark gray dome matches the thunderclouds at the top of the frame and the lake at the bottom. Below the clouds the sky is slate blue, while the castle's facing wall is ivory and beige. Rather than overshadowing everything below, the dark clouds permit a partial light that imparts a gray tone to the trees and lawn and accents the violet flowers on the silver reeds. The trees are alive in the gusts from the approaching storm, and they have an irregular rather than a geometric symmetry that surrounds, cradles, and integrates the man-made structure.

The interior scene in the next cut is just as beautiful. Light floods in from a large window on the left to illuminate a spacious room with the small, formal figures of Bullingdon, Reverend Runt, and Graham staring down at a table where Lady Lyndon is signing bills. Once again the visual tone counterpoints the emotional one. Though the color is as absent from Lady Lyndon's life as it is from her face in subsequent close-ups, the long shot's light, shadow, and color create another "Vermeer." The white light from the window at the left is balanced by the bright white fireplace on the right. The burnished brown hardwood floors are vividly offset by a narrow orange drapery vertically hanging at the left border, an orange chair in the center where Graham sits, and another orange chair on the far right next to the fireplace. A violet chair in the left foreground echoes the violet reeds of the last frame and the coat of Barry's second in the previous "Vermeer."

The fourteen-second duration of this frame implies that the film's cinematic eye transcends its narrative. The characters seated in the shadows either look down at the table or away from the light that outlines their faces.

Now that Bryan and Barry are gone, Lady Lyndon's face is as ashen as her dress, and her only function is to maintain the family's material possessions and herself as Bullingdon's Oedipal prize. Sitting with downcast gray eyes in a gray dress under a large mound of gray hair, the neutrality of her person is transferred to the black letters of her signature on the thick, gray paper. But even as a ghost Lady Lyndon retains her grace. After she silently sighs upon signing Redmond's annuity, Bullingdon senses her emotion and turns toward her. Through his spectacles he directs us to take another look at Lady Lyndon. The next close-up reveals a surviving beauty that Barry did not appreciate and Bullingdon cannot possess. As she looks down to resume the mechanical ritual her life has become, her face and the fluidity of her motion are as lovely as ever.

The film ends with a reprise of the splendid interior that began the scene. During this final display of color, the "female" Schubert Trio modulates to a minor key just before its last note synchronizes with the last word of the epilogue: "It was in the reign of George III that the aforesaid personages lived and quarreled. Good or bad, handsome or ugly, rich or poor, they are all equal now." But then, abruptly, a full orchestra resoundingly asserts the "male" determination of the Sarabande as the credits begin. Juxtaposed to the serene delicacy of the landscapes and painterly interiors, the violent energy associated with duels and battle is sublimated into cosmic harmony, a balance formerly associated with Beethoven's Ninth Symphony in *A Clockwork Orange*. And as in *2001*, the color, beauty, and violence of *Barry Lyndon* are subsumed in the pure potentiality of a white-lettered black screen.

Notes

1. See Walter Kaufmann, *Nietzsche: Philosopher, Psychologist, Antichrist* (Cleveland and New York: World, 1956), 213.

2. Kaufmann, *Nietzsche*, 227.

3. Kaufmann, *Nietzsche*, 235.

4. Kaufmann, *Nietzsche*, 359.

5. Sigmund Freud, "Totem and Taboo," in *The Basic Writings of Sigmund Freud*, ed. and trans. A. A. Brill (1913; New York: Modern Library, 1965), 807–930.

6. Sigmund Freud, *Civilization and Its Discontents*, ed. and trans. James Strachey (1930; New York: W. W. Norton, 1962), 79.

7. William Makepeace Thackeray, *The Luck of Barry Lyndon*, ed. Martin Anisman (1844; New York: New York University Press, 1970).

8. *Barry Lyndon*, DVD, directed by Stanley Kubrick (1975; Burbank, Calif.: Warner Bros. Home Video, 2001), chapter 2.

9. *Barry Lyndon*, DVD, chapter 3.

10. *Barry Lyndon*, DVD, chapters 5–7.

11. *Barry Lyndon*, DVD, chapter 10.

12. *Barry Lyndon*, DVD, chapter 12.

13. *Barry Lyndon*, DVD, chapter 13.

14. *Barry Lyndon*, DVD, chapter 14.

15. See Marcel Dunan and John Roberts, eds., *Larousse Encyclopedia of Modern History* (New York: Harper & Row, 1964), 168–170.

16. *Barry Lyndon*, DVD, chapter 14.

17. *Barry Lyndon*, DVD, chapter 17.

18. *Barry Lyndon*, DVD, chapter 20.

19. *Barry Lyndon*, DVD, chapter 22.

20. *Barry Lyndon*, DVD, chapter 25.

21. *Barry Lyndon*, DVD, chapter 30.

22. *Barry Lyndon*, DVD, chapters 33, 36.

23. *Barry Lyndon*, DVD, chapter 37.

24. Stanley Kubrick, interview by Michel Ciment, *Kubrick: The Definitive Edition* (New York: Faber & Faber, 2001), 170.

25. *Barry Lyndon*, DVD, chapter 2.

26. *Barry Lyndon*, DVD, chapters 18, 40.

27. *Barry Lyndon*, DVD, chapter 3.

28. *Barry Lyndon*, DVD, chapters 23, 25.

29. *Barry Lyndon*, DVD, chapter 4.

30. *Barry Lyndon*, DVD, chapter 34.

31. Herman Melville, *Moby-Dick*, ed. Harrison Hayford and Hershel Parker (1851; New York: W. W. Norton, 1967), 169–170.

32. *Barry Lyndon*, DVD, chapter 34.

33. *Barry Lyndon*, DVD, chapter 20.

34. *Barry Lyndon*, DVD, chapter 40.

35. *Barry Lyndon*, DVD, chapter 44.

36. *Barry Lyndon*, DVD, chapter 45.

37. *Barry Lyndon*, DVD, chapters 7, 9, 39.

38. *Barry Lyndon*, DVD, chapter 45.

39. *Barry Lyndon*, DVD, chapter 46.

~

CHAPTER FIVE

Projecting Light
The Shining

The Shining is first and foremost a fairy tale. Kubrick and Diane Johnson read Bruno Bettelheim's *The Uses of Enchantment* while preparing the screenplay, and judging from what Kubrick told Penelope Houston in 1971 about his predilection for fairy tales, the idea was probably his.[1] Bettelheim's book was published in 1975, and its subject as well as its Freudian approach to the genre must have appealed to Kubrick:

> There is a widespread refusal to let children know that the source of much that goes wrong in life is due to our very own natures. . . . The dominant culture wishes to pretend, particularly where children are concerned, that the dark side of man does not exist. . . . Psychoanalysis was created to enable man to accept the problematic nature of life without being defeated by it, or giving in to escapism. . . . This is exactly what fairy tales get across to the child in manifold form: that a struggle against severe difficulties in life is unavoidable, is an intrinsic part of human existence. . . . Most children now meet fairy tales only in prettified and simplified versions which subdue their meaning and rob them of all deeper significance—versions such as those on films and T.V. shows, where fairy tales are turned into empty-minded entertainment.[2]

But in a fairy tale and in *The Shining*, the mirror of experience that children will have to enter is not exclusively negative or threatening. The film's major critics have been so mesmerized by Jack Nicholson's performance that they assume evil triumphs in the end despite Wendy and Danny's escape. The film's last frame of Jack reincarnated at a 1921 Overlook soiree seems to

Richard T. Jameson to be Kubrick's real view of humanity and of his audience: "Illumination is poisonous: we cannot learn: 'we have always been here.' . . . The face grinning imbecilically out at us is our own."[3] And for Alexander Walker the innocents' salvation seems intentionally ironic: "To a confirmed skeptic like Kubrick, who believes man has little capacity to learn from his past and none at all to shape a rational future for himself, the best that can be said is that [the end of *The Shining* is] an illustration of random odds at work whose outcome is a little less pessimistic than might have been predicted."[4]

In spite of the fact that Jack is foregrounded through much of the picture, the pivotal character is actually Danny, not only because he is clairvoyantly present in many scenes where the camera focuses on Jack, but because he mirrors the spectator, Kubrick's target and actual subject. In *The Shining* Kubrick extends the evolutionary theme of *2001* and *A Clockwork Orange* in fairy-tale form. Danny and the spectator receive the Star Child's vision and the artist's insight, while Jack gradually regresses into an archetypal fusion of cannibal-giant and big, bad wolf. Of course, Jack is us (as Jameson observes), but so is the recognizing intelligence of the film that explores the worst in human nature in order to demonstrate the best.

Figure 5.1. Danny prefigures the Star Child, humanity's best hope. The large eyes and ears of Bugs Bunny on his shirt and the giant teddy bear pillow to his right suggest in-spired strength. *Courtesy of Warner Bros./Photofest © Warner Bros.*

Figure 5.2. Jack threatens humanity's end. He becomes a fairy-tale fusion of cannibal-giant and killer ape. *Courtesy of Warner Bros./Photofest © Warner Bros.*

Kubrick's attraction to fairy tales is consistent with his evolutionary hope. Bettelheim emphasized that stories not only "give full recognition of difficulties" but also "suggest solutions." For a child the promise of a happy ending is an assurance that "even the meekest can succeed in life," and this is why Lewis Carroll called his Alice saga "the love-gift of a fairy tale."[5] Kubrick's films are meant to nurture adults. They conform to Bettelheim's idealized definition of a psychoanalysis that refuses to be defeated by the apparent pessimism of its insight: "Freud's prescription is that only by struggling courageously against what seem like overwhelming odds can man succeed in wringing meaning out of his existence." The experience of the story alerts the spectator to the nature and direction of the destructive impulses that threaten to possess him, as they have so obviously enslaved others. And with the progression of individual insight, one person at a time, the films suggest "what the next steps in the development toward a higher humanity might be."[6]

Kubrick's concern for humanity's future may have accounted for a disagreement with Johnson over Danny's fate: "We decided that somebody obviously had to die because it was a horror film. . . . I thought it should be Danny, the child, but Kubrick was much more tender hearted than I and said, 'Oh, no, impossible.'"[7] Johnson's comment need not be taken as archly ironic, especially in the film's Bettelheim context. *The Uses of Enchantment* had received high praise upon its publication in 1975. Harold Bloom called it "a splendid achievement, brimming with useful ideas . . . and most of all overflowing with a realistic optimism and with an experienced and therapeutic good will."[8] In 1978 Kubrick gave the book to Johnson to suggest the direction he wanted the story to take, just as he had given Joseph Campbell's *The Hero with a Thousand Faces* to Arthur C. Clarke in preparation for the cowriting of *2001*.[9] Both Campbell and Bettelheim shared a faith in the power of storytelling to save the individual from psychological (and spiritual) entropy.

The "hero" Campbell discovered through comparative mythology is courageous and fortunate enough to live out the full range of human potential. Odysseus travels from the security of domestic stability through the ugly brutality of killing to an awareness of the whole cycle that he then conveys in art. He would not have been a hero if he had been content with unquestioned peace (like Paris), with the glory and exhilaration of war (like Achilles), or the illusion of justice and vindication (Menelaus and Agamemnon). To find absolute psychological security in any concept of good fortune is a form of regression, and eventually a trap where the mind stagnates and the feelings wither. From *2001* through *Eyes Wide Shut*, Kubrick followed Campbell's distinction between "victories" that appear to achieve dominance and "rebirths" that sustain the human spirit:

> Within the soul, within the body social, there must be—if we are to experience long survival—a continuous recurrence of birth (*palingenesia*) to nullify the unremitting recurrences of death. For it is by means of our own victories, if we are not regenerated that the work of Nemesis is wrought. . . . Peace then is a snare; war is a snare; change is a snare; permanence a snare. When . . . death closes in . . . there is nothing we can do, except . . . be dismembered totally, and then reborn.[10]

The achievement and even the conviction of any finite ideal is, in Campbell's view (and in Bettelheim's and Kubrick's), a failed surrogate for the tranquility of death, an end to the stress of having to adapt to the shocks and changes that keep the mind alive: "The most permanent of the dispositions of the human psyche are those that derive from the fact that, of all animals, we remain the longest at the mother's breast. Human beings are born too soon. They are unfinished, unready as yet to meet the world. Consequently their whole defense from a universe of dangers is the mother, under whose protection the intra-uterine period is prolonged."[11]

The major danger in all of Kubrick's post-2001 films is stopped growth and regression. Bettelheim observes that many fairy-tale heroes fall asleep and are reborn, stimulating a wish in the listener "for higher meaning in life: deeper consciousness, more self-knowledge, and greater maturity."[12] Jack, on the other hand, tells Danny that he wants to stay in the Overlook "for ever and ever and ever"; shortly after the ax-murdered Grady girls invite Danny to play with them "for ever and ever and ever."[13] The death that counts in Kubrick's films is the death of the mind and spirit, and Danny's survival at the end affirms the power of art that his paranormal gifts reflect.

Danny is The Shining's Star Child. His clairvoyance and precognition correspond to a story's telescoping of fictional time into present experience, and to Campbell's hero "who has been able to battle past his personal and historical limitations to the generally valid, normally human forms."[14] When Kubrick described the potential abilities of extraterrestrial beings in the context of 2001, he might also have been speaking of the power of art in its transcendence of time and space, even though art is still dependent on sensory forms: "They would possess the twin attributes of all deities—omniscience and omnipotence. These entities might be in telepathic communication throughout the cosmos and thus be aware of everything that occurs. . . . They might possess complete mastery over matter and energy; and [by tapping every intelligent mind], they might develop into an integrated collective consciousness."[15]

In a later interview on The Shining, he expressed the hope that scientists would eventually prove the existence of ESP, and though the discovery would not "be quite as exciting as, say, the discovery of alien intelligence in the universe, it [would] definitely be a mind expander."[16] The paranormal communication between Danny and Dick Hallorann, the ability to shine, resembles a film's ability to bypass explicit statement and to speak, soul-to-soul, through images and symbols. Kubrick intends his films to jump-start the spectators' media-stalled psychological growth and to confer on some of them his unflagging drive to experiment.

In an interview appended to the Eyes Wide Shut DVD, Steven Spielberg said that the way Kubrick told stories was "sometimes antithetical to the way we are accustomed to receiving stories." He added that Kubrick "wanted to change the form" of cinematic narrative and that Kubrick told him he had only begun to do that in 2001. Spielberg did not quite agree, and praised Kubrick for exploring different genres and taking new artistic risks in every film. Even after fifteen viewings of The Shining, even knowing "what's right around the corner," Spielberg could still be surprised all over again: "I don't know anybody else who possesses that kind of magic."[17]

In *The Shining* and the two films to follow, Kubrick's heroes are explorers. Joker goes to Vietnam, not to protest the war, but to learn to be his best self in the worst of all possible worlds. Alice falls into a nightmare vision of futile monotony that courage and love enable her to escape. A "Flyer" jacket and an "Apollo" sweater identify Danny as an astronaut leading us into a vision of evil that may be as alien to the naive as a fairy-tale setting is to a child. The film's opening frames conform to Bettelheim's description of "deliberate vagueness" at the start of a fairy tale, symbolizing a departure from ordinary reality—something hidden to be revealed in old castles, forbidden rooms, or "impenetrable woods."[18]

However, the primary visual source of the overture is *2001*. Kubrick leads the spectator toward the alien room of the inner self where crucial transformations occur: they may turn us forward toward the Star Child's contemplative vision or backward toward Moonwatcher's ecstatic assertion, and the roles this time are filled by Danny and Jack. Before the opening credits appear, an aerial shot of a still, cold mountain lake reflects the surrounding mountains like a mirror. The camera's descent resembles Bowman's descent over the mountains of Jupiter—as if the Star Child has returned to earth to observe the present state of humanity and to take us through the looking glass to view the fears and motivations that society is constructed to deny. The mirror will be a recurring motif in the film, always revealing what most people do not care to see but what the gifted child (Carroll's Alice or Kubrick's Danny) wants and needs to know.

In *2001* Dr. Floyd is repeatedly confined in visual boxes that reflect his compulsion to control rather than explore. Jack's first entrance to the Overlook, like Floyd's entry to the space station, reveals a controlled environment symbolized by the ubiquitous presence of rectangles and squares: tables, paneled windows, chairs, sofas, and the rows of tiny mailboxes at the front desk.[19] It is a societal order that purports to bring security, but instead produces chaos and violence. The manager, Mr. Ullman, is the perfect servant of this order, a less obvious ghost of the European class system that has produced the monstrous butler, Delbert Grady. The traditional, subjugated servant is content to find superiority by emulating or vicariously sharing in the triumphs of his superiors. Ullman's perfect grooming and slick manner mirror the wealthy guests he serves, but his tiny office reveals the scope of his bureaucratic soul. Jack and Ullman's assistant, the lugubrious Mr. Watson, are seen from the back of the room in square-shouldered suits, sitting in square-backed chairs, facing the small paneled squares in the window behind the desk.[20] The grouping is perfectly symmetrical, and the shot recalls Floyd's briefing to the assembled scientists on Clavius, even down to the small American flag on the desk to Ullman's right.

While Floyd serves the national imperative of colonizing new territory for America, Ullman serves the descendants of those who pushed the limits of lebensraum in the nineteenth century. *The Shining* warns that every past horror will inevitably recur—ax murders, wars, holocausts—just as the happy ending of one fairy tale lasts only until we are plunged into the next. Jack's caretaking predecessor, the wife and child murderer Charles Grady, shares the mind of the spookily obsequious butler, Delbert Grady. Both have a compulsive need to "correct" any threat to the social illusion that secures their status. Charles Grady foreshadows Jack's Dr. Hyde transformation because he absorbs the ruthless power seeking of the rich and famous, surrounded as he is by the trappings of their prestige. Periodically, well-adjusted individuals of every social class need an occasion to fight or support a war that kills others to affirm that they are protected from chance and death. Of course, all such acts in the general sense are as psychotic as those of an ax murderer because those who attempt to stave off their death through violence usually speed their own.

As in *A Clockwork Orange*, the other form of death that concerns Kubrick is spiritual. Ullman has a waxy, mannequin look, and his reference to the Grady atrocity lacks feeling because he only wants to accomplish his personnel task as efficiently as possible, to be optimally "useful," as HAL puts it. His assistant, Watson, has a sallow, somber appearance that exudes Dickensian menace. The tragicomic ironies associated with Ullman become apparent later when he takes Jack and Wendy on a tour of the hotel and its grounds:

> Oh this old place has had an illustrious past. In its heyday it was one of the stopping places for the jet set, even before anybody knew what a jet set was. We've had four presidents who stayed here, lots of movie stars. . . . [Wendy interjects] Royalty? [Ullman replies] All the best people. . . . Construction started in 1907. It was finished in 1909. The site is supposed to be located on an Indian burial ground, and I believe they actually had to repel a few Indian attacks as they were building it.[21]

Of course the "best people" in a Kubrick film (*Paths of Glory, Dr. Strangelove, Barry Lyndon, Full Metal Jacket, Eyes Wide Shut*) are clearly the worst people, but the real satiric edge here is the reversal of the Indian burial ground cliché. In the Hollywood scenario the angry Indian ghosts wreak havoc from beyond the grave, while in *The Shining* the ghosts of the supplanters destroy the souls of their own descendants. The Overlook's large ground-floor rooms are decorated with wall hangings that imitate Navajo and Apache designs, and an Edward Curtis sepia print of a chief hangs prominently in one of the hallways. These trophies of victory are accentuated by the taxidermic monstrosities of large elk and buffalo heads, killed in part to destroy the Indians' food supply or, Teddy Roosevelt–style, to demonstrate the manhood of the killers. In an obituary tribute Diane Johnson noted that the Indian burial ground reference expressed an intent to "assail racism" but that elaboration of the theme "fell by the way."[22]

Later when Jack furiously hurls a tennis ball against the wall next to the buffalo skull, the film connects his individual need for triumph with America's fear-driven slaughter of savage beasts and pagan people. The heroes of the frontier were no more able to recognize their relation to these other living beings than Charles Grady or Jack Torrance are able to recognize their families in the act of killing them. In the European paradigm Saint George righteously slays the dragon, while in the Homeric precedent Greeks and Trojans nobly hack themselves to death. The glorious conquests of physical nature that Western civilization appears to have achieved have been partly impelled by the crude servitude to instinct that moved Moonwatcher to kill. And the hotel, haunted by the ghosts of its murderous past, is the world at its present stage of evolution.

Nevertheless, *The Shining*, like *Alice in Wonderland*, is a "love-gift" that preserves the vision of those with the capacity to see. Without the guerrilla resistance of storytelling, every human eye would be stolen by the Sandman of socialized value that Freud adapts from E. T. A. Hoffman in "The Uncanny."[23] The psychological (in some societies, the physical) fate of dissidents is symbolized by the murder of Charles Grady's daughters, who wanted to burn down the hotel. When Delbert Grady briefs Jack on his mission in the red men's room, he sets up the opposition between Danny and Hallorann on one side and those who serve the spirit of the place on the other. Hallorann's race helps to symbolize his alienation, but the film links those who can shine regardless of social definition against those who can't. Delbert Grady's link to Charles Grady lies in their rage to silence doubts about a system that rewards their subservience:

> *Grady:* Did you know, Mr. Torrance, that your son is attempting to bring an outside party into this situation? Did you know that?
>
> *Jack:* No.
>
> *Grady:* He is, Mr. Torrance.
>
> *Jack:* Who?

Grady: A nigger.

Jack: A nigger?

Grady: A nigger cook.

Jack: How?

Grady: Your son has a very great talent. I don't think you are aware how great it is. That he is attempting to use that very talent against your will.

Jack: He is a very willful boy.

Grady: Indeed he is, Mr. Torrance. A very willful boy. A rather naughty boy, if I may be so bold, sir.

Jack: It's his mother. She, uh, interferes.

Grady: Perhaps they need a good talking to, if you don't mind my saying so. Perhaps a bit more. My girls, sir, they didn't care for the Overlook at first. One of them actually stole a pack of matches and tried to burn it down. But I corrected them, sir. And when my wife tried to prevent me from doing my duty, I *corrected* her.[24]

Grady's use of "racism" as a rationale is comical. To begin with, the delivery is crack-up material when his British "niggah" is immediately followed by Jack's incredulous hard *r*'d "a nigger?" As a liberal Boulder schoolteacher, Jack is not prejudiced against black people. His immediate family serves as a personal scapegoat that parallels group hatreds among the human family. Jack is entrusted with an ennobling mission—to kill his family as the Overlook's founders killed Indians and thus to objectify his superiority as America's founders did by reducing "niggers" to three-fifths of a person.

Danny sensed that the Overlook was a scary place before he got there, and Wendy catches up after the vampiric crazy woman bites Danny on the neck. When Jack kisses that same woman in Room 237, she captures his soul, and he returns to Wendy to tell her he has seen nothing. Even though he has touched a horror, his denial represents an equally frightening capacity to keep a satanic promise: be loyal and patriotic, do your duty, and regardless of the bloody facts, you will be immune to fear:

Wendy: Whatever the explanation is, I think we have to get Danny out of here.

Jack: Get him out of here?

Wendy: Yes.

Jack: You mean just leave the hotel?

Wendy: Yes. (*Danny envisions the hotel elevator lobby again filling with torrents of blood splashing out of the elevator.*)

Jack: (exploding in rage) This is so fucking typical of you to create a problem like this when I finally have a chance to accomplish something—when I'm really into my work! I could really write my own ticket if I went back to Boulder now, couldn't I? Shoveling out driveways, work in a car wash. Doesn't that appeal to you?

Wendy: Jack . . .

Jack: Wendy, I have let you fuck up my life so far, but I am not gonna let you fuck this up![25]

Having finally found the success he craved in the film's final frame, Jack becomes a mirror of our own worst selves. After being frozen in the maze as a visible beast, he is reborn in a dimensionless black and white photo of celebrity and wealth. The sequence suggests that both images portray the same monster. While Danny and some spectators escape, Jack's growth has been stopped in a tabloid fantasy of heaven. Details in the photograph identify the place as hell for those with eyes to see. A crowd of beautiful people, "the jet set before there was a jet set," surrounds Jack in the photograph that fills the frame after the zoom-in. Everyone is either looking forward or facing inward toward Jack, the murderer at the heart of the revelry. Below him, the caption is deliciously ironic: "Overlook Hotel, July 4th Ball, 1921." The numbers are symbols of independence, and their combination evokes an archaic expression, innocently popular at the time, "free, white, and twenty-one." The words are written on Jack's lower torso as if to identify that he has finally made it.[26]

While Jack's right hand is raised in joyful greeting, a man with a mustache and glasses reaches his left hand over onto Jack's right arm. The detail suggests that he still is not free, that someone or something else still controls him. Similarly, a woman to his left appears about to touch his shoulder. Appropriately, the next woman on his left has steel bands just above her knees with a chain between them. Kubrick told Michel Ciment that "the ballroom photograph at the very end suggests the reincarnation of Jack."[27] Despite the happily-ever-after ending, Danny will have to live with a ubiquitous majority of Jacks for the foreseeable future. The film does not differentiate between the actual jet set and those who worship them as "the best people." Only the alienated are saved.

Danny's paranormal gifts might have remained unused or psychologized away had his circumstances been different. Odysseus would never have transmitted wisdom in stories had he not been exiled for twenty years, and he never could have contributed to the freedom of his family had he not suffered. If reality were universally pleasant, stories that enable continuing growth in the real world would not be told. The ideal receiver of a fairy tale's gift must in some fundamental way be hungry enough to need the story's nourishment. In reply to Ciment's query about Danny's "evolution," Kubrick replied, "Danny has had a frightening and disturbing childhood. Brutalized by his father and haunted by his paranormal visions, he has had to find some psychological mechanism within himself to manage these powerful and dangerous forces. To do this, he creates his imaginary friend, Tony, through whom Danny can rationalize his visions and survive."[28]

In *The Shining* Kubrick makes Danny the vehicle of his vision. Wendy, on the other hand, is Danny's foil, an ordinary child who, like many parents, is unsuited for the protective role she tries to play. The ignorant or naive parent cannot protect a child from unknown and unforeseen dangers. When Wendy first appears seated at the kitchen table with Danny in their Boulder apartment, she is reading *The Catcher in the Rye*. It is de rigueur reading for the wife of a high school English teacher, as it was for those members of Kubrick's audience that he especially hoped to reach. Through Holden Caulfield, an updated Huckleberry Finn, Salinger skewered social pretension. But Wendy worships everything that provoked Holden's disgust. During the introductory tour of the Overlook she gushes to Ullman that the hotel is "beautiful," "fantastic," and that she "has never seen anything like it." She enthuses about the "authentic" and "gorgeous" Indian designs, accenting the irony of their acquisition, and disingenuously exclaims, "As a matter of fact this is the most gorgeous hotel I've ever seen."

Her ecstatic response to being permitted to set foot in the Gold Ballroom pathetically reflects celebrity worship in general, especially in light of the film's view of the Overlook's past occupants. The hotel's guests hold fans like Wendy in contempt, as does Ullman, for her sincere admiration and starry-eyed awe:

> *Ullman:* We eh . . . brought a decorator in from Chicago just last year to refurbish this part of the hotel.
>
> *Wendy:* Oh well he sure did a beautiful job. Pink and gold are my favorite colors.[29]

When Wendy finally sees the hotel's underlying horror at the end, the glimpse of the man in the bear suit performing fellatio echoes Holden's experience in the Edmond Hotel, where his window view of other rooms reveals a transvestite and a couple spitting drinks at each other, prompting Holden to reflect that although he is "a sex maniac" he doesn't "understand sex at all."[30]

The line's larger implication is that Holden doesn't understand life at all, and *The Shining's* overt horror film conclusion suggests that Wendy and the mass audience are mostly Holdens. This is partly expressed through the comic echoes of *Psycho*, when Wendy knocks Jack down the steps, when the soundtrack shrieks after Hallorann's murder, and when she encounters look-alikes of Norman Bates's mother, not just in one chair, but sitting grouped around a table. The empty eye sockets of these ghosts reflect the blindness of "ghost story and horror film addicts," Jack's label for Wendy in the initial interview with Ullman. Audiences that want to be scared by *Psycho* don't want to be scared by the more immediate reality of becoming zombies.

For Kubrick, true horror is a monotonous repetition of personalities and events. *The Shining's* ghosts are threatening because they "correct" any deviation from a structure maintained by alpha dominance. During the introductory tour of the hotel, Ullman tells Jack and Wendy that "by five o'clock tonight you'll hardly know anyone was ever here." Wendy's response, "Just like a ghost ship, huh?" evokes the legendary ship the *Flying Dutchman*, whose captain must expiate a crime by sailing forever without coming to port. However, the ghosts that claim Jack cannot confine Danny, and some of the spectators may not be left behind with Jack in the final frame.

Hallorann initiates Danny into knowledge of their timeless situation:

> I'm scared of nothing here, [but] you know Doc, when something happens it can leave a trace of itself behind . . . say like if someone burns toast. Well, maybe things that happened leave other kinds of traces behind. Not things that anyone can notice, but things that people who shine can see. Just like they can see things that haven't happened yet. Well, sometimes they can see things that happened a long time ago. I think a lot of things happened right here in this particular hotel over the years, and not all of them was good.[31]

But, of course, the things that were good continue to be in the communication that is occurring at that moment. Stephen King thought the film version of his story failed because he understood Kubrick to have expressed a disbelief in ghosts and in hell: "He didn't seem to want to get behind the concept of the ghost as a damned soul." He reported that Kubrick told him that the idea of ghosts was "always optimistic" because it "presupposes life after death," and so King thought that Kubrick meant Jack's final fate to be "a happy ending."[32] That Kubrick did not spell out or have a chance to elaborate on his ironic comment about ghosts seems obvious. He probably employed the traditional metaphors of ghosts and hell to image people and conditions that are clearly real, much as Shakespeare did in *Macbeth*, and he was probably sincere when he reportedly said that *The Shining* would be "the scariest horror movie of all time."[33]

The initial scene between Danny and Wendy in the bright child-friendly kitchen of their Boulder apartment warns us that the future is always dangerous:

Danny: Do you really want to go and live in that hotel for the winter?

Wendy: Sure, Danny, it will be lots of fun.

Danny: Yeah, I guess so . . .

Wendy: What about Tony? He's looking forward to the hotel, I bet.

Danny: (While eating his sandwich he wiggles the forefinger of his left hand and speaks with a different voice.) No, I ain't Mrs. Torrance.

Wendy: Oh come on, Tony. Don't be silly.

Danny: (as Tony) I don't want to go there, Mrs. Torrance.

Wendy: Well, how come you don't want to go?

Danny: (still as Tony) I just don't.

Wendy: Well, let's just wait and see. We're all gonna have a real good time.[34]

Although her maternal instinct is strong, Wendy's inability to recognize menace is widely shared. Kubrick and Johnson made her less sophisticated than in King's novel, and Shelley Duvall's persona is more childlike than maternal. She and Danny initially appear together seated at the kitchen table eating identical peanut butter and jelly sandwiches while they immerse themselves in fiction—Danny's cartoons and Wendy's *Catcher in the Rye*. They are ingesting unconscious experience from the stories that will become actual experience later in the film. They are both dressed in red and blue, and Wendy's jumper covers an outfit that resembles red flannel underwear or feety pajamas. As if to signify oral regression, a recurrent motif, Wendy's cigarette burns next to a coffee cup imprinted with cute animals. While she tells Danny that Tony is mistakenly apprehensive about the hotel, a golden bottle of Joy detergent stands prominently behind her on a kitchen shelf directly to her left.

Wendy has decorated the hallways and Danny's room with paintings, decals, and toys of contemporary children's culture, loving expressions of an attempt to give him a wholesome inner life. But for adults these images are consumer products, like the detergent, intended to shield the child from ugly realities that the parents avoid confronting. In translating Bettelheim's idea of literary influence to cinema, Kubrick used popular cartoon images even though Bettelheim had scorned them as mindless entertainment. In the initial scenes in Boulder a large image of Bugs Bunny appears on the front of Danny's shirt.[35] Bugs is riding a magic carpet, and he is surrounded by stars. Kubrick may have chosen Bugs Bunny as a guide for *The Shining's* Star Child because the character has an edgy quality that corresponds to a preference for defiant satire over Salinger's comic lament. On the series that Danny is watching on TV, *The Bugs Bunny/Road Runner Hour,* Bugs boldly confronts bullies while the Road Runner's speed enables him to dodge pursuers until they stupidly harm themselves. Danny clearly resembles Road Runner at the end of the film, and Tony is brave and smart like Bugs.

The only parts of Bugs that initially show on Danny's shirt are his long ears. Later we see his wide-open eyes. Bugs's survival depends on his abilities to see, hear, and notice more than his adversaries. As a result his actions are quick and bold, and his speech radiates Bronx chutzpah. Whenever his dogged hunter, Elmer Fudd, is just about to catch him, Bugs taunts him with the famous line, later repeated by Dick Hallorann to Danny, "Ehh, what's up, Doc?" Bugs's adventures could take him into outer space where he battled Marvin the Martian or (via the magic carpet) to the strange Freudian space of a Baghdad harem where he hid Aladdin's lamp from a greedy sheikh.

In another episode Bugs has a close call with one of the most formidable of traditional fairy-tale characters. As usual, of course, he saves himself from becoming someone's dinner and, in the process, rescues two of his admiring fans, Hansel and Gretel, before "Witch Hazel" can pop them in the oven. But near the end of *The Shining* when Danny retraces his footprints in the maze's snow, he resembles the Road Runner whose salvation always depends on a combination of his own speed and an omniscient narrator's magic. Just as Elmer Fudd always pursues but never catches Bugs, so Wile E. Coyote persistently and delightfully fails to snare his prey. In one episode Wile leans into a hole he is digging to catch Road Runner and falls right through the bottom into the path of an oncoming train. Another time Wile scales a cliff and attempts to drop a boulder on Road Runner as he drinks from a water cooler that Wile has set in his path. Road Runner gets his drink and accelerates away with his usual breakneck speed while Wile, who has rushed down so excitedly he beats the boulder to the spot, senses his danger too late to avoid being driven into the ground by his own device. He ends up sealed inside the water cooler, like the Big Bad Wolf in the horse trough of Red Riding Hood's grandmother or the fireplace of the third little pig.[36]

On the open door to the bedroom from which we view Danny brushing his teeth, two decals from Charles Schulz's *Peanuts* foreshadow the saving power of Danny's resourceful imagination. At the bottom right of the frame,

Snoopy, the dream-spinning beagle, stands blissfully on roller skates, safely framed by a rainbow arch. Directly above him his tiny bird friend, Woodstock, rises into the clouds on a rainbow-colored hot air balloon.[37] The skates suggest Snoopy's mental mobility, and the colors of the rainbow fit the many guises his imagination shapes. These include Joe Cool, Literary Ace, Flashbeagle, Vulture, and Foreign Legionnaire. But in his most vividly daring exploits as "World War I Flying Ace," he outsmarts and outfoxes his nemesis, the historically famous Red Baron. The official *Peanuts* website describes him as "a modern icon of intelligent exploration."[38]

In 1968, the year *2001* was released, and shortly after the Apollo program was launched, the National Aeronautics and Space Administration selected Snoopy as its official mascot, and ever since he has appeared on NASA decals, bumper stickers, posters, cards, and pins. A special "Silver Snoopy" pin is awarded to recognize engineers and other NASA employees who have made crucial contributions to the safety of manned flights.[39] For the scene in the bathroom where Danny consults Tony in the mirror, the link between imagination and safety could not be exemplified better than in Snoopy. Beneath the rainbow arch of his dreams Snoopy can skate with his eyes closed. Directly above him his tiny best friend is about to soar above the clouds. Where Snoopy leads by spinning stories and inventing games, Woodstock follows though "his flying and logic are erratic," and his size makes him (as the official *Peanuts* website puts it) "an accident waiting to happen." Appropriately, he types and takes shorthand because he receives inspiration from Snoopy as a spectator does from a film, and in this way goes on to take flight himself.

Danny's Snoopy is Tony. At the outset he tells Danny that Jack will call momentarily to say that he got the job and that the place Tony dreaded is now an unavoidable destination. The camera cuts to Wendy placidly washing dishes next to her bottle of Joy and a half-gallon carton of milk. When she answers the phone, Jack calls her "babe," and the appearance of the room suggests that she and Danny feel secure and well taken care of. There are books everywhere, on the floor, on the tables, and on top of the TV as if to suggest that this is a civilized space. Above the TV a photograph of a cute brown and white dog, held aloft by its owner, overlooks a TV image of a world where innocence is protected by a white-hatted good guy, like the one in the center of the small screen (centered in the larger frame), facing down a taller black-hatted foe.[40]

That view of the world exists in the family room, a surface space, while back in the inner space of the bathroom the camera slowly pushes in toward the mirror until Danny and Tony fill the screen. They are expressing an essential narrative tension, the desire of the storyteller to protect the child from knowing more than he can handle versus the necessity of preparing him for everything that life brings. When Danny begs him to explain why he doesn't want to go to the hotel, Tony's sheltering impulse is expressed by his firm "no" and by a visual image of withdrawal when Danny's index finger closes into his fist. But Danny's instinctive need to know the dangers life will bring is expressed by his sudden change from begging to commanding his genie to tell.

Tony responds with the recurrent montage of a river of blood overwhelming elevator doors that should secure upward movement, the advance of civilization. The image of the look-alike Grady girls suggests the anonymous replication of slaughtered children, while Danny's silent scream mirrors the film's witness to past, present, and future reflections of historic horror. Still, the recurrence of the image suggests impermanence, as does the black screen transition to a scene that once again pictures the counter impulse to foster life.

That impulse is personified in the film as feminine by the psychiatrist who helps Wendy try to soothe Danny after he awakens from the traumatic dream that Tony delivered.[41] Though Wendy and the doctor express the love that Jack and the Overlook's builders lack, they cannot implement that love by muffling it in the easy deceptions of clinical psychology. Accordingly, the doctor's kindly voice sounds under the black screen before she appears, as if her intention to repair Danny's "delusion" cannot dispel recurrent darkness. Her actual line, "Now hold your eyes still, so I can see," suggests the reductive attempt of science to safely box a fairy tale's vision. What the doctor sees in Danny's eyes is literally on the surface; she cannot see what Danny has seen and is therefore ill equipped to help him.

The decor of Danny's bedroom evokes the film's definition of itself as a fairy tale among fairy tales. Their prominence implies Wendy's unconscious sense of fiction's collective power to arm her child. Protective feeling is immediately imaged in the large brown and gold teddy bear pillow directly to Danny's right. The benevolent red-mouthed face is larger than Danny's and suggests the whole range of imagined protectors from the personal Tony to the collective Bugs Bunny, now more visible on his shirt than it was in the kitchen scene. In the shots where we see Danny from the back with the psychologist leaning over him, Snoopy reappears, this time on the pink and blue curtains over a shelf that contains books, games, and a running shoe. Every element in the room contributes to Danny's escape in the end—the physical ability to run complemented by the ability to concentrate conferred by the games, and the hope to prevail against overwhelming odds, as Little Red Riding Hood finally does even after the wolf swallows her.

A picture of the wolf in a red cap appears on a vertical board directly to Wendy's right in the shots taken from the back of Danny's bed. Wendy is still wearing her red leotard and blue jumper, and a Goofy doll wearing a red shirt and blue bib overalls in the center of the bookshelf to her left reflects her incompetence. But Goofy also exemplifies Wendy's salient virtue—the courage to persist in the face of failure. The Disney website describes him as always "trying to do things that he goofs up," and yet remaining "cheerful and undaunted."[42] With particular relevance to the Pollyanna side of Carter-era America, Goofy appeared in post-1960s cartoons as a suburban family man with a wife and children. Though Goofy would certainly seem incapable of caring for a family, he always muddles through, and so does Wendy. In the pantry where she has trapped Jack, Delbert Grady tells him, "Your wife appears to be stronger than we imagined, Mr. Torrance. Somewhat more resourceful, she seems to have got the better of you."[43]

When the doctor tells Danny to rest in bed for the rest of the day, her general advice corresponds to the physically based psychology that Kubrick had satirized in A Clockwork Orange. She explains that Danny's hysteria after his vision of the gory flood is the "the result of emotional factors [that] rarely occur again." But the film means to say that these visions rarely occur in "normal" people who cannot or will not face the probability that the worst of the past will repeat itself. Wendy is hugely relieved and immediately draws out her pack of cigarettes, offers the doctor one, and begins to smoke. The sequence connects the doctor's vocal stroking to the oral satisfaction of the cigarette and suggests the shallow nature of psychology's solution to the problem of evil.

Oral regression also soothes Danny. Until the vision in the mirror, Tony had consistently calmed Danny's fears, and at five years old he naturally describes his source of comfort as the little boy who lives in his mouth and hides in his stomach. Danny's response associates the comfort of storytelling with that of food, and fairy tales were originally delivered as vocal comfort directly from the mouth of the teller to the (sometimes literally) open mouths of the listeners. Thus Danny, as the incipient artist, associates his internal storyteller with the mouth and stomach, in the sense of both satisfaction and nourishment. Tony comes to life in Danny for the same reason that grown-ups tell tales—to alleviate fear and pain:

Doctor: Did he adjust well to school?

Wendy: No. He didn't like it too much at first, and then he had an injury [when Jack dislocated his shoulder], . . . I guess that's about the time when I first noticed that he was talking to Tony.[44]

Danny's real protectors are of little help. When Wendy and the psychologist emerge from Danny's room, a picture of two of Snow White's seven dwarfs hangs at the back of the hallway in the center of the frame. The picture, along with a decal of a running dwarf on Danny's door, suggests the well-intentioned but inadequate power of parents like Wendy and institutionalized gurus like the doctor to alert children to dangers they themselves do not recognize. The evil queen in "Snow White" hates her stepdaughter because she is jealous of her beauty. The story warns that children are at bottom a threat to all parents, no matter how loving or well intentioned, because they are a constant reminder of the aging process and of mortality. Snow White's stepmother can stop time only if she remains forever more beautiful than her daughter. Since this is impossible, parents will need to displace the resulting desperation into some form of mental or physical aggression, and most do manage to avoid harming their own children.

Because they act out what normal parents repress, Snow White's privileged stepmother and Danny's socially impotent father are psychotic exceptions. Fearing that she cannot be "the fairest in the land" if the young beauty lives, the queen orders her huntsman to take Snow White to the woods and kill her. But the huntsman proves compassionate, and the queen's maddening mirror relates, to her furious dismay, that Snow White is alive and well with the seven dwarfs. Though they have warned her not to let anyone in the house, the queen, posing as a peasant peddler, entices Snow White into eating a poisoned apple, whereupon she drops dead.

The dwarfs take her to the mountains and place her in a glass coffin because they cannot bear to bury her: "Snow White lay there in the coffin a long, long time, and she did not decay, but looked like she was asleep, for she was still as white as snow and as red as blood, and as black-haired as ebony wood." There she is discovered by a handsome prince who persuades the dwarfs to let him take her away: "I cannot live without being able to see Snow White. I will honor her and respect her as my most cherished one." His servants carry her away on their shoulders, but when one of them stumbles, the piece of poisoned apple pops out of her throat: "Not long afterward she opened her eyes, lifted the lid from her coffin, sat up, and was alive again. 'Good heavens, where am I?' she cried out."[45]

While Snow White is lovingly trapped within the glass coffin, she is as good as dead, but even when she was alive her foster parents could not help her grow beyond their tiny bounds. The idea that well-meant restriction may be unwitting exposure is suggested further by the title of a book in the Boulder apartment: *The Wild Child*.[46] Kubrick is alluding to the François Truffaut film about a French doctor's adoption of an eleven-year-old feral child discovered in the woods in 1798. A debate ensues after the boy seems to be in-corrigible at an institute for the deaf where he has been placed. Some of his teachers believe that he must be mentally defective, since the light of reason was thought to be divinely implanted. Others, like Itard, the kindly doctor who discovered the boy, believe that children are innately "wild" and that an inclination toward culture must be learned. After patiently tutoring the boy, Itard appears to have proved his point. However, in the film's crucial and most moving scene the boy makes a mad dash toward the woods and disap-pears before he finally returns to his father and his home. Truffaut seems to say that though human beings may yearn for perfect freedom, they must live within the limits of the human condition and within the strictures of an im-perfect society.[47]

However, by questioning social norms *The Wild Child* places itself outside them, suggesting that outward acquiescence cannot quell the creative spirit celebrated by Truffaut in other films. Danny's paranormal gift, like a story-teller's symbolic imagination, sets him apart and preserves his difference, his "wildness," from the normalizing standards of psychology. That is why "Tony" tells Danny never to talk about him, because Danny instinctively knows that the collective superego will do everything it can to purge modes of thought that might upset the status quo. But, as in *Clockwork*, that purgation is para-doxically effected by absorption. In *The Shining* the luxury hotel that caters to the needs of its celebrity guests parallels the paradise that, in Bettelheim's view, beckoned Hansel and Gretel: "Regression to the earliest, 'heavenly' state of being—when on the mother's breast one lived symbiotically off her—does away with all individuation and independence. It even endangers one's very existence, as cannibalistic inclinations are given body in the fig-ure of the witch."[48]

When Hallorann takes Wendy and Danny through the Overlook's kitchen, Wendy's comment connotes the psychological danger of being trapped in a fantasy of wealth and power:

Wendy: Yeah. This whole place is such an enormous maze, I feel I'll have to leave a trail of breadcrumbs every time I come in.

Hallorann: Don't let it get you down Mrs. Torrance—it's big but it still ain't nothing but a kitchen . . . a lot of the stuff you'll never have to touch.

Wendy: I wouldn't know what to do with it if I did.[49]

The kitchen's bounty stands for the whole paradise of the Overlook that Wendy does not know enough to dread. Just as she has missed the point of Holden Caulfield's disgust with the phony glamour she adores, so she forgets that birds ate the breadcrumbs Hansel had strewn to guide him and his sister back to an inhospitable home. Even if Hansel's trail had remained, the children would only have returned to the continuing danger of a stepmother who finds her family to be an intolerable impediment to her needs.

Wendy's "trail of breadcrumbs" reference to "Hansel and Gretel" occurs just before Hallorann inventories the hotel's lavish pantry: "We got canned fruits and vegetables; canned fish and meats; hot and cold cereals—Post Toasties, Cornflakes, Sugar Puffs, Rice Krispies, Oatmeal, Wheatina, and Cream of Wheat. We got a dozen jugs of black molasses, we got sixty boxes of dried milk, thirty twelve-pound bags of sugar." In the film's self-referential fairy-tale context, the wow-factor of affluence has an air of menace:

> When [Hansel and Gretel] approached the little house they saw that it was built of bread and covered with cakes, but that the windows were of clear sugar. "We will set to work on that," said Hansel, "and have a good meal. I will eat a bit of the roof, and you, Gretel, can eat some of the window. It will taste sweet." . . . Then a soft voice cried from the parlor: "Nibble, nibble, gnaw. Who is nibbling at my little house?" The children answered: "The wind, the wind." The old woman had only pretended to be so kind; she was in reality a wicked witch, who lay in wait for children, and had only built the little house of bread in order to entice them there. When a child fell into her power, she killed it, cooked and ate it, and that was a feast day with her.[50]

In *The Shining*, Jack becomes the equivalent of both the wicked stepmother and the witch, the resentful or exploitive parent. But his ultimate fate represents what would have happened to Hansel and Gretel had they lacked the intelligence and courage to escape. Like some of Odysseus's greedy men, gobbled by the Cyclops, Jack's desire for infantile omnipotence results in a death that is physical in the narrative and potentially spiritual for the spectator. Bettelheim explains the danger of becoming lost in fantasies of pleasure: "The gingerbread house [the Overlook] is an image nobody forgets: how incredibly appealing and tempting a picture this is, and how terrible the risk one runs if one gives in to the temptation. . . . The house stands for oral greediness and how attractive it is to give in to it."[51]

The pantry's wealth is based on the ruthless ascension of the hotel's builders and owners, and suggestions of murders, past and present, immediately intrude. Among the mind-boggling numbers of rib roasts, hamburgers, turkeys, and pork roasts, Hallorann puts special emphasis on "lamb" by asking Danny if he likes it. Subliminal connotations of slaughter begin to fill the scene. When Hallorann first begins to communicate to Danny telepathically, an eerie ringing ensues as Danny stands transfixed next to a large box of

Willapoint Minced Clams. Later Jack tells Wendy about his horrible dream of chopping his family to pieces, and when Wendy later locks him in the pantry he wakes up among cartons of sliced peaches, pimento pieces, and tomato puree.

As Hallorann shines the question, "How'd you like some ice cream, Doc?" the sound becomes ominously deeper, partly because Danny has never met anyone before with his powers, and partly because Hallorann is standing next to a can of Calumet Baking Powder with an Indian head trademark. As Hallorann conveys a kindred spirit to Danny, the film conveys a warning to protect viewers like-minded enough to get the message. A large part of America's prosperity was built upon the slave labor of Hallorann's forebears, and the Overlook literally rests upon the graves of dead Indians.[52]

The storyteller serves as the real parent to children whose parents lack the wisdom to prepare them for life. Ullman has just introduced Hallorann to Jack and Wendy when his secretary brings Danny in. She says he was looking for them outside, and we understand that he has been frightened by his vision of the Grady girls in the recreation room and that he is seeking his parents for comfort. But Jack's line immediately implies that comfort is no more likely to be given to Danny by the powers that be than it was to the world in *Dr. Strangelove*: "Dan, did you get tired of bombing the universe?" The line unconsciously reflects Jack's aggression, but Danny's blue jacket with the orange-lettered "Flyers" on the back identifies him as an explorer rather than a leader. The cartoon images of Snoopy and Woodstock foreshadow this, and Danny's ESP abilities to travel through time and space connect him to David Bowman and the symbolic use of blue and orange in *2001*.

In the semicircle formed after Danny joins the group, Danny and Hallorann stand at corresponding positions from each end, and the dark blue jackets and light blue shirts that both wear set them apart from the brown and gray outfits of the others.[53] In the subsequent scene where Hallorann explains to Danny how he knew his parents called him "Doc," he assumes the role of the special protector that children find in strong fictional characters, such as Bugs Bunny: "I can remember when I was a little boy, my grandmother and I could hold conversations entirely without ever opening our mouths. She called it 'shining,' and for a long time I thought it was just the two of us that had the shine to us. Just like you probably thought you was the only one. But there are other folks, though mostly they don't know it, or don't believe it."[54] As Danny and Hallorann sit at the table in the kitchen, both rest their hands on the table with their fingers interlocked, just as their minds are interlocked in a way that others cannot see.

Like Tony refusing to say why he doesn't want to go to the hotel, Hallorann tries to protect Danny's innocence by telling him to stay out of Room 237. But Hallorann's order to stay out is the storyteller's invitation to enter. Bettelheim points out that the tale of Little Red Riding Hood is especially frightening because the heroine is actually swallowed, whereas the witch only planned to devour Hansel and Gretel. When the narrator (through the agency of a hunter) removes Red Riding Hood from the wolf's body, her reaction reflects the right response to a scary story: "Ah, how frightened I have been; how dark it was inside the wolf's body." The spectator following David Bowman to Jupiter empathically trembles with him before they are given to understand the value of their fear. Using verbal metaphors that anticipate *The Shining*'s visual ones, Bettelheim affirms the necessity and purpose of fictional immersion: "Having been projected into inner darkness [Little Red Riding Hood] becomes . . . appreciative of a new light [illuminating] the emotional experiences she has yet to master, and those to avoid because they as yet overwhelm her."[55]

The "wild and destructive wolf [in "Little Red Riding Hood" and "The Three Little Pigs"] stands for all asocial, unconscious, devouring powers against which one must learn to protect oneself."[56] Fairy-tale deaths are typically not mourned, and Hallorann's murder does not cancel the film's hope for its viewers. People die unjustly, and Jack, a pretentious cynic and an avid reader, laughs at that obvious fact just before his ax shatters childish illusion: "Little pigs, little pigs, let me come in. Not by the hair on your chinny chin chin."[57] In mocking the story, Jack is as inattentive to his role in it as Wendy had been when she forgot that Hansel's trail of breadcrumbs failed to lead backward into safety. She sobbingly pleads with Jack when he menaces her on the stairs, "I just want to go back to my room." In the end she proves to be as resourceful as the third little pig: she knocks Jack down the stairs with a baseball bat; she cuts Jack's wrist and sends Danny down the snow bank to safety; she keeps her wits about her through a series of supernatural shocks; and she pilots herself and her child off to safety in a vehicle that resembles a space ship.

Just before Danny is shown reaching toward the doorknob of Room 237, we see Wendy in the kitchen spooning fruit cocktail into a large bowl. As she licks the sugary juice off her finger, the radio announcer prognosticates a historical future based on the cycle of the seasons shown in the opening frames: "I want to go outside and lie in the sun. Yet to our north and to our west, it is snowing and cold, and it's moving right here towards Colorado, right now as we talk. It's incredible." Unfortunately, a pessimistic forecast of events is all too credible, but as the announcer wraps it up, he snaps his fingers twice as a lead-in to the clicking sound of Danny's Big Wheel.

From floor level the steadicam's low-angle view of Danny exaggerates his smallness relative to the space in which he travels, and the color scheme matches that of *2001*. His sweater, like David Bowman's space suit, is red-or-ange, while his overalls and the back of his "ship" are blue. When he comes to the door of Room 237, it looms over him as the monolith did over Moon-watcher and Floyd. Like them, Danny stops and slowly extends his hand upward toward a locked door he is unready to enter.[58]

Ciment sees the end of *The Shining* as the victory of "the 'child of light' over the forces of darkness, of intelligence over instinct, of Theseus, the solar hero, over the Minotaur."[59] After a brief blue-tinged snow shot of the hotel's outer space, Danny is shown kneeling with toy trucks in the center of a dark orange hexagon in the carpet. He is rapt in his play and making engine sounds when a green tennis ball rolls directly into his space. As in *2001*, evolutionary awareness must supplant technological toys. When Danny stands, his sweater again identifies him with Bowman. On a blue background a large white rocket surrounded by yellow suns points upward toward Danny's head. The black-lettered word "Apollo" stretches vertically from Danny's stomach to his neck to confirm Ciment's view that he is a "solar" hero. Below the rocket the horizontal letters "USA" refer to the contemporary space program that prefigures the imaginary one of *2001*. Danny gathers his courage and advances toward Room 237—"Mom, are you in there?"

Just before a brief dissolve to Wendy tinkering with the basement furnace, the open door of Room 237 reveals large circles of light thrown by a table lamp seen inside a full-length mirror, and the two, taken together, are the film's primary symbols of insight and expression. In retrospect, they reflect Kubrick's intent to therapeutically distance "Mom" from naive adults. In a post-*2001* interview he told Eric Nordern: "As a child matures he sees death and pain everywhere about him, and begins to lose faith in the ultimate goodness of man. . . . But if we can accept the challenges of life within the boundaries of death—however mutable man may be able to make them—our existence as a species can have genuine meaning and fulfillment. However vast the darkness, we must supply our own light."[60]

According to Vincent LoBrutto, Kubrick "had begun to develop a treatment for *The Shining* when he learned that [Diane] Johnson was giving a course at the University of California at Berkeley on the Gothic novel. She seemed to be the ideal collaborator."[61] Because the Gothic novel was the favorite prose form of the English Romantics, Johnson was probably familiar with the landmark study by M. H. Abrams, *The Mirror and the Lamp: Romantic Theory and the Critical Tradition.*[62] The title "identifies two common and antithetic metaphors of mind, one comparing the mind to a reflector of external objects, the other to a radiant projector which makes a contribution to the objects it perceives."[63] The metaphoric mirror derives from Plato and dominates Western literature through the eighteenth century, while the lamp is a prevalent romantic image.

For Plato the attempt of art to imitate reality was doomed to failure because the only true reality was the world of eternal "ideas" that could be apprehended but not conveyed. The world perceived by the senses was composed of shifting shadows, perceived through a glass darkly. As Abrams puts it, "A mirror image is only a simulacrum of an object, forced to represent three dimensions by two; hence the lowly status of art as mere appearance far removed from truth."[64] Aristotle, on the other hand, believed that nature was both real and imitable, and his influence prevailed in artistic practice and theory until the eighteenth century.

In "On Poetry in General" (1818), William Hazlitt combined the mirror and the lamp to demonstrate how the Romantic poets rejected Aristotelian imitation to reflect "a world already bathed" in an "emotional light" they had themselves "projected."[65] As a precedent Abrams cites El Greco, who anecdotally refused to leave a darkened room because "the daylight distanced his inner light."[66] And as an example he cites Coleridge's ode "Dejection," where the poet, overwhelmed by the "inanimate cold world of the ever-anxious crowd," suffers the loss of his "genial spirits" and his "shaping power of imagination." But when he recovers, he once again becomes "a source of light" that can convert "matter-of-fact into matter-of-poetry."[67]

In *The Shining*, lamps are associated with "the shine" and foreshadow the affirmation of Wendy and Danny's escape. They also imply disparities of perception. Mirrors and lamps are especially prominent after the cut to Hallorann's Miami room immediately following Wendy's hysterical interruption of Jack's hallucinated conversation with Lloyd, the bartender: "Danny told me . . . he saw this crazy woman in [Room 237's] bathtub. She tried to strangle him."[68] A black screen immediately follows, preceding a close-up of Hallorann's tabletop TV where the montage introducing the Miami evening news contains subliminal warnings. The clips suggest the difference between the film's psychological explorations and the potential danger of televised "reality." Following an aerial shot of Miami a huge plane with the swept-back wings of a bomber soars upward. The montage then shifts to color pictures that represent potential victims of primitive human drives.

The image of a lighthouse immediately precedes an almost imperceptible reverse zoom until the bottom border of the TV screen becomes visible. The sequence and the reflexivity accentuate the protective purpose of fairy tales in Kubrick's post-*2001* films. In quick succession we see a woman searching through plants along the beach, a baby in a stroller waving American flags, and two police officers standing next to the enlarged rectangular light on the top of their car. Instead of appearing in its natural red, the light looks like a purple "screen" with two symmetrical "stars" inside it. Behind the officers in the top center of the screen, the bright tail of a Pan Am jet draws the eye to its logo, a blue image of the endangered earth. The flying motif evokes both the threat of *Dr. Strangelove* and the potential for transcending it in *2001*. Immediately after the shot of the plane the shadowy figure of a child emerges from the open door of a school bus seen from the side at an odd, low angle. Then an image of small studio monitors seems to echo the superficiality of HAL's BBC interview, while hands on a keyboard offer information that is as useless as Jack's typing.

The artificial symmetry of the next frame invites interpretation. Hallorann's bare feet propped on a pillow framing the TV rhyme with a similar shot of Danny's feet during the doctor's attempt to diagnose him, and both characters represent art's ability to convey experience denied in the "real" world. On both sides of the desk next to the TV, two table lamps throw a dull light against the back wall where a painting shows a sitting, bare-breasted black woman in a large sun hat against a gray and white background. After cutting to a close-up of Hallorann's face, the camera again zooms slowly backward until we see another symmetrical arrangement of similar objects, but the difference between the two walls highlights the difference between literal and symbolic modes of thought. Instead of viewing the scene straight-on, the camera is positioned to Hallorann's right, creating a larger sense of space. The lamps on the nightstands send up large, bright cones of light, and the books beside them may imply "literary" levels of meaning.

The painting centered in the frame directly over Hallorann's head also pictures a nude black woman, but while the woman over the TV leans back on her right hand, this woman kneels upright with her back and feet arched. She wears no shielding hat and her body is taut with power against a radiant orange background. This field of orange stands directly over the elegant dark blue of Hallorann's pajamas.[69] Orange also associates him with Danny as he is about to be seen, and both wore dark blue jackets during their initial meeting in the Overlook's kitchen.

The camera now cuts back to the opposite side of the room where a now visible "Glen Rinker" announces that a South Florida heat wave has created a problem that is "just the opposite" of the blizzard he has been describing in Colorado. Just as Danny can shine through ordinary perceptions of time and space, so the culturally informed spectator can hear the metaphorical convention of "weather" to describe states of feeling and cycles of events. One particular line makes it clear that the message shining through the words alludes to Jack's lack of love, while another implies a connection between individual and collective aggression: "Officials in Colorado tell Newswatch at least three people have been killed by exposure to freezing winds. . . . The National Guard might be called out to clear streets and roads."

The antitheses of temperature may also suggest that despite repeated and virtually predictable "exposure" to coldhearted crime or justified war, peacetime denial is so extreme that it will suppress the self-knowledge necessary to avert the mass deaths feared in *Dr. Strangelove* and imaged in *Barry Lyndon* and *Full Metal Jacket*. Kubrick himself summed up the newscast's other references to blocked highways, frozen railroad tracks, and closed airports: "One of the ironies in the story is that you have people who can see the past and the future and have telepathic contact, but the telephone and the short-wave radio don't work, and the snowbound mountain roads are impassable. Failure of communication is a theme which runs through a number of my films."[70]

But the films also demonstrate forms of communication that do not fail. Paranormal communication may be rare, but the symbolic communication it represents is not. The camera tracks forward until Hallorann's face fills the frame. An eerie ringing sound keynotes mysterious revelations just as it did in *2001*, and as it waxes the everyday voice of the TV wanes and vanishes. Hallorann's brow furrows, his mouth opens, and his eyes widen as he begins to receive Danny's vision.

The wide eyes and open mouth also recall Danny's wide-eyed scream the first time he saw the river of blood in the Boulder bathroom and reflect the mesmerized attention of the spectator to the scene that follows. When Hallorann's trembling increases and the ringing gets louder, the camera cuts to the open door of Room 237, identified by the red-numbered key hanging from its ring, just as before when Danny entered. This time, however, we see into the room from the opposite side, and another full-length closet mirror appears frame left directly behind the key. The table lamp that was reflected in the first mirror is now directly visible in the center of the frame. The doubling effect of the two mirrors is accentuated by the now visible presence of the room's twin doors, both standing open with their shiny doorknobs symmetrically reflecting light.

Figure 5.3. Hallorann's wide eyes and open mouth mirror the spectators, as he shines Danny's vision of Jack and the crazy woman. *Courtesy of Warner Bros./Photofest © Warner Bros.*

When Danny entered the forbidden room the first time, we did not see him attacked by the crazy woman. This time his "second sight" takes Hallorann and the spectator with him, so that Kubrick can convey a specific image of what makes human beings crazy. The clairvoyant vision also suggests that symbolic narrative provides insights blocked in ordinary discourse. Because the crazy woman assaults and later shines through Danny, she represents a threat to innocence, the knowledge of good and evil rather than evil in and of itself.

Hallorann's earlier injunction to "stay out" cannot and should not be observed. The narrator of a fairy tale leads children into just enough danger to help them learn. But the story should not be so frightening that they recoil into traumatized denial. Similarly, Kubrick's hint of comedy provides sufficient distance from horror-show clichés to make the scene a preparation for tragic situations that every adult will encounter. The distance is initially present in a self-referential allusion to *2001* when the camera cuts from Hallorann in his bed to Danny shaking in *his* bed; Bowman shook like this just before he entered Jupiter space, and his space suit was the same shade of red-orange as Danny's sweater. The specific cinematic repetition may be read as an archetypal version of birth pangs before the "fall."

As soon as the camera enters Room 237 we notice that the split-level suite is luxurious compared to Hallorann's room, yet its colors and lighting are unsettling and repellent. The deep green of Hallorann's bedding, along with his dark blue pajamas, were appropriately strong and beautiful. Here the pink sofas on the light green and purple–patterned carpet are faded and sickly, especially in contrast to the previous scene. As the camera pans left and ascends the steps five more lamps throw enough light to view the room, but their shades allow only a downward glow while Hallorann's lamps threw huge haloes on the wall behind his bed.

The entrance into Room 237 is a downward progress into psychic space. There is the entrance through the open door, then the first room, the second room above the split-level steps, and finally the bathroom where the "crazy" secret resides. Instead of going directly toward the bathroom door on the second level, the camera first pans left to show two lamps on either side of the king-size bed. The light from these lamps shines both upward and downward, the one on the far side is reflected in a large vertical mirror directly to the right of the bathroom door, as if the camera has gone out of its way to reiterate these symbols. The mirror that will reveal Jack's soul is lit by the lamp of the narrator's light. In The Shining's mirror, evil cannot intimidate because it is so stupid and absurd.

To achieve the wisdom of a fairy tale's perspective on giants and monsters, the film must guide the viewers through a mind-opening portal. The vertical mirror just before the bathroom door contributes a through-the-looking-glass dimension immediately before the camera closes in on the door. Instead of passing straight through, the camera comes up so close that the frame becomes a black screen for four seconds. As in 2001, the black screen transition signals a fear of death in a character, and an awareness of that fear in the spectator.

A painting of a fox to the left of the door balances the mirror on the right. The color of Jack's jacket is a slightly darker orange than the fox's fur. If Jack is a wolf to Danny and Wendy elsewhere in the story, he is no more than a fox to a panther in the scene that follows. The crazy woman emerges from the tub without bending from the waist. As she steps out she sets each long, powerful leg down slowly and silently. Despite Jack's perception that her blatant nudity must be a sexual advance, the woman is not conventionally sexy. She is as tall as Jack, and her androgynous, square-shouldered frame, short hair, and unblinking eyes suggest that, like Lloyd the bartender and Delbert Grady, she is one more form of the Overlook's collective evil.

After Jack comes to meet her and they face each other in profile, she dips her head down for a moment as if she were measuring her prey. Then she slowly raises her hands up the sides of his open jacket. When she reaches his neck, she extends her fingers for a moment before she draws his head in for the kill. Up to this point Jack has stood mesmerized and motionless. His enthrallment mirrors a certain kind of spectator. A *Clockwork Orange* had suggested that cinema may assault an audience; this scene reflects a film's power to corrupt.

When the door swings open we enter an overtly theatrical space. The gold arch over the bathtub is like a proscenium, and when the woman draws the shower curtain back, her full frontal nudity seems to fulfill the film's R-rated promise. As she advances, Jack's moronic smile satirizes a mass audience that is finally getting what it paid for. Five cuts to Jack during the woman's approach reveal the limits of his "background." In each cut a blurred mirror holds a dim lamp seen through the open door behind him. Increasing exposure to pornography dulls perception and is a major cause of the mind-death that concerns Kubrick in *Eyes Wide Shut.* (He explores other causes in *Dr. Strangelove, 2001, A Clockwork Orange,* and *Full Metal Jacket.*) Jack's inability to write reveals that he cannot fantasize on his own. His dream come true is a trite fantasy, and in the kiss to come he will continue the poisonous sucking that sickened him long before he entered the room.

When the woman reaches Jack, the frame centers them beneath the tub's proscenium arch. The image is redolent of erotic cliché. Next to the open curtain the area inside the room's innermost space behind the tub is backlit, while the area in front, closer to the audience, is relatively dark. After the kiss begins, the cut to a close-up loses the theatrical symmetry and accelerates Jack's loss of control. As the strange music swells, the ecstasy of erotic bliss will morph into panicky shock. People may seek relief from having to measure themselves socially or economically through physical pleasure, violent spectacle, or religious fervor. Jack's sexual encounter leads spectators to an area of self-awareness that most would prefer not to enter. The desire for erotic escape and Jack's desire to attain perfect security as a murderous agent of the "hotel" are motivated by the same need.

When people hurl themselves into a patriotic fervor preceding a war, the emotion is even stronger than that elicited by sexual escape. Jack will eventually do the bidding of the hotel because human beings apparently need to periodically kill members of their own species in order to stave off the fear of death. The crazy woman scene implies that sexual freedom cannot sublimate violence because it cannot kill death. No matter how guilt free, sex cannot replace society's need to commit legalized murder.

When Jack senses the woman's transformation and looks in the mirror, he sees an image of universal decay. She is ancient, toothless, and covered with ambiguous brown stains from feces or disease. But the tone of the scene turns comic when the woman pursues Jack like a carnival spook with open arms and faux laughter. In the discussions she held with Kubrick on Freud's "The Uncanny," Diane Johnson was impressed by the idea that dolls and puppets "are scary."[71] Freud wrote that "a feeling of the uncanny" arises from "doubts whether an apparently animate being is really alive; or conversely, whether a lifeless object might not be in fact animate" as in "waxwork figures, or ingeniously constructed dolls." Added to these is "the uncanny effect of epileptic fits, and of manifestations of insanity."[72] Three nonsequential cuts to the woman in the tub escalate this effect. In the first she lies prone on her back with her eyes open; in the second she rises like a board; and in the third she sits awake like Dracula in his coffin. Jack is bitten because he cannot distinguish between a vamp and a vampire, while Danny's clairvoyance allows us to see what Jack cannot. As Jack backs away, his mouth opens, his arms spread, and he begins to shake. In the crosscuts Danny too is shaking, but his eyes do not blink and his lips are tightly closed.

Because Danny's parents fail as guides, and because he is isolated from other children and nurturing adults, he has created a personal storyteller to keep him intact. In the Boulder bathroom where Danny first appears, he asks "Tony" to tell him what will happen next. Tony knows the general future will be bad, based on past experience, and as the personification of Danny's special precognition, he knows that Jack will "phone Wendy up in a minute" to tell her he got the job. Danny's powers resemble the creative process. He cannot plan the future, and though he may have a general sense of where he is going, each phase becomes clear one step at a time.

"The Uncanny" also seems to have shaped the relation between Danny and Tony. Freud praises Otto Rank's exploration of "the connections that the 'double' has with reflections in mirrors, with shadows, with guardian spirits, with the belief in the [immortal] soul."[73] Danny invents Tony, as a storyteller invents characters. And just as a writer becomes his characters in the act of writing them, so Freud describes a mental process where the subject substitutes "an extraneous self for his own." Then when Hallorann receives the events in Room 237 through Danny's eyes, he reflects a spectator's empathy. Freud defines telepathy as a form of doubling, because each party "possesses knowledge, feelings, and experience in common with the other," creating an "interchanging of the self."[74]

According to Freud the "primary narcissism of the child" invents guardian spirits to preserve the ego and deny death: "But when this stage has been surmounted, the 'double' reverses its aspect. From having been an assurance of immortality, it becomes the uncanny harbinger of death."[75] In his grandiose ambition to become a writer, Jack longs to join an elite that seems to be above death. Nobody wants to be like everyone else, because everyone else dies. The doubled servants named Grady (Charles and Delbert), and their doubled daughters, imply a universal motive for murder. For some to be immortal, others have to die, as the Indian art and the animal heads in the hotel lobby silently proclaim. Unfortunately, according to Freud, this illusion has a future: doubling is "marked by . . . repetition of the same features or character-traits or vicissitudes, [and] of the same crimes . . . through several consecutive generations."[76]

The persistence of the past in *The Shining* threatens to confirm the dead-end conclusion of *Dr. Strangelove*. But unlike that film, *The Shining* has characters we care for and respect. After Jack exits Room 237 and retreats backward down the dark hallway, the scene dissolves to Hallorann trying to telephone the Overlook.[77] For a moment both images are simultaneously on the screen, as if to balance the destructive and creative powers each represents. The deep blue shadows in Hallorann's room complement his blue pajama top and strikingly offset a bright table lamp, centered in the doorway of a pine-walled back room.

Hallorann's call "cannot be completed as dialed." It may represent the failed communication Kubrick referred to as a major theme of his films, but the centralized position and brightness of the lamp represent communication that works—the telepathy that resembles the symbolic language of film. In the immediate cut to the Torrance apartment, Hallorann's lamp becomes another lamp, in the same position in the frame, on the bed stand between the bed and the open bathroom door. Even though Wendy is beside herself with worry for Danny, this lamp (in conjunction with the overall "shine" motif) seems to foreshadow survival. It is prominent later when Danny alarms Wendy by calling out "REDRUM" from his bedroom, and again when he writes the word on the apartment door. In this scene the lamp's placement next to the bathroom door counterpoints the film's signature horror of Jack smashing that door with his axe. The open door also frames an image of the window with the piled-up snow that enables Danny's slide to safety.

Although Hallorann does not deserve to die any more than Danny does, his murder does not confirm the film's pessimism. Just after we see the balloon-filled hallway to the Gold Ballroom where the Overlook will claim Jack, the scene cuts to Hallorann in the same frame with the blue shadows and the bright lamp. Just as Bowman dies to become the Star Child at the end of *2001*, Hallorann's care and courage are ultimately transferred to Wendy, Danny, and the spectators. Immediately after his last phone call and a title card indicating that the narrative has jumped to the next morning, a

Figure 5.4. **The mirror and the lamp are symbols of insight and hope. Even as Danny writes the reversed letters for "murder" on the bedroom door, the background glass reflects the centered lamp.** *Courtesy of Warner Bros./Photofest © Warner Bros.*

shot of the plane taking him to Denver fills the screen.[78] The angle and the framing exaggerate its size, and its orange and blue stripes, along with Hallorann's blue scarf and orange shirt, again recall the predominant colors of *2001*.

In the comfort of the plane's cabin Hallorann is assisted by a flight attendant just as Floyd was on the space shuttle, but the next leg of his journey is as perilous as Bowman's was aboard the *Discovery*. After landing at the Denver airport, Hallorann is once again seen on the phone arranging for a snowcat to get him up the storm-blocked road. Knowing that Danny is in danger, Hallorann does everything he can to get through to him, first by phone to the ranger station, finally by making the treacherous drive himself.

In these actions he reflects the film's purpose of "getting through" to human beings endangered by ignorance of their own nature. Since he cannot explain how he knows that Danny is threatened, he tells the garage owner that the people taking care of the hotel have "turned out to be unreliable assholes" and that Ullman told him "to go up there and find out if they have to be replaced." The lie contains thematic truth: the people responsible for protecting society from war, racism, and social injustice—the caretakers—are insanely blind to the disparity between their self-image and what they do.

Verbal and visual metaphors of storm, cold, and fog suggest that "leaders" can no more change the human condition than they can control the weather.

The car radio reports that the storm has occurred so early in the season that the usual winter preparations have not been made. The airports and roads are closed, and "the national weather service has declared a stockman's and traveler's advisory for all areas outlying the Denver metro region—get the cows in the barn." The cold corresponds to the state of mind that periodically changes peaceful, civilized citizens into killers, performing duties enjoined by the powers that be. And the warning to shelter livestock is ironic, given a collective psychosis that cannot be kept outside. As the announcer reiterates, "Yeah, they're just not prepared."

In the continuing human analogue, travelers must negotiate their way with limited visibility in a fog of ignorance. An overturned truck suggests that some do not make it, mentally or physically, but the flares along the border of the road and a policeman with a flashlight indicate an intention to help. Looking through Hallorann's windshield with the rearview mirror in the center of the frame, we see a capsule image of what we have seen and can expect to see on the screen and in life: surrounding darkness, innocent victims, and an effort to shed light, however limited, on the road ahead.[79]

As in *2001* Kubrick creates an experience rather than a statement. Hallorann's approach to the hotel implies a conventional expectation of rescue that is not fulfilled. But his death, like that of Bowman, is meant to enable an expansion of vision rather than simple irony. When Hallorann switches to the snowcat, he is as alone as Bowman was in his space pod prior to entering an alien space. The headlights and blinking amber lights on the windshield approach the camera in a similar way, the only illumination in the gray darkness of the snow and the black clustered pines that wall the trail.[80]

Inside, Hallorann's anxious face shakes from the bumps, just as Bowman's did when his space pod hurtled through the Star Gate. But while Bowman's death was mystical, Hallorann's is horribly familiar. Just before the snowcat's final approach, Kubrick's comic distance locates Jack standing in the pantry next to diabolically labeled boxes of "sliced peaches" and "pimento pieces." The ghost that enables mayhem is another version of the natural imperative that turns *Clockwork*'s Alex into a terrorist. In the end the metaphors converge: killer ghosts return as inevitably as killer storms.

In an interview after *2001*, Kubrick reflected on why most people suppress the "gnawing" fear of death: "Why . . . should [a person] bother to write a great symphony, or strive to make a living, or even to love another, when he is no more than a momentary microbe on a dust mote whirling through the unimaginable immensity of space."[81] There is no logical answer; there is only an instinct to perpetuate life that is strong enough to counteract the equally strong impulse to destroy it. Freud generalized these opposites as Eros and Thanatos, and Kubrick personified them as Jack and the Overlook's ghosts versus Hallorann and Wendy.

Correspondingly, cinematic images of light subtly mitigate darkness. As Jack menaces Wendy on the stairs, Danny clairvoyantly views the scene and hears Jack's voice as if he were speaking underwater: "What do you want to talk about? Maybe it was about Danny. I think we should discuss what should be done with him."[82] In the cut to Danny watching from the kitchen table where Wendy left him, his mouth is open, his eyes are wide with terror, and in the orange pajamas that match Bowman's space suit, he has entered the ultimate nightmare of every child. The Hansel and Gretel scenario has become real. One parent wants to kill him, and the other appears powerless to stop it.

Once again he sees the river of blood gushing from the elevators, but this time it overwhelms the frame, splashing up against the camera lens as the chairs in the hallway begin to float. In the midst of this hopeless vision a cone of light suddenly appears, shining from the right of the elevator and expanding toward the left, like the light from a movie projector. Then a bright pink vertical rectangle containing white vertical bars appears in the center of the cone. The blood on the bottom of the frame is almost black, but the projected light deepens to a rich rose-red. It is a reflexive image of the film's affirmation. Works of art represent the other side of the human coin, and their intellectual and aesthetic qualities counter brutality.

A shot of Hallorann about to enter a narrow corridor of trees immediately precedes Danny (as Tony) hoarsely repeating "redrum" at Wendy's bedside as she continues to sleep.[83] She comes to full awakening only after she sees "redrum" reversed in the mirror. The preliterate Danny conveys a message in code that his unconscious dictates, just as the film speaks directly to the viewer's unconscious in images spontaneously produced by the artist's imagination. As before, the mirror has a dual effect: it frightens because it reveals a hidden evil, but it reassures because it warns of threats we otherwise would not see.

Jack's evil intentions appear in several mirrors, but Danny becomes Tony in others, and his power to live is ultimately stronger than Jack's ability to do harm. In the archetypal finale, intelligence beats the odds. Danny's vision overwhelms Jack's might, just as Odysseus triumphed over the Cyclops, David over Goliath, and Bowman over HAL. At the climax of the chase through the maze, Danny backs into his own footprints, leaps to the side, covers the displaced snow with his hands, and hides in the hedge until Jack passes. He then runs back the other way to the exit and escapes.[84] Perhaps Tony inspires hiding the footprints, but why does Danny think of doing it at this particular place in the maze? In an early scene just after the family had settled in at the hotel, Wendy and Danny walked through the maze, so that the way out remains in his unconscious. But many viewers fail to notice that when Danny makes his final break for the opening, he is going back the way Jack has just come.

Danny's strategy is every bit as incredible for a five-year-old as his ability to write "murder" in the bedroom mirror. As an inexplicable impulse in a life-or-death situation, it resembles Bowman's release of the "explosive bolts" that hurl him back into the *Discovery* after HAL had pronounced it impossible. If Danny had run directly toward the opening, he would have shown Jack the way out and been overtaken outside. This way he not only escapes, he traps Jack inside. The ax murderer is left as helpless as the wolf in the third little pig's pot, or the witch after Gretel pushes her into the oven.

As Jack moves forward through the maze, the rectangle of light at the end of each tunnel always recedes. Symbolically, he can never reach the light, never pass through the monolith to be born anew. His lurching slows and his speech slurs until he dies as he had he had lived: frozen forever in the monotonous role of Jack the Dull Boy. For Kubrick, death occurs when the mind ceases to grow. The image of ice-crusted doom morphs naturally into the coda's photo of Jack, triumphant, stillborn forever in black and white.

That is as far as some human beings will ever go. If the species is to survive, a sufficient number of its members must change and evolve. In the final section Jack represents the worst of the human past. His ax stands for the enduring weapon, from bone clubs to nukes, and his inarticulate screams express the futility of distancing death through violence. He must be supplanted by a species whose strongest drive is to see more and shine what they see.

After the snowcat begins to move, the lights on the hotel grounds and in the windows give the effect of stars, while the headlights once again evoke a spacecraft. When it swings around, the headlights blur into a white rectangle haloed brilliantly by turquoise light. Then after passing a tall, old-fashioned streetlamp that moves right to left across the foreground, it "takes off" by ascending a nearly vertical rise.

The camera then reverses direction. Dance music plays as it tracks in toward a wall of photographs.[85] When it stops before the one in the center, we recognize "the reincarnation of Jack," as Kubrick put it, on a day and year that ironically connote independence: July 4, 1921. Two dissolves bring

Jack's face closer as he simultaneously recedes in time. The song plays for the last twenty-four seconds of the shot, continues through a ten-second black screen, and concludes one minute and thirty seconds into the final credits. Then for the final forty-four seconds muffled applause and talking from the dance floor merge with the sounds of the spectators leaving the theater. Though this may be taken to identify the audience with the dancers, there is a difference: The song's title, "Midnight with the Stars and You," suggests transition and ascent, and while the Overlook's ghosts will remain forever as they are, the viewers of this cinematic fairy tale may change and grow.

Notes

1. Stanley Kubrick, interview by Penelope Houston, "Kubrick Country," *Saturday Review*, December 25, 1971; repr. in *Stanley Kubrick: Interviews*, ed. Gene D. Phillips (Jackson: University Press of Mississippi), 114.

2. Bruno Bettelheim, *The Uses of Enchantment* (New York: Vintage, Random House, 1989), 8–9, 24.

3. Richard T. Jameson, "Kubrick's *Shining*," *Film Comment*, July/August 1980, 32.

4. Alexander Walker, Sybil Taylor, and Ulrich Ruchti, *Stanley Kubrick, Director: A Visual Analysis* (New York: W. W. Norton, 1999), 312.

5. Lewis Carroll, *Alice's Adventures in Wonderland and Through the Looking Glass*, intro. Morton N. Cohen (1865; New York: Bantam, 1981), 101.

6. Bettelheim, *The Uses of Enchantment*, 26.

7. Diane Johnson, interview by Donald Williams, "An Interview with Diane Johnson," C. J. Jung page *Film Review*, www.cgjungpage.org/index2.php?option=content&do_pdf=1&id=490.

8. Harold Bloom, review of *The Uses of Enchantment*, by Bruno Bettelheim, *New York Review of Books*, July 15, 1976.

9. See Arthur C. Clarke, *Lost Worlds of 2001* (1972; Boston: Gregg Press, 1979), 34; see also Vincent LoBrutto, *Stanley Kubrick: A Biography* (New York: Donald I. Fine, 1997), 266, 413.

10. Joseph Campbell, *The Hero with a Thousand Faces*, 2nd ed. (Princeton, N.J.: Princeton University Press, 1968), 16–17.

11. Campbell, *The Hero with a Thousand Faces*, 6.

12. Bettelheim, *The Uses of Enchantment*, 214.

13. *The Shining*, DVD, directed by Stanley Kubrick (1980; Burbank, Calif.: Warner Bros. Home Video, 2001), chapters 15, 16.

14. Campbell, *The Hero with a Thousand Faces*, 20.

15. Stanley Kubrick, interview by Eric Nordern, *Playboy*, September 1968; repr. in Phillips, ed., *Stanley Kubrick: Interviews*, 50.

16. Stanley Kubrick, interview by Michel Ciment, *Kubrick: The Definitive Edition* (New York: Faber & Faber, 2001), 181.

17. Steven Spielberg, interview by Paul Joyce, "Remembering . . . Stanley Kubrick . . . Spielberg on Kubrick," July 22, 1999, in "Special Features," *Eyes Wide Shut*, DVD, directed by Stanley Kubrick (1999; Burbank, Calif.: Warner Bros. Home Video, 2001).

18. Bettelheim, *The Uses of Enchantment*, 62.

19. *The Shining*, DVD, chapter 2.

20. *The Shining*, DVD, chapter 3.

21. *The Shining*, DVD, chapter 8.

22. Diane Johnson, "Stanley Kubrick (1928–1999)," Obituary, *New York Review of Books*, April 22, 1999.

23. On the use of "The Uncanny" by Kubrick and Diane Johnson in preparing the script, see Dennis Bingham, "The Displaced Auteur: A Reception History of *The Shining*," in *Perspectives on Stanley Kubrick*, ed. Mario Falsetto (New York: G. K. Hall, 1996), 290.

24. *The Shining*, DVD, chapter 24.

25. *The Shining*, DVD, chapter 25.

26. *The Shining*, DVD, chapter 39.

27. Kubrick, interview by Ciment, 194.

28. Kubrick, interview by Ciment, 192.

29. *The Shining*, DVD, chapter 8.

30. J. D. Salinger, *The Catcher in the Rye* (New York: Bantam, 1964), 62–63.

31. *The Shining*, DVD, chapter 10.

32. Stephen King, *American Film*, September 1986; quoted by Vincent LoBrutto, *Stanley Kubrick: A Biography* (New York: Donald I. Fine, 1997), 414.

33. See Jameson's reference to Kubrick's comment as apocryphal in "Kubrick's Shining," 243.

34. *The Shining*, DVD, chapter 2.

35. *The Shining*, DVD, chapters 2–5.

36. For summaries of every episode of *The Bugs Bunny/Road Runner Hour* during the 1971–1972 season, see the article by Kevin McCorry at looney.goldenagecartoons.com/tv/bugstweety/.

37. *The Shining*, DVD, chapter 4.

38. Official *Peanuts* website, www.unitedmedia.com/comics/peanuts/.

39. Joyce Johnson, curator of SAIC Information Services, NASA website, "Silver Snoopy Award," www.hq.nasa.gov/osf/sfa/snoopy.html.

40. *The Shining*, DVD, chapter 4.

41. *The Shining*, DVD, chapter 5.

42. "Goofy," disney.go.com/characters/mickey/html/meet/goofy.html.

43. *The Shining*, DVD, chapter 31.

44. *The Shining*, DVD, chapter 6.

45. Jacob and Wilhelm Grimm, "Little Snow White," in *Children's and Household Tales*, trans. D. L. Ashliman (1857), www.pitt.edu/~dash/type0709.html.

46. *The Shining*, DVD, chapter 6.

47. See Graham Barron, review of *L'Enfant Sauvage* [The Wild Child], Apollo Movieguide Review, www.apolloguide.com/mov_fullrev.asp?CID=3314&Specific= 4055.

48. Bettelheim, *The Uses of Enchantment*, 161.

49. *The Shining*, DVD, chapter 9.

50. Jacob and Wilhelm Grimm, "Hansel and Gretel," in *Children's and Household Tales*, trans. Edgar Taylor and Marian Edwardes (1857), www.logicalviewinc.com/hanselandgretel/Story.asp.

51. Bettelheim, *The Uses of Enchantment*, 161.

52. On the Calumet can and *The Shining*'s Indian motif, see Bill Blakemore, "The Family of Man," *San Francisco Chronicle*, July 29, 1987.

53. *The Shining*, DVD, chapter 8.

54. *The Shining*, DVD, chapters 8–9.

55. Bettelheim, *The Uses of Enchantment*, 180–181.

56. Bettelheim, *The Uses of Enchantment*, 42.

57. *The Shining*, DVD, chapter 33.

58. *The Shining*, DVD, chapter 17.

59. Ciment, *Kubrick*, 146.

60. Kubrick, interview by Nordern, in Phillips, ed., *Stanley Kubrick: Interviews*, 73.

61. LoBrutto, *Stanley Kubrick*, 412.

62. M. H. Abrams, *The Mirror and the Lamp: Romantic Theory and the Critical Tradition* (New York: Oxford University Press, 1953).

63. Abrams, *The Mirror and the Lamp*, viii.

64. Abrams, *The Mirror and the Lamp*, 34.

65. Abrams, *The Mirror and the Lamp*, 52.

66. Abrams, *The Mirror and the Lamp*, 43.

67. Abrams, *The Mirror and the Lamp*, 67–68.

68. *The Shining*, DVD, chapter 21.

69. On blue and orange as exemplifying a perfect harmony of complementary opposites on the standard color wheel used by artists and color theorists, see Faber Birren, *Color and Human Response* (New York: Van Nostrand Reinhold, 1978), 58–59.

70. Kubrick, interview by Ciment, 188.

71. Johnson, interview by Williams, *C. J. Jung page Film Review*.

72. Sigmund Freud, "The Uncanny," in *The Standard Edition of the Complete Psychological Works of Sigmund Freud*, vol. 17, ed. James Strachey, Anna Freud, Alix Strachey, and Alan Tyson, trans. James Strachey (1919; London: Hogarth Press, 1955), 226.

73. Freud, "The Uncanny," 234–235.

74. Freud, "The Uncanny," 234.

75. Freud, "The Uncanny," 235.

76. Freud, "The Uncanny," 234.

77. *The Shining*, DVD, chapter 21.

78. *The Shining*, DVD, chapter 27.

79. *The Shining*, DVD, chapter 27.
80. *The Shining*, DVD, chapter 31.
81. Kubrick, interview by Nordern, in Phillips, ed., *Stanley Kubrick: Interviews*, 72.
82. *The Shining*, DVD, chapter 29.
83. *The Shining*, DVD, chapter 32.
84. *The Shining*, DVD, chapter 38.
85. *The Shining*, DVD, chapter 39.

CHAPTER SIX

~

Painting It Black
Full Metal Jacket

Full Metal Jacket is part fairy tale, part Jungian myth. In his foreword to the screenplay, Kubrick's coscreenwriter, Michael Herr, reported that Kubrick was "single-minded" about "the old and always serious problem of how you put into a film or a book the living, breathing presence of what Jung called the Shadow."[1] In a postfilm interview Kubrick himself was unusually explicit: "We're never going to get down to doing anything about the things that are really bad in the world until there is recognition within us of the darker side of our natures, the shadow side."[2] He offered a related Jungian insight to Gene Siskel: "I suppose the single improvement one might hope for in the world, which would have the greatest effect for good, would be an appreciation of the Jungian view of man by those who see themselves as good and externalize all evil."[3] And in one of his film's key scenes the hero, Private Joker, speaks the auteur's mind:

Colonel: Marine, what is that button on your body armor?

Joker: A peace symbol, sir!

Colonel: Where'd you get it?

Joker: I don't remember, sir!

Colonel: What is that you've got written on your helmet?

Joker: "Born to Kill," sir!

Colonel: You write "Born to Kill" on your helmet, *and* you wear a peace button. What's that supposed to be? Some kind of sick joke?

Joker: I don't know, sir!

Colonel: You don't know very much do you? You better get your head and your ass wired together or I *will* take a giant shit on you. Now answer my question or you'll be standing tall before the man.

Joker: I think I was trying to suggest something about the duality of man, sir!

Colonel: The what?

Joker: The duality of man, the Jungian thing, sir!

Colonel: Whose side are you on, son?

Joker: Our side, sir![4]

Jung himself put it this way:

> Evil, without man's ever having chosen it, is lodged in human nature itself . . . as the equal and opposite partner of good. . . . The dualism does not come from this realization; rather we are in a split condition to begin with. It would be an insufferable thought that we had to take personal responsibility for so much guiltiness. We therefore prefer to localize the evil with individual criminals or groups of criminals. . . . One must ask oneself how it is that for all our progress in the administration of justice, in medicine, and in technology, for all our concern for life and health, monstrous engines of destruction have been invented which could easily exterminate the human race.[5]

But Kubrick is not a Jungian per se, and he combines Jung's overall perspective with a "a Freudian thing" in the film's opening section, where Sergeant Hartman is the ultimate caricature of Freud's "anal character": "A child initially experiences tension from the buildup of fecal material. When the pressure upon the anal sphincters reaches the critical level, they open and expel the waste products from the child's food. Since this discharge of tension is pleasurable, severe toilet training establishes a lifelong displacement of anal release into emotional expulsions of rage and violence."[6]

In *Dr. Strangelove* the main joke is usually perceived as the popular one of the early 1960s, that bombs and missiles are phallic symbols. However, that film also alludes to the anal basis of military violence. When General Turgidson first appears, he cannot answer the phone because he is, as his girlfriend puts it, "tied up in the powder room." Later he tells the president that the bombers' approach to their target will cause real trouble "when the spaghetti hits the fan" and that when they drop "all their stuff," it will "cause a bit of a stink."[7] General Ripper's preservation of his bodily fluids is usually thought to refer exclusively to his fear of sexual impotence, but he is lodged in "Burpleson Air Force Base," a name connoting constipation. When group captain

Mandrake tries to cajole Ripper into releasing the world-saving code, he rec-
ommends drinking water to prevent being "rancid and clotted." Ripper, of
course, prefers to be rancid and clotted, since he believes the alternative is
death. When he is forced to surrender the base, he blows his brains out in the
bathroom.

After discovering that Ripper's code word can recall the planes that are
about to nuke Russia, Mandrake is confronted by one of the attack forces,
Colonel "Bat Guano."[8] Brandishing his rifle as if to spray guano on Mandrake, the colonel delays the crucial call to the president. Mandrake con-
vinces him to back down by pulling rank: "The Court of Inquiry on this'll
give you such a pranging, you'll be lucky if you end up wearing the uniform
of a bloody toilet attendant." Desperately needing change for the phone,
Mandrake orders Guano to "shoot off" the lock of the Coca-Cola machine.
As Guano bends to pick up the jackpot of coins, the machine fires a jet
stream of brown Coke into its assailant's face.

During *Full Metal Jacket's* planning stage, Kubrick subscribed to *Maledicta*,
"a journal of scatological invective and insult,"[9] but the film's unrelenting
wave of scatological words and images is far removed in tone from
Strangelove's sprightly jokes:

Hartman (to Cowboy): Were you about to call me an asshole?

Cowboy: Sir, no sir!

Hartman: How tall are you, Cowboy?

Cowboy: 5'9", sir!

Hartman: I didn't know they stacked shit that high. Are you trying to squeeze
an inch in on me somewhere? Bullshit! It looks to me like the best part of you
ran down your mama's thigh and ended as a brown stain on the mattress.[10]

Freud attributed the repulsiveness of feces to evolution. When human beings assumed an upright posture, olfactory stimulation no longer determined
their ability to find food and avoid enemies. The "higher" senses of sight and
hearing took precedence. As a result, civilization prevented regression to a
weaker stage of evolution by making animal smells taboo. The evolutionary
advance of the species is protected by the toilet training of children:

The *excreta* arouse no disgust in children. They seem valuable to them as being a part of their own body which has come away from it. Here upbringing insists with special energy on hastening the course of development which lies
ahead, and which should make the excreta worthless, disgusting, abhorrent,
and abominable. Such a reversal of values would scarcely be possible if the

substances that are expelled from the body were not doomed by their strong smells to share the fate which overtook olfactory stimuli after man adopted the upright posture. Anal eroticism, therefore, succumbs . . . to the "organic repression" which paved the way to civilization.[11]

The circles of Hartman's hell are organic, descending through the "homo," to bloblike animals, to vomit, and finally to feces at the end of the line: "If you survive recruit training, you will be a weapon, you will be a minister of death praying for war, but until that day you are pukes; you are the lowest form of life on earth; you are not even human fucking beings. You are nothing but unorganized, grab-asstic pieces of amphibian shit." In order to rise to an inviolable heaven of male being, Hartman preaches a doctrine of inanimate salvation. To win is to waste the enemy—to lose is to become waste: "Your rifle is only a tool. It's a hard heart that kills. If your killer instincts are not clean and strong, you will hesitate at the moment of truth. You will not kill. You will become dead marines. And then you will be in a world of shit, because marines are not allowed to die without permission."[12]

These lines foreshadow the evolution of the hero, Private Joker, one of only three marines in the film's second half who does not follow orders. While his comrades spew bullets at an unseen enemy, Joker is the only one brave enough to look an "enemy" in the face and waste her—out of compassion. And he is the only marine in the film who remains mentally and emotionally alive at the end "in a world of shit" that is bigger than Vietnam. The film's other misfit is not so lucky. In the opening scene Hartman chokes Private Pyle for a "smile" that he cannot wipe off, because it is the natural contour of his mouth. He slaps him repeatedly in the face for confusing his right and left shoulders during drill, and later after an unspecified infraction, he forces Pyle to march behind the rest of the outfit with his pants down around his ankles and his thumb in his mouth.

This particular form of humiliation plays on unconscious fears of regressive weakness in the other recruits. After Hartman discovers a jelly doughnut in Pyle's footlocker, he threatens the whole group because they have failed "for not giving Private Pyle the proper motivation."[13] They are made to do push-ups while Pyle is forced to stand between them eating the doughnut. He had told Hartman that he took the doughnut because he "was hungry." It is an infantile response to abuse, another version of the thumbsucking Hartman had forced him to act out, and it is his last pacifier as the weak persona that the others fear to be.

Hartman had conferred the name "Gomer" on Pyle as an insult, comparing him to Gomer Pyle, television's clownish marine. The title character of the long-running sixties sitcom was a gentle enlistee whose incompetence continually frustrated his short-fused sergeant, Vince Carter. But Carter's ego was susceptible to Gomer's foolish praise, and the two became unlikely friends. Though Gomer frequently annoyed his superiors on the base, he was neither harmed nor humiliated. In the film the nickname's irony is enhanced by Pyle's real name, "Leonard," which evokes the retarded giant, Lennie, from Steinbeck's *Of Mice and Men*. When Hartman assigns Joker to be Pyle's mentor—"He'll teach you everything; he'll teach you how to pee"—Joker resembles George, Lennie's caretaker. He not only helps Pyle to negotiate the obstacle course, he teaches him to make his bed and lace his boots. Following the jelly doughnut incident we see Pyle pathetically telling Joker that everybody hates him. Joker tells him he "looks like shit" and buttons his shirt, but like Lennie's George, he has mixed feelings about his charge. (Vincent D'Onofrio, who played Pyle, also played Lennie in an off-Broadway production.)[14]

In the night scene that immediately ensues, the light in the bunkhouse is a cold slate blue. We are made to see the Jungian dark side in these blue "shadows," the side that Joker knows abstractly from his reading, but that he here begins to know as a nightmare come true. In a scene that echoes the water hole attack in "The Dawn of Man," the first shot is a close-up of the "blue" blanket's weave with indentations that make it look like sand.[15] Then we see hands wrapping a bar of soap in a white towel that becomes the ape-man's bone. The hands test the weapon by rapping it twice on the bed. Kubrick described this "night attack" as an atavistic trace: "Probably way back [aggression and xenophobia] did serve a survival purpose. One way to improve the survival of the hunting band is to hate any suspect outsiders." And generalizing its thematic implications for the film as a whole, he added, "Nationalism is, I suppose, the equivalent of what held the hunting band together. But with atomic weapons the evolutionary programming that served Cro-Magnon man now threatens our existence. . . . International Law still offers little in resolving conflict, [and] fighting, certainly between nuclear powers, offers only the possibility of extinction."[16]

Joker hangs back until the others have struck their "motivating" blows. Even when his turn arrives, Cowboy has to order him to join in, "Do it, do it!" Pyle's eyes have been closed during the whole attack, but as Joker hesitates Pyle opens his eyes and turns his head to see that his big brother, his only protector up to now, is about to strike him. Joker clenches his teeth and hits Pyle once. Pyle cries even louder, and Joker beats him five times with a vehemence resembling that of the bone-bearing apes when they wield their weapons for the first time. Before Cowboy retreats to the cover of his bunk, he leaves Pyle with the parting words, "Remember it's just a bad dream, fat boy." For Joker it is the first in a series of awakenings. As he lies on the lower bunk just below the sobbing Pyle, he tightens his mouth and slowly raises his hands to his ears. In *2001* Floyd and the team that accompanied him to the moon covered their ears against the monolith's unbearable ringing, as if its message were still beyond their range. Joker's unreadiness appears in the darkness of his shadowed eyes, the same dormancy that lay under the ape-men's ridged brows.

At the end of basic training Hartman assigns the recruits to their new positions. Most go to the infantry, and all are proud of having "graduated." Joker is the exception. He is proud of having made it through basic training, but his first job suggests that he will achieve a "graduation" they will not:

> *Hartman (reading):* 4212—Basic Military Journalism . . . Basic Military Journalism?
>
> You gotta be shittin' me, Joker. You think you're Mickey Spillane? You think you're some kind of fuckin' writer?
>
> *Joker:* Sir, I wrote for my high school newspaper, sir!
>
> *Hartman:* Jesus H. Christ! You're not a writer, you're a killer!
>
> *Joker:* A killer, yes, sir![17]

The camera immediately cuts to a close-up of Pyle. His head is tilted down, his dead eyes are rolled upward, and he *has* become the absolute killer Joker will never be. He indicates his transformation when he does not answer after Hartman calls his name, "Pyle . . . Gomer Pyle, you forget your fucking name?"

The camera then cuts to the next scene where Joker's voice-over suggests that he has evolved from killer to writer in a future extending beyond the end of the film: "Our last night on the island. I draw fire watch." Although Pyle shot Hartman in the bunk room in Gustav Hasford's novel,[18] Kubrick moved the action to a place that is consistent with the idea of anal release. After drawing out the words, "Hi . . . Joker," Pyle begins to load the golden brown bullets into the rifle's dark brown magazine that he holds between his legs. The light on Joker's helmet and on the wall behind him confers the cold blue quality that helps the audience to feel the distance that is necessary to recognize the metaphor. The scene refers the film's title to the anal basis of "shooting" and makes virtual synonyms of "combat marine," "grunt," and "turd":

> *Joker:* Are those . . . live rounds?
>
> *Pyle: (still sitting on the toilet)* 7-6-2 millimeter, *(snaps one in)* full . . . metal . . . jacket.

Joker: Leonard, if Hartman comes in here and catches us, we'll both be in a world of shit.

Pyle: I am . . . in a world . . . of shit![19]

The world of shit is then immediately shown to be that of all the recruits when Pyle springs to his feet and presents arms, following each move of the rifle from shoulder to shoulder with a ritual roar: "Right shoulder, huuuh! Left shoulder, huuuh!" Then the words "Lock and load!" prepare for the cathartic result.

As Leonard intones the marine creed, "This is my rifle . . . my rifle is my life," Hartman bursts from his door and shouts to the gathering others who have been roused from sleep, "Get back in your bunks!" After he enters the latrine the fearsome aspect of the scene merges with the comic-grotesque, just as it does in *A Clockwork Orange* and *The Shining*. Before we see him clearly, we hear Hartman's voice anticipating the murder of innocence heard in the mouseketeer chorus of the film's final scene: "What is this Mickey Mouse shit?" Then he appears, a short man in white boxers and a gray sleeveless sweatshirt, absurdly wearing his hat, as if to show that sergeant bluster can no longer cover human frailty: "What in the name of Jesus H. Christ are you animals doing in my head?"

Then comes a series of questions that shrilly escalate as he confronts a situation he cannot compute: "Why is Private Pyle out of his bunk after lights out? Why is Private Pyle holding that weapon? Why aren't you stomping Private Pyle's guts out?" Joker prevents the scene from tipping into the ludicrous, not so much through his words, as through the fear in his voice: "Sir, it is the private's duty to inform you that Private Pyle's rifle has a full magazine. It is locked and loaded, sir!" At the same time, Joker's formal response creates satiric distance. His respectful "sir" adds irony to the metaphor of a "full magazine . . . locked and loaded," especially since Pyle has taken so much shit from Hartman.

The idea behind this scene is pure Freud, and the anal metaphor carries the scene. Just before he blows Hartman away, Pyle sounds a sigh of relief as if a long constipation were about to end. Strangely, the sigh is inhaled rather than exhaled. Then he releases a single round. In the sequence of frames starting at 44:08, the flash from Pyle's rifle cuts to the film's last view of Hartman, standing with his mouth wide in a final shout, and, for a split second, still unbloodied. After his red "bodily fluid" spurts out and he crumples to the floor, Pyle takes a deep breath and finally exhales a silent sigh of pure pleasure.

Figure 6.1.   Just before he blows Hartman away, Pyle inhales an ecstatic sigh. *Courtesy of Warner Bros./Photofest © Warner Bros.*

He then raises the rifle to point at Joker, who survives because he can hold in his fear. Gently, Joker says, "Go easy, Leonard, go easy man"—just before Pyle sits down on the toilet, cracks the rifle butt on the floor, and "goes" by squeezing off a second round into his mouth. As scatology the metaphor is comic, but the act itself is shocking and tragic. The saving grace is Joker's horrified "Noooo!" just as Leonard puts the rifle in his mouth. From first to last Joker's surviving ability to think, feel, and reject regression represents humanity's best hope.

The film's final image of Pyle shows his mouth wide open in death as his head tilts backward against the top of the toilet tank. But while Hartman's mouth was open as he spewed out a last gasp, Pyle's is passively open in death. He dies as the helpless receptacle of a system that made him eat shit. And his spotless white T-shirt blending with the white toilet and white tiled wall represents his lethal innocence. The myth of heroic bloodshed has become the wasted blood splattered on the wall. The scene cuts once to Joker's shaken face before a final shot indelibly frames Pyle as the Freudian "maker" of war.

Just before Pyle's image fades, Joker's wide eyes and open mouth foreshadow his ability to creatively transform the experience he absorbs. Together he and Pyle constitute a duality of human potential. The two are repeatedly seen together apart from the group, with Joker as Leonard's mentor. Both are singled out, one by retardation, the other by precocity. Both are verbally raped by Hart-man, enabling them to out-tough the other marines by killing close-up, looking their targets directly in the eye. But while Pyle kills to expel fear and rage, Joker "wastes" an enemy at close range in an act of premeditated euthanasia. Ironi-cally, the deed earns him the respectful adjective "hardcore" from his fellow marines near the film's end.[20] The audience must also be hardcore if they are to see as Joker sees, without succumbing to disgust and despair.

Joker encounters two major shadow figures in the film: Sergeant Hartman and a fellow marine he meets in Vietnam shortly after he is reunited with Cowboy. Animal Mother acts and thinks (to the extent he can be said to think) upon aggressive instincts that training had no need to sharpen. Un-like Pyle he is a born killer. He approaches Joker with contempt in his voice and an eerie stare that is scary but not psycho. Nor is it "the thousand-yard stare" of a civilian traumatized by combat. Rather, combat has enabled him to express what he was born to do. Like *Clockwork*'s Alex, he has a natural gift for improvising violence, and he is the only marine at rest who is still covered with ammo (full metal jackets) from his bandoliers to the back of his helmet. He is also the only marine besides Joker to have something written on his helmet, "I am become Death." The whole line from the *Bhagavad Gita* (11:32) reads, "I am become Death, the Destroyer of Worlds," and was re-portedly quoted by J. Robert Oppenheimer after the first atomic bomb was dropped on Hiroshima in 1945.[21]

The shot/reverse shots of Animal Mother and Joker facing off provide a striking image of Jungian duality: Animal Mother carries a rifle while Joker carries a camera. Animal Mother's unblinking eyes threaten abrupt attack, while Joker looks out steadily from his glasses. Animal Mother's words con-vey contempt for language, while Joker jabs back with mocking wit:

Animal Mother: You a photographer?

Joker: No, I'm a combat correspondent.

Animal Mother: Oh, ya seen much com-bat?

Joker: I've seen a little on *T . . . V.*

Animal Mother: Yoou're a real comedian.

Joker: Well, they call me "the Joker."

Animal Mother: Well I got a joke for you, I'm gonna tear you a new asshole.

Joker (in his John Wayne voice): Well, pilgrim, only after ya eat the peanuts outta my she-it.

Animal Mother: You talk the talk. Do you walk the walk?[22]

As in the scene with the colonel, camera angles in shot/reverse shots make Matthew Modine's Joker look even taller than he naturally is. He draws himself up to his full height in the profile shot of the two where his John Wayne voice tells Animal to eat shit. And he easily tops each of Animal's insults to get an appreciative rise out of the other marines. But Animal has no buttons for Joker to push, and his sinuous body language threatens a sudden strike. Even when he challenges Joker physically to "walk the walk," his voice betrays no excitement. Joker tightens his lips as Cowboy holds him back while a black marine comes over to lead Animal away, soothing him with flattery as if he were his keeper: "Hey, you may not believe it, but under fire Animal Mother's one of the finest human beings in the world. All he needs is someone to throw hand grenades at him the rest of his life." Animal smiles, backing off as if indifferent. He has enjoyed the challenge. He would have enjoyed the fight. He throws an offhand insult at his buddy, "Thank God for the sickle cell," which Eightball fondly ignores as if Animal were an irritated pet. Altogether, the scene reveals an unevolved pleasure in assault, semicomically in Animal, given his name, and even in Joker when his testosterone is stirred. While Animal exhibits a precivilized hostility to moral

Figure 6.2. Eightball calls off Animal Mother, Joker's alpha opposite. Covered in bullets, Animal embodies pure aggression, but the camera angles accent Joker's superior height and evolving maturity. *Courtesy of Warner Bros./Photofest © Warner Bros.*

hypocrisy, Joker balances his own alpha-alienation with verbal power and intelligence. In energy and independence Animal and Joker stand apart from the others as the ape-man leader did at the "Dawn of Man."

When Animal single-handedly charges an enemy sniper near the end of the film, his killer instinct proves its crisis value, just as Bowman's did when he defied HAL. In the preliminary screenplay Joker's description (not in the film) indicates that he recognizes his former adversary as Ardrey's armed ape: "Animal Mother hoists his B-60 machine gun and charges for the street crossing. He fires blind. He lopes along with the fluid grace of a meat eater. His chin is dripping saliva. Animal Mother is a predator attacking. He wants warm blood to drink. Animal Mother wants human flesh to tear apart and devour. Animal Mother doesn't know what the hell he's doing. He thinks he's John Wayne."[23]

Joker's John Wayne imitations express his duality. The scene in the press hutch begins with Joker reading a book. He puts it down, stretches, and complains, "I am fucking bored to death, man. I got to get back in the shit. I ain't heard a shot fired in anger in weeks." The action reminds the audience of his intelligence (he has a book), while the words show that he is still immature and untested. After Payback (who is reading a girlie magazine) teases him for trying to sound tough, Joker once again uses his John Wayne voice as a defense: "Listen up, pilgrim. A day without blood is like a day without sunshine." The whole exchange indicates that Joker still shares a whistle-in-the-dark swagger with the others.[24]

In a voice-over from the preliminary screenplay that was later dropped, Joker refers to a particular Wayne vehicle: "Beatings, we learn, are a routine element of life on Parris Island. And not that I'm-only-rough-on-'um-because-I-love-'um crap in Mr. John Wayne's *Sands of Iwo Jima*."[25] Wayne's dark side surfaces in *Sands* when the film's hero, Peter Conway (John Agar), unsuccessfully challenges the Wayne character's order not to risk rescuing a wounded man. As a dehumanized military machine, Sergeant Stryker is so focused on taking the Japanese-held island that he is indifferent to the fate of individual soldiers. The inability of Cowboy to control his men in a similar situation is a measure of the difference between attitudes toward authority in the two films and between World War II and Vietnam. But the biggest difference is Kubrick's deliberate removal of sympathy from every sergeant and officer in *Full Metal Jacket*.

Conversely, Stryker's humanity is affirmed near the end when we learn that his wife left him and that he has no children. His vulnerable side appears during a furlough when he has a touching affair with a street woman in Hawaii. By the end of the film his men have come to like and respect him, and he is shot and killed shortly after the film reaches an apex of patriotism in the famous flag-raising scene. The best in Stryker then rises from the ashes in the person of Conway, who sheds his cynicism to become a born-again patriot.[26]

Kubrick made Joker the anti-Conway just as he made Hartman the anti-Wayne. In a post–*Full Metal Jacket* interview he made the same point about another film:

> [*An Officer and a Gentleman*][27] clearly wants to ingratiate itself with the audience. So many films do that. You show the drill instructor really has a heart of gold—the mandatory scene where he sits in his office, eyes swimming with pride about the boys and so forth. I suppose he actually is proud, but there's a danger of falling into what amounts to so much sentimental bullshit.[28]

Clearly, Kubrick and Herr considered Wayne's influence on American culture to be anything but benign. In the same speech in the preliminary screenplay where Joker compares Animal Mother to a bloodthirsty ape, he also connects him to Wayne: "Animal Mother doesn't know what the hell he's doing. He thinks he's John Wayne." Herr had previously written about how "all the kids who got wiped out by seventeen years of war movies before coming to Vietnam . . . were actually making war movies in their heads, doing little guts-and-glory Leatherneck tap dances under fire, getting their pimples shot off for the networks."[29] In another report a soldier told the writer: "I was seduced by World War II and John Wayne movies."[30]

Even in 1968 after huge demonstrations had occurred at the Democratic convention in Chicago and on the mall in Washington, and after innumerable draft card and flag burnings, John Wayne's *The Green Berets* (1968) grossed $11 million at the box office. The song that played over the closing credits, "Ballad of the Green Berets," sung by Sergeant Barry Sadler, was a top-ten hit for months.[31] In the film Wayne (Colonel Mike Kirby) leads his super soldiers on a dangerous mission to capture a North Vietnamese general. They are accompanied by a Joker-like journalist, who begins as a cynic, but after observing what perils the soldiers face, he too becomes a fervent commie hater.[32] Herr's direct experience of Vietnam influenced his explosion of the Wayne myth in a passage from the preliminary screenplay (omitted from the film), where marines watching *The Green Berets* in a PX movie theater laugh uproariously at an absurdly attired Wayne "in tailored tiger-stripe jungle utilities, wearing boots that shine like black glass." When Wayne orders an Asian actor to kill the Vietcong, a marine in the audience yells, "You fuckin' asshole, *you* kill stinking Cong. I wanna go home now!" They think this is "the funniest movie they have seen in a long time."[33]

Kubrick and Herr undoubtedly included the PX screening to show the general cynicism of grunts on the ground in Vietnam. Even in World War II Wayne was booed during a USO appearance because the troops resented his posture as an unscathed hero.[34] Whenever Joker's experience diverges from war movie clichés, he imitates or mentions Wayne, but his lines in the preliminary screenplay either differ in wording from lines in the film or are used in different situations: when Sergeant Gerheim (Hartman) initially berates the recruits, Joker uses his John Wayne voice to say, "I think I'm going to hate this movie"; and when Cowboy is deflated because Animal Mother has openly defied his order not to charge, Joker consoles him with "Mother was lucky. . . . He had a John Wayne wet dream."[35]

In the preliminary screenplay Joker says, "Is that you, John Wayne? Is this me?" only once, when the squad is joking to keep up their nerve in a desperate combat situation. In the film Joker's John Wayne question is his first line in the film. It expresses not only intelligent cynicism but an actual courage that makes him part–John Wayne. After Hartman punches him in the stomach, he does not crumple but manages to keep one foot squarely on the ground as he sinks to one knee. When Hartman orders him to show his "war face," Joker roars back to prove that he is a killer, worthy of the sergeant's "beloved corps."[36] At the end Joker does indeed prove that he can kill, but for a purpose that his training did not intend.

Even after Joker has experienced combat, his last John Wayne imitation shows that he has not become what he had called "the phony tough" or "the crazy brave." When the television crew points its cameras downward at the grunts resting on the ground, the others take their cue from him and have fun claiming roles for themselves. The camera crew looms large in very low angle shots from the marines' point of view as if to symbolize their lack of individual importance. As they speak, stretchers carry the wounded across the screen before them, while tanks belch fire into a field where smaller fires burn in the distance:

Joker: Is that you, John Wayne? Is this me?

Cowboy: Hey start the cameras. This is "Vietnam: The Movie."

Eightball: Yeah, start the cameras. Joker can be John Wayne; I'll be a horse.

Donlon: T.H.E. Rock can be a rock! (*gesturing to his right*)

T.H.E. Rock (*pulling up his trouser leg*): I'll be Ann-Margret.

Doc Jay: Animal Mother can be a rabid buffalo.

Crazy Earl: I'll be General Custer.

Rafterman: Who'll be the Indians?

Animal Mother: Hey, we'll let the gooks play the Indians![37]

The reflexive "Western" references from John Wayne to General Custer place the film in a historical context that helps to universalize its portrait of war. The killing of nonwhite enemies of the United States has always been rationalized as the necessary extermination of a subhuman threat—from redskins to Japs to gooks.[38] On March 16, 1968, Lieutenant William Calley ordered the slaughter of 347 unarmed civilians in the village of My Lai. The military tribunal, sensitive to antiwar pressures, asserted that the perpetrators were misfits or that they had gone berserk from combat fatigue. Ironically, the similar murder of three hundred Lakota (Sioux) noncombatants at Wounded Knee, South Dakota, in 1890 earned each member of the Seventh Cavalry (Custer's former outfit) a Congressional Medal of Honor.

Calley's comments at his trial may have influenced the portrayal of the marine in Cowboy's platoon who kept the North Vietnamese Army corpse as a companion. In the TV interview, that marine answers a leading question with the reply, "Do I think America belongs in Vietnam? I don't know, I belong in Vietnam, I can tell you that." His casual response presents an image of a loyal soldier with a sense of patriotic purpose. Calley too described himself as a "run-of-the-mill average guy." When asked why he had volunteered to come to Vietnam, Calley replied that he "really felt he belonged" there. And when asked how he could have turned so many people into corpses, Calley showed that he had come to understand the intended effect of his indoctrination: "We weren't in My Lai to kill human beings, really. We were there to kill *ideology* that is carried by—I don't know. Pawns. Blobs, Pieces of Flesh, and I wasn't in My Lai to destroy intelligent men. I was there to destroy an intangible idea."[39]

Like Calley, who "felt superior there" as the "big American from across the sea" ready to "sock it to these people here," the corpse-keeping marine only half-comically tells his comrades that they are living in "great days" and that they are "jolly green giants" walking the earth.[40] The reference to the logo of a canned vegetable company (Jolly Green Giant) is intercut with a shot of Rafterman, Joker's diligent photographer, snapping a picture of the gruesome scene that *Stars and Stripes* would obviously never print.

The media satire accentuates the Eichmann-like banality that helps to disguise the shadow. The media image of the grunts as average men, just following orders, was trenchantly exposed in a 1970 Academy Award–winning documentary, *Interviews with My Lai Veterans*, directed by Joseph Strick. In a scene that may well have influenced Kubrick, a group of soldiers described how their messmates hung, scalped, and otherwise mutilated their victims. One soldier related that his buddies cut off ears even if they weren't sure whether the corpse was a Vietcong: "If they got the ear, it was a VC." Another explained that the trophies were "like scalps" because "some people were on an Indian trip over there," and still another added that the troops "wiped the whole place out" because of what he called "the Indian idea . . . the only good gook is a dead gook."[41]

The sentiments echo the Seventh Cavalry's vengeful payback for Little Bighorn in the Wounded Knee massacre and, in particular, the massacre of a peaceful Cheyenne village at Sand Creek, Colorado, in 1864. The officer in charge, Colonel J. M. Chivington, exhorted his men to "kill and scalp all; big and little; nits make lice." One of Chivington's coerced half-Indian guides described a scene that resembled My Lai:

> Some thirty or forty squaws collected in a hole for protection . . . a little girl about six years old went out with a white flag on a stick. She was shot and killed. . . . I saw one squaw cut open with an unborn child lying by her side. I saw the body [of another woman] with the privates cut off, and I heard a soldier say he was going to make a tobacco pouch out of them.[42]

Following Bettelheim, Kubrick suggests that parents who transmit denials of humanity's dark side assure continuing destruction. In the first scene in the *Stars and Stripes* press room, the details of the set constitute a collage of insipid television programs that sweeten war.[43] Other details reflect and counterpoint specific voices in the film. The first shot has the cynical, laid-back editor, Lieutenant Lockhart, centered in the frame reviewing copy. Directly over his head is a banner in marine orange and gold that proclaims, "First to go. Last to know. We will defend to the death our right to be misinformed." Directly in front of him sits a large black telephone that the camera angle exaggerates. The frame externalizes a collective mind that distorts language to skew the truth.

In a scene set against a background of civilian suffering and politically sanctioned murder, familiar objects in the room have a bizarre resonance. The icon of American innocence, Mickey Mouse, appears over Joker's left shoulder just as the editor tells Joker to fictionalize some "kills" to prove that America is winning the war. The red, white, and blue–clad Mickey doll sits on a white stool on the windowsill, his right arm raised in a white-gloved greeting. To Mickey's left stands a Minnie Mouse doll, and to her left a decapitated Mickey head faces her in profile. While Mickey raises his friendly wave to us, we see the deaths of body and mind that denial of the shadow can cause.

The Mickey Mouse ideal is an ironic motif in the film from Hartman's outraged question—"What is this Mickey Mouse shit?"—to the mouseketeer song that concludes the film. In his earliest incarnation—Disney's *Steamboat Willie* (1928)—Mickey was a mischievous joker, but parental demand converted him into the paragon of childhood role models. He became the ultimate Mr. Nice Guy, doing everything well, always a benefactor, and never a threat to himself or others. The first "Mickey Mouse Club" began in 1929. It met at Saturday matinees for cartoons and games, in-group passwords and handshakes, and a club song. The later TV version of the club introduced the famous mouseketeers in 1955, followed by revivals in 1977 and 1989. Today Mickey is still the presiding figure at Disney theme parks around the world. The presence of Mickey in a war movie is especially pointed in that his name was code for the American campaign in Europe during World War II, a war of idealism in a relatively innocent America. The decapitated Mickey head on the windowsill suggests that a red, white, and blue mouse can no longer protect his children, psychologically or physically.[44]

The wall that Joker faces on the opposite side of the room is plastered with artifacts that sanitize war. Directly to the right of the banner that reads "First to go. Last to know" sits Snoopy, the beloved beagle from Charles Schulz's comic strip *Peanuts* (also pictured on Danny's bathroom door in *The Shining*). In the subsequent pressroom scene Snoopy is over Joker's head as he feigns sleep during Lockhart's alarm bulletin: "Charlie has hit every major military base in Vietnam and hit 'em hard."[45] Directly beneath that picture in the previous scene was a strange black and white drawing of another *Peanuts* character, Charlie Brown. Charlie was shown frontally in a military cap with a sword in his left hand, and his gaping mouth was a black hole in the same kind of "war face" Hartman had goaded Joker to show. The picture probably disappeared in the subsequent pressroom scene because Kubrick cut the film's final montage from the preliminary screenplay. In it shots of Joker as a marine firing his rifle alternate with Joker as an eight-year-old boy, firing his toy rifle. When Joker, the marine, is fatally shot by a barrage of machine-gun fire, the eight-year-old Joker "clutches his chest in mock agony" and starts to fall before he is suspended in a freeze-frame that resembles a famous Spanish Civil War photograph by Robert Capa: "But this picture is of an eight year-old boy."[46]

Lieutenant Lockhart dramatically circles the room to announce that rumors of the Tet Offensive he had earlier denied have become devastatingly true: "The enemy has used the Tet Ceasefire to launch an offensive all over the country. He has hit every major military target in Vietnam. In Saigon the United States Embassy has been overrun by suicide squads. Khe Sanh is standing by to be overrun." In the final cut of the film Kubrick supplemented the screenplay's description of disaster with Lockhart's insistence on the propaganda job his own squad will now have to hustle: "In strategic terms Charlie's cut the country in half, the civilian press is about to wet their pants, and we've heard even Cronkite's gonna say the war is now unwinnable. In other words it's a huge shit sandwich, and we're all gonna have to take a bite."

The scatological reference recalls the basic training motif that war "wastes" (kills) on a massive scale ("a world of shit"). In contrast the bulletin boards intersperse *Playboy* pictures with cute cartoon and TV characters, as if to underscore an absurd denial of the military's methods and ultimate purpose. Several pictures of pop culture sergeants provide ironic contrasts to Hartman and, taken together, provide a collective disguise for the film's portrayal of basic training as child abuse. A picture of Sergeant Orville P. Snorkel from the cartoon strip *Beetle Bailey* appears in the right-center of the frame. Snorkel was constantly taking his insatiable anger out on the strip's title character, Private Beetle Bailey. The frequent punches that Beetle absorbed from the sergeant never injured or traumatized him. Mort Walker's purpose was to show the catch-22 aspects of bureaucracy based on his World War II experience. Nevertheless, the cartoon's introduction helped to boost support for the Korean War in a society dominated by patriotic veterans.[47]

Next to the wide-mouthed, shouting Snorkel is a photograph of Sergeant Ernie Bilko, portrayed by Phil Silvers in *The Phil Silvers Show*, a vastly popular TV sitcom of the 1950s. Unlike the angry whip-'em-into-shape sergeants of most military drama, Bilko was a con man who ran the motor pool at a small Kansas army camp. Though the setting was martial, the show's viewers saw nothing that reminded them that a base's raison d'être is to prepare adolescents to kill. Bilko spends his time devising various money-making schemes, including "midnight cruises on landing craft, tank rides, poker games, and deals with service stations for spare parts or jeep tires."[48]

Another popular media character, who was anything but dumb and sweet, is also pictured on the wall in the center of the frame. Charlie McCarthy was *the* American ventriloquist's dummy in the 1930s, '40s, and early '50s. His creator, Edgar Bergen, gave him a disrespectful wit that was invigorating for those times. Because he was supposed to be a child and because he was exempt from human shame, Charlie could come on to women in ways that were ahead of his time, and he articulated social frustrations by boldly asserting equality with those "above" him. He always addressed his "parent" as

"Bergen," and when a woman asked Bergen how he could talk without moving his lips, Charlie interjected, "You're asking the wrong person!"⁴⁹

Charlie's presence in the room corresponds to Joker's. As Lieutenant Lockhart describes the dire situation the Americans face as a result of Tet, the other reporters voice their alarm while Joker sits slumped in his chair, eyes closed, like a bored high school student. Suddenly Joker sits up alertly and gets a Charlie-sized laugh from the reporters with "Does this mean Ann-Margret's not coming?" For the first time Lockhart's face betrays anger. With the American position and his own security now threatened, Joker's sarcasm has finally hit a nerve. But Lockhart's retribution is disproportionate, revealing that he too is a killer. Joker's "assignment" is a potential death sentence: "Joker, I want you to get straight up to Phu Bai, Captain January will need all his people. And Joker you will take off that damn button. How's it going to look if you get killed wearing a peace button." Realizing the danger, Joker asks the lieutenant to reject the request of his photographer, Rafterman, to go along. Lockhart's argot-laden reply barely disguises his malice: "Vanish, Joker, most ricky-tick and take Rafterman with you. You're responsible for him." As it does throughout the film, marine-speak truncates feeling. When the lieutenant uses "vanish" as an imperative, he implies that if Joker and Rafterman die, Joker's "attitude" will have earned its just desert.

The Mickey Mouse dolls on the windowsill accent the danger. In the first pressroom scene, all the dolls were together over Joker's left shoulder. They now frame him. Mickey is over his right shoulder while Minnie and the decapitated head are on the left. Mickey is thus separated from Minnie, and the head of an anonymous mouse "casualty" is severed from its body. Other details achieve the same perspective. There are two pictures of mothers and children on one of the bulletin boards to the right of the Charlie McCarthy picture: one is a color photograph of a mother cradling a naked infant; the other, above it and to the right, is a black and white shot of a mother kneeling next to a small child underneath a sign that reads "Vietnam." Immediately after Joker's banishment the scene abruptly cuts to the roaring helicopter where a psychotic soldier shoots Vietnamese women and children on the ground for sport.

Kubrick's background score presents other forms of innocence, denial, and delusion. Even pop music that purports to be knowing and cynical contributes to a numbing of individual awareness without which, Jung believed, societies could not change. If psychological introspection really is the only way to advance the species, then incessant noise may finish us off before we resort to nuclear weapons. The subtext of the songs in *Full Metal Jacket* "shines" for those who can still hear and see. Each song matches or counterpoints its context. Kubrick explained that the songs were selected for histor-ical accuracy (1962–1968) and for content "that played well with a scene."[50] The Nancy Sinatra song "These Boots Are Made for Walking" (1966) starts during the black screen dividing Pyle's sprawled body from the bright sun of a Saigon street. The downward drone of an electric guitar and soft drumbeats last for sixteen seconds while pedestrians and motorbikes swirl by. The hard beats start when a prostitute starts walking toward Joker and Rafterman seated at a café table. In perfect rhythm with the drumbeat, all of her move-ments resemble animal display—from her body-flaunting march to her walk-ing in place as they haggle about a price.[51]

Then, after stealing Rafterman's camera, a young Vietnamese performs a karate display before jumping on the back of his friend's motorcycle, as if to deter Joker and Rafterman from pursuit. Joker appreciatively apes the thief in the same way he mocks macho aggression with his John Wayne imitation. As the thieves zoom off, a white-uniformed traffic officer on a square platform above a traffic island waves his arms to maintain the orderly flow of traffic. The image is nicely ironic since the thief's aggressive display, like the war, nullifies morality and law. The policeman's waving parallels that of the "criminal" as well as Joker's imitation—civil restraint, untamed violence, and the artist's satirical mimesis are reflected simultaneously in this sequence, just as they are in the film as a whole. Joker's mockery shows his distance from the knee-jerk aggression implicit in the song's threat to "walk over" an un-faithful lover. Considering the eventual outcome of the war, it is not certain who is being walked over. The only thing certain is that every war is a set-back for humanity.

The next song, "Chapel of Love" (Dixie Cups, 1964), plaintively asserts love and proposes marriage, while playing under a bunkhouse scene where Joker and the other "grunts" exchange insults over which of them is a vir-gin to combat.[52] Another *Stars and Stripes* reporter, Payback, looks up from a sex magazine as he responds to Joker's complaint about the boredom of inaction and his desire to "get back in the shit": "Joker thinks the bad bush is between an old mama-san's legs." When the reporters realize that the booms they hear are incoming shells of the Tet Offensive rather than the fireworks of the Tet holiday, they grab their rifles and run to the front line. This is Joker's initiation to the violence he said he craved: "A! I hope they're just fuckin' with us. I ain't ready for this shit." By ending when the alarm siren drowns it out, "Chapel of Love" sets up a Strangelovian gag: Joker wanted real fireworks, and after the shooting stops he has had his honeymoon. Until the final showdown with Animal Mother over the dy-ing sniper, Joker is married to war.

The sex-violence joke continues in "Wooly Bully" (Sam the Sham and the Pharaohs, 1962), the song that plays during Joker's confrontation with Animal Mother.[53] In his later work Freud reversed his original belief that aggression was sexually based: "The tendency to aggression is an innate, independent, instinctual disposition in man . . . [that] opposes the program of civilization."[54] When Joker is reunited with Cowboy, he immediately gains status in the unit as a journalist who can make them "famous." Sensing that Joker is another alpha figure who might challenge his dominance, Animal assumes the "crazy-brave" persona that has made him valuable to the group. Their "dance" to the background strains of "Wooly Bully" echoes the apes' leaping display at the water hole in 2001.

In the song, Matty told Hatty about something with two big horns and a wooly jaw. The horns are suggested by the winged pagoda that looms over Animal's head. Its fluted surface echoes the bullets on the "bully's" bandolier and on the back of his helmet with its hanging straps that symmetrically frame his face. Before each verse the guitars pound an introductory crescendo. At the end of the speech by the soldier who keeps the enemy corpse, the notes ascend again, but this time they are followed by the rumble of tanks in an abrupt cut to the next scene. The aggressive instinct has made its usual transition from words ("I'll git ya!") to acts, when the marines advance with rifles at the ready and the tanks belch fire.

After the Battle of Hue, the song "Surfin' Bird" (Trashmen, 1963) suggests a transition from apocalyptic action to entropic noise signaling the end of music, language, and civilization. The lyrics consist almost entirely of nonsense syllables. Kubrick said he selected the song because it expressed satiation. After accomplishing two kills, the face of the marine who kept the corpse is "euphoric . . . and so he's got this look on his face, and suddenly the music starts and the tanks are rolling and the marines are mopping up."[55] During the news interview the "bird" is the pea-green chopper that ferries off the wounded. But the colloquial metaphor becomes a thematic one when a tank's gunfire begins just as the song's last verse descends to a lip-gurgling finale.[56]

The song plays under the dialogue when the marines claim their roles (John Wayne, General Custer, etc.), but after Animal Mother says, "We'll let the gooks play the Indians," its "words" are replaced by the loud whirr of the ascending "bird" as the scene ends. The sequence is identical to the replacement of "Wooly Bully" by tank fire between DVD chapters 24 and 25. Words descend to animal-cry lyrics before disappearing altogether in the exultant roar of mechanical "progress," as if the ape's bone in 2001 now has a voice. (Kubrick's dry response to the Rolling Stone interviewer's enthusiasm is worth noting: Cahill: "Of the music in the film, I'd have to say I'm partial to Sam the Sham's 'Wooly Bully,' which is one of the great party records of all time. And 'Surfin' Bird.'" Kubrick: "An amazing piece, isn't it?")[57]

The film's last song, The Rolling Stones' "Paint It, Black" (1966), plays under a ten-second black screen after the last scene and continues through the credits:

> I see a red door and I want it painted black,
> No colors anymore I want them to turn black.
> I see the girls walk by dressed in their summer clothes,
> I have to turn my head until my darkness goes.
> I look inside myself and see my heart is black.
> I see my red door and it has been painted black.
> Maybe then I'll fade away and not have to face the facts.
> It's not easy facin' up when your whole world is black.[58]

While the black screens in *2001* suggested progress, this song seems to imply regression. The lyrics are about inner darkness welling up to destroy subtle shades of thought and feeling. But in *2001* black preceded advance, and unlike "Surfin' Bird," "Paint It, Black" contains insight, poetry, melody, and rhythm. Kubrick's vision from *Strangelove* on makes a connection between personal humiliation and an infantile rage to destroy the world. In Kubrick's concluding image, the marines march off into the sunset as Joker, in his final voice-over, says that though he "is in a world of shit," he is "not afraid." In "Paint It, Black" Jagger and Richards put it this way: "If I look hard enough into the settin' sun, / My love will laugh with me before the mornin' comes." Despite a strong desire for denial, the singer cannot turn away from self-knowledge.

From his first appearance in the film, Rafterman's incorrigible innocence makes denial irrelevant. As a photographer he can absorb, but he cannot filter or interpret. When Rafterman first appears, he is seated next to Joker at a street café table in Saigon in the first Vietnam scene following the basic training sequence. The prostitute's greeting defines both marines, "Hi, baby!" and her English come-on sounds like baby talk— "suckee, suckee" and "me love you long time." Then in haggling over the price, Joker complains that "five dollars is all my mom allows me to spend." But the girl is also a child and stifles a cough throughout the scene. In an aside Joker tells Rafterman that half the prostitutes in the country have TB and the other half serve South Vietnamese officers. As expendable tools the marines too are in imminent danger. The prostitute echoes the come-on that has brought them to Vietnam: if you give Uncle Sam what he wants, he will "love you long time."

Rafterman continually sucks on Marlboros, a cigarette distinguished by its cowboy icon, "the Marlboro Man," a John Wayne variant. Joker does not smoke and needs neither a macho image nor a patriotic conviction to make him feel safe. The two mirror antithetical recipients of the story. Rafterman is the successfully socialized "normal" child, conscientiously carrying out his assignment as he picks up his camera and motions Joker and the girl to pose together. When his camera is stripped from him by the Vietnamese teenager, he looks surprised because, as he complains in the next scene, he thought he had come to Vietnam "to help these people." His inability to protect his "camera" foreshadows the dehumanizing effect of the combat pictures he continually snaps. In the next chapter he and Joker pass a group of marines standing in a circle tossing a basketball, a detail that advances the fairy-tale motif of children in peril. Rafterman complains that he hates his nickname and wants the "trigger time" his training promised: "I wanna get into the shit."[59]

Although adolescents usually have a hard time imagining their own mortality, Joker already has an inkling of what they will witness later. But he does not realize that Rafterman will suffer a different kind of death than the one he tries to protect him from: "If you get killed, your mom will find me after I rotate back to the world and she'll beat the shit out of me." Though his bones do not splinter and his blood does not spurt, the person that Rafterman was disappears. In the reporters' hutch, one of the correspondents, Payback, tells Rafterman that Joker has "never been in the shit" because his eyes don't reveal the evacuation of mind and feeling that real tough guys have: "He ain't got the . . . thousand-yard stare. . . . It's like you've really seen beyond. I got it. All field Marines got it. You'll have it too." Rafterman replies ingenuously, "I will?"[60] Payback is unwittingly right about both Rafterman and Joker. By the end of the film Rafterman has passed "beyond" the bounds of civilized illusion, while Joker, showing equal courage, keeps his soul in his body and never gets the stare.

After being banished by Lieutenant Lockhart, Joker and Rafterman are ferried into the combat zone on a chopper. Its door gunner fires for sport at fleeing civilians on the ground, chanting "git some, git some, c'mon, c'mon" using the same words and rhythm as "Wooly Bully." When Joker asks him, "How can you shoot women and children?" Rafterman stifles an urge to vomit, as if to suggest revulsion though he may only be airsick. The gunner's response is memorable: "Easy, you just don't lead 'em so much."[61] Kubrick told coscreenwriter Michael Herr that the language of the film should aim for "poetic truth" rather than naturalism, that it should have a fabulous quality. In this case the words were ready-made. Although the gunner's line is worthy of an ogre, Herr referred to it as a "famous" commonplace among the grunts.[62]

As the hero of the fable Joker is not shaken by what he hears and sees. He instinctively refrains from judgment as he gathers experience and strength. Kubrick cut the preliminary screenplay version of the scene where Joker as a more conventional hero kills two South Vietnamese officers who throw Vietcong captives out of the helicopter.[63] In the final version Joker grows into his story gradually. Kubrick opens Joker's eyes as if he were adjusting a camera lens. They are still not fully open when the film ends. Conversely, Rafterman's mind is incorrigibly closed from the start. He diligently photographs dead civilian bodies and snaps off a series of shots of the marine who keeps the body of the dead "NVA gook" as if he were a go-getting paparazzo.[64] These sights do not diminish his programmed patriotism. When the marines look down into a pit holding two dead comrades, Rafterman is the only one who can fall back on slogans: "Well at least they died for a good cause . . . freedom."[65]

In the shit, however, Rafterman talks the talk and walks the walk. His scary aspect in the final scene does not stem from the fact that he finally gets his kill, but from his high-pitched exultation. Aping Cowboy's riff on the Lusthog Squad, Rafterman boasts, "Am I a life-taker? Am I a heartbreaker?"[66] Seen in profile with his knees bent and his rifle extended from his groin, he grotesquely thrusts his pelvis in and out as he crows, "I saved Joker's ass. I got the sniper. I fucking blew her away."[67] Kubrick may have adapted this image of displaced sexuality from a verbal hint in the preliminary screenplay during further action after the sniper's death: "Several artillery rounds crash into the ruins, raising a pillar of smoke. 'Lookit! Lookit that!' Rafterman says. 'That's sex! That's pure sex!'"[68] His line praising Joker for sharing in the glory of his kill—"Joker, we're going to have to put you up for the Congressional Medal of . . . ugly"—is delivered in a grotesque falsetto bleat that aurally reflects a memorable comment made by Gustav Hasford in *The Short-Timers*: "The ugly that civilians choose to see in war focuses on spilled guts. To see human beings clearly, that is ugly. To carry death in your smile, that is ugly. War is ugly because the truth can be ugly and war is very sincere."[69]

But since *Full Metal Jacket* is not an antiwar film, per se, and because it is about the duality rather than the ugliness of man, it includes much that is beautiful. Kubrick was fascinated by the emergence of the best human traits in situations that the worst traits have brought about:

> There are obviously elements in a war film that involve visual spectacle, courage, loyalty, affection, self-sacrifice, and adventure, and these things tend

to complicate any anti-war message. War memoirs show us that many of the men who aren't destroyed by the horror and stresses of combat, at least in retrospect, view their participation in the war as the greatest moments of their lives. Didn't General Robert E. Lee say, "It is fortunate that war is so terrible or we should grow very fond of it?"[70]

As Kubrick told Gene Siskel, the ugliest human being in the film is the helicopter door gunner.[71] But the visual imagery before and after he brags of his kills—157 dead gooks and fifty water buffalo—is the most beautiful in the film. Though Lieutenant Lockhart has banished Joker and Rafterman to the shit, the small black shadow of the helicopter, seen from the helicopter door, initially passes over a landscape of green jungle vegetation under a slate blue sky with gray-blue mountains in the background. The "bird" is literally a shadow when we first see it, a black harbinger of death as it passes through a frame that is rose pink and slate blue from the early morning light. At 58:42 the large white sphere of the sun is three-quarters visible as it appears at the center of the frame, rising above the blue clouds.[72]

As the helicopter crosses the sun, its windows are illuminated like those of the various spacecraft in 2001. As the descent begins the point of view shifts to within, echoing Bowman's descent into Jupiter space and the opening shot of The Shining. Encroaching shadows adumbrate discoveries on the

Figure 6.3. The helicopter carries both Joker and a door gunner who shoots women and children for sport. In this shot their duality is reflected by the ominous black chopper passing through the luminous blue sky. *Courtesy of Warner Bros./Photofest © Warner Bros.*

ground. Just before the cut to Rafterman's sickened face, a large shaded area in the clouds and a view of the horizon suggest duality: Exactly one-half of the tree rim on the right side is brightly illuminated, while the left half is entirely black. Upon landing Joker and Rafterman enter a strangely beautiful scene. As they run through high golden grass, the background is lit by pink-orange flames under a slate blue sky matching the colors of the sky in the preceding scene.

Continuing the same paradox, Crazy Earl, the marine who kept the corpse of the dead North Vietnamese soldier, is blown up by a booby-trapped white rabbit. Certainly Crazy is one of the ugliest characters in the film, but the subsequent efforts to save and protect him by Doc Jay, Cowboy, and Joker have a beautiful quality that is reinforced by the aesthetics of the scene. At 1:27:23 the three marines on either side of the dying man form a symmetrical tableau with Cowboy and Joker kneeling on either side of Doc who is just below them in the center, desperately applying CPR. The "life-takers" are now intently affirming life. They are framed by the vertical walls of two bombed-out buildings, and their three helmets form a perfect triangle. The early morning light shines directly on Doc's helmet in the center as he attempts to infuse life, while Crazy's helmet lies directly in front of him to the right. Behind them orange and gold fires send up slate blue smoke under a white sky. The scene's subject and coloring resemble the action paintings of J. M. W. Turner.[73]

Kubrick's emphasis on heroic altruism recurs in the scene where Doc Jay goes out to tend to the mortally wounded Eightball against Cowboy's order. After Doc is fatally shot, Animal Mother charges out to the wounded men, again defying Cowboy. Gene Siskel considered Animal Mother to be the most contradictory character in the film: "We find ourselves cheering Animal's bravery . . . even though we [initially] despise the sight of him, covered in bandoliers of bullets." Kubrick responded, "Courage is appealing, isn't it." Later in the interview he added, "I don't see the characters in the story in terms of good or evil, but in terms of good *and* evil. The only character in the story who seems absolutely beyond the pale is the helicopter door-gunner."[74]

When Joker says that they "can't just leave" the dying sniper for the rats, Animal's alpha instinct to preserve dominance takes over: "Hey, asshole, Cowboy's wasted. You're fresh out of friends. I'm runnin' this squad now. I say we leave the gook for the mother-lovin' rats." Seeking the support of the other marines and free from civilized restraints, Animal intuitively voices the emotional justice of revenge. But Joker's residual hatred for the sniper vanishes as quickly as it arose. As the only character with whom the audience can identify and as the narrator, Joker represents an evolution toward empathy and a refusal to add to the atrocities he has seen. His reply actualizes John Wayne courage even as it augurs a mature and humane intelligence: "I'm not tryin' to run this squad. I'm just sayin' we can't leave her like this."[75]

The scene in the preliminary screenplay is significantly different. There Animal does not initially object, "I don't care. Go on and waste her." At first Joker refuses, but the sniper's persistent begging prompts him to go ahead and fire. After another marine praises Joker for being "one hard dude," Animal is infuriated. First, he beheads the sniper's corpse: "Rest in pieces, bitch." Then he thrusts the head into the face of each marine, saying, "Now who's hard, motherfuckers?" Finally, with Freudian precision he puts his machine gun over his shoulders and walks directly to Joker. "Nobody shits on the Animal, motherfucker. Nobody."[76] By removing Animal's response from the finished film, Kubrick deprived the killer ape of the last word. The highlighting of Joker's eyes as he prepares to shoot suggests a crucial transformation. As Penelope Gilliatt put it, "We seem to be watching the passage of a lifetime's sensibility."[77] Even though Joker proves that he is hard, he does not become ugly. The paradoxical act of mercy killing shows that his feelings remain.

The object of Joker's compassion has a far more important role in the film than she did in the screenplay where she falls dead from a rooftop immediately after Rafterman kills her. The scenario describes her as "a young girl, no more than seventeen years old, a slender Eurasian angel with dark, beautiful eyes, which, at the same time are the hard eyes of a grunt."[78] In the finished film the sniper's eyes are hard only when she is firing at Joker inside the building. Otherwise they are wide with shock, fear, and pain. As an outsider and underdog, she echoes Pyle, whose marksmanship had been praised by Hartman as the one thing he did well. And despite the devastation she wreaks upon the squad, the audience cannot help but be impressed by her cool nerve, especially after she is revealed to be a woman.

Every preceding reference to women has reduced them to a sexual function, beginning with Hartman's initial compliment to Joker just before he punches him in the stomach: "You can come over to my house and fuck my sister." The line is actualized when a pimp on a motorcycle offers the heartbreakers a girl who appears to be about fifteen.[79] In the barracks women were part of the blur of "amphibian shit" that the marines were made to believe they could transcend. But even though his dying words are "I can hack it," Cowboy's body involuntarily trembles while blood and saliva flow from his mouth. Before Joker shoots the sniper, Animal says, "fuck her" and "waste her." To die is to be fucked or turned into shit. But the sniper dies at her own request, retaining the human dignity that Joker, her partner in the film's thematic battle, preserves. Kubrick did the same for the audience by keeping Joker alive at the film's end, contrary to the original plan to begin and end the story with his death.

Kubrick's satire is protective of the viewers and unmerciful to his targets. One reviewer put it this way: "*Full Metal Jacket* finds Stanley Kubrick behind the lens with lethal intent, camera locked, loaded, and ready to fire."[80] Before we see the sniper, the film makes us want to destroy an instrument of death. Once she appears, our sympathies are reversed. We do not realize she is a woman until, braids flying out to the sides, she makes a balletic, slow-motion pivot toward Joker. Her black shirt and a black and white checked scarf enhance her beauty. Suddenly, the ugliness of aggression has become the beauty of the good fight. She has not been trained to be a killer, and she has not been reduced to a uniformed tool. Kubrick transmits her fortitude directly into Joker, enabling him to break Animal's primitive hold.

After the sniper shoots Cowboy, a burning building appears just as the marines reverse their focus from killing to preserving life.[81] Its shape recalls *2001*'s monolith, though Kubrick denied a conscious insertion, calling the resemblance "an extraordinary accident."[82] In any case the building appears so emphatically and enduringly in Cowboy's death scene that no thoughtful viewer can ignore it. The flames on its right side are insignificant in themselves, since fire and smoke are visible in every scene after the door gunner says, "Ain't war hell?" Here, however, the burning building is the only source of light in a scene that is emotionally gripping and visually beautiful. While the building burns in the center of the frame, its flames are surreally reflected by a miniature fire that appears to be burning inside Joker's left upper arm as he cradles Cowboy. It shifts to cover Joker's heart as he gently lays his best friend down. When his head is over Cowboy's face, the bull's-eye on the left side of his helmet is centered in the frame directly over a magnified pair of binoculars under his arm. The bull's-eye recalls the eye of Joker's flashlight that appeared on Hartman's door just before Pyle's suicide, and like both Pyle and Hartman, Cowboy dies blindly.

Following an ironic pietà, the building remains visible for fifteen seconds as the marines rise ritually, one by one. For a moment it disappears as Animal comes around the corner to join them, but then it reappears for twenty-nine seconds, centered between the four marines now standing with their heads bowed. It disappears for a final time just before a head and shoulders shot of Animal centers the word "Death" on his helmet, as he says, "Let's go get some payback."

The next shot shows Joker slowly lifting his head and modulating his expression from sorrow to resolve, "OK." The word "Kill" is now seen on *his* helmet, and when the marines approach the sniper they form a line that re-sembles the apes' sneak-up on the water hole as Animal, like Moonwatcher, turns and waves them on. It seems that enlightenment will have to wait as long as mankind agrees to become Death. But that does not mean that change will never come to the species, and that it cannot occur now in the individual. In the final scene numerous marines, including Joker and Rafter-man, appear as dark shadows marching toward the sunset through a fiery night. As they pass, two more buildings burn under a patch of blue sky.[83] Then the sky lightens until the buildings are fully lit by a large bright fire at the base of the one on the right.

Hartman's constant degradation of women had unconsciously aimed to drive the recruits back from genital desire to the anal pleasures of explosive release: "You will give your rifle a girl's name, because this is only pussy you people are going to get. Your days of finger banging old Mary Jane Rotten-crotch through her purty pink panties are over! You're married to this piece, this weapon of iron and wood, and you *will* be faithful!"[84] His barrage suc-ceeds with Pyle and Rafterman but fails with Joker. The triumph of sexuality over perverse violence, Eros over Thanatos, is part of the hopeful quality of the film's last speech. The "monoliths" burn brightly in the center of the frame just as Joker says,

> My thoughts drift back to erect-nipple wet dreams
> About Mary Jane Rottencrotch
> And the great homecoming fuck fantasy.
> I am so happy that I am alive,
> In one piece.
> And sure—
> I'm in a world of shit,
> Yes,
> But I am alive,
> And I am not afraid.[85]

Notes

1. Michael Herr, foreword to *Full Metal Jacket: The Screenplay*, by Stanley Kubrick and Michael Herr (New York: Alfred A. Knopf, 1987), v.

2. Stanley Kubrick, quoted by Penelope Gilliatt, "Mankind on the Late, Late Show," *Observer* (London), September 6, 1987.

3. Stanley Kubrick, quoted by Gene Siskel, "Candidly Kubrick," *Chicago Tribune*, June 21, 1987; repr. in *Stanley Kubrick: Interviews*, ed. Gene D. Phillips (Jackson: University Press of Mississippi), 184.

4. *Full Metal Jacket*, DVD, directed by Stanley Kubrick (1987; Burbank, Calif.: Warner Bros. Home Video, 2001), chapter 22.

5. Carl G. Jung, *The Undiscovered Self* (New York: New American Library, 1957), 110–111.

6. Sigmund Freud, *Civilization and Its Discontents*, ed. and trans. James Strachey (1930; New York: W. W. Norton, 1962), 47.

7. *Dr. Strangelove*, DVD, directed by Stanley Kubrick (1964; Burbank, Calif.: Warner Bros. Home Video, 2001), chapters 4, 22.

8. *Dr. Strangelove*, DVD, chapter 21.

9. See Michael Herr, *Kubrick* (New York: Grove Press, 2000), 45.

10. *Full Metal Jacket*, DVD, chapter 2.

11. Freud, *Civilization and its Discontents*, 47n.

12. *Full Metal Jacket*, DVD, chapter 7.

13. *Full Metal Jacket*, DVD, chapter 8.

14. See Vincent LoBrutto, *Stanley Kubrick: A Biography* (New York: Donald I. Fine, 1997), 465; and Matthew Modine, *Full Metal Jacket Diary* (New York: Rugged Land, 2005), 55.

15. *Full Metal Jacket*, DVD, chapter 9.

16. Kubrick, quoted by Penelope Gilliatt, "Mankind on the Late, Late Show."

17. *Full Metal Jacket*, DVD, chapter 13.

18. See Alexander Walker, Sybil Taylor, and Ulrich Ruchti, *Stanley Kubrick, Director: A Visual Analysis* (New York: W. W. Norton, 1999), 330.

19. *Full Metal Jacket*, DVD, chapter 14.

20. *Full Metal Jacket*, DVD, chapter 37.

21. According to a colleague, however, Oppenheimer actually said, "Now we're all sons-of-bitches." See Judith Flanders, "When Pink Was Far from Rosy," review of *American Prometheus: The Triumph and Tragedy of J. Robert Oppenheimer*, by Kai Bird and Martin J. Sherwin, *Spectator* (London), January 23, 2008.

22. *Full Metal Jacket*, DVD, chapter 23.

23. The preliminary 1985 version, "Full Metal Jacket: A Screenplay: Based on *The Short-Timers*, by Gustav Hasford," by Stanley Kubrick and Michael Herr, has been posted on the Kubrick site by its webmaster, Roderick Munday. It is a facsimile 8½ × 11 inch photocopy of the original. See the Kubrick site, www.visual-memory.co.uk/amk/doc/0065.html.

24. *Full Metal Jacket*, DVD, chapter 18.

25. Kubrick and Herr, "Full Metal Jacket: A Screenplay," the Kubrick site.

26. *Sands of Iwo Jima*, DVD, directed by Allan Dwan (1949; Vancouver, British Columbia: Lions Gate Home Entertainment, 1998).

27. *An Officer and a Gentleman*, DVD, directed by Taylor Hackford (1981; Hollywood, Calif.: Paramount Pictures, 2000).

28. Tim Cahill, "The *Rolling Stone* Interview: Stanley Kubrick," *Rolling Stone*, August 27, 1987; repr. in Phillips, ed., *Stanley Kubrick: Interviews*, 198.

29. Michael Herr, *Dispatches* (New York: Alfred A. Knopf, 1977), 169.

30. Mark Baker, *Nam: The Vietnam War in the Words of the Men and Women Who Fought There* (New York: Quill, 1981), 12.

31. See Chester A. Yosarian, "The United States Army's Green Berets: History Re-evaluated, Corrected, and Respected," 1996, at earthllink.net/~ amerwar/.

32. *The Green Berets*, DVD, directed by John Wayne and Ray Kellogg (1968; Burbank, Calif.: Warner Bros. Home Video, 1997).

33. Kubrick and Herr, "Full Metal Jacket: A Screenplay," the Kubrick site.

34. See Yosarian, "The United States Army's Green Berets," earthllink.net/~ amerwar/.

35. Kubrick and Herr, "Full Metal Jacket: A Screenplay," the Kubrick site.

36. *Full Metal Jacket*, DVD, chapter 2.

37. *Full Metal Jacket*, DVD, chapter 27.

38. The term "gook" came from "goo-goo," as applied to people of the Philippines by American troops in 1915; see Richard Drinnon, *Facing West: The Metaphysics of Indian-Hating and Empire-Building* (New York: New American Library, 1980), 455.

39. Richard Hammer, *The Court-Martial of Lt. Calley* (New York: Coward, McCann & Geoghegan, 1971), 391–392; quoted by Drinnon, *Facing West*, 456.

40. *Full Metal Jacket*, DVD, chapter 24.

41. *Interviews with My Lai Veterans*, written and directed by Joseph Strick (Los Angeles: Laser Film Corporation, 1970); see Drinnon, *Facing West*, 456–457.

42. Quoted by Ralph Andrist, *The Long Death: The Last Days of the Plains Indians* (New York: Macmillan, 1993), 90–91; on Kubrick's use of Native American motifs in *The Shining*, see Bill Blakemore, "The Family of Man," *San Francisco Chronicle*, July 29, 1987.

43. *Full Metal Jacket*, DVD, chapter 17.

44. See "The Biography of a Mouse," www.mickey-mouse.com/themouse.htm.

45. *Full Metal Jacket*, DVD, chapter 19.

46. Kubrick and Herr, "Full Metal Jacket: A Screenplay," the Kubrick site.

47. See *Beetle Bailey*, King Features website, and "*Beetle Bailey* at 50," *Jefferson City News Tribune*, September 6, 2000, www.newstribune.com/archives/.

48. See John Vogel, "Plot Summary for the *Phil Silvers Show* (1955)," Internet Move Database, www.imdb.com/title/tt0047763/plotsummary.

49. See "Charlie McCarthy: Welcome to Snerdville," www.snerdville.com/characters.htm.

50. Kubrick, interview by Cahill, in Phillips, ed., *Stanley Kubrick: Interviews*, 193.

51. *Full Metal Jacket*, DVD, chapter 16.

52. *Full Metal Jacket*, DVD, chapter 18.

53. *Full Metal Jacket*, DVD, chapter 23.

54. Sigmund Freud, *Beyond the Pleasure Principle*, ed. and trans. James Strachey (1920; New York: W. W. Norton, 1990); quoted by Robert Ardrey, *The Territorial Imperative* (New York: Atheneum, 1966), 294.

55. Kubrick, interview by Cahill, in Phillips, ed., *Stanley Kubrick: Interviews*, 193.

56. *Full Metal Jacket*, DVD, chapter 27.

57. Kubrick, interview by Cahill, in Phillips, ed., *Stanley Kubrick: Interviews*, 193.

58. Mick Jagger and Keith Richards, "Paint It, Black," 1966, Renewed, ABKCO Music, Ltd., www.abkco.com.

59. *Full Metal Jacket*, DVD, chapter 17.

60. *Full Metal Jacket*, DVD, chapter 18.

61. *Full Metal Jacket*, DVD, chapter 20.

62. Herr, *Dispatches*, 35.

63. Kubrick and Herr, "Full Metal Jacket: A Screenplay," the Kubrick site.

64. *Full Metal Jacket*, DVD, chapter 24.

65. *Full Metal Jacket*, DVD, chapter 28.

66. *Full Metal Jacket*, DVD, chapter 23.

67. *Full Metal Jacket*, DVD, chapter 37.

68. Kubrick and Herr, "Full Metal Jacket: A Screenplay," the Kubrick site.

69. Gustav Hasford, *The Short-Timers* (New York: Bantam, 1979), 175–176.

70. Kubrick, quoted by Siskel, in Phillips, ed., *Stanley Kubrick: Interviews*, 186.

71. Kubrick, quoted by Siskel, in Phillips, ed., *Stanley Kubrick: Interviews*, 187.

72. *Full Metal Jacket*, DVD, chapter 20.

73. *Full Metal Jacket*, DVD, chapter 31.

74. Kubrick, quoted by Siskel, in Phillips, ed., *Stanley Kubrick: Interviews*, 182, 187.

75. *Full Metal Jacket*, DVD, chapter 37.

76. Kubrick and Herr, "Full Metal Jacket: A Screenplay," the Kubrick site.

77. Gilliatt, "Mankind on the Late, Late Show."

78. Kubrick and Herr, "Full Metal Jacket: A Screenplay," the Kubrick site.

79. *Full Metal Jacket*, DVD, chapter 30.

80. Rita Kempley, Review of *Full Metal Jacket*, *Washington Post*, June 26, 1987.

81. *Full Metal Jacket*, DVD, chapter 35.

82. Kubrick, interview by Cahill, in Phillips, ed., *Stanley Kubrick: Interviews*, 194; see also Walker, Taylor, and Ruchti, *Stanley Kubrick, Director*, 340.

83. *Full Metal Jacket*, DVD, chapter 38.

84. *Full Metal Jacket*, DVD, chapter 4.

85. *Full Metal Jacket*, DVD, chapter 38.

~

CHAPTER SEVEN

Directing Dreams

Eyes Wide Shut

Michel Chion, Alexander Walker, and Mario Falsetto have commented briefly on Kubrick's use of color. Chion observes that "white is everywhere" in Kubrick's films, and though he says it is important he does not say why. His only specific observations apply to *2001*, where red represents the interior of the human body and black brings out "the immensity of the void."[1] Walker also highlights white and red. In *2001* HAL's red eye is "the traditional color of an alarm signal," and red is "an ominous and magical illumination" that suffuses the screen as Bowman disconnects HAL.[2] Red is also the "keynote" of *Eyes Wide Shut* where it indicates "various moods," though only one is specified: in the lobby of Victor's apartment, red suggests that Bill is "entering a furnace that will consume him." *The Shining* also has a "blood red" keynote, though the blizzard at the end is a "whiteout" in keeping with the murderous tone. In *A Clockwork Orange* Walker feels that white "signals danger" and is so dominant that "the film would lose nothing if shot in monochrome." In *Barry Lyndon* Walker limits white to its representation of Barry's cold marriage.[3] Except for an additional observation that green and white combine to create the "eerie yet tranquil" atmosphere of the bedroom at the end of *2001*, Walker does not comment further on specific colors.

Mario Falsetto offers an extensive description of the "highly determined color scheme" in *Eyes Wide Shut*, such as in the party scene at Ziegler's mansion: "the golden hues of the downstairs public spaces" in contrast to the "colder gray/blue tones of the private space" of the upstairs bathroom; the "precise use" of red and green in the Christmas decorations; the "excessive lighting" of "thousands of tiny lights [in] the party space"; and, in the orgy scene, the blue iron gates, the black-cloaked male guests, Red Robe's crimson outfit, and the gold paint of the rooms. In the climactic scene in Ziegler's study, he finds the red pool table "so conspicuous that one could jokingly claim it is the main character." For Falsetto the film's intricate color patterns reinforce "a poetic rendering of Bill's consciousness and often stand in for his emotions."[4] Though he does not read meaning into the colors of particular scenes, he does quote a comment by Federico Fellini suggesting that color may be more than mood: "Colors in a dream [in *Juliet of the Spirits*] are concepts, not approximations or memories. . . . In a dream color is the idea, the concept, the feeling, just as it is in a truly great painting."[5]

That critics have not delved more deeply into Kubrick's use of color is surprising, since he was as much a cinematographer as a director, and after *2001* he was renowned for scientific interests that directly affected his filmmaking. The metaphor of color as complexity of mind has a physiological basis. Color has no objective existence. It is created by the perceiving eye. Dogs, for example, see only in black and white. The colors of the spectrum perceived by human beings emerge when light strikes the eye, producing a chemical change in the liquid that covers the retina. In the case of color, what we are determines what we see. *2001* uses color to express evolution. The film's opening sequence has few bright colors, while the closing sequence contains a rapid transformation of virtually every color visible to the human eye. Using the monolith as key, black is the color of evolutionary potential throughout the film. (For Jung, black was the "germinal phase of all processes.")[6] A three-minute overture of black screen precedes the rising sun over the crescent moon, the opening title, and the ascending notes from Richard Strauss's *Also Sprach Zarathustra*.

Then, after the title, the screen remains black for fifteen seconds before we see the bright orange sun rising over the still benighted desert.[7] This orange becomes the symbol of pure energy that propels the natural world, an orange arising from black potentiality, preceding a serene blue intelligence that appears most strikingly in the steady eyes of David Bowman and the larger than human eyes of the Star Child. (Studies have shown red-orange to be the most exciting color to the nerves of the eye, while blue and orange are harmonious, complementary opposites on the standard color wheel, first devised by Michel Chevreul.)[8] In the film's final section, "Jupiter and Beyond the Infinite," the black monolith becomes dark blue as it guides Dave closer and closer to a transfiguring rebirth.[9] (Wassily Kandinsky felt that "the darker the shade [of blue] the stronger is its call into the Infinite, the stronger is the yearning for . . . the Transcendental.")[10]

When the mature David Bowman walks from the bathroom toward his "last supper" just prior to his own transcendence in the alien room, he wears a square-shouldered black robe and holds his arms straight down at his sides, resembling the monolith,[11] and recalling Kubrick's comment that the monolith's element of travel was "inner space."[12] In *Eyes Wide Shut* the emblematic opening shot of Alice dropping her black dress to the floor suggests another version of the monolith. (The same shot is also the inside cover of the DVD.) Then in the opening scenes both she and her husband dress in black until the crucial bedroom scene where they are differentiated as she begins to advance. After Alice angrily accuses Bill of implying that no strange man would talk to her unless he wanted sex, Bill replies that it's not "quite that black and white, but I think we both know what men are like." The rest of the scene and the film will accentuate the irony of this statement, since he is the one who sees the world in simple contrasts. Kubrick uses black and white to express a deeper dichotomy: as in *2001*, black is the symbol of potentiality and growth, while the white of naked bodies in *Eyes Wide Shut* represents regression, initially to infantile pleasure, and ultimately to mental death when Bill leans down as if to kiss the naked corpse of a woman that he mistakenly believes has saved his life.

The black clothing and white nakedness of Bill and Alice at the beginning of the film suggest that the characters are naive and unformed. The antithesis of their blank innocence is the "rainbow" of color that suffuses the film, an image that celebrates complexity of vision, the affirmation of maturity and experience over dangerous illusions. As in *Barry Lyndon*, the most advanced vision available to the spectator is the film as a whole rather than the understanding of any individual character, and Kubrick expresses this by celebrating existence through color, providing an affirmative wisdom that immature egotism cannot see.

Kubrick's association of black with birth and white with death reverses archetypal convention. Sergei Eisenstein had done this in *Alexander Nevsky* where the brave, defending Russians wear black and gray, while the barbaric invading Germans wear white, and although Kubrick considered that film to be a "dishonest" political polemic, he respected Eisenstein's theoretical writings. In a 1959 interview after *Paths of Glory*, he commented that although "the black and white contrasts of *Alexander Nevsky* do not fit all drama," they effectively express conflict in war movies, and that Eisenstein's experimentation with black and white explored "the possibilities of film."[13]

Eisenstein derived his color theory from an analysis of the novels of Nikolay Gogol (1809–1852).[14] In "On Color" he noted that in a realistic novel like *Dead Souls*, color aided characterization, that is, Gogol associated a particular "range of colors" with individual characters. In his fantasy novel, *The Terrible Vengeance*, on the other hand, he used color symbolically, as Kubrick does in adapting Schnitzler's *Dream Story*. Eisenstein added that dramatic conflict in Gogol "shows through in color" and that "the very clash of colors becomes an arena of the struggle."[15]

Coincidentally, Eisenstein's prediction for the future of cinema paralleled Kubrick's development of color in the six films after *Dr. Strangelove*: "From the monkish asceticism of a narrow range of colors—black, gray and white— we are heading rapidly towards a full-blooded palette, a complete rainbow of color." Significant uses of the word "rainbow" occur in *Eyes Wide Shut*'s screenplay, and its visual texture fulfills Eisenstein's hope that the cinema would eventually express "black and white" conflicts (as in his planned film about racial strife starring Paul Robeson) "in all the multicolored diversity of the colors of real life." In *Eyes Wide Shut* the "black and white" division is clear: regressive assertions of dominance versus creative self-awareness, but the colors of "real life," the "intermediate colors" of Gogol's realistic stories, are subordinated to the "palette of pure primary colors" that Eisenstein admired in those works "whose subject matter is fantasy."[16]

Eisenstein credited Gogol with making color "integral to the total visual and aural conception of his subject matter" and applied this idea to the nascent development of color in his own art: "The moving image in color is no mere piece of frivolous amusement but a force capable of profound psychological revelation."[17] Recollections by several of Kubrick's technical collaborators on *Eyes Wide Shut* suggest that Kubrick was aiming to make color provoke an interpretive response. Chester Eyre, the director of operations at the laboratory that developed the film stock, said that Kubrick "had a fixed idea about the color of each sequence, and he would strive with you to obtain that color, even it had no relation to the preceding sequence."[18]

Eyre's concept of "relation" may have been purely formal, and when he says that "Kubrick was always focused on the mood that could be achieved with a certain color," he may have assumed that all directors use color for mood, while Kubrick may actually have been striving to make color "integral . . . to his conception of the subject matter," as Eisenstein put it. Eyre goes on to describe a method of working that lends credence to discerning themes through color relationship, such as black and white, or blue and orange:

> He would look at what had been shot the previous day, mentally adjust the colors, write the specifications on the camera sheets he had given to us, and then request certain color combinations that he'd devised with Larry Smith on the set. Normally it's left to the laboratory to assess the color of the negative. A

filmmaker might ask us to print something a certain way—say, dark and red—but Stanley was asking for specific *combinations* of colors.[19]

Eyes Wide Shut cinematographer Larry Smith implied that Kubrick was using colors that were appropriate for expressionistic fantasy in the same way that Eisenstein believed Gogol used them: "The blue we used was very saturated, much bluer than natural moonlight would be, but we didn't care about that—we just went for a hue that was interesting."[20] A passage from the film's source novel, Arthur Schnitzler's *Dream Story*, suggests a possible origin of Kubrick's "interest": Albertine, the Alice prototype, describes the sky in her dream as "far bluer and more expansive than in the real world."[21] Smith added that "it was an over-the-top blue, but it complemented the orange light very nicely and gave those scenes an intriguing look." (Kubrick was probably aware of Newton's 1666 discovery that light passing through a prism formed a band of color or "spectrum" that he later arranged into a "color wheel." In Chevreul's revision, colors directly opposite each other on the wheel, such as blue and orange, are considered complementary.)[22]

Smith refers to antitheses that ultimately balance each other in the film's complete experience: "If we were dealing with the orange hue, I'd simply dim down the household bulbs to get a warmer feeling. Most of the movie is at either extreme—either very rich and warm, or very blue and cold."[23] The polarities Smith observed correspond to a critical debate over Kubrick's effect and intent. As Smith intuits, Kubrick fostered the "blue" understanding that some feel make his films overly cerebral *and* the "warmer feeling" that many critics have missed. As in psychoanalysis, the impact of a Kubrick film is rigorous, painful, and—ideally—therapeutic.

While Kubrick shared a taste for detachment with storytellers like Shakespeare, Brecht, and Twain, and psychoanalysts like Freud, Jung, and Bettelheim, he may have been further confirmed in following this natural bent by an apparent interest in Eastern philosophy. In 1964 when Arthur C. Clarke first worked with Kubrick on *2001*, he had already been living in Sri Lanka, a primarily Buddhist country, for eight of the fifty-two years he resided there before his death in 2008. Possibly through Clarke, probably through Campbell and Jung, and given his own taste and temperament, Kubrick knew the *Bhagavad Gita* well enough to add two of its most notable passages to *Full Metal Jacket* and *Eyes Wide Shut*. Neither were included by his screenwriters.

The *Bhagavad Gita* is an epic poem in the sixth book of the *Mahabharata*, one of India's most sacred texts, composed and elaborated by anonymous storytellers between 400 BC and AD 400. In *Full Metal Jacket* Kubrick put a phrase from it on Animal Mother's helmet, "I am become Death," and in

Eyes Wide Shut he added a passage in Hindi, spoken over and over again by "Red Robe," the erotic cult leader at the orgy Bill observes: "To protect men of virtue and destroy men who do evil, to set the standard of sacred duty, I appear in age after age."[24] Members of the Hindu community in Britain and the United States were outraged by the placement of the passage in an immoral context. The *Bhagavad Gita* is the Indian "Bible," read devoutly by millions of people and used publicly in India to administer oaths of office and to swear in courtroom witnesses.[25] The objections resulted in the passage being posthumously replaced in the *Eyes Wide Shut* DVD with a bizarre chant that sounds something like the reversed music soundtracks that fundamentalists search to detect satanic blasphemies. The original passage, however, has a significant bearing on the theme of *Eyes Wide Shut* and on Kubrick's overall philosophy. On the surface Kubrick's intent would seem to be simple irony, given the satanic speaker, but the context of the verse suggests the creative purpose that Red Robe counteracts.

In the *Gita* the line is spoken by the god Krishna to the warrior prince Arjuna immediately before the onset of a massive battle. Like Odysseus, Arjuna is a storied archer, and like him he is initially reluctant to go to war. While Odysseus tried to escape conscription because he did not want to leave his family, Arjuna does not want to fight because many of the opposing warriors are his relatives. In both stories the hero learns that he must be psychologically ruthless whether or not he has to physically kill. And at the same time, that ruthlessness preserves his power to be compassionate toward those who must live in a world that alternately depresses and horrifies. Krishna urges Arjuna to follow his example of constant work in the face of eternally recurrent evil.

In *Full Metal Jacket* the words on Animal Mother's helmet partially quote Krishna's definition of himself as the transcendent agent of eternal process: "I am become Death." The whole passage reads, "The Supreme Lord said: I am death, the mighty destroyer of the world, out to destroy. Even without your participation all the warriors standing arrayed in the opposing armies shall cease to exist. Therefore, you get up and attain glory. Conquer your enemies and enjoy a prosperous kingdom. All these [warriors] have already been destroyed by me. You are only an instrument, O Arjuna."[26] In *Full Metal Jacket* Joker must kill to survive, but his compassion is uncorrupted and demonstrated toward Pyle, Rafterman, Cowboy, and the female sniper. His helmet, combining the words "Born to Kill" with a peace symbol, conveys more than just a simple message about the duality of man. It expresses the idea behind Kubrick's desire to make a war film without a political or moral agenda, to consider war as a "phenomenon," as Herr put it.

Taken together the two passages imply that the seeming cruelty of Kubrick's satire kills what must be killed with understanding in order to advance the spirit. The implied philosophy resembles that of the *Odyssey*, and both works significantly diverge from the Christian ideal of turning the other cheek. Buddhist compassion includes reverence for all living things and a recognition that those capable of becoming enlightened must be willing to trust their own integrity and to live without guilt "in a world of shit."

The distance that offends some of Kubrick's critics can be recognized as the hardness necessary to perform the work prescribed by Krishna for Arjuna. Those who receive the satirist's barbs cannot be made worse than they already are, but their vulnerability to exposure and ridicule can hearten others, overwhelmed, as in fairy tales, by gigantic folly: "Your foes . . . are already killed by me. Be just my instrument, the archer at my side."[27] Another archer, Odysseus, encountered giants, multiheaded monsters, and kings whose stupidity was as vast as their power. Part of the fearsomeness of the foe is the seeming universality and inevitability of the evils each generation presents. The individual feels the worthlessness and absurdity of a personal existence and turns away from the specter of merged anonymity (as in Alice's dream of interchangeably fucking couples).[28] This is the nightmare of countless arms, eyes, and mouths that Arjuna sees when he beholds Krishna just before the god identifies himself as the life process, encompassing the manifestation and disappearance of every disparate form.

Another major Eastern myth may inform the second emblematic image of *Eyes Wide Shut*. The picture of Alice on the DVD cover evokes the female role in the creation story of Tantric Buddhism, a legend dating back to the sixth century AD. At the world's beginning the god Shiva and his mistress Shakti are locked in a blissful embrace unconscious of their difference. Their eyes are closed like those of newborn infants or lovers in a state of arousal. But suddenly the earth where they sit begins to shake, causing Shakti to open her eyes for the first time since her creation. The quake in the earth and within Shakti has been triggered by the adversary of the gods, Ravana, trying to escape his imprisonment beneath the sacred mountain, and although Shiva quickly stills the trembling with a mere stamp of his foot, Shakti had felt fear for the first time and was irremediably awake.

Following her separation from Shiva, Shakti assumed the role of Maya, a dancer so skilled that the objects she portrays appear to be solidly real and separate from each other, fascinating Shiva to the point where he forgets that all existence is a unified field and that Maya's creations have no separate reality: "Maya produces the world; she is the mother of our individual, swiftly transitory lives [that] are fraught with sufferings and guilt, shortcomings, cruelty, and absurd infatuations, nevertheless they are unique manifestations of divine energy."[29]

Alice Harford is Kubrick's Maya archetype. Her "foolish infatuation" sets the story in motion and leads to its serious revelations. Maya "expresses [Shiva's] secret nature and unfolds his character."[30] Like Shiva and Shakti, Bill and Alice are initially one, but the seeds of separation are already present in Alice as she articulates a fantasy that shatters the Edenic innocence of their marriage. In the film's first bedroom scene after Victor's party, a close-up profile shot shows Bill and Alice about to kiss. His face is shadowed and his eyes are closed, while her face is illuminated and her right eye warily targets the viewer. The scene takes place in a mirror, and when Alice turns in the midst of a passionate kiss, she looks directly at herself and simultaneously at the audience. The mirroring suggests the self-knowledge that Alice and some spectators instinctively seek. Though the image may provoke simple voyeurism—Nicole Kidman being exposed in a private moment—the psychological context suggests an incipient awareness threatening conventional images of sexual passion, marital bliss, and social status.[31]

Alice's drive to understand herself is especially evident in the second bedroom scene where Kubrick and the screenwriter, Frederic Raphael, significantly changed the motivation and tone of Alice's confession from that of her counterpart in *Dream Story*. Albertine and her husband, Fridolin, tease each other about their flirtations at the party, "exaggerated the extent to

Figure 7.1.   The image in the bedroom mirror evokes the film's title. While Bill's eyes are closed, Alice's stay open, foreshadowing her escape from a constricting role. *Courtesy of Warner Bros./Photofest © Warner Bros.*

which their masked partners had attracted them, made fun of the jealous stir-
rings the other revealed, and lied dismissively about their own." In the film
Bill never admits being attracted to the two seductive models, while Alice
never says (even untruthfully) that she was attracted to the aging roué she
danced with.[32]

While Albertine and Fridolin go on to frankly describe instances of being
attracted to other people, Bill denies flirting with the models, because he "is
married" and because he "would never lie" or "hurt" her. Alice is angrier at
Bill's evasions than she is jealous about anything he actually said or did. She
denies Bill's smug remark that "the pot is making [her] aggressive" and accuses him of hypocrisy, because as she will soon reveal, she herself was so attracted to a stranger on a previous occasion that she almost sacrificed her
marriage for a one-night stand. When she says she only wants "a straight
fucking answer" and that she is "just trying to find out where [he's] coming
from," she voices the film's questioning of the monogamous ideal, a societal
reassurance of the superego's complete control, similarly questioned in each
preceding Kubrick film. On the surface Alice seems to be angry about conveniently male definitions of infidelity: "Millions of years of evolution, right?
Right? Men have to stick it in every place they can, but for women . . . it is
just about security and commitment and whatever the fuck else!" But, as
usual, Kubrick is less concerned with social evolution than with the expansion of inner space.

Kubrick derived the intensity of Oedipal fears in his male characters from
Freud, but the optimistic structure of his films came from Campbell and Jung.
Jung frequently commented on the irony of regarding the biblical fall as a
curse. In 2001 Kubrick portrayed the first weapon as the magic enabler of human emergence. For Jung the myth of Adam and Eve described "the dawn of
consciousness":

> Problems . . . draw us into an orphaned and isolated state where we are aban-
> doned by nature and are driven to consciousness. There is no other way open
> to us; we are forced to resort to conscious decisions and solutions when for-
> merly we trusted ourselves to natural happenings. Every problem, therefore,
> brings the possibility of a widening of consciousness, but also the necessity of
> saying goodbye to childlike unconsciousness and trust in nature.[33]

Jung reads the feminine power to weaken preexisting states of perfection
as the preeminent creative drive. While men fixate on perfection, women
yearn for completeness. Accordingly, he conceives the feminine nature as
fundamentally artistic, capable of the creation of experience that cannot be

absolutely known or understood, that always retains an aura of mystery: "For, just as completeness is always imperfect, so perfection is always incomplete, and therefore represents a final state which is hopelessly sterile. '*Ex perfecto nihil fit*,' say the old masters, whereas the *imperfectum* carries within it the seeds of its own improvement. Perfection always ends in a blind alley, while completeness by itself lacks selective values."[34] Selective values, including Bill's idealized concepts of marital love and fidelity, can lead to evolutionary dead ends, not only for a marriage but for the social contract that Kubrick criticized in Rousseau and satirized in *A Clockwork Orange*.[35]

In the eight-second shot immediately following the three-card black and white opening credits (Cruise-Kidman-Kubrick), and just before the title (*Eyes Wide Shut*), Alice is the emblem of the film itself, a carrier of aesthetic power in the service of evolution. The image is stylized. Seen from behind, Alice has just tried on a black dress in preparation for a Christmas party. She steps gracefully to her right in synch with the recurrent Shostakovich waltz that plays under the credits, slips off the right strap, then the left, pushes the

Figure 7.2. In the emblematic opening shot, Alice disrobes with distinct movements that convey her strength. Her courageous confession and traumatic dream expose the sexual dangers a "liberated" culture denies. *Courtesy of Warner Bros./Photofest © Warner Bros.*

dress off her hips with both hands, kicks out the right leg, then the left, and, standing naked with her legs and arms at symmetrical angles, stands looking down as the image ends. These movements are choreographic—clean and distinct. They establish her strength of character and along with other elements of the image, signal entrance to a work of meticulous design.[36]

Beige room dividers stand in the foreground, each topped by twin Doric columns, suggesting a stage, while in the background tied orange drapes frame a Venetian-blinded window resembling a theater curtain. Their reflection in a full-length mirror at the left is illuminated by an intervening floor lamp, below which two racquetball racquets rest. The mirror and the lamp reiterate a visual motif used in *The Shining* where, in contrast to a mirror of objective realism, Kubrick's cinematic lamp illuminated universal subjectivities.[37] The symbolism of the mirror becomes explicit later when Bill takes a cell phone call from Alice in Domino's apartment in front of a mirror that reflects the title of a book on the table below it: *Studies in the Mirror*.[38]

A second book on Domino's table, *Introduction to Sociology*, is anticipated by the racquets in the opening image. The racquets foreshadow Victor Ziegler's thanking Bill for referring him to an osteopath, "the top man in New York," for a racquetball injury. "Victor" occupies a dominant position in the primate hierarchy of contemporary Manhattan where Bill, like Redmond Barry, occupies a midlevel position. The film means to bring its spectators to an awareness of this mechanical (albeit biological) system, so that they may consciously reject it and avoid becoming dominoes in an alpha game. This necessitates a rigorous process of self-examination, a continual challenge in life that is mirrored microcosmically by the difficult experience of the film itself. Just as Odysseus endured as the sole survivor of his voyage, spectators able to experience the beneficial effects of *Eyes Wide Shut* must endure its slow pace and their frustration when the film does not fulfill sentimental or erotic expectations. Its antiromantic love story masks the artist's love for the "children" he guides, and after a black screen transition that signals growth as in *2001*, a six-second shot of the cold, taxi-filled streets foreshadows the Odyssean necessity of leaving every shelter that succeeds the womb.

While the first shot of Alice showed her standing naked in a brightly lit space, the first shot of Bill reveals him standing in a darkened bedroom alcove, swaddled in his black tux and illuminated only by the cold blue outdoor light that shines through another window, framed again by theatrical orange curtains.[39] While Alice brings hidden realities to light, Bill never emerges from the darkness of his fears and social illusions. Accordingly, the initial lighting visually contrasts the inward capacities of both characters at their entrance.

Eyes Wide Shut continues Kubrick's tendency to focus on the persistence of childish traits in adults. In fact, at the same time he was planning and writing *Eyes Wide Shut*, he was simultaneously working on *A.I.*, his version of *Pinocchio*, about a robot boy who wants to be human so that he can earn his mother's love, and "The Aryan Papers," based on Louis Begley's novel *Wartime Lies*, about a nine-year-old Jewish boy who avoids capture in Nazi-occupied Poland.[40] Kubrick worked on all three films between 1990 and 1995. In addition to featuring actual children such as Danny Torrance, or virtual children such as Pyle and Rafterman, Kubrick depicted a supine Frank Poole in diaperlike white shorts being tended by HAL, while his parents gush over him on a videophone; then there are Alex de Large being nourished by the milk-plus of human cruelty and Redmond Barry tossed between Oedipal rage and filial need. Kubrick also gave Napoleon Oedipal overtones in his obsessive jealousy over Josephine, and the unrealized screenplay began and ended with close-ups of the emperor's childhood teddy bear.[41]

But *Eyes Wide Shut*'s connection between infantile need and sexual obsession is most directly anticipated by *Lolita*. That is the essence of Nabokov's Freudian joke about Humbert's obsession with a female child; it satirizes the romantic and infantile fixation of a man on a particular woman. When he begs the visibly pregnant Lolita to leave her husband and run off with him at the end, he is a man in love with an abstract perfection that is actually experienced only in the womb or at the breast. A romantic idealist like Humbert can only wait "for the rest of his life," as he puts it, to recover that unattainable bliss:

> It's not too late . . . don't tell me that it's too late because it's not too late. If you want time to think it over, that's perfectly all right with me, because I've waited already for three years and I think I could wait for the rest of my life if necessary. You're not giving anything up. There's nothing here to keep you. . . . You're not bound to him in any way, as you are bound to me by everything that we have lived through together—you and I.[42]

Whereas the experience Humbert has "lived through" has not changed him, Lolita has become the kind of mother she herself never had. In her final scene she is in late and visible pregnancy, a far cry from the sex kitten image that captured Humbert and that Quilty attempted to capture. In the novel Humbert dies of a heart attack and Lolita dies in childbirth, but Kubrick enables her to endure and prevail as the kind of heroine he would draw more fully in Alice. Both women maintain a protective attitude toward their children and their less developed husbands, and both maintain focus and composure as the major male characters tearfully break down: "I'm going to have his baby in three months. . . . I've wrecked too many things in my life. I can't do that to him. He needs me. (*Humbert places his head in his hands and begins to sob uncontrollably. She scolds him.*) Oh, come on now, don't make a scene. Stop crying! He could walk in here at any minute. Will you please stop crying?"[43]

Unlike Humbert, Bill Harford's tears may be therapeutic; at least the final scene leaves open that possibility. At the outset, however, the fortysomething doctor has the depth of a fifteen-year-old behind his professional mask. His first line, "Honey, have you seen my wallet?" shows that he is used to being looked after by a doting mom, and when he tells his wife that they are "running a little late" (for Victor's party), the line speaks to both characters' immaturity. But Alice is brighter and more sensitive than her husband, and she is a step nearer the Star Child in the final scene. In our first view of her after the emblematic opening she is sitting on the toilet, a decidedly unexpected counter to the erotic prerelease trailers and stills. However, this image and the later instance where she leaves Bill to go to the bathroom at the party associate her with a process of purging cultural limitations that have stifled her growth.

When she and Bill emerge into the hallway, the bedroom goes dark in a black screen transition, while in the first of several corridor shots, we see them passing into larger spaces that subliminally express growth. This first corridor is lined with Christiane Kubrick still lifes that connote the human capacity to celebrate rather than control existence. The represented flowers are cultivated rather than wild, and along with the paintings themselves, their creation and placement convey a sense of discrimination and protective nurture. As they step into the living room, Bill asks Alice for the name of the babysitter, even though she has just mentioned it in the bathroom when she asks him if he left her the phone and pager numbers. In this sphere Alice is the adult, the nurturer, the responsible partner. Directly over her right shoulder behind the Christmas tree hangs a painting of a wide golden road ascending between thick stands of dark green trees. It remains visible for thirty seconds, just before Bill and Alice head off into an Oz that is as spooky as the Overlook's ballroom.

The male pursuit of wealth and the female pursuit of romance aim toward the proverbial, nonexistent pot of gold "somewhere over the rainbow." The idea is driven home in the next scene where the two undulant models serpentinely address Bill's innocence:

Gayle: Do you know what's so nice about doctors?

Bill: Usually a lot less than people imagine.

Gayle: They always seem so knowledgeable.

Bill: Oh, they are very knowledgeable about all sorts of things.

Gayle: But I bet they work too hard. Just think of all they miss.

Bill: You're probably right. Now, where exactly are we going . . . exactly?

Gayle: Where the rainbow ends?

Bill: Where the rainbow ends?

Nuala: Don't you want to go where the rainbow ends?

Bill: Well, now that depends where that is.

Gayle: Well, let's find out.[44]

The decor of the Harfords' apartment seen in the first two minutes immediately indicates that Alice, with her experience as an art gallery manager, values the rainbow for its own sake, while her focused, good-boy husband does not. In addition to accentuating the film's child and growth motifs, the presence of Helena in the opening scene associates proportion and color with maturity: her coloring book, crayons, and crude drawing of a man offset the large finished paintings of red, blue, and green gardens radiating against the rear wall, in bright deep focus illuminated by the chandelier.

In teaching Helena to delight in nature and color, Alice bestows a dream of the world that makes life more interesting than fearful. At the same time, the balletic abridgement of E. T. A. Hoffman's "The Nutcracker and the Mouse King," which Alice allows Helena to see, prepares the child to resist visions of the world that disproportion and pollute it. At an Austrian family's annual Christmas party, a little girl named Clara receives a nutcracker doll dressed like a soldier from her benevolent uncle, Drosselmeier, a teller of magical tales. Just as Helena asked not just to stay up for *The Nutcracker*, but until 1:00 a.m., Clara wants to stay up all night with her gift, as if she senses that its story is vital to an awareness that will keep her alive. Her parents send her to bed, and her dream, as if it were directed by Drosselmeier (and as Kubrick intends in the dreams and dreamlike parts of *Eyes Wide Shut*), reveals truths about the adult world that waking reality conceals.

A mouse king kidnaps Clara and shrinks her to his own size, so that the Christmas tree looms hugely and the room itself expands into a space large enough to admit unknown threats. But just as her captive compression seems unbearable, her Nutcracker Prince personally defeats the Mouse King and his regiment, scattering the enemy troops as if they were once again mice. The Prince then takes Clara on to Candyland, where a chorus of dancing sweets, each representing a different part of the world, caters to her visual and gustatory delight. Finally, this Freudian family dream is complete, when Clara and her omnipotent lover are joined by the maternal Sugar Plum Fairy. Clara thinks she has reached happily-ever-after until she wakes up, surrounded by her real family on Christmas Day. Like Dorothy returning from Oz, and like Alice at the end of the film, Clara will discover her nativity to a real world that may be imperfect but that can no longer be circumscribed by authority or convention.[45]

The separate seductions tried on Bill and Alice at Victor's party are attempts to draw them into their seducers' dreams. The Harford apartment reflects Alice's maternal instinct to protect her family from the mental bondage symbolized by the film's other interiors. Bright primary colors are notably absent from the Ziegler mansion. Its gold-lit windows in brownstone walls are matched by the gold crosswalk lines on the brown street and the yellow taxis that recurrently will carry Bill into alien space. The immediate cut to Bill and Alice inside shows them walking in a corridor, paralleling the previous shot in their apartment, except that this corridor is colorless. The ivory walls are lined by symmetrical brown glass cases with interior shelves holding ranks of antique vases and plates, symbols of entrenched wealth and power confined in tight boxes as opposed to the flourishing natural things on Alice's walls.[46]

Rounding the corner they are met by their aptly named host, "Victor," the alpha male Bill personally serves. Mounted on the wall behind them, a huge brown, pink, and gold eight-pointed star with a white center gleams conspicuously, as if to indicate that Bill and Alice are beginning their odyssey through inner space. The impression is heightened by the starlike curtain of white lights directly behind Victor, just behind the grand winding staircase that later leads to the reductively merged pleasures of bedrooms and art galleries. In an alcove at its base a statue of a winged god carrying a maiden foreshadows Victor's capture of Mandy, the morsel he has chosen to sample for the evening.

The scene involving Bill, Victor, and Mandy pictures the subservience of sexuality to power as seriously repulsive, but the exchange between Sandor and Alice has a comic tone even though its villain represents a similar menace.[47] Throughout Alice's dance with Sandor, the large eight-pointed stars and the curtains of white lights form the backdrop rather than the colored lights of the Christmas trees, and the colors of the room have the golden cast that Wendy admired in the Overlook ballroom. Sandor evokes the Overlook's ghosts in that his speech and manner are anachronistic, and he has the predatory, exploitive purpose that characterizes the "house." But when he announces himself as "Hungarian," as if to make himself exotically attractive, the hint of sarcasm in Alice's response, "I'm American," deflates his suavity and begins to make him absurd.

Immediately and too soon after introducing himself, Sandor waltzes into a hilariously oily shtick: "Did you ever read the Latin poet Ovid on *The Art of Love?*" In the first book of the *Ars Amatoria*, Ovid's formulae for sexual conquest are initially couched in metaphors of the hunt: in order to "catch [his] hare," the experienced amorist knows where to "hang nets" or "spread birdlime," just as the fisherman knows the seasonal movements of his prey.[48] Through some unrevealed privilege Sandor has entrée to soirees where beautiful, wealthy women abound, and he follows his mentor's advice to be bold in initiating conversation with his quarry, because she will be disappointed if he retreats. As a simple machine, much less complex than HAL, Sandor's memory contains only one book. His gestures of taking Alice's glass, insouciantly downing the contents, and then kissing her hand are not original: "Fix well thine eyes on her and so confirm the message of thy love. Ofttimes, without a word being spoken, the eyes can tell a wondrous tale. When she has drunk, be thou the first to seize the cup, and where her lips have touched, there press thine own and drink."[49]

But Alice knows Ovid as well as he, and she senses what she later learns the hard way: that promiscuity is a repetitive nightmare and that over-the-rainbow fantasies of sexual perfection can be outgrown. To Sandor's opening salvo she replies, "Didn't [Ovid] wind up crying his eyes out in some place with a very bad climate?" At the age of thirty-five Ovid was banished from Rome shortly after he completed *The Metamorphoses*, and immediately after he published *The Art of Love*. The cause may have been the scandalous nature of the latter book, but it was also rumored that he had an affair with the granddaughter of the emperor, since she was banished in the same year. He was never to return to the setting that had stimulated his major works, and he died after a largely unproductive exile at the age of sixty in a remote Roman outpost on the Danube River—realizing, all too late, that creativity flourishes best when the artist's working conditions are firmly rooted (e.g., Shakespeare in London, Faulkner in Oxford, Kubrick in St. Albans). For the artist whose work is his life, even more than for the ordinary person, there's no place like home.[50]

Art and its misuses comprise a major theme in the scene at the Zieglers'. Immediately after the opening Ovid exchange, Sandor looks for another opening by asking what Alice does, and when she answers that she managed an art gallery that went broke, he offers to help her through his "friends in the art game." For Sandor and the powerful males he emulates, every activity is a competitive game, and having discovered Alice's interest in art, he invites her upstairs to see Victor's collection of Renaissance bronzes. At its best art expresses intangible experience in visible form, but only for those spectators capable of perception. During their dance Alice's eyes are brightly expressive, highlighted by eyeliner, continually moving and reflecting light. Sandor's eyes are largely invisible, dark holes like those of Moonwatcher and the Overlook ghosts that resemble Norman Bates's mother. He is a being with no depth, no soul, expressing an ancient biological impulse mechanically refined by much practice and a few books. The same is true for Bill's purveyors of the rainbow's end. His eyes are also dark as Gayle initiates the come-on by recalling how he removed a speck from her eye during a photo shoot.

Shortly afterward Bill twice tells the overdosed Mandy to open her eyes and repeats "look at me" five times, but we never see Mandy's eyes in the scene. As Bill speaks to her she appears in profile with her head turned away from the camera, and in brief frontal shots afterward her eyes are small black holes that reflect no light. Anticipating her later appearance as a naked corpse, her nudity in this scene is necrophilic, recalling both the Gogol reference to dead souls in A Clockwork Orange and the female sex-tables at the Korova Milk Bar. As Bill questions Victor about her condition, the shot/reverse shots contrast Mandy's sprawled body on the chair to a painting of a pregnant nude directly behind Victor. The woman in the painting lies on a bright red flower-patterned fabric, but she has a sad expression on her face. While Mandy's body is lifeless and soulless, this woman's body carries life, but the painting's spatial context suggests despair over the surroundings of her inner life and the ugliness of the world her child would inherit.[51]

That world is like the nightmare of "The Nutcracker," absurdly disproportioned and ruled by a Mouse King. The green-paneled, gray-tiled room recalls the color and floor pattern of 2001's alien room, but that room had an aesthetic grace that prefigured transformation, whereas the ugliness of Victor's room parallels the polluting substances in Mandy's body and can contribute only to death. Nothing in the room coheres. The green-paneled walls trimmed in elegant brown wood and the plush brown chairs suggest a law office, but exposed toilets, sinks, and tubs represent the primitive, biological drives that underlie the civilized surface of Victor's world, and the incongruous mock fireplace suggests the artificiality of the association between wealth and refinement.

Correspondingly, the first view of Domino's apartment reveals a messy kitchen containing a bathtub, as if to express immaturity and underlying confusion.[52] While Mandy's name connotes childishness, Domino's name implies replication. Eventually we learn that she has become HIV positive, and the physical death of both victims may symbolize the metamorphoses of mind that produce "zombies," as Kubrick put it in his New York Times letter defending *A Clockwork Orange*.[53] The pregnancy of the woman in Victor's painting suggests the danger to children that storytelling aims to correct by restoring proportion to a topsy-turvy world. Mandy's red hair echoes that of Bill's daughter, Helena, and Bill's eyes are visible and clear while he revives and admonishes her, as if he were speaking to a child. In this brief space of adult concern, Bill is at his best, and the scene prepares us for the possibility that he is inwardly alive here, lucky to be alive at the end, and potentially still alive in the future that the film's ending projects.

The differentiated fate of women alike in physical beauty also expresses the importance of individual growth: Mandy regresses and Alice evolves. Mandy primitively gravitates toward the most powerful male as she perceives him, while Alice struggles and succeeds at becoming her own person. The alternative is the soul death of replication, Gayle and Nuala as a single entity, echoing the identical Grady sisters of Danny's vision, Domino as a "piece" in the "sociological" game, and Sandor as the beta male, hardly distinguished from an animal endlessly seeking a roundabout way to perpetuate his genes.

Victor has a similar attitude toward Mandy. He complains to Bill that he doesn't want to let her recuperate for another hour because she might be discovered, but Bill firmly insists and tells him to have someone take her home. Bill respects his medical responsibility to protect and perpetuate life. In his professional role he is nurturing and sincere. The other denizens of Victor's ballroom focus only on infantile pleasure and the temporary omnipotence of successful seduction. Bill may be naive in his jealous rage over his wife's unacted fantasy, but his basic decency is accented in contrast to Nick Nightingale's desertion of responsibility as a doctor and a father. (He has a wife and four boys in Seattle that he rarely sees.)

Just as Sandor has no inkling of the value and purpose of art, so Nick wants to know if Bill is still in "the doctor business." In a Kubrick film, innate rather than environmental qualities usually determine character difference. Evolving characters such as Joker and Lolita show concern for other human beings, while regressive ones like Animal Mother and Humbert do not:

> *Bill:* You know what they say, once a doctor always a doctor.
>
> *Nick:* Yes, or in my case, never a doctor, never a doctor.[54]

Their opposition as human types is suggested by the contrasting colors of their jackets: Bill's black one suggests evolution and growth, while Nick's white one connotes regression and death.[55]

Nick later brags about his gig as a blindfolded pianist for upscale orgies where the real reward (and the limit of his vision) is a peek at naked women when the blindfold slips. In Kubrick's world an artist can either assume responsibility for psychological development and physical survival, or evade it in stupefying escapes. When Bill says he never understood why Nick "walked away" from medicine, Nick replies, "It's a nice feeling, I do it a lot." None of the characters in *Eyes Wide Shut* actually kills anybody, though there is some suspicion later that Victor may have had something to do with Mandy's death. But Nick's neglect of his family, Bill's obsession with revenge to the point that he cannot attend to Helena, and Alice's confession that she would have sacrificed Bill and Helena for one night with the naval officer suggest an analogy between murder and forgetting someone's existence. The addiction metaphor as a regression to the breast, made overt through Mandy's habit and Victor's later comment on her "great tits," is apparent in the self-staging of the sex scene in the Harford apartment after the party.

Nick's "walking away" extends to cinema that seeks absolute fulfillment in voyeurism rather than awareness. After Victor's party, Bill and Alice erotically perform by watching their naked embrace in the mirror, giving themselves the Chris Isaak song "Baby Did a Bad Bad Thing" as a soundtrack. The song extends Nick's metaphor and foreshadows Alice's fantasy in its allusion to walking away from one's lover. The use of the word "baby" in the title qualifies the word "bad" in different ways. Kubrick does not mean to say that voyeurism, per se, is evil, but he does make clear that in excess, it can cause irreversible regression. As the nude Alice removes her earrings in front of the mirror, a Christiane Kubrick still life of sunflowers, gourds, and blue flowers hangs next to the mirror over her right shoulder. Its blue and gold are reflected in a vase directly beneath it, and the orange spot on the gourd rhymes with bright orange candles to the right of the vase. Few in the audience will notice the painting and its reflection when they are being offered the anticipated delight of Nicole Kidman's body, pleasantly bathed in pink light. Their lack of awareness, and an invitation to awareness on a second viewing, may be symbolized by the removal of both earrings and glasses, reflexive symbols of staying alert in a scene that deliberately lacks erotic excitement.

The monkeys that preferred looking at pictures of dominant monkeys to getting fruit juice correspond to spectators who come to the film for a peek at Tom and Nicole.[56] Many moviegoers unwittingly sacrifice their minds and senses for the rush of vicarious narcissism that the scene portrays. The Harfords are attempting to retain the excitement of being strangers to each other, seeking arousal in the mirror as if they are watching someone else, "walking away" from consciousness and responsibility in contrast to the kind of sex that Alice's postenlightened line and the film's last word suggest. Human beings need to "fuck" as an act of loving and creative expression rather than to get fucked in a needy pursuit of pleasure that can spell the end of life and growth.

Alice's impulse to explode the notion that good sex is bliss leads first to divisive cruelty and finally to wisdom. The greatest danger of sexual obsession lies in the neglect of children, and the stopping of their growth by adults who have stopped their own. Bill has apparently reached a maximum level of competence as a general practitioner, ministering to the Manhattan elite. But in his personal life, he thinks of himself as a good husband and a good father without ever thinking about what it means to be good in those roles. He remains locked in the frame of the mirror that Alice looks beyond as the first bedroom scene ends.

Just after a close-up of Alice with her eyes open and an intervening six-second black screen, silver elevator doors part to admit Bill to his office on Monday morning. The shot echoes a similar sequence in 2001 where a black screen precedes a silver door sliding open to admit Dr. Floyd to a lounge containing a pink-suited flight attendant, the equivalent of Bill's receptionist.[57] Floyd resembles Bill in his smug professional confidence and in his sense of himself as a loving parent. When his six-year-old daughter (played by Vivian Kubrick) asks via videophone if he can attend her birthday, he has to decline since he is literally in outer space, and when she asks if he can get her a phone for a present, he misses her plea for more contact: "We've got lots of telephones already."[58]

As a doctor constantly on call, Bill too spends much time away, and a reminder of Helena appears immediately after he enters in a strange painting of a dark-skinned woman in a gold robe with an orange headscarf facing a blue door. A large black number 7 (Helena's age) stands against a white background in the painting's center. Its bright primary colors recall the Christiane Kubrick pieces in the Harford apartment: bright orange vertical lines resembling flames stand under the number, warmly complementing the blue background. Directly beneath, a smaller painting of strewn toys shows an upended, smiling Raggedy Ann doll in the foreground, her red hair mirroring Helena's, smiling out at Bill as he passes. To the right of that painting a small sepia photo of a boy in a snowsuit under an unlit Christmas tree stands on the counter, suggesting again a timeless need for parental warmth, just before Bill passes a long cobalt waiting couch beneath blue and white windows that look like ice.

A cut to Alice and Helena at breakfast in the kid-friendly Harford kitchen accentuates a cold/warm, male/female contrast reminiscent of The Shining, where Wendy nourishes Danny while Jack, far less successfully than Bill, pursues his ambition of securing status by serving the rich. The shot reveals Alice to be a more sophisticated mother than Wendy as she reads the Times through her glasses with a serious expression. Directly above her a large still life of golden apples again suggests her artistic sensibility and may additionally connote the temptation she will soon describe to her husband. As in *The Shining*, though less obviously, a TV cartoon contains a warning: "'Twas the night before Christmas, and all through the house, not a creature was stirring, not even a mouse." The parent who discovers Santa in the poem undergoes no strengthening trial, and the message is one of lavish gifts awaiting children who have only to keep their eyes peeled for unearned rewards, foreshadowing Helena's innocent greed in the concluding scene at the upscale toy store. Though the tub of I Can't Believe It's Not Butter shows that Alice is health savvy, the cartoon clip suggests the stunting effect of cultural dreams that reduce adults to sleepwalking mice.

Continuing crosscuts show both parents attending to dependants. But Bill's examinations are impersonal and routine, and his smooth bedside manner is offset by the cold silver and white setting of the examining room and the colorless portraits of Victorian doctors on the back wall. In contrast, Alice and Helena are suffused by subtle rhythms of color and light that suggest a process of growth, the world taking on color. The visual textures rather than their mundane actions and sparse dialogue foreshadow the distinction between Alice's need for change and Bill's need for stasis in the following scene. At the end of a typical day their sameness appears, as it had at the party, in the color of their clothes. Before putting Helena to bed and retiring to their own room, Bill wears a gray T-shirt and Alice a gray sweater.[59]

In a Kubrick film individual understanding leaps beyond prevailing inertia. Kubrick's coscreenwriter, Frederic Raphael, initially questioned the transposition of Schnitzler's novella because "many things [had] changed since 1900, not least the relations between men and women," and in particular, "underlying assumptions, which are dated . . . about marriage, husbands and wives, the nature of jealousy."[60] Kubrick's refusal to agree is consistent with his anthropological perspective, and he had been planning to film *Dream Story* for decades before he hired Raphael. In a 1968 interview he was asked if "romantic love" would be "unfashionable" by 2001:

The basic love relationship, even at its most obsessional, is too deeply ingrained in man's psyche not to endure in one form or another. It's not going to be easy to circumvent our primitive emotional programming. Man still has essentially the same set of pair-bonding instincts—love, jealousy, possessiveness—imprinted for individual and tribal survival millions of years ago, and these still lie quite close to the surface, even in these allegedly enlightened and liberated times.[61]

When Alice questions the idea that "millions of years of evolution" have established a male right to promiscuity and a female need for commitment, Kubrick explicitly alludes to the biological programming that still determines social rank. Bill's "obsessive" need to revenge himself through sexual conquest, after his wife confesses her attraction to a rival male, is an attempt to restore the hierarchical position he feels he has lost. At Ziegler's party, the men wear black while the host's wife displays Victor's rank in bright red. When money replaced land as the mode of male power in the nineteenth century, male plumage was replaced by female adornment. The first image of Alice in the film shows her taking off a fancy dress and foreshadows her shedding of the role that is defined by how she looks rather than what she sees. The babysitter sends her off to the party with "You look amazing," and Victor greets her with "Look at you! God, you're absolutely stunning," adding that he doesn't "say that to all the women," although his wife's demurral implies that for Victor, women are undifferentiated, valued only for prestige-conferring physical beauty.

Alice's refusal to accept her role in the film's exposed primate hierarchy is initially symbolized by the black dress that equalizes her status with the black-clad males at the party. Nick Nightingale is the only male wearing white, signifying his subservient rank, and when Bill later chooses a costume to wear to the orgy, he is careful to select a black cloak and hood, even after the shop's owner suggests he choose "something more colorful," a "clown, officer, or pirate" costume that would have made him the modern equivalent of a Shakespearean "low character."[62]

Robert Ardrey's *African Genesis* was an acknowledged influence on *2001* and *A Clockwork Orange*, and it may have implicitly influenced *Eyes Wide Shut*. Ardrey compared human societies to those of other species that allowed a male to get the best female "his rank could afford."[63] Because females have a low status among primates generally, they obtain favors from the males they belong to through forms of prostitution: after stealing a piece of fruit from under the nose of a dominant male, the female monkey "will promptly present her behind" to keep him occupied or distracted while she devours her prize.[64] Mandy had ambitions as an actress but is so far gone in her failure to gain rank in that way, or through secure attachment to a dominant male, that she gives herself to Victor to maintain her supply of drugs. He values her only for her "great tits." Alice's first line in the film is an inquiry about "how she looks," and when she accuses Bill of "not even looking," he replies, "You always look beautiful." In fact, Bill trusts that his investment in Alice will pay unlimited dividends because she is a sure thing. He does not need her beauty, per se, as a sexual stimulant for himself because he is primarily stimulated by her effect on other men and the reassurance that they envy him for his power to attract such a valuable mate. His smug pleasure over Sandor's desire "to fuck my wife" ignites Alice's rage over the primitive role she continues to play for Bill after "millions of years of evolution."

When Bill daydreams the erotic encounter between Alice and the naval officer, he imagines her engaged in the "primate prostitution" he unconsciously projects from their own relationship. After extended foreplay in his sequence of black and white fantasies, Alice invites the officer to enter from behind, as if to suggest Bill's atavistic pain at being replaced by a more powerful ape.[65] Ardrey observed that the female experience of adultery involved fewer head-on collisions with other instincts than occur in the psyche of her more distracted mate.[66] Her paramount instinct to protect the young maintains her stability when a "pair bond" breaks, while the inability to control his mate implies a male's sexual impotence and social castration. In a primitive situation his physical security would be threatened because rivals would be emboldened by his inability to protect his possession. This unconscious basis of jealousy accounts for Bill's desperation to restore his status, an emotion that Kubrick assured Raphael had not changed in a million years, much less since 1900.

When Alice's confession is interrupted by a phone call informing Bill that one of his patients just died, he tells her, "I guess I better go over and show my face," a phrase suggesting that he is already unconsciously ashamed of his marital failure. Alice is clearly not ashamed, but still winding down from her anger at his hypocrisy and disturbed over her own possession by sexual feelings she could not control. Her obsession is mirrored in the bizarre come-on Marion Nathanson offers Bill at her father's deathbed. Though she and Bill "hardly know each other," as Bill puts it, Marion confesses her long-standing love for him and shockingly kisses him on the lips even though she is engaged to Carl, a math professor, who has just received an appointment at the University of Michigan. Despite her husband's intellectual prestige, Marion perceives Bill as the more powerful male for no discernible reason. Upon his arrival, Carl turns out to be a handsome man, taller than Bill with a similar haircut, and tenderly concerned for Marion's loss. As a stranger to another woman he too might be an ideally powerful male, just as the anonymous naval officer had been for Alice.

But at this point in the story surpassing Carl will not compensate for Bill's humiliation because Marion is not beautiful, and seducing her presents no challenge. Moreover, Carl is not high enough in the social hierarchy to represent a potency Bill can exceed. When he leaves the Nathanson apartment, he smashes his fist into his hand as if he needs the purifying catharsis of a fight, and momentarily he meets a pack of roving males that mirror his social demotion and the physical frustration it evokes.[67]

The college students who accost him on the street are like the young males of an animal group preparing themselves to fight each other to replace the present generation of primal fathers. Though the students' sweatshirts identify them as intelligent enough to attend Yale, they are still unproven adolescents, having not yet cleared a social niche for themselves as Bill has. But Bill's sexual humiliation has returned him to their level, and as they approach one of them seeks prestige among his peers by boasting of getting a woman so excited that she did a "Mexican lap dance" on his face and "left scars on the back of [his] neck." For these boys conquest is more important than orgasm, and though they are not about to rape and kill, their male bonding and aggression resemble similar groups in A Clockwork Orange and Full Metal Jacket.

Ardrey believed that innate aggression enables man to effect two primary drives: territoriality and dominance. When the students spot Bill, they seize an opportunity to express these drives by taking possession of the sidewalk from an inferior male whom they arbitrarily identify as homosexual, because their own heterosexuality is the only social power they have achieved. Having passed puberty, college entrance, and in the case of the boy who knocks Bill off the sidewalk, a football game or two, they need to convince themselves they are no longer little boys by distinguishing themselves as superior men. They need Bill to be gay for the same reasons the students in Dream Story need Fridolin to be Jewish. In their eyes males of those groups may have the appearance of men but are no more than women in comparison to "real men." Expressing a similar need in himself and his low-ranked recruits, Full Metal Jacket's Sergeant Hartman verbally castrated any male who was not a marine.

Lacking other forms of ownership, the college boys try to dominate any space they occupy. The scene proceeds from the same emotions that drive the marine recruits to "motivate Pyle" and Alex to humiliate people just because he can. They abandon their sex talk as readily as Billy Boy's gang ignores their prospective rape victim, because the assertion of dominance and territory are stronger drives than sex. Though the Yalies are socially inhibited enough not to actually beat Bill, their "hey, hey, he-he-hey" directly echoes the inarticulate excitement of Alex's droogs as they gear up for violence.

The actual assault is initiated by the biggest boy football-blocking Bill into a parked car and continues in barely sublimated verbal derision, as the word "faggot" is repeated with intense rage through clenched teeth. Subsequent insults evoke Sergeant Hartman's calling his recruits "ladies," the contempt of the marine "hunting band" for "suspect outsiders" (as Kubrick put it),[68] and the robotic compulsion of men so biologically and culturally driven to compete that they remain lifelong adolescents: "What team's this switch hitter playing for?" "The pink team." "Merry Christmas, Mary," and (pointing to another kid's presented ass) "prime cut o' meat, baby," and, finally, as they are leaving, "I got dumps that are bigger than you."

Defining itself by contrast, a human gang relegates outsiders to subhuman status. Without the support of having gained himself a trophy wife, Bill feels the way Hartman said recruits should feel before they become full-fledged marines: "Until that day you are pukes; you are the lowest form of life on earth; you are not even human fucking beings. You are nothing but unorganized, grab-asstic pieces of amphibian shit."[69] As they exit, the New Haven horde asserts its territorial imperative—"Go back to San Francisco where you belong"—accentuating Bill's exile from where and who he was.

But even his lost status was an illusion. Near the end when he is stalked by a bald man in an overcoat, he stops to buy a paper next to a street sign that reads "Wren Street."[70] Martin Scorsese had thought that "Wren Street" was part of the film's dream motif, since no such street actually exists in Greenwich Village.[71] But in view of Bill's failure to gain admittance to the upper echelons of Manhattan society, despite his butlerlike willingness to make "house calls," he is no more than a wren to an eagle in comparison to the dominant males privileged to attend the orgy.[72] And the danger he faces from the big boys perched atop the corporate and political structure stems from the public discovering them to be disguised "droogies," as Alex aptly calls the prime minister who buys his silence at the end of Clockwork.

Rather than being an object for competing males to prize, Alice reverts to her primitive power to choose a mate and in the process accelerates advanced awareness. She knows nothing about the man she wants so badly other than that he is a naval officer, but this identity externalizes her own need to explore. Nora and Mandy seek men who represent status and security, but Alice wants her life to be an odyssey rather than a conquest. Her daughter's name, "Helena," symbolizes Alice's aspiration for her daughter when she named her—to be a woman men would fight for. But Alice has reached a point in her life when she is becoming a determining subject of her experience rather than a passive object or the body in the mirror.

In the second bedroom scene Alice is still a child, but she is no longer naked as a baby.[73] While her husband's torso is still uncovered, Alice wears a pink teddy, and an intervening scene shows her doing a reverse strip as she puts on a black bra while the camera moves upward from her buttocks toward her sensitive, bespectacled face. The differing degrees of nudity in the second bedroom scene correspond to phases of maturity. Bill wants Alice to console him for his hard work and monogamy, to be his "teddy" bear. Alice has apparently needed marijuana for a while to sustain this role, as suggested by her accessing the stash and rolling the joints. But the pot fails to work as Bill uses his usual techniques to arouse her, and she breaks away from these fogged consolations when Bill says that Sandor wanted to have sex with her because she is "a very beautiful woman."

As she disengages herself and stands up, her next line is a non sequitur, but it reflects what has apparently been troubling her for a long time: "So . . . because I'm a beautiful woman the *only* reason any man wants to talk to me is because he wants to fuck me! Is that what you're saying?" And when Bill answers that it's not "quite that black and white," subsequent dialogue suggests that he is the one confined to categories and clichés. Alice is unconsciously infuriated because she is beginning to realize why Bill values her, especially because he is not really listening to her attempt to define herself and their relationship. At the moment he is frustrated because the sexual gratification he was about to enjoy has been interrupted, and he is angry and impatient with her for changing the subject from his pleasure to her seemingly irrelevant concern with how she is perceived. His family and professional lives are locked safely in small conceptions of his virtue that he takes pains to preserve rather than question.

When Alice doubts that he or his naked female patients ever have sexual thoughts, he answers that a nurse is always present and that "sex is the last thing on this hypothetical fucking woman patient's mind," because "she's afraid of what I might find." The line suggests that middle-class morality protects Bill from seeing his own duality as securely as a nurse protects the patient, and as a mother protects a baby. He is the one who is afraid of finding out what Alice has already discovered in herself. Accordingly, the use of color in the scene defines character and expresses Alice's expanding mind. Bill's black and white mind is matched by his black shorts, bare torso and legs, topped by a boyish thatch of thick black hair. He is repeatedly seen next to a black phone and a black and white lamp to the left of the bed.

When he first appears he is sitting on the edge of the bed responding to Alice's question about whether he "fucked" the two girls at the party. Behind him the cold blue light of pain and recognition shines through the bathroom window. It is an "over-the-top blue," as cinematographer Larry Smith called it, and its unreality establishes it as a symbol of subjective experience in a scene that begins the film's entrance into dreams. The scene begins with Alice as a male fantasy of sexual solace and emotional warmth. She is lying on a maroon bedspread leaning back against a flowered maroon headboard with her eyes closed and her mouth open. Red-gold hair falls on either side of her face; her pale gold skin harmonizes with her light pink teddy; and her voice and movements are languorous from the pot. The scene's first frames present her as the supreme sex symbol the prerelease publicity promised she would be.

But her first words are jarring and hostile, countering the seductive image. When she asks if Bill "happened to fuck" the two girls, she accents the *k*, beginning a breakout from her marijuana haze that symbolizes a long-suppressed anger. When Bill tries to sweet-talk Alice by using "fuck" to arouse her, he unwittingly triggers Alice's realization that her grooming (pictured extensively in previous scenes) has invited a mind-fuck that she will no longer accept. When she sits up on the bed, the small painting on the pink wall behind them once again shows a light-colored road leading through light green fields toward a stand of dark green trees under a transitional orange sky. As with the similar painting in their living room, the image suggests the journey that both Harfords will take into a nightmare Oz of the unconscious. The orange sky recalls the evolutionary transitions of *2001*, and the dark green of the fields matches the color of transformation in that film's alien room.

Like Bowman, Joker, and Danny, Alice leads the evolutionary way. When she breaks away from Bill and stands up, she assumes a dominance in the scene that is visually continued even after she sits on the floor, through low camera angles of her and high ones of Bill. While her husband crouches in dull light on the bed, Alice initially stands framed by the pink bathroom doorframe that matches her pink teddy. Behind her the cerulean blue provides a dynamic contrast, as if to accent an activity of mind no longer fogged by the pot. Throughout the rest of the scene Bill remains stationary on the bed, while Alice uses her body expressively. Still standing in the doorway, she initially taunts his sexual frustration with subtle movements of her hips as she mocks his hypocritical denial of extramarital attraction. After moving to her left, she sits briefly on the bench in front of the mirror that had begun to reflect her capacity for introspection in the previous bedroom scene.

When Alice stands again, she moves to "center stage," backed by the blue window and orange drapes that framed her emblematic nude image after the opening titles. There she will deliver the speech that changes their lives and exposes the biological imperatives that must be modified and managed if the human "family" is to survive. Like Danny in *The Shining*, Alice has less screen time than her more backward relative, but her monologue is central to Kubrick's vision that humanity's survival depends upon recognizing and managing regression. Just as Danny's ESP transcends time and space, Alice's sexual discovery represents all impulses that threaten the human family—not just sexual ones.

As different as they are, sexuality and aggression promise to satisfy infantile longings for perfect security and omnipotence. At the same time that Alice dreamed of being possessed by the naval officer and freed from her adult identity, she simultaneously functioned lovingly as a wife and mother. After sending Helena to the movies with a friend (a detail reflecting her own escapism), she and Bill made love and discussed their child and their future, as if these objective concerns were the whole reality. In the course of her recollection Alice's infantile dream is replaced by an adult reflection on the paradox of her feelings: "And I thought if he wanted me, even if it was for only one night, I was ready to give up everything. You, Helena, my whole fucking future. Everything. And yet it was weird because at the same time you were dearer to me than ever and . . . at that moment my love for you was both tender and sad."[74]

Her compassion for Bill shows that she senses the threat posed to her loved ones from a powerful destructive force in herself. Though this central message is generally implicit in *Strangelove*, *Clockwork*, and *Barry Lyndon*, it is closer to the threshold of a character's consciousness in Joker and Alice than in previous films. After her rage settles and she sits on the floor, she presents a narrative that potentially betrays the other human beings dependent on her, as well as the best in herself.

The speech progresses as a paradigm of spiritual evolution, from an initial tone of cruel revenge, to a reverie of exploration, and back to a series of self-questioning reflections on the puzzling contradictions she felt. She describes the attraction as something that came over her, strong enough to take possession of her mind and yet at the same time not stronger than the counter impulses to nurture, preserve, and protect. Though Bill is literally higher than she because he is sitting on the bed, the camera remains below her as she sits on the floor through the rest of the scene, suggesting that her self-awareness in comparison to Bill's is like that of an adult to a child.

The shot/reverse shot close-ups during the monologue express the same contrast. Alice's hair is swept back off her forehead, while Bill's is covered by a thick shock of boyish hair. But the most striking difference between the two is in the expressiveness of their eyes. Bill's are dark brown and shadowed like Moonwatcher's, while Alice's Bowman-like blue ones express fluctuations of consciousness from light to dark and back toward light. When she says that her brief fling would have destroyed "her whole fucking future," she closes her eyes so that the end of her development as a human being is imaged as inner darkness. But as she continues she reaches the crucial revelation that her love and compassion remained alive, even as part of her tried to destroy them. And when she says, "my love for you was both tender and sad," her eyes intensify, her brows come down, and her mouth closes. (Bill's remains open throughout the speech.)

Her facial change expresses a transition from oral infantile craving toward a mature awareness of sexuality's power to destroy. She may also be sad for herself because she had not intended harm before she was unexpectedly overwhelmed. The lines also foreshadow her tender embrace of her husband after she describes her nightmare vision of fucking couples in a subsequent scene. In that dream she had laughed at him and was still laughing when he awakened her. Both scenes thematically forgive human beings for atavistic subjection, as long as it remains unconscious.

Alice's instinct to evolve counters her backward instinct to promiscuously select the best progenitors (however absurdly they are perceived, as with Nora in *Barry Lyndon*). At the end of the speech that impulse is "gone," and she is "relieved." The phone call informing Bill of Lou Nathanson's death coincides with the death of her obsession. While Bill stares, still mesmerized for three and a half rings, Alice exhales away her adolescent dream, dying in one phase to emerge into a larger mental and emotional space. When she looks up after Bill tells her who had called, her eyes are blankly open, but her mouth is firmly closed. She is spent but not deflated or depressed, and we sense that she will survive the nightmare to come. It will bring her still more disturbing revelations, but like Private Joker she has the right stuff to keep her humanity intact in a corrupting environment. Her steady eyes contrast sharply to Marion's darting, frightened ones in the next scene, when that distraught woman confronts her obsession with Bill versus her impending marriage.

The paralysis of sexual obsession is pointedly expressed in Alice's description of being transfixed by the naval officer's glance: "I could not move." As with the Ovid allusion, the line may derive from the classical scholarship of Kubrick's cowriter, Frederic Raphael.[75] When Medea first sees Jason, the naval officer in search of the golden fleece at her father's court, she too "cannot move." But after marrying him and returning to his kingdom, Jason discards her for another woman, and Medea in a jealous rage kills their children. The Medea allusion is reinforced by the name of Nick Nightingale's hotel, the "Hotel Jason," where Bill pursues his quest to discover the owners of supreme value in his own society.[76]

Alice's behavior in the bedroom after she questions Bill about the models and his female patients reveals a vicious potential and implies that desire and jealousy can be lethal, negating the humanity of the enslaved person. The

Medea syndrome represents a self-absorption that can kill the parental instinct, thereby "killing" the child. In the end Alice makes a choice, to protect her family rather than to satisfy her id's need for omnipotent pleasure and her ego's need to prove that she is not her husband's property. She transcends being a fighter for a particular group—in this case oppressed women—and becomes an advocate for man- and womankind. In her next major scene Alice narrates the dream she had of an orgy that parallels Bill's appearance at the mansion. But just as Freud and Schnitzler thought dreams to be more fundamentally real than the defensively structured experience of waking reality, so Kubrick makes Alice's reaction to what she has seen more mature and compassionate than that of her husband.

In the same way that mirrors multiply the ugly monotony of couplings at the mansion, Alice's dream in her second monologue is a nightmare of replication. In Schnitzler's *Dream Story*, Albertine's parallel dream recapitulates the novel's themes, but her narrative differs from Kubrick's truncated version in tone and emphasis. At the start Albertine finds herself inexplicably alone in a mountain villa on the day before her wedding, as if she were "an actress coming onto the stage." She expects her role to be that of a bride, but when she looks for her wedding dress, she finds instead a collection of "resplendent operatic costumes." Unlike the men at Bill's orgy, the devotees at Fridolin's mansion change from their black cloaks to bright-colored courtiers' clothes, and in the dream Fridolin suddenly arrives, rowed in by galley slaves, "richly dressed in gold and silk." Albertine then dons the garb of a princess, and they go for a walk through a radiant mountain meadow.

But just before they "felt it was time to rejoin the world of everyday society" (to wake up), their clothes disappear. Horrified, she blames Fridolin for the humiliation, and he, as if "fully conscious of [his] guilt," flees down the mountain to a nearby city to buy "the most gorgeous" clothes and jewelry. The replacement of the wedding dress with the oriental costumes connotes the replacement of the monogamous ideal with promiscuous display, and Fridolin's initial image as a fairy-tale prince suggests the security Albertine feels because her husband is highly ranked in the social hierarchy. But the sudden exposure of their naked vulnerability culminates in their being merged with a mass of anonymous humanity. Instead of a Romeo and Juliet pairing of unique soul mates, she discovers to her "all consuming shame" and then her relief that she has escaped the strain of containing sexual impulse, and she feels happily separated forever from a husband still strenuously trying to retain a separate, superior self.

When her ideal lover (the Dane she had been so taken by at the seaside resort) appears to her, his metamorphoses suggest that her sexual attraction was primary and that its object could have been anybody. He appears and disappears from behind a cliff "two, three or perhaps a hundred times" and is "always the same person, yet always someone different." As identity dissolves so does time and space, and Albertine's merging encompasses past, present, and future. She tries to flee this death of herself as a distinct person, but finds instead an analogue of religious salvation after she and her lover lie down together in the meadow.

Their lovemaking then becomes collective and anonymous, a "single wave" of copulation that gives Albertine a feeling of ecstatic liberation similar to that of the devotees at Fridolin's orgy, an ironic analogue to the heavenly absorption of all souls in God:

> I had long since—how strange such temporal notions seem!—ceased to be alone in the meadow with that man. But whether there were three or ten or a thousand couples there beside myself, whether I could see them, and whether I gave myself to that man only or to others as well, I could not say. But just as that earlier feeling of horror and shame transcended anything conceivable in a wakeful state, it would be equally hard to conceive of anything in normal conscious life that could equal the freedom, abandon, the sheer bliss I experienced in that dream.[77]

The rest of the dream describes the return and punishment of Fridolin, echoing Bill's humiliation at the orgy but providing a metaphysical dimension that Kubrick decisively omits. Here the film's Mysterious Woman is the Princess of the Land who offers to redeem Fridolin if he becomes her paramour. He refuses because he has pledged to remain true to Albertine for "all eternity." For rejecting the princess he is condemned to death, and as he ascends the hill toward his "crucifixion," his scourging evokes Albertine's scorn. While she sits, "reclining in the arms of [her] lover among the other couples," she is absorbed into a mind-set that is more robotic than erotic. The dream ends as her husband is about to be crucified for exposing the waking world's sustaining lie: that salvation from death and suffering can be conferred by illusions of sexual possession and social rank.

Whereas Albertine's dream occurs primarily in the open space of a mountain meadow, Alice's begins "in a deserted city" where she and Bill immediately appear naked, as if to reduce Schnitzler's layered stripping of identity to a concise image of a civilization deserted by the walking illusions that people it.[78] Kubrick and Raphael selected Albertine's being anonymously fucked in the midst of myriad rutting couples as the essence of her dream. The rest, particularly the extended ridicule of Fridolin's idealism, is omitted as is the reiteration in the dream of the connection between sexuality and dominance.

These themes are treated sufficiently in other parts of the film, but Alice's second major scene spotlights the quality of her character rather than simply making her a mouthpiece for the story's themes.

Albertine's affect regarding her dream is barely mentioned. Just before she embraces the Dane and joins the "three or ten or thousand" other couples, she hides her face in her hands. Alice, on the other hand, has an intense emotional reaction, and while both Schnitzler and Kubrick affirm the curative effect of self-knowledge, Alice's transformation is visceral rather than intellectual, involving her whole being. Bill's entrance to the bedroom reveals a subjective space suffused in blue light. In the earlier bedroom scene where Alice confessed her attraction to the naval officer, the blue light had been behind her and outside the window, in stark contrast to the sexual glow of the maroon bedframe, the orange curtains, the pink walls, and her pink teddy. Here she wears the same teddy, but the outer blue of mature distance and understanding is now inside the room. Even her skin and hair are blue, though Bill's are not.

After asking Bill to lie down, Alice sits up and begins to tell the dream, assuming a visually superior position as she leads the way into an inner space too dangerous for her "child." Nicole Kidman's acting recognizes a tragic dimension in the ugly absurdity she describes, and as she speaks, the film regards her nuanced performance as its most beautiful human element to this point. She begins by holding her hand to her forehead, as if to cover the self-knowledge her words expose, and her hands move randomly for a moment expressing the chaos of her feelings. After a momentary cut to Bill lying completely immobile, his face now resembling the mask he wore at the orgy, her hand covers her mouth as if she doesn't want to continue. Her whole physical instrument registers subtleties of pain and pity, compared to the Mysterious Woman's mask and hollow voice and the vacancy of Mandy's eyes.

Kubrick had described Jack Nicholson's performance in his scene with "Lloyd," the bartender, as "incredibly intricate, with sudden changes of thought and mood—all grace notes."[79] Kidman's performance in this scene achieves that level. When Alice says she "felt wonderful" after Bill left to get their clothes, the words express freedom from guilt. At the same time her vocal tone and body language convey deep remorse: her profile is shadowed, and she lowers her head as she begins to describe "lying in a beautiful garden stretched out naked in the sunlight." The contrast between the visual and verbal images mirrors the spectators' having temporarily obscured their individual egos to illuminate their collective selves. She remains upright until she says the naval officer laughed at her. Then she lies down and sobs into the pillow as if completely humiliated, giving Bill a fleeting sense of power.

Assuming dominance he rolls himself into a sitting position, and taking on a professional air, he says gently, "Why don't you tell me the rest of it?" After she demurs, saying "it's too awful," the brief reverse shot shows him looking down at her and saying in one of the film's crowning ironies, "It's only a dream." The words express smug superiority, but he is not seen from the low angle that would be Alice's POV, and the camera implies that she will not humbly follow his lead. Her protective strength is restored as she sits up and embraces him, even as her words speak of betrayal. Initially, the embrace is a profile shot with each of them facing the opposite way. After she begins with "he was kissing me," a brief cut to Bill shows him looking over her shoulder with the same mesmerized expression he wore in the earlier bedroom scene when she confessed her desire. Similar cuts are made when she says she doesn't know how many men she was with and when she wanted to make fun of him as his dream-self imperturbably looked on. The cruelty of her own dream-self contrasts sharply to her waking affect in the scene. As her love for Bill dies in the dream, her waking love revives in the tightening of her embrace, her sighs, and the anguish of her face in the blue light.

Except for brief cuts, the dream narrative unfolding in the profile shot distinguishes between the film's vision and that of the everyday world. When Bill's face is seen briefly in the cuts, its expression is blank, masklike, uncomprehending. In the profile shot his head is hidden behind his wife's, facing darkness, while her whole body is illuminated by the blue wisdom of the dream. Here especially, Kubrick diverges from Freud and agrees with Jung. Instead of having Alice's dream represent a surrender to the id that therapy and the superego must repair, Alice has returned with a life-enhancing tale to tell.

The embrace in profile creates a Janus-faced image of the individual and the species—Bill as the dark, uncomprehending ego, Alice as the inspired urge to explore inner space. After the last close-up of Bill looking over her shoulder, Alice releases Bill, and putting her hand to her forehead and over her shadowed eyes to muffle the pain, she concludes by saying that she was still laughing at Bill in her dream when he woke her up. As she speaks she is weeping, and when she embraces Bill again, her head is hidden for the first time behind his, suggesting that the truth of dreams in this dream story will once again recede.

Kidman's tour de force solo of horror, sorrow, and compassion is accompanied by sad violins providing a slightly eerie atmosphere that is melancholy rather than bizarre. The music begins to get louder when she says the naval officer laughed at her and reaches its loudest point when she says, "Everyone was fucking, and then I was fucking other men." It softens again when she says, "I wanted to make fun of you," providing more counterpoint to her dev-astating words, and diminishes to silence just as she covers her mouth before the scene ends with a fade to black.

The preceding black screen in the film occurred just after Bill and Alice embraced in the mirror following the porn fantasy they created for them-selves after Victor's party. Here her sobs continue under the black screen for eight seconds before the cut to a sunlit, taxi-filled Manhattan street. Kubrick's sparing uses of this form of transition are emphatically different. The first dissolves a shallow collective dream that the spectator has paid to see. Pornography contains no surprise. But the second underscores Alice's compassionate response to her cruel dream as a decisive advance.

Alice is able to accommodate contradictions that the "normal" socially conditioned person cannot. Her incorporation of opposites is externalized by parallel shots of the apartment interior following Bill's two returns from the mansion. The second entry occurs just after Bill receives the ominous warn-ing to give up his inquiries for his "own good" while standing outside the mansion's barred, blue gate. In the second bedroom scene, Alice's pink teddy had externalized the secure sexual warmth Bill expected and was denied when the tone shifted to the unadmitted truths symbolized by the cold blue windows. Now, after the disturbing revelation of her dream played entirely in blue, she wears her glasses and a pink blouse as she patiently helps Helena with her homework.[80]

The dialogue begins with familiar lines that only serve to heighten Bill's inner confusion:

Alice: Hi.

Helena: Hi, Daddy.

Bill: Any calls?

Alice: Dr. Sanders and Mrs. Shapiro.

While he struggles to maintain the pretense of daytime concerns, Alice easily makes the transition from the strange frontier of the dream world to the nur-turing necessities of home. When Helena proudly announces that she got all her math problems right, the ironic subtext contrasts Alice's ability to recover from her "adventure," as she puts it in the concluding scene, and Bill's inability to ac-cept what has happened. When she asks if he is hungry, the implied answer is yes, hungry to restore the absolute confidence he enjoyed before.

Once again Alice is the mature protector, while Bill needs help in solving his emotional problems as much as Helena does with her math. Bill's potential failure to reach the adulthood Alice displays is suggested by Helena's request after he says he has to go out again right after dinner: "Am I gonna get a puppy for Christmas? He could be a watchdog," expressing her need for Bill to play the role that is even more necessary to his survival than to hers. On his way to the kitchen to get a beer, his abdication of responsibility is suggested when he passes a painting of a small potted tree with pink blossoms under a rainbow sky of orange, red, and purple light. The plant may symbolize Helena and her need for the life-sustaining warmth and light he should supply.

Instead, the oral consolation of a beer indicates his infantile need, but as he absorbs its coldness in the dull light of the kitchen, the crosscuts to Alice and Helena in the warm dining room highlight the prime cause of his frozen state: Alice (still working on Helena's math) says, "Joe has two dollars fifty. Mike has one dollar and seventy-five cents. Joe has how much more money than Mike." The words coincide with Bill's feelings of inadequacy, measured in his society by the money that secures sexual possession. He has lost his wife and been humiliated by overwhelming social, economic, and physical power at the mansion, and when Alice asks if the problem is "a subtraction or an addition," the subtext conveys Bill's sexual and social losses.

After a brief cut to Alice and Helena, a slow zoom-in to Bill is accompanied by a voice-over of Alice telling her dream: "And there were all these other people. Hundreds of them everywhere, and everyone was fucking." Then the camera cuts back to a three-quarters close-up of Alice, resting her chin on her hand and smiling at Bill with a loving look. Her smile exactly coincides with "And then I was fucking other men, so many, I don't know how many I was with." A brief cut back to Bill's tight-mouthed answering smile is followed by a final image of Alice, touching her hand to her neck as she relishes the moment before looking serenely back toward Helena.

The repetition of zoom-ins expresses the interior of each character—self-concerned jealousy versus familial devotion. Alice can forgive herself and will forgive Bill because her soul can adapt to change and transform it to deeper love, while Bill, like HAL before him, cannot compute contradiction. Kubrick is concerned with psychic entropy, and the screenplay foreshadows this kind of death when Bill becomes aware of physical dangers, first with the discovery that Domino is HIV positive, and then when he is followed by the bald "Stalker," the elite cabal's implied enforcer. In the latter scene he stops to get a newspaper with the headline "Lucky to Be Alive" at the corner of "Wren Street," the name that Martin Scorsese noted does not appear on the Manhattan map. Kubrick apparently invented the name to suggest Bill's social rank and vulnerability. In *The Shining* Jack wore a T-shirt of an eagle swooping down with extended talons, as Wendy, his innocent prey-to-be, served him breakfast. Here the bald man in the overcoat is the eagle and Bill is the wren. When he takes refuge in a coffeehouse named Sharkey's, the metaphor changes to suggest that he is a small fish swimming, as Victor says later, "way out of [his] depth."

Bill is no more important to the Victors of the world than Mandy, the hooker he revived in Victor's bathroom. Both are simply servants, Bill's medical degree and upscale apartment notwithstanding. Seated at Sharkey's he reads a newspaper account of Mandy's collapse from an overdose, and Kubrick means Bill's prior warning to Mandy—"You can't keep doing this"—to reflect his own situation and to connect with "Lucky to Be Alive." Obsessive jealousy and pornographic fantasy quickly become addictions that can break down and destroy the conscientious doctor and upright family man. The article's text moves progressively toward the camera until part of it reveals that Mandy was accompanied to the room by two men, recalling Nick Nightingale's escorted departure from the Hotel Jason, and that she was avidly pursuing a career in acting aided by "many important friends in the fashion and entertainment worlds."[81]

The death of mind that Mandy suffered before her physical death, and that now threatens Bill, is reflected in his initial dialogue with the receptionist after he goes to the hospital to examine her:

Receptionist: Her name again?

Bill: Curran. Amanda Curran.

Receptionist: C-U-R-R-A-N.

Bill: Yes.

Receptionist: Miss Amanda Curran?

Bill: That's right.

Receptionist: I'm sorry, doctor. Miss Curran died this afternoon.

Bill: She died this afternoon?

Receptionist: Yes, at three forty-five this afternoon. I'm sorry.

The repetitious dialogue is visually supplemented by the continual revolving of the door in the background. (Michel Chion observes forty-six examples of "parroting" in the script from the first instance, "[Gayle:] Where the rainbow ends. [Bill:] Where the rainbow ends?" to the last, "[Bill:] Forever? [Alice:] Forever? [Bill:] Forever." He adds that parroting shows how words can reduce individuality because they "belong to everybody" and because "language is not thought," but only "a succession of words.")[82]

The next cut visually conveys Bill's suicidal pursuit. A corridor shot reverses earlier ones that open into larger spaces. This one follows Bill from behind as he recedes toward a vanishing point that becomes the morgue, a gleaming silver room lacking complexity and color. In addition to the silver walls that mirror nothing, the reduction of mental space is indicated by the banked rows of corpse-containing body drawers. After the attendant slides Mandy out, the full frontal nudity of her ultra-pale corpse continues the association of erotic addiction with mental death. The voice-over that plays in Bill's mind as he bends down, as if to kiss the corpse, reveals what has driven Bill to view Mandy's body and indicates his inability to distinguish women in any way other than as wife or whore. He believes that Mandy is the Mysterious Woman who "saved" him at the mansion, and as his face approaches hers he hears her saying that she could not reveal herself "because it could cost me my life and possibly yours."

Even though Victor later confirms Bill's wish to believe that the two women are one, his tone suggests that he is expediently answering a leading question and telling Bill what he wants to hear. The credits indicate that the women are different people, played by different actresses: Mandy by Julienne Davis and the Mysterious Woman by Abigail Good. Good is taller and more statuesque than Davis, and as editor Nick James of *Sight & Sound* wryly observed, "They have different pubic hair."[83] Bill's inability to differentiate suggests a dulling of perception to the same blank whiteness Kubrick associated with death in *Barry Lyndon*, here imaged in the pallor of Mandy's corpse. The visual image of Bill leaning down toward Mandy's face expresses his near brush with death, and it is accompanied by ominous piano music that builds as he comes closer to her face.

Ironically, Mandy's red hair parallels that of Alice, the character most able to make distinctions, most alive emotionally as a wife and mother, and most intellectually perceptive as an observer of hypocrisy and a connoisseur of art. After Bill exits the morgue, the reverse corridor shot leads into an expanding space lined with bright abstract paintings, a Star Gate echo foreshadowing his return to Alice, and the potentiality of following her lead toward health and wholeness. At this point his cell phone rings, issuing a summons from Victor, who unintentionally will help him to reject the ugliness and artificiality of the world he had aspired to join.

The awakening Victor provides is accompanied by subtle cinematic elements of space and color. Continuing the corridor motif from the hospital, an attendant leads Bill on a long fifteen-second walk to Victor's study. The corridor's pink walls are elegantly ominous in their resemblance to those that trap Jack Torrance in the Overlook Hotel. Like Jack, Bill is given to understand that he lives in a more dangerous place than he imagined, but thanks to Victor, crude as he may be, Bill is not absorbed into the corruption that eventually possesses Jack. Instead he is warned to leave well enough alone, accept his status as a small fish, and return to his family in one piece.

Though Victor can wisely counsel physical self-defense, his example and outlook would destroy Bill if he took them to heart. The ambivalence of Victor's role is conveyed by the contrast between the ugliness of his language— "prick," "cocksucker," and "asshole"—and the color harmonies of his brightly colored space. The first glimpse reveals rich golden brown walls hung with expensive-looking period paintings. They surround an arresting red pool table illuminated by a light fixture holding three extremely bright green shaded lights. However, the central thematic feature is a triptych of large blue windows in the center of the back wall.[84] Their color, theatrically curtained borders, and placement directly over a radiator echo the background of Alice's shattering confession in the Harford bedroom. The discovery motif—Alice later refers to their "adventures"—is accentuated by the large model of a three-masted schooner centered directly below a second blue window that appears at key points in the dialogue.

As before, blue is associated with a distanced understanding that may just be beginning for Bill but is already established in the audience. After Victor pours Bill a drink, the first window remains prominent in the frame for three minutes, while the second is visible throughout the two-minute shot/reverse shot sequence that begins when Bill learns that Victor saw him at the party and later had him followed. The crosscuts to his open-mouthed amazement echo a similar expression during Alice's confession. Victor walks away from the window when he begins to excoriate Nick Nightingale for leading Bill astray, but the window motif returns when the blue triptych forms the whole background to Bill's intensely felt repetition of his earlier question and Victor's affirmative reply: "The woman lying dead at the morgue was the woman at the party."

Throughout the thirteen-minute dialogue Cruise masterfully conveys Bill's attempt to maintain his arrogant façade as his adult identity is dismantled piece by piece. The range of gradations includes sucking up to Victor upon entering; briefly assuming his masterful doctor pose when he thinks he has been called about a medical problem; nervous denial when told that Victor knew where he was the previous night; hanging his head when Victor tells him he saw him at the party, followed by a pathetic attempt at compo-

Figure 7.3. Embarrassed and angry, Bill grips the pool table after Victor tells him that he doesn't realize the danger he was in. *Courtesy of Warner Bros./Photofest © Warner Bros.*

sure, "Victor, what can I say?"; nasal exhaling somewhere between a laugh and a sob after Victor says he had him followed; the repeated placing of hand to forehead as if to soothe fractured assumptions about the people he thought he knew and his place among them.

After Victor tells Bill of his failure to play a role he naively believed his social sophistication had achieved—"Those people arrive in limos and you showed up in a taxi"—he crosses his arms tightly across his body, and holding his hand against his cheek and then closing his eyes with his fingertips, he shakily repeats, "There was a . . . there was a . . . woman there, who, erh . . . tried to warn me."[85] His need to believe in her saving grace ironically merges erotic fixation with Oedipal need. Holding his right hand to his right cheek as if he has been slapped, and extending his right hand toward Victor as if he were striking back, he "sees" an opening. Discovering inconsistency seems to be a triumph to a mind limited by logic, and Bill's righteous anger echoes HAL's calm confidence: "Do you mind telling me what kind of fucking charade ends with somebody turning up dead?" But his body wilts again when Victor tells him, "That whole play-acted 'take me' phony sacrifice that you've been jerking yourself off with had nothing to do with her real death."[86]

The scene ends with an image of Bill standing with arms tightly crossed in front of Victor whose hands are paternally placed on his shoulders. His own potential mental death is ironically figured in Victor's concluding line: "Listen Bill, nobody killed anybody. Someone died. It happens all the time. Life goes on. It always does until it doesn't." Then in a stunning cut we see a close-up of Bill's blue-lit mask lying expressionless on a purple pillow just before the camera moves right to reveal Alice peacefully sleeping.[87] Kubrick means to say that being alive is synonymous with a vital inner life, and that a death of spirit, invisible beneath the mask, can occur long before respiration stops.

In the next cut Bill opens the apartment door and follows the familiar route past the green and gold paintings in the hallway, past the Christmas tree in front of the blue-lit windows, and past the bright flower paintings into the kitchen to open a beer. This time, however, the familiarity of his home, like all the taken-for-granted aspects of his life, lacks the promise of shelter because it is counterpointed by the Ligeti piano line that accompanied his fearful retreat from the Stalker and his stunned discovery of Mandy's death in the newspaper. The music's driving repetition creates suspense, heightens intensity, and signals an approaching dramatic climax. It softens as he opens the beer and remains a quiet undertone through a dissolve to his opening the bedroom door. Then after stopping completely for a beat, the respite is shattered by a single punishing note that accelerates as it pounds the ears sixteen times in rapid succession. It transforms to a trill in the cut to Alice still asleep next to the mask, but as the camera cuts to a close-up of Bill bending his knees to sit on the bed, the trill, though still heard, yields to the Stalker theme, booming in bass fortissimo. The effect is like a final blow to a rubber-legged fighter. The music accompanies Bill's redemptive return to infancy, letting up as he lays his head on Alice's breast, fading further as he starts to weep, and stopping completely just after he says "I'll tell you everything" a second time.

Kubrick's conclusion is very different from Schnitzler's. In the novel both characters calmly reflect on the night's events, firmly assuring their future and that of their daughter. Like Kubrick, Schnitzler does not recount the substance of Fridolin's confession, ending the novel with the couple still in bed as dawn breaks. Unworldly in comparison to her husband, as befits a fin de siècle wife, Albertine's "impassive" face is that of a wise child. Her "large bright eyes" reflecting "the day [that] now seemed to be dawning" express saintlike forgiveness and faith. This demeanor never wavers as Fridolin, far more composed than Bill, asks "hesitantly yet full of hope" what they should do. Taking his head in her hands and "pillowing it tenderly against her breast," Albertine says they are "truly awake at least for a good while," and when Fridolin wants to add "forever," she whispers cryptically, "Never enquire into the future."

Having prudently delivered this mild caution, the novel ends with a celebration of familial bliss: "Both lay there in silence . . . dreamlessly close to one another—until, as every morning at seven, there was a knock upon the bedroom door and with the usual noises from the street, a triumphant sunbeam coming in between the curtains, and a child's gay laughter from the adjacent room, another day began."[88]

Kubrick's ending is more problematic. The need to diverge from Schnitzler was suggested early on by cowriter Frederic Raphael: "It's a good story, but it's not a great one. Its final irony is a little too neat. You start with the parents with their little girl, and you end with them and her. It's cute, but it turns all that happens into a dark tale that gets tied up with a bow. There's not much progression."[89] Apparently taking this to heart, Kubrick altered the affect of the characters after the husband's confession. In his version the morning-after occurs in another room with the couple fully clothed, and a significant "progression" is conveyed cinematically, through light, color, and acting. Though husband and wife both look as though they have cried themselves out, their language and lighting are strikingly opposed.

The cut from the dark blue bedroom reveals Alice in three-quarters closeup wearing a pale blue sweater matching the color of her eyes. Behind her, vertical lines of pink, gold, and orange in shallow focus harmonize with her dark red hair and flushed pink skin. In her upright left hand, prominently displaying her wedding ring, she holds a cigarette, providing a stark contrast to the pot-smoking scene where she had inflicted so much pain. In that scene her husband had tried to seduce her by calling her "a very beautiful woman," just as Sandor had done at the party. Nick Nightingale extolled the beauty of the women at the mansion to Bill, but when the spectator is given his privilege, clichéd images of full-breasted, full frontal nudity are anti-erotic and bizarre. Nicole Kidman's beauty is most apparent in the film when she is wearing glasses, or has just awakened.[90]

The film displays the disparity between the pinup ideal and what an eye wide open sees. In this scene Alice is just recovering from crying all night (as Kidman did in preparing for the shoot), but has not "cried [her] eyes out," as she recalled of Ovid, mocking the expertise of Sandor's model. Rather, she has cried out the rage and suffocation that had trapped her in the bedroom mirror and has overcome the paralyzing effect of erotic fantasy: "He glanced at me [and] I could hardly move."[91] Since her dream, however, she has taken a quantum leap, and in the end Kubrick lets her speak for him.

Figure 7.4.　Alice looks lovingly at Bill, while helping Helena with math. Her glasses set her apart from him and mark the self-knowledge she eventually gains. *Courtesy of Warner Bros./Photofest © Warner Bros.*

Figure 7.5.　Joker too wears glasses, as he tells the incredulous colonel that his "Born to Kill" helmet and peace button refer to "the duality of man." He and Alice embody the evolutionary hope that connects their films. *Courtesy of Warner Bros./Photofest © Warner Bros.*

The soft morning light on her face accentuates her progress when the camera cuts to Bill still slumped in darkness. The three-quarters profile shot shows him on a dark red sofa wearing black pants, a matching black sweater, with only the back of his neck receiving light from a window behind him. Though there are three cuts to each of them during the eighty-five-second scene, most of the sequence frames Alice. Rubbing her fingers together as if still distraught, she brings herself back to the concerns of the moment and begins to lead Bill toward responsible maturity: "Helena's gonna be up soon. She's uh . . . (long pause, struggling, before the cut to Bill as she finishes the line) she's expecting us to take her Christmas shopping today." Still in darkness, Bill's wordless response tells us that he feels drained and helpless and that he will need to rely on his wife's strength. A sudden cut to the upscale toy store reveals significant changes in both characters.[92]

In contrast to the preceding scene, the toy store set is an explosion of color and movement, perhaps another Star Gate leading to Alice's evolved vision. In its complex gradations of primary colors and pastels, it is also another "rainbow," echoing the paintings in the apartment that reflect the vitality of Alice's inner life. Her advance is also shown in the toning down of surface glamour. Her black turtleneck and camel coat completely cover her body, accentuating the inner "color" that shines from her eyes and through the glasses that connote mature insight. In contrast, Bill's eyes remain nervous and dark. At first his arms are defensively crossed, and the continual bowing of his head suggests that he is desperately thinking of something to say. By emphasizing Kidman's superior height through her hairstyle and careful positioning, the camera supplements her dominance in the dialogue. She is the first to speak:

Alice: That's nice (as Helena looks at a miniature pram).

Helena: I could put Sabrina in here.

Alice: Yeah.

Helena: It's really . . . pretty.

Alice: It's old-fashioned. (And after Helena has run off and discovered a huge teddy bear) He's big.

Helena: I hope Santa Claus gets me one of these for Christmas.

Helena expresses Mandy's dream and that of the pre-enlightened Alice—to be "pretty" and to attract a "big" man. But the film has shown that these achievements produce the equivalent of stuffed animals rather than human beings with inner lives. The Sabrina reference was timely in that Sydney

Pollack's remake of Billy Wilder's classic 1954 *Sabrina* had been released in 1995, while Kubrick and Raphael were preparing the script.[93] (At that time, of course, they could not have known that Pollack would replace Harvey Keitel as Victor Ziegler in 1997.)[94] The story is a fairy tale about the daughter of a Long Island chauffeur enchanted by the lives of the rich people her father serves. After a year in Paris as a fashion intern, she returns as a radiantly beautiful woman (Audrey Hepburn or Julia Ormond) and is courted by the younger of the estate's two owners (William Holden or Greg Kinnear), the Prince Charming she had worshipped from afar. But the older brother (Humphrey Bogart or Harrison Ford) prefers that the prince marry the daughter of a business partner to achieve a lucrative family merger and decides to woo Cinderella himself as a cynical diversion. Of course, he falls in love and Sabrina chooses him: "It is here," as Roger Ebert said, that the film "ventures into Freudianism." But the film does not belabor this implication, and Ebert found it interesting as "escapism about escapism. Sabrina is escaping into this movie world as much as we are."[95]

Before the exchange with her mother, Helena tries to catch floating soap bubbles, visual equivalents of the ephemeral dreams that gave Bill and Alice so little substance in themselves and in their marriage. The miniature baby carriage that might hold her Sabrina doll is an "old fashioned" container, big enough for a Hollywood fairy tale but not for a Bettelheim one.[96] The selection suggests that Helena thinks of herself as her mother's doll and wants to imitate her guidance. Her next choice, a Barbie doll, suggests how far Alice herself has come and how she may now be able to guide Helena to a richer and wider view. An analogy to her straitjacketed role in relation to her husband is concisely described in Jung's essay on "Marriage as a Psychological Relationship": "The simpler nature works on the more complicated like a room that is too small, that does not allow him enough space. The complicated nature, on the other hand, gives the simpler one too many rooms with too much space, so that she never knows where she belongs."[97]

Here, with the gender pronouns reversed, is the impetus to Alice's need to break out of the role she could no longer play for Bill, and a new equilibrium of contained and container that plays out in the rest of the scene. In addition to being shorter than Alice, Bill's reduction is conveyed by his clothing. For the first time in the film other than the bedroom scenes, he is tieless, and beneath his overcoat he wears a dark red sweater in place of the consistent black and white uniform that had reflected his simplistically imagined rank. In addition to the open collar, his open topcoat conveys a loss of certainty, especially because Alice's coat is closed and her neck is covered by the black turtleneck.

Bill shrinks a little more when he thrusts his hands in his coat pockets and opens the coat just at the point when he asks Alice what they should do. The impression of boyish innocence is consistently conveyed in the film by the shock of black hair that hangs over his forehead in every scene except the opening ones at Ziegler's party and in his medical office. Conversely, Alice's forehead is always exposed as if to suggest her greater capacity for reflection. (This contrast is enhanced by a baldness motif associated with threats to Bill's innocence: by Milich complaining of hair loss against a background of wigged mannequin heads at Rainbow Fashions; by a bald attendant who hands Bill a warning upon his return to the mansion; and by the shaved-head figures of the doorman at the Sonata Café and the Stalker on Wren Street.)

Bill's mussed hair may also signal a curative disintegration. Michael Herr described the negative sexuality of *Eyes Wide Shut* as a portrayal of spiritual malaise rather than puritanical censure: "As a not so pure product of the sixties, I've often wondered whether over the long run the sexual freedom of those years didn't numb more genitals than it inflamed, more than all the prohibitions of all the decades that went before . . . what if freedom isn't just another word for nothing left to lose, but something that's lost whenever you mistake a carnal matter for a spiritual matter?"[98]

By the end of the film Alice has learned not to make that mistake. Early on she saw through her persona and wanted more. After shattering the mirrored bliss of her marital dream, she had a dream vision of sexual merger that seemed to be a nightmare. But by enduring the dream and not losing her capacity to love, she finally learns to creatively channel her dark side, just as Joker did in Vietnam. In the end her exploration makes her a uniquely feminine avatar of Campbell's hero with a thousand faces.[99]

At the same time she is a fragile human being, and the combination of Kubrick's direction and Kidman's acting makes her struggle admirable because it clearly isn't easy. Throughout the toy store dialogue, Alice needs to rise to the occasion because Bill's exposure has reduced him to her second child. Just at the point that he asks her what she thinks they should do, Helena shows her "a fairy doll," a toy not haphazardly present on the set but a specific symbol written into the script.[100] With a strained smile at Helena, Alice can only repeat the question twice before she can begin to form an answer, and the doll suggests the magical transformation she must undergo to protect those whose spiritual survival depends on her. The scene's power lies in the struggle she undergoes to give birth to this larger self. Her initial parroted response—"What do I think?"—had been used earlier by other characters to connote vapidity; now it is used contrastively to indicate serious reflection.

Throughout the dialogue, long pauses, facial expressions, and head movements make her responses more thoughtfully expressive than Albertine's immediate and relatively prosaic solution. After Helena is out of earshot and a second "what do I think," there is a nine-second pause before she sighs deeply and begins to deliver the film's key thematic lines. Though she has shaky moments, her eyes are as courageously unwavering as Redmond Barry's were in combat, and her vocal tone is intelligently firm rather than sentimentally forgiving:

> *Alice:* Maybe, I think, we should be grateful *(six-second pause)* . . . grateful that we've managed to survive through all of our adventures, whether they were real or only a dream.
>
> *Bill (after a six-second pause he seems to understand her answer as forgiveness and replies with tentative hope):* Are you . . . are you sure of that?
>
> *Alice (shaky again at having to pronounce a certainty she cannot affirm; she rolls her eyes for a split second, sighs, places her hand to her forehead, touches her finger to her eye under her glasses, and shakes her head; then after putting her hand to her forehead as if reluctant to reply hurtfully, she looks him directly in the eye and begins to speak):* Only as sure as I am that the reality of one night, let alone that of a whole lifetime, can ever be the whole truth.
>
> *Bill (delivering the line as a tentative question, rather than a rueful reflection as Fridolin does):* And no dream is ever just a dream?
>
> *Alice (another six-second pause, and after looking down for a beat, she looks up resolutely):* The important thing is we're awake now, and hopefully for a long time to come.[101]

After Bill romantically adds, "Forever," Kidman again conveys the sense that these are not just empty pronouncements but difficult insights to feel and express. With a pained negative shake of her head, she asks him not to "use that word—it frightens me." In the cut to Bill, his eyes show fear, his mouth is open, and he takes a deep breath as if preparing himself to be hurt by what she says next. Seeing his response, Alice's maternal strength returns and her tone is once again firm and assuring: "But I do love you, and you know . . . there is something very important we need to do as soon as possible." After Bill asks, "What's that?" Alice pauses for four seconds and delivers the film's last line: "Fuck."

The word's unexpectedness in this context creates a distance from the kind of kiss-and-make-up ending of a film like the one Alice is watching just before and after her phone call interrupts Domino's orchestrated kiss.[102] In the first cut to the Harford kitchen, the small TV plays a scene from Paul

Mazursky's *Blume in Love* (1973) where George Segal, separated from his wife, Susan Anspach, comments on a Venetian waiter's saying "You're welcome," in response to his "Grazie": "If I were Italian, he would have answered me in Italian."[103] The clip parallels Bill's cluelessness in Domino's kitchen, while a subsequent cut ironically foreshadows Kubrick's ending by showing Segal and Anspach walking hand in hand into a future assured by the unfaithful husband's pained regret and the wronged wife's hard-won maturity. (Mazursky had acted in Kubrick's first feature, *Fear and Desire*, 1953.)[104]

In her own hard-won maturity Alice has come to understand sexuality's power to shatter psychic balance within and between human beings. That may be why "Fuck" is her last line and the film's final word. In the second bedroom scene Bill uses it once to try to seduce his wife, and both characters use it repeatedly to vent their frustration. As a colloquial adjective, the word expresses anger: "fucking this," "fucking that." As an active singular verb, it expresses aggressive dominance: Alice fucks Bill by narrating her extramarital attraction, and Bill tries to fuck her back by fucking someone else. Except for this scene where both characters use the word increasingly as their anger escalates, "fuck" is not heard again until Ziegler peppers his speech with obscenities in his last dialogue with Bill. The words contribute to the ugly brutality of Victor's character and assume an air of menace when Ziegler verbally roughs up Nick Nightingale:

> And then I remembered seeing you with that prick piano player, Nick whatever-the-fuck his name was at my party. . . . If he hadn't mentioned it to you in the first place, none of this would have happened. I recommended that little cocksucker to those people and he's made me look like a complete asshole. . . . OK, he had a bruise on his face. That's a hell of a lot less than he deserves.[105]

The implication is that however friendly Victor may seem at the moment, Bill's punishment could be worse since he knows more about his patient than Nick knew about any of the individuals at the orgy.

At the end of the scene Victor tells Bill that "Mandy" was not harmed for protecting him at the mansion and that she only had her "brains fucked out. *Period.*" But for Kubrick life does not go on if people's minds are fucked by the Ludovico treatment of addictive fantasy. In making "fuck" his film's period, Kubrick erases its obscenity by turning it into an active verb with a plural subject. In a post-*Shining* interview, Kubrick reflected on "failure of communication" as one of his major thematic concerns.[106] Though it is spoken in a context of gentle revelation, Alice's closing word is nothing less than a demand for authentic exchange. *Eyes Wide Shut* is the director's final effort to intimately involve his viewers, making them see and realize themselves anew.

Notes

1. Michel Chion, *Kubrick's Cinema Odyssey* (London: British Film Institute, 2001), 79.

2. Alexander Walker, Sybil Taylor, and Ulrich Ruchti, *Stanley Kubrick, Director: A Visual Analysis* (New York: W. W. Norton, 1999), 224.

3. Walker, Taylor, and Ruchti, *Stanley Kubrick, Director*, 233.

4. Mario Falsetto, *Stanley Kubrick: A Narrative and Stylistic Analysis* (Westport, Conn.: Greenwood Press, 1994), 137–138.

5. In Peter Bondanello, *The Cinema of Federico Fellini* (Princeton, N.J.: Princeton University Press, 1992), 299; quoted in Falsetto, *Stanley Kubrick*, 139.

6. Carl Jung, quoted in J. E. Cirlot, *A Dictionary of Symbols*, trans. Jack Sage (New York: Philosophical Library, 1962), 55.

7. *2001: A Space Odyssey*, DVD, directed by Stanley Kubrick (1968; Burbank, Calif.: Warner Bros. Home Video, 2001), chapter 3.

8. On red-orange, see Faber Birren, *Color and Human Response* (New York: Van Nostrand Reinhold, 1978), 58–59; on the color wheel, see Birren, *History of Color in Painting* (New York: Reinhold, 1965), 142.

9. *2001*, DVD, chapter 28.

10. Wassily Kandinsky, *Concerning the Spiritual in Art* (1912; New York: Dover, 1977), 39; on blue as "darkness made visible," and its religious connotations, see Cirlot, *A Dictionary of Symbols*, 52.

11. *2001*, DVD, chapter 30.

12. Stanley Kubrick, interview by Joseph Gelmis, "The Film Director as Superstar: Stanley Kubrick," in *The Film Director as Superstar* (Garden City, N.Y.: Doubleday, 1970); repr. in *Stanley Kubrick: Interviews*, ed. Gene D. Phillips (Jackson: University Press of Mississippi), 91.

13. Stanley Kubrick, interview by Colin Young, "The Hollywood War of Independence," *Film Quarterly* 12, no. 3 (Spring 1959): 4–15; repr. in Phillips, ed., *Stanley Kubrick: Interviews*, 7; for Eisenstein's own comments on black and white in *Alexander Nevsky*, see Sergei M. Eisenstein, "Color and Meaning," in *The Film Sense*, ed. and trans. Jay Leyda (New York: Harcourt Brace, 1947), 142; for Kubrick's negative comments on that film, see Maurice Rapf, "A Talk with Stanley Kubrick about *2001*," *Action*, January/February 1969, repr. in Phillips, ed., *Stanley Kubrick: Interviews*, 79; on Kubrick's youthful interest in Eisenstein, see Vincent LoBrutto, *Stanley Kubrick: A Biography* (New York: Donald I. Fine, 1997), 37.

14. See my comments on the Gogol reference in *A Clockwork Orange*, this volume, chapter 3.

15. S. M. Eisenstein, "On Color," in *Selected Works*, vol. 2, ed. Michael Glenny and Richard Taylor, trans. Michael Glenny (London: British Film Institute, 1991), 263.

16. Eisenstein, "On Color," 263.

17. Eisenstein, "On Color," 263.

18. Chester Eyre quoted by Stephen Pizzello, "A Sword in the Bed: Cinematographer Larry Smith Helps Stanley Kubrick Craft a Unique Look for *Eyes Wide Shut*, a Dreamlike Coda to the Director's Brilliant Career," *American Cinematographer*, October 1999, www.theasc.com/magazine/oct99/sword/.

19. Eyre, quoted by Pizzello, "A Sword in the Bed," www.theasc.com/magazine/oct99/sword/.

20. Larry Smith, quoted by Pizzello, "A Sword in the Bed," www.theasc.com/magazine/oct99/sword/.

21. Arthur Schnitzler, *Dream Story*, trans. J. M. Q. Davies (1926; London: Penguin Books, 1999), 241.

22. See Birren, *History of Color in Painting*, 110.

23. Smith, quoted by Pizzello, "A Sword in the Bed," www.theasc.com/magazine/oct99/sword/.

24. *The Bhagavad-Gita: Krishna's Counsel in Time of War*, 4:7–8, trans. Barbara Stoler Miller (New York: Bantam, 1986), 50.

25. See Salil Tripathi, "Enraged by Madonna and Nicole," *New Statesman*, September 20, 1999, www.saliltripathi.com/articles/20Sept1999NewStatesman.html.

26. *The Bhagavad Gita*, 11:32–33, trans. Ramanand Prasad, eawc.evansville.edu/anthology/gita.htm. The Stoler Miller translation does not use the word "Death." It reads, "I am time grown old, creating world destruction, set in motion to annihilate the worlds; even without you, all these warriors arrayed in hostile ranks will cease to exist. Therefore, arise and win glory! Conquer your foes and fulfill your kingship! They are already killed by me. Be just my instrument, the archer at my side" (*The Bhagavad-Gita: Krishna's Counsel in Time of War*, 11:32–33, 104–105).

27. *The Bhagavad-Gita*, trans. Barbara Stoler Miller, 11:28–33, 104.

28. *Eyes Wide Shut*, DVD, directed by Stanley Kubrick (1999; Burbank, Calif.: Warner Bros. Home Video, 2001), chapter 24.

29. Heinrich Zimmer, *Myths and Symbols in Indian Art and Civilization*, ed. Joseph Campbell (Princeton, N.J.: Princeton University Press, 1972), 207.

30. Zimmer, *Myths and Symbols*, 199.

31. *Eyes Wide Shut*, DVD, chapter 5.

32. *Eyes Wide Shut*, DVD, chapter 6.

33. Carl G. Jung, "The Stages of Life," in *The Portable Jung*, ed. Joseph Campbell, trans. R. F. C. Hull (1930; New York: Viking, 1971), 4–5.

34. Carl G. Jung, "Answer to Job," in *The Portable Jung*, ed. Joseph Campbell, trans. R. F. C. Hull (1930; New York: Viking, 1971), 561.

35. See this volume, chapter 3.

36. *Eyes Wide Shut*, DVD, chapter 1.

37. See the discussion of M. H. Abrams, *The Mirror and the Lamp: Romantic Theory and the Critical Tradition* (New York: Oxford University Press, 1953), and its influence on *The Shining*, this volume, chapter 4.

38. *Eyes Wide Shut*, DVD, chapter 12.

39. *Eyes Wide Shut*, DVD, chapter 1.

40. Louis Begley, *Wartime Lies* (New York: Alfred A. Knopf, 1991).

41. Gene D. Phillips and Rodney Hill, *The Encyclopedia of Stanley Kubrick* (New York: Checkmark Books, 2002), 263.

42. *Lolita*, DVD, directed by Stanley Kubrick (1962; Burbank, Calif.: Warner Bros. Home Video, 2001), chapter 41.

43. *Lolita*, DVD, chapter 41.

44. *Eyes Wide Shut*, DVD, chapter 4.

45. E. T. A. Hoffman, "The Nutcracker and the Mouse King," in *The Best Tales of Hoffman*, ed. and trans. E. F. Bleiler (1816; New York: Dover, 1979), 130–182.

46. *Eyes Wide Shut*, DVD, chapter 2.

47. *Eyes Wide Shut*, DVD, chapter 3.

48. Publius Ovidius Naso (Ovid), *The Love Books of Ovid*. Book 1: *The Art of Love*, trans. J. Lewis May (New York: Rarity Press, 1930), www.sacred-texts.com/cla/ovid/lboo/index.htm.

49. Ovid, *The Art of Love*, www.sacred-texts.com/cla/ovid/lboo/index.htm.

50. See Betty Radice, *Who's Who in the Ancient World* (Baltimore: Penguin, 1973), 180–182; and Sir William Smith, *Smaller Classical Dictionary*, rev. E. H. Blakeney and John Warrington (New York: E. P. Dutton, 1958), 207–208.

51. *Eyes Wide Shut*, DVD, chapter 5.

52. *Eyes Wide Shut*, DVD, chapter 11.

53. See this volume, chapter 3.

54. *Eyes Wide Shut*, DVD, chapter 2.

55. See this volume, chapter 2, on Kubrick's association of black with growth, and chapter 5, on the association of white with failure and death. Cf. Eisenstein's similar reversal of the positive associations of black and white, mentioned in this chapter.

56. See this volume, chapter 3.

57. *2001*, DVD, chapter 7; see this volume, chapter 2.

58. *2001*, DVD, chapter 6.

59. *Eyes Wide Shut*, DVD, chapter 6.

60. See Frederic Raphael, "Onward and Upward with the Arts, 'A Kubrick Odyssey,'" *New Yorker*, June 14, 1999, 40.

61. Stanley Kubrick, interview by Eric Nordern, *Playboy*, September 1968; repr. in Phillips, ed., *Stanley Kubrick: Interviews*, 67.

62. *Eyes Wide Shut*, DVD, chapter 14.

63. Robert Ardrey, *African Genesis* (New York: Atheneum, 1961), 92.

64. Ardrey, *African Genesis*, 136.

65. *Eyes Wide Shut*, DVD, chapter 16.

66. Ardrey, *African Genesis*, 135–136.

67. *Eyes Wide Shut*, DVD, chapter 10.

68. See this volume, chapter 6.

69. *Full Metal Jacket*, DVD, directed by Stanley Kubrick (1987; Burbank, Calif.: Warner Bros. Home Video, 2001), chapter 2.

70. *Eyes Wide Shut*, DVD, chapter 31.

71. Martin Scorsese, interview in *Stanley Kubrick: A Life in Pictures*, DVD, directed by Jan Harlan (1999; Burbank, Calif.: Warner Bros. Home Video, 2001).

72. *Eyes Wide Shut*, DVD, chapter 2.

73. *Eyes Wide Shut*, DVD, chapter 6.

74. *Eyes Wide Shut*, DVD, chapter 7.

75. See Roger Clarke, "Putting the Knife into Stanley: A Review of *Eyes Wide Open* and *Dream Story*," review of *Eyes Wide Open: A Memoir of Stanley Kubrick*, by Frederic Raphael, and *Dream Story*, by Arthur Schnitzler, *Independent* (London), August 2, 1999; see also Michel Chion's reference to Raphael's collaboration on Greek and Latin translations, *Eyes Wide Shut* (London: British Film Institute, 2002), 17.

76. See Thomas Bulfinch, "The Golden Fleece—Medea," in *Bulfinch's Mythology: The Age of Fable*, www.sacred-texts.com/cla/bulf/bulf16.htm.

77. Schnitzler, *Dream Story*, 62–66.

78. *Eyes Wide Shut*, DVD, chapter 24.

79. Stanley Kubrick, interview by Michel Ciment, *Kubrick: The Definitive Edition* (New York: Faber & Faber, 2001), 188.

80. *Eyes Wide Shut*, DVD, chapter 29.

81. *Eyes Wide Shut*, DVD, chapter 32.

82. Chion, *Eyes Wide Shut*, 70–71.

83. See Charlotte O'Sullivan, "Body of Evidence," *Independent* (London), August 27, 1999.

84. *Eyes Wide Shut*, DVD, chapter 33.

85. *Eyes Wide Shut*, DVD, chapter 34.

86. *Eyes Wide Shut*, DVD, chapter 35.

87. *Eyes Wide Shut*, DVD, chapter 36.

88. Schnitzler, *Dream Story*, 98–99.

89. Raphael, "Onward and Upward."

90. *Eyes Wide Shut*, DVD, chapters 24, 29, and 36.

91. *Eyes Wide Shut*, DVD, chapter 7.

92. *Eyes Wide Shut*, DVD, chapter 37. The "stage directions" throughout this scene are mine rather than those of the published screenplay.

93. *Sabrina*, DVD, directed by Billy Wilder (1954; Hollywood, Calif.: Paramount, 2001); *Sabrina*, DVD, directed by Sydney Pollack (1995; Hollywood, Calif.: Paramount, 2002).

94. See David Hughes, *The Complete Kubrick* (London: Virgin, 2000), 247.

95. Roger Ebert, review of *Sabrina*, directed by Sydney Pollack, *Chicago Sun Times*, December 15, 1995.

96. See this volume, chapter 4.

97. Carl G. Jung, "Marriage as a Psychological Relationship," in *The Portable Jung*, ed. Joseph Campbell, trans. R. F. C. Hull (1930; New York: Viking, 1971), 171.

98. Michael Herr, *Kubrick* (New York: Grove Press, 2000), 78.

99. See this volume, chapters 2 and 4.

100. See Stanley Kubrick and Frederic Raphael, *Eyes Wide Shut* (New York: Warner Books, 1999), 163.

101. *Eyes Wide Shut*, DVD, chapter 37; the "stage directions" are mine.

102. *Eyes Wide Shut*, DVD, chapter 12.

103. *Blume in Love*, DVD, directed by Paul Mazursky (1973; Burbank, Calif.: Warner Bros. Home Video, 2007).

104. See Hughes, *The Complete Kubrick*, 17.

105. *Eyes Wide Shut*, DVD, chapter 33.

106. Kubrick, interview by Ciment, 188.

~

Afterword

After her husband's death, Christiane Kubrick invited several interviews to correct negative stereotypes created by the British tabloid press:

> All those awful stories . . . that he sprayed the grounds with insecticide because he was so afraid of intruders. This was a man who loved his animals, so how could he do such a thing? That he shot people and tried to pay them off because they are bleeding. Please? How could he not be hurt by this kind of lie? That he hated women, was phobic, obsessive, weird. I flinch, when I see all these things repeated about Stanley the so-called crazy man.[1]

Kubrick's oldest daughter, Katharina, recalled how her sister, Anya, once remarked that "the more she reads about daddy the more she thinks that Howard Hughes was probably a perfectly normal person." When asked if any of the books on Kubrick were equally unreliable, Christiane singled out Frederic Raphael's *Eyes Wide Open: A Memoir of Stanley Kubrick* (New York: Ballantine, 1999) and John Baxter's *Stanley Kubrick: A Biography* (London: HarperCollins, 1997).[2]

As coscreenwriter of *Eyes Wide Shut*, Raphael spent considerable one-on-one time with Kubrick. The objectionable passages of his memoir, describing the director as physically timid, penny-pinching, and secretive, are gratuitous and transparently reflect the author's own insecurities and obsessions. Nevertheless, Raphael's memoir is professionally informative when he comments on inherent differences between a writer and a director in conceiving a story. Baxter, on the other hand, had no direct access to Kubrick and often relied on the testimony of coworkers with a personal ax to grind. Aside from the errors of fact that members of Kubrick's family were in the best position to notice, Baxter spread the misanthropy smear from the man to the work:

> In Kubrick's films, love dies, ambition dies. Power conquers all, but that too is fleeting. There remains only, always and forever, the eye. And yet, how much can a single eye see? Kubrick's view of life is as monocular as that of his camera. Alone in his hoarded isolation, eye glued to his photographic peephole, glimpsing the world in flashes, he's forced to infer personality from an overheard conversation, guess at character from a movement, a shadow. In adolescence, Kubrick chose the life of the eye and the mind over that of the soul and the spirit. Concentration on so narrow a view of the world will yield its insights, but they risk being circumscribed and arid. That he should come at the end of his career to make *Eyes Wide Shut*, a film about two self-involved people and their fantasies, has a sour suitability. As light dims, a lens can become a mirror, reflecting back to the voyeur an image of himself.[3]

No wonder Baxter incensed the family, since this caricature of self-absorption was so contrary to their experience. Kubrick's reluctance to travel heightened the legend of the world-hating hermit, and the family made that issue the core of their defense. Christiane told Patrick Amory of *Paris Match* how Kubrick did not limit his personal life to the immediate family:

> *Amory:* People say he was a recluse and a hermit, and yet you describe him as convivial. Astonishing, *n'est-ce pas?*
>
> *Christiane:* The "hermit" loved nothing more than to talk with people. Our house was always a place for friendly professional meetings. He loved to meet my artist friends, or my daughters' friends—musicians and students. He spent hours on the telephone, and many of his friendships were exclusively by phone. It is true that he didn't like to leave [his home in] Childwickbury House, and the love and comfort of his family, but he was still very outgoing. His close friends used to say, "Before there was an internet, there was Stanley Kubrick."[4]

Anya told Peter Warren of the *Scottish Sunday Express* that the family was so important that "when filming in Ireland for *Barry Lyndon* became a necessity, we all traveled together like a gypsy caravan, dogs and all! It's very strange to find ourselves defending this desire to be with his family and if possible at home. I thought it was what most dads wanted." Phillip Hobbs, Katharina's husband, commented that Kubrick's "idea of bliss" was to work in his office "with one eye on his wife painting out in the garden," and Anya added that Stanley liked "to be able to emerge from his office and walk straight into the family kitchen and then back to his desk."[5]

Perhaps Kubrick's concern for his family and friends was a microcosm of his concern for humanity's future. The family is the primary focus of attention in *The Shining* and *Eyes Wide Shut*, and children or childlike adults are major characters in the six films discussed here. Children were also the protagonists of Kubrick's unfinished projects, *A.I.: Artificial Intelligence*, about a robot boy who wants to be human, and *Aryan Papers*, about a nine-year-old Jewish boy hiding in Poland during the Holocaust.[6] In 1968, during a post-*2001* interview, Kubrick commented on the cultural future of the family bond:

> *Eric Nordern:* Do you think that by 2001 the institution of the family, which some social scientists have characterized as moribund, may have evolved into something quite different from what it is today?
>
> *Kubrick:* One can offer all kinds of impressive intellectual arguments against the family as an institution, its inherent authoritarianism, etc., but when you get right down to it, the family is the most primitive and visceral and vital unit in society. You may stand outside your wife's hospital room during childbirth muttering, "My God, what a responsibility! Is it right to take on this terrible obligation? What am I really doing here?"; and then you go in and look down at the face of your child and—zap!—that ancient programming takes over and your response is one of wonder and joy and pride. It's a classic case of genetically imprinted social patterns. There are very few things in this world that have an unquestionable importance in and of themselves and are not susceptible to debate or rational argument, but the family is one of them.[7]

2001 portrayed the evolving mind of the human family as a whole, while subsequent films concerned the success or failure of individuals to know themselves. Cinema at its best strives for consciousness, and Kubrick may have hoped that his spectators would come to see what his characters don't see, or are only beginning to see, and be moved to go on from there. According to Christiane, the director's rehearsal of *Eyes Wide Shut*'s leading actors mirrored this quest: "Nicole and Tom spent a great deal of time here in our house during the shooting. . . . In order to play their roles they had to analyze themselves, dissect themselves. And because Stanley was like a grandfather to them . . . a strong confidence was born between them. Stanley believed in both of them, and trusting him, they gave him all they had." Kubrick later told Christiane that he was especially moved during the bedroom scenes, because Cruise and Kidman were not content to simply shed their clothes but courageously stripped away their "skins," achieving a "complete nakedness" of "being."[8]

Kubrick enabled these extraordinary performances by allowing the actors to embark on their own course of self-discovery rather than trying to dictate that course:

> Stanley cleared the set and allowed Tom and Nicole to watch themselves on a monitor. He did not remain seated in front of them. He directed from a distance, allowing them to discover the finest nuance, the perfect gesture. He would repeat the scene over and over . . . "Let's go again, try something different." I know that Nicole and Tom would say they were inspired to search for the best, to seek their absolute limits. And in Stanley's eyes it was absolutely essential that they were a couple in real life. When they would cry, or touch, or smile, it was marvelous. Because they agreed to play the game Stanley proposed, they were able to explore all that was possible.[9]

Cruise and Kidman's subsequent divorce does not undercut Kubrick's message and intent. There is no guaranteed happy ending for Bill and Alice either, but for many spectators the experience of *Eyes Wide Shut* could lead to the awareness Kubrick sought to bestow on individuals ready to run the risk. In the end Alice is strong enough to know that her clarity may be transient, and rightly so if growth is to continue: "The important thing is we're awake now, and hopefully for a long time to come."[10] Kidman delivers these lines in a phony room of sleep-inducing toys. Lewis Carroll liberated his Alice by allowing her to see the absurdity of Victorian society, to be in it but not of it. The same is true for those spectators who may become unique versions of humanity's best self. They are the storyteller's children, and they are Stanley Kubrick's hope.

Notes

1. Christiane Kubrick, quoted by Sean O'Hagan, "I Flinch, When I See All These Things Repeated about Stanley the So-Called Crazy Man," *Observer* (London), April 17, 2005.

2. Nick James, "At Home with the Kubricks," *Sight & Sound*, September 1999, 12.

3. John Baxter, *Stanley Kubrick: A Biography* (London: HarperCollins, 1997), 4.

4. Christiane Kubrick, interview by Patrick Amory, *Paris Match*, September 9, 1999; my translation.

5. Anya Kubrick and Phillip Hobbs, quoted by Peter Warren, "I Flinch at Those Stories about Crazy Stanley," *Scottish Sunday Express* (Glasgow), July 11, 1999.

6. After Kubrick's death *A.I.* was directed and released by Steven Spielberg in 2001. On the genesis of that film, see *The Encyclopedia of Stanley Kubrick*, by Gene D. Phillips and Rodney Hill (New York: Checkmark Books, 2002), 6–8; on the source and plan for *Aryan Papers*, see Vincent LoBrutto, *Stanley Kubrick: A Biography* (New York: Donald I. Fine, 1997), 497–499.

7. Stanley Kubrick, interview by Eric Nordern, *Playboy*, September 1968; repr. in *Stanley Kubrick: Interviews*, ed. Gene D. Phillips (Jackson: University Press of Mississippi, 2001), 67.

8. Christiane Kubrick, interview by Amory, *Paris Match*.

9. Christiane Kubrick, interview by Amory, *Paris Match*.

10. *Eyes Wide Shut*, DVD, directed by Stanley Kubrick (1999; Burbank, Calif.: Warner Brothers Home Video, 2001), chapter 37.

~

Synopses

2001: A Space Odyssey (1968)

The film has three parts. In the first, "The Dawn of Man," a group of apelike prehumans spends every waking moment grazing on plants. They are defenseless against predators, and a leopard is shown dropping on one from a cliff and carrying him off. They do, however, exhibit aggressive displays toward other groups when both approach a watering hole at the same time. One morning they wake to discover a towering, black, rectangular object standing upright in the ground outside their cave. Their leader approaches it and finally summons the nerve to touch it. Evidently inspired by this contact, he suddenly understands that the bones he rummages among in the next scene can be used as weapons. From this point on he and his band become the earth's supreme predators, killing and eating tapirs for meat and driving a rival band from the watering hole with lethal blows of their bone clubs. Following earth's first murder, the leader euphorically hurls his club toward the sky where it suddenly becomes a space ship orbiting the earth three million years later.

In the rest of the first section the ape leader is replaced by his dominant counterpart, the scientist Dr. Heywood Floyd. After adroitly concealing the purpose of his mission from several Russian diplomats, he leads a group of scientists to the moon to investigate a black "monolith" identical to the one that inspired the apes. Protected by his space suit, Floyd reaches a gloved hand toward its silver edge, echoing the gesture of his ape ancestor. At this point the object emits a sound so piercing that it drives the scientists to cover their ears.

In the film's second section, "Jupiter Mission, Eighteen Months Later," the spaceship *Discovery* speeds toward Jupiter on a mysterious mission, carrying astronauts David Bowman and Frank Poole and their loyal servant, the brilliant 9000 model computer, HAL. But when HAL appears to have made a mistake about a mechanical function, the astronauts decide to disconnect him, since all of the ship's functions, including life support, are under HAL's control. HAL "overhears" them by reading their lips, and in a primitive survival-of-the-fittest battle, kills Poole by cutting his lifeline during a spacewalk repair. HAL, in turn, is killed by Bowman when the astronaut prevails in an "inspired" attack that HAL cannot compute.

After the film's second murder, Floyd appears to Bowman in a prerecorded message on a television screen to tell him that HAL alone knew the purpose of the mission. In the film's last section, "Jupiter and Beyond the Infinite," Bowman speeds toward Jupiter in a space pod through a magnificent array of space phenomena, led by the black monolith that floats ahead. In the last scene he finds himself in a strange room, furnished in eighteenth-century style. He ages quickly, dons a black dressing gown with square shoulders, and sits down to consume a luxurious last supper.

Next, we see him as a very old man lying on a bed, about to die. When he extends his arm upward, echoing the gesture of Floyd and the ape leader, the monolith appears at the foot of the bed. Then, in place of Bowman, the Star Child appears on the bed in a womblike globe. The camera advances directly into the monolith where its blackness becomes a night sky full of stars, with the blue orb of the earth to the left and the Star Child in his globe to the right. To the ascending strains of *Also Sprach Zarathustra*, the Star Child slowly turns his head to the right and gently directs his large, blue-eyed gaze into the camera as the film ends.

A Clockwork Orange (1971)

In a futuristic London of the late twentieth century, Alex and his teenage gang of droogs—Dim, Georgie, and Pete—gear up for a night of mayhem by drinking drug-laced milk at the Korova Milk Bar. Subsequent scenes show them beating an old drunk, vanquishing a rival gang, and joyriding in a stolen car. They end the evening by horrifically raping a writer's wife in her home, while her badly beaten husband is forced to watch. After returning to the Korova for a nightcap, Alex raps Dim across the thighs for blowing a raspberry at a female opera singer when she launches into an impromptu aria at a nearby table.

The leader's improbable love of classical music is shown in detail after he returns to his immaculate room, where the face of his hero, Ludwig van Beethoven, is stamped on the window shade. Alone in his sanctuary with Basil, his pet snake, Alex masturbates blissfully to the sounds of Beethoven's Ninth Symphony while fantasizing violent scenes from horror movies. After a brief visit from his social worker, Mr. Deltoid, the next morning, Alex goes to a record shop where he meets two teenage girls, both of whom he promptly beds in his room, while the camera and the soundtrack, playing the William Tell Overture, race in fast motion.

Later that evening his droogs complain that Alex is not a grown-up leader because he has abused Dim and because his night forays have not produced any cash. While he and the droogs are walking at dockside the next day, classical music heard from an open window inspires Alex to quell their rebellion by savagely knocking Dim and Georgie into the marina with his cane. Later, however, the droogs get their revenge by knocking Alex unconscious with a milk bottle after he emerges from a burglary, where he has accidentally killed a wealthy woman he had only intended to rob.

Taken into custody immediately, Alex is sent to prison, but his intelligence and cunning soon enable him to gain the favor of the prison chaplain, who gives him a comfortable job in the prison library. There he imagines scenes of sex and violence while reading about them in the Bible. Undeterred by the chaplain's warning that "when a man ceases to choose, he ceases to be a man," Alex seizes an opportunity to escape by volunteering to undergo the "Ludovico treatment," an experimental conditioning program that uses drugs and cinematic images to make the subject violently ill at the sight of violence. After being humiliated before visiting dignitaries in a theatrical demonstration of his inability to answer abuse, Alex is released but finds himself homeless when his parents refuse to take him in, having already rented out his room.

Alone and feeling suicidal on the streets, Alex is viciously attacked, first by a horde of homeless men, like the one he had earlier beaten, and then by Georgie and Dim, who have become policemen. Barely conscious in the rain, Alex drags himself to a country house that turns out to be the home of the couple he and his droogs had raped and beaten. The wife has died as a result of the assault, and the writer, Frank Alexander, has become a socialist advocate of the deprived masses. Thinking Alex to be "another victim of the modern age," he takes him in. But when Alex sings "Singin' in the Rain" in the bathtub, the same song he had sung during the rape, the writer knows who he is and determines to get revenge. After intense grilling, the writer and his compatriots discover that Alex becomes unbearably ill whenever he hears Beethoven's Ninth Symphony, the background score to the Nazi propaganda films he had been forced to watch during the treatment. Trapping Alex in an attic room, the writer has his revenge when the booming music drives Alex to "snuff it" by jumping from the window.

Under the black screen that immediately follows, Alex's voice-over begins just before his bandaged feet appear on a hospital bed: "I fell hard but I did not snuff it. Oh no, if I had snuffed it, I would not be here to tell what I have told. I came back to life, after a long black, black gap of what might have been a million years." He is nursed back to health by government edict because of public outcry against his dehumanizing punishment. With great fanfare and a slew of photographers, the chief government minister comes to the hospital to strategically confer compensation: an "interesting" job with a salary that takes his suffering into account, as long as he agrees to be publicly grateful to the very party that had ordered the Ludovico treatment in the first place.

As a special surprise, the minister has a magnificent stereo wheeled into the room, and to the rhapsodic sounds of the final "Ode to Joy" chorus of Beethoven's Ninth, he and the minister smilingly offer thumbs-up to popping flashbulbs. In the film's final shot Alex shows that he is "cured, all right" by returning to the synesthetic ecstasy he had enjoyed in his bedroom. As the Ninth surges to a climax, a fantastic cinema image shows Alex and a naked, black-gloved model performing an orgiastic ballet in a heavenly white space, while an elegant crowd of Edwardian ladies and gentleman delightedly applauds.

Barry Lyndon (1975)

In 1750s Ireland, Redmond Barry's mother has raised him by herself because his barrister father was killed shortly after his birth in a duel. While he is still an adolescent, his cousin, Nora Brady, sexually toys with him until the arrival of a British officer, Captain John Quin, whose military manliness, absurd but seemingly authentic to a country girl, in addition to his marriage offer of 500 pounds a year to her family, brings about an engagement that maddens Redmond with jealousy. He challenges Quin to a duel and apparently kills him, so that he must immediately leave for Dublin to avoid arrest. On the road Redmond is soon relieved of his horse, purse, and pistol by the renowned highwayman John Feeney, leaving him with no choice but to join the British army.

After proving his mettle in a boxing match against a regiment bully, he is reunited with Captain Jack Grogan, an old family friend, and his second in the duel. Grogan tells him to write to his mother, even though Redmond is ashamed of losing her money. Then Grogan relates the startling news that Nora's brothers loaded his dueling pistol with a globe of wax to secure Quin's "five hundred a year," enabling the stunned buffoon to marry Nora after all. Redmond soon ships out to fight in the Seven Years' War, where Grogan is lethally wounded. Under fire, Redmond carries his dying friend from the battlefield and passionately weeps for the loss of the only father he has ever known. After several battles and bouts of looting, Redmond becomes depressed by the lot of the common soldier and manages to escape with the clothes and horse of an officer into the German countryside. There he returns briefly to his pastoral roots during a stay of several months with Lischen, an attractive German girl whose husband is away fighting. Finally tiring of the rural routine and of Lischen, he departs for Bremen, determined to gain passage back to Ireland and to permanently attain the rank of gentleman.

But as soon as he reaches the main road, Redmond is intercepted by a troop of Prussian soldiers. Their leader, Captain Potzdorf, tells Redmond that he is going in the wrong direction and that he should ride with them to find his way. Potzdorf quickly realizes that Redmond's declared identity as "Captain Fakenham" is preposterous and impresses him into the Prussian army where the lot of the common soldier is much worse than among the British. But in a fortunate battlefield accident, Redmond frees Potzdorf from the fallen beam of a burning building and bears him to safety on his back, just as he had carried Grogan. As a result Potzdorf rewards him by releasing him from the infantry and enlisting him to serve a fellow Irishman, believed by the Prussians to be a British spy.

The Chevalier de Balibari, however, is an independent gambler rather than a spy, and the homesick Redmond, touched by the chevalier's Irish accent, weeps as he had for Grogan and regards the sympathetic older man as another father. They escape the Prussians by switching clothes and then travel through Germany and France to bilk wealthy noblemen at cards. Their trick is to have Redmond peek at the opponent's hand while pretending to serve drinks, and then signal the chevalier in a subtle code. If a nobleman refuses to make good his inevitable loss, Redmond enforces payment in duels that he always wins. Eventually, however, the round of cards, duels, and constant traveling becomes oppressive, and when the opportunity presents itself at a Belgian castle, he cold-bloodedly seduces the wife of Sir Charles Lyndon, a crippled British lord, who dies of apoplexy in a jealous rage.

The second part of the film opens with Barry's marriage to Lady Lyndon and concerns the decline and fall of his aristocratic dream. Lord Bullingdon, Sir Charles's son, hates Barry for stealing his beloved mother. His hatred grows after Barry twice canes him, once for refusing the respect of a dutiful kiss when he is about twelve, and later at about fifteen for starting to spank Barry's natural son, Bryan, when the seven-year-old has pestered him at study. Two years later Bullingdon has his revenge by staging an eloquent verbal attack during a concert at the castle. With Shakespearean flourish he recounts Barry's infidelities toward his mother, the "ruffian's" corporal punishments, and Barry's scheme to make Bryan the titled heir of the Lyndon estate. When the enraged Barry erupts from his chair and hurls Bullingdon to the floor, the guests gasp in consternation, and it takes nearly every man in the room to restrain him.

From this point on Barry loses all standing among the lords he has squandered the family fortune to join and is rejected even by friends he had earnestly impressed. His passion for Lady Lyndon had always been attached to her rank and money, and he is consoled only by the genuine love he feels for his son, Bryan. But when Bryan suffers a fatal fall from a horse, Lady Lyndon temporarily loses her sanity and turns to religion, while Barry turns to drink. Barry's mother tries to shore up what little is left of the Lyndon wealth by firing Reverend Runt, Lady Lyndon's spiritual adviser, and Bryan's former tutor. The minister goes for succor to Bullingdon, who realizes that although he is unsuited for it, he must challenge Barry to a duel if he is ever to recover his usurped estate.

Unlike Barry's first duel with Quin, where both parties turn and fire simultaneously at ten paces, this duel proceeds according to a formal rule of alternating shots. Bullingdon wins the coin toss and goes first but clumsily misfires and must await Barry's shot as a stationary target. But Barry, determined to recover his reputation as a gentleman, fires into the ground, giving Bullingdon a second opportunity for "satisfaction." With a lucky shot Bullingdon wounds his stepfather in the leg, and Barry is carried to a nearby inn where a surgeon determines he has no alternative but to amputate the leg below the knee to save the patient's life. After luring Barry's mother to the inn with news of her son's wound, Bullingdon is able to bar her return and finally rid himself of the "Barrys of Barrydom." He finalizes his victory by offering Barry an annuity if he will leave England forever and threatens debtors' prison if he refuses. Barry has no choice but to accept and, left (as at the outset) with only his devoted mother, returns to the continent to "resume his former profession of a gambler," but "without his former success."

In the film's last scene, the color and passion that Barry's energy had given the film is gone. Bullingdon has regained his mother, the prize he had most desired, but she is a pale ghost of the beauty she had been. She looks sadly at Barry's annuity check before signing it in an endless process of bill paying that signals a transition from the overtly savage life of eighteenth-century dueling and class dominance to the commercial hierarchy of the nineteenth century.

The Shining (1980)

In 1970s Colorado, aspiring writer Jack Torrance is interviewed at the storied Overlook Hotel to be its caretaker for the winter off-season when it is empty and snowed in. He is undeterred by the manager's tale of a former caretaker, Charles Grady, who was driven mad by "cabin fever" and in the winter of 1970 killed his wife and two daughters with an ax before turning a shotgun on himself. Jack tells Mr. Ullman to "rest assured" that nothing like that could ever happen to him and that he welcomes an isolation that will give him ample time to write. The scene shifts back to the family apartment in Boulder, where his wife, Wendy, and Danny, their psychic five-year-old son, are sitting at the kitchen table. While he eats a peanut butter and jelly sandwich and she smokes, Danny says that he and "Tony," his imaginary friend, do not want to go to the hotel. Shortly thereafter, he sees a vision of an elevator gushing blood in the bathroom mirror.

But Jack accepts the job, and soon after they arrive, Danny meets the chef, Dick Hallorann, who shares Danny's clairvoyant and telepathic abilities to "shine," as he says his grandmother called it. He tells Danny that his fear of "something bad" in the hotel does not apply to the present, but that bad things have happened there in the past, and that their aura remains "like the smell of burnt toast." He does, however, tell Danny to avoid Room 237 at all costs.

Although Jack had an alcohol problem when he was a teacher in Vermont and once accidentally broke Danny's arm in a drunken rage, his demeanor at the outset is loving and urbane. Two giveaway moments in the car on the way to the hotel foreshadow his later behavior. First, he is disproportionately angry at Danny for saying he is hungry after being told to eat before they left, and then, despite Wendy's protective demurral, he seems wickedly pleased to tell him about the Donner Party's cannibalism in mountains like the one they are ascending. A month later, Jack's frustration at being unable to write, aggravated by his underlying instability and social isolation, has him hurling a tennis ball against the lobby wall where animal heads and expropriated

Indian rugs signify the aggressive nature of the hotel's former guests. He has the first of his transforming visions when, like a giant in a fairy tale, he looks down at the tiny figures of Wendy and Danny walking through a model of the outdoor hedge maze at the very moment they are actually doing so.

From this point on he becomes increasingly abusive toward Wendy and withdraws for a time to his room without dressing or shaving. Upon emerging, he begins to visit the ghost of Lloyd, the hotel's bartender, who serves him drinks on the house and treats him like a celebrity. He also gets royal treatment from the butler, Delbert Grady, at a hallucinated 1920s soiree in the hotel ballroom. (Delbert has the same last name as Charles Grady, the ax murderer, and may share his nature.) The butler tells Jack that his two daughters felt as Danny does about the hotel and that he had to "correct" them after they tried to burn it down. Meanwhile, Danny is exploring the hotel on his Big Wheel when he is abruptly halted in a corridor by two ghostly girls who invite him to "come and play." Eventually, despite Hallorann's warning, Danny is tempted to enter Room 237 where he says "a crazy woman bit him on the neck," leaving visible marks.

Danny's terror is transmitted telepathically to Hallorann in Miami, and when Jack at Wendy's urging goes to investigate Room 237, Danny and Hallorann clairvoyantly see him discover a seductive naked woman in the bathroom. As they kiss, Jack looks in the mirror and recoils in horror when he sees that she has become a filthy, rotting crone. Jack tells Wendy that he saw nothing in Room 237, and the two argue about leaving the hotel immediately to protect Danny. Although Jack says he is about to accomplish some important writing, he actually feels entrusted by the hotel's powers-that-be to accomplish a great mission that he soon comes to believe will begin with the murder of his wife and son.

After Wendy has discovered that the prolific pages he has typed contain only one sentence—"All work and no play makes Jack a dull boy"—he menacingly pursues her up a stairway where, armed with a baseball bat, she knocks him out and locks him in the kitchen pantry. But after Delbert Grady supernaturally sets him free, Jack disables the snowcat vehicle, Wendy's only means of escape, and then uses an ax to split the bathroom door where she and Danny are hiding. Wendy stops him temporarily by stabbing his hand through the door with a kitchen knife and sends Danny sliding down a snowbank from a window opening that is too small for her to squeeze through.

Dick Hallorann flies in from Miami to attempt a rescue, but Jack kills him with the ax as soon as he enters the lobby. Danny runs back into the hotel looking for Wendy and runs back out into the snow-filled hedge maze after Jack just misses him hiding in a pantry cupboard. While Wendy searches for him inside, she encounters a series of spectral visions: a tuxedoed man with a cracked skull holding a martini and saying "great party"; a waiter serving cocktails to a drawing room of skeletons; a kneeling person in a bear costume looking up at her from the foot of a bed after being interrupted giving oral sex; and finally the image of the elevator gushing blood that Danny has repeatedly seen.

While Wendy goes outside to continue her search, Jack, drooling like a rabid wolf, limps out into the maze, but Danny eludes him because he has been through the maze before with Wendy and because he is inspired by "Tony" to double back to the correct exit, while Jack runs past him toward the wrong one. When Danny emerges, Wendy scoops him up and they escape in the snowcat that Hallorann had just driven in, while Jack, unable to find the exit, bestially screams for Wendy's aid before freezing to death. In the film's last brief sequence, he reappears inside the hotel lobby, elegantly groomed and frozen forever in a black and white photo surrounded by glamorous admirers, including a woman in leg chains. The photograph is dated July 4, 1921, ironically suggesting that he has been eternally enslaved by pride, greed, and the American dream.

Full Metal Jacket (1987)

In 1968 South Carolina at the famed Parris Island marine base, the abusive but effective Gunnery Sergeant Hartman whips his recruits into shape for combat duty in Vietnam. He is particularly hard on a slow-witted innocent named Pyle whom he verbally and physically humiliates for failures on the obstacle course and for sneaking a jelly doughnut into his locker. He also physically assaults Joker, the film's narrator, for mocking him with a John Wayne imitation, but he respects Joker's courage and intelligence and assigns him to be Pyle's mentor. For all his incompetence elsewhere, Pyle turns out to be an ace on the rifle range, but Hartman's effectiveness as a trainer of killers backfires when Pyle turns psychotic. While on night watch Joker discovers Pyle with his loaded rifle sitting on top of a toilet in the latrine. Hearing voices, Hartman enters angrily in skivvies but still wearing his hat: "What are you animals doing in my head?" and "What is your major malfunction, numbnuts?" Pyle fires two rounds, instantly killing Hartman, and then to Joker's agonized "Noooo!" sits back on the toilet, puts the barrel in his mouth, and blows his brains out.

The scene abruptly shifts to Vietnam where Joker, now a reporter for *Stars and Stripes*, and Rafterman, his fresh-faced, gung-ho photographer, dicker with a Da Nang prostitute while another young Vietnamese steals the camera, prompting Rafterman to comment, "We're supposed to be helping them, and they shit all over us every chance they get." The two get their first taste of action when a truck bomb crashes through the gates of their base, but this is only a mild foretaste of the "world of shit" they will enter after the *Stars and Stripes* editor, Lieutenant Lockhart, banishes them to the combat zone because Joker reacts sarcastically to his grave announcement of the Tet Offensive: "Does this mean Ann-Margret's not coming?"

Joker and Rafterman are flown in on a helicopter carrying a door gunner who shoots women and children for sport. Then Joker has two significant confrontations before encountering the enemy. First, a posturing noncombat colonel castigates him for wearing a helmet with the words "Born to Kill" next to a peace button. "What's that supposed to mean?" he sputters. Joker replies that it's about "the duality of man, the Jungian thing, sir." That duality is demonstrated when Joker faces off with Animal Mother, a member of the outfit that includes Cowboy, his best buddy from Parris Island. Animal, in crossed shoulder belts of bullets, derides the bespectacled, camera-carrying Joker for being a "combat correspondent," while Joker mocks his macho tone in his John Wayne voice. They trade escalating insults to the delight of the others, until another marine calms Animal and defuses the situation.

Joker and Rafterman then accompany the Lusthog Squad, and after a battle near Hue city, the unit is interviewed by a television crew, while the wounded are ferried off in choppers. Cowboy says he hates Vietnam because "there's not one horse in the whole country." Animal says they should "send us more guys, and maybe bomb the hell out of the North." Joker says he came to Vietnam "to meet interesting and stimulating people of an ancient culture and kill them" and "to be the first kid on my block to get a confirmed kill." When the squad leader, Crazy Earl (so named for keeping and conversing with a Vietcong corpse), is bizarrely killed on patrol by a booby-trapped toy rabbit, Cowboy replaces him.

During a break from fighting, the platoon purchases a fifteen-year-old hooker, who has to be convinced to include Eightball because soul brothers are "too beaucoup." Eightball unzips his pants to convince her otherwise, but Animal asserts his dominance by being the first to take her into an abandoned movie theater, saying "all fucking niggers must fucking hang," but not to worry, he'll "skip the foreplay." Their respite is short, however, and on their next patrol a deadly female supersniper makes every shot count (like Hartman's lauded models, Charles Whitman and Lee Harvey Oswald), first killing Eightball and Doc Jay, barely missing Animal, and finally nailing Cowboy.

After Cowboy dies in Joker's arms, Animal leads a "payback" assault on the sniper's position in a bombed-out building. When they reach it, the crack shot turns out to be "a slender Eurasian angel . . . not quite five feet tall," as an early screenplay draft describes her. After Rafterman fatally shoots her and exults—"Am I a life-taker? Am I a heartbreaker?"—she appears to be in great pain and begs to be shot. Animal, now the squad leader, orders the men to move out and leave her for the "mother-lovin' rats." When Joker objects that they "can't just leave her," Animal accuses him of trying to run the squad and challenges him to shoot her at point-blank range. Joker rises to the occasion and demonstrates a fundamental decency, uncorrupted by the horrors he has seen. His first and only confirmed kill is achieved out of compassion. As the film ends he and his unit march off into a darkening sunset, singing the Mickey Mouse anthem. In his voice-over Joker says that though he is "in a world of shit," he is glad to be alive and not afraid of what he may have to face in the world or in himself.

Eyes Wide Shut (1999)

At a party given by his ultrarich patient, Victor Ziegler, affluent Dr. Bill Harford flirts with two models while his beautiful wife, Alice, dances with Sandor Szavost, a comically seductive Hungarian roué. Before they leave, Bill is called upstairs to revive a call girl named Mandy, who has overdosed on drugs after servicing Victor in his elaborate bathroom. She is naked and comatose when he arrives, but she seems comforted by his kind rebuke, "You can't keep doing this." At home that night the Harfords undress and perform erotically for themselves in their bedroom mirror. In a seemingly disturbed moment, Alice interrupts a kiss to turn her gaze straight into the camera.

The next night in their bedroom, while slightly high on pot, Alice asks if Bill "happened to fuck" the models at the party. Bill, in turn, asks what Sandor wanted, and Alice answers that he wanted to take her upstairs to have sex, "right then and there." Bill is turned on to think that another man found his wife so attractive, but Alice is irritated that he is not jealous and snaps out of her high to demand why. When Bill smugly replies that she is his wife and he knows she would never be unfaithful, Alice becomes enraged over being reduced to a trophy and over Bill's assertion that "women don't think like that."

When he denies ever having sexual feelings while examining his female patients, Alice's rage at his hypocrisy impels her to recall an attraction to a naval officer she saw while they were vacationing on Cape Cod. Bitterly, she tells Bill that she would have deserted him and their daughter for just one night with the stranger. Bill appears to be in shock as Alice, in a semitrance, puzzles over her conflicted emotions—how she fantasized about the officer and at the same time felt that Bill was "dearer to [her] than ever." The ringing phone abruptly breaks into Alice's reverie and Bill's nightmare with the news that a patient, Lou Nathanson, has just died.

Bill feels obligated to go to the Nathanson apartment, where in a bizarre turn, the dead man's thirtysomething daughter, Marion, passionately kisses Bill on the lips, declaring that she is hopelessly in love with him even though she is about to leave for the University of Michigan where her fiancé, Carl, has an appointment in the math department. Moments later, Carl, a handsome man with a haircut resembling Bill's, arrives and tenderly embraces Marion. After shaking his hand, Bill leaves on a note of consoling propriety as if nothing untoward had happened.

Outside on the wet winter streets, he smacks his gloved fist into his hand as he thinks about Alice, when suddenly six rowdy college students accost him, shove him against a parked car, and tell the "faggot" he should "go back to San Francisco where [he] belongs." Moments later, Domino, an attractive young prostitute, invites him to her apartment for "a little fun." Inside, they are just beginning to kiss, when Alice calls Bill on his cell phone, thinking he is still at the Nathansons'. She casually asks how long he will be gone and says she is going to bed, as if her traumatizing confession had not occurred. Still fully clothed, Bill decides to leave, and after paying Domino, returns to the street.

Continuing to walk, rather than hailing a cab, he passes the Sonata Café, a jazz club where Nick Nightingale, the old friend and dropout from medical school he had met at Victor's party, is the visiting pianist. Between sets Nick tells Bill that he has a private gig at 2:00 a.m. for mysterious employers who insist that he play blindfolded. Their parties always occur in a different place. When Nick intriguingly adds that the blindfold sometimes slips to reveal bevies of amazing women, Bill begs to go along, but Nick refuses because he has been sworn to secrecy. As a favor to an old friend, however, he informs Bill that everyone in attendance wears a disguise and that the password for admission is "Fidelio."

Bill immediately proceeds to Rainbow Fashions, a costume shop, where the owner, Mr. Milich, unimpressed by Bill's claim to be the doctor of the previous tenant, lets him in after bargaining for two hundred dollars over the rental price. Before Bill can retrieve his overcoat and leave with his costume, a strange scene unfolds involving two Japanese men in their underwear wearing women's wigs and Milich's pubescent daughter, wearing only a bra and panties. Milich, apparently enraged, threatens the men with arrest, calls his daughter "a little whore," and chases her until she hides behind Bill, where she whispers something in his ear.

As Bill rides in a taxi across a bridge and toward the suburban mansion where the party is being held, he continuously fantasizes black and white scenes of Alice and the naval officer having sex, as if he were watching a porn film. After being admitted, he thinks himself safely incognito in his hooded black cloak and classic Greek mask. First, he witnesses a weird ritual involving kneeling women wearing only G-strings. They hold hands in a circle around a man in a red-hooded robe, who swings a censer and chants incomprehensibly.

When the chant stops, the women rise and walk to assignations with individual onlookers. The tallest and most statuesque walks directly to Bill to tell him he is in great danger and should leave immediately. Before he can react, a masked man takes the woman away, and Bill wanders from room to room to witness an orgy that includes a variety of sexual acts and actors, playing for an equal number of voyeurs. When the statuesque woman comes to warn him a second time, Bill asks who she is and asks her to go with him. She refuses, saying it could cost both their lives. At that point another masked attendant enters to tell Bill that his waiting cab driver urgently needs to talk to him.

The man leads Bill away, but instead of going to the outer door they enter the balconied ballroom where the introductory ritual had occurred. The man in the red robe sits in the center, circled by a large audience. After beckoning Bill to enter the circle, he demands the password. Bill calmly answers, "Fidelio," but "Red Robe" replies that he has given the password for admittance, not the password for the house. When he cannot supply it, the man orders Bill to remove his mask. He complies, but Red Robe then demands that he remove his clothes as well, or he will be forcibly stripped. Suddenly the statuesque woman appears on the balcony and announces that she "is ready to redeem him." The leader accepts her sacrifice but tells Bill that if he reveals what he has seen, there will be dire consequences for him and his family. Bill nods his assent, but before departing asks what will happen to the woman. Red Robe replies that her fate is sealed and that "when a promise is made here, there is no turning back."

Bill arrives home before daylight and upon entering the bedroom discovers Alice talking in her sleep. He wakes her, and she says that she has had a nightmare. Initially, she refuses to tell it because "it was too awful," but he persuades her because it was "only a dream." At the dream's outset she and Bill find themselves naked in a beautiful garden. After Bill departs to retrieve their clothes, the naval officer appears. He initially laughs at Alice but then makes love to her among hundreds of other fucking couples. Soon she is fucking countless other men, and when Bill returns with the clothes, she laughs at him, knowing he can see her. When she finishes relating the dream, Bill seems dazed, but Alice has been overwhelmed by a wave of remorse, grief, and protective love. She embraces him, as if she were comforting a child, as the scene ends.

The next day Bill searches for Nick Nightingale. A waitress at the lunch counter next to the Sonata Café first refuses but then accedes to Bill's request for Nick's address, after Bill says that he has medical test results that Nick needs to know. At Nick's hotel, the male desk clerk tells Bill that Nick left at 4:30 a.m. with two tough-looking men and that he had a bruise on his cheek. The clerk is obviously attracted to Bill, but, ironically, the first sexual opportunity Bill has had since Domino holds no attraction. Bill then goes to Rainbow Fashions to return the costume and is shocked to find the two Japanese men civilly bidding farewell to Milich at the counter, while his daughter stands beside him in a bathrobe. Bill says he thought that Milich was going to have the men arrested, but the owner enigmatically replies that "things change," and then, putting his arm around his daughter, tells Bill to return if he wants anything else, "and it needn't be a costume." As with the desk clerk, this offer of attainable sexual satisfaction is not one he can accept.

Once again, Bill takes a taxi to the mansion, this time in broad daylight, but still fantasizing the black and white "film" of his wife having sex with the naval officer. Once there, he approaches the barred gate and peers in. A car comes down the driveway, and an elderly man with a grim expression gives Bill a note that warns him to stop asking questions or else. Late that night Bill leaves his sleeping family and goes to his office. Desperate to counteract the doubts sown by his wife's near infidelity, being called a "faggot" on the street, and his humiliation at the mansion, he tries to call Marion Nathanson. When Carl answers, Bill hangs up. Then he returns to Domino's apartment where Sally, her equally attractive roommate, tells him Domino is gone and will not return. Although Sally seems to be aroused when Bill unbuttons her shirt, she abruptly pushes him away and, sitting down with him at the table, proffers the "devastating" news that Domino is HIV positive.

Bill hastily departs and on the now night-darkened street observes himself being followed by a large man with a shaved head. When he turns the corner and stops at a newsstand to buy a paper, the man stops at the corner and stares at him. Alarmed, Bill ducks into a coffeehouse named Sharkey's. Seated at a table he picks up the paper headlined "Lucky to Be Alive" and notices an article about an ex–beauty queen named Amanda Curran, who overdosed in a hotel room. He immediately goes to the hospital and, after claiming to be her doctor and asking for her room number, is informed that she died that afternoon. He then goes to the morgue to view her nude body and discovers that she is the woman he revived in Victor's bathroom. In the corridor on the way out he receives a phone call summoning him to the Ziegler mansion.

In a long dialogue transpiring around a bright red pool table, Ziegler tells Bill that he was present at the orgy, witnessed Bill's exposure, and had him followed for his own safety. He tells him that some of the richest, most powerful people in the city are regular attendees and will stop at nothing to prevent exposure. Victor falsely confirms Bill's mistaken belief that the woman who "redeemed" him was Mandy, the girl he revived at the party, and that her seeming sacrifice was part of an elaborate charade to intimidate him. He assures Bill that she was not harmed, that afterward she only "had her brains fucked out," and that since her hotel room was locked from the inside, she died as a junkie rather than a victim of murder.

Crestfallen, Bill leaves and returns to his apartment. Upon entering the bedroom, he sees the mask that he had forgotten to return to Rainbow Fashions staring up from his pillow beside the sleeping Alice. Breaking into tears, he lays his head on his wife's breast, saying he will tell her everything. The next morning he sits abjectly across from Alice, whose tear-stained face shows the effect of hearing about the near-disaster her cruel confession caused. The concluding scene takes place in an upscale toy store, where they have promised to take Helena, their seven-year-old daughter, Christmas shopping.

As Helena wanders excitedly among the toys, Bill asks Alice what they should do. Alice answers that they should be glad they have survived their "adventures," that she still loves him, and that the reality of one night or even a lifetime "can never be the whole truth." She implies that their marriage may have a better chance of lasting because they "are awake now, and hopefully for a long time to come." But when Bill adds, "Forever," Alice says the word frightens her, as if to say that they must not repeat their original mistake of overconfidence. The first step, she says, is to do one thing as soon as possible. Bill asks what that is, and Alice's one-word reply—"Fuck"—is the film's concluding line.

Bibliography

Abrams, M. H. *The Mirror and the Lamp: Romantic Theory and the Critical Tradition.* New York: Oxford University Press, 1953.

Adler, Jerry. "Mind Reading." *Newsweek,* July 5, 2004.

A.I.: Artificial Intelligence. DVD. Directed by Steven Spielberg, 2001. Universal City, Calif.: Dreamworks and Warner Bros., 2002.

Altman, Robert. Voice-over to clips from his films upon winning an honorary Oscar at the 2006 Academy Awards. ABC Television, March 5, 2006.

Andrist, Ralph K. *The Long Death: The Last Days of the Plains Indians.* New York: Macmillan, 1993.

Ardrey, Robert. *African Genesis.* New York: Atheneum, 1961.

———. *The Territorial Imperative.* New York: Atheneum, 1966.

Armetz, Aljean. "Man Was a Killer Long before He Served a God." *New York Times,* August 31, 1969.

Bailey, Andrew. "A Clockwork Utopia: Semi-Scrutable Stanley Kubrick Discusses His New Film." *Rolling Stone,* January 1972, 20–22.

Baker, Mark. *Nam: The Vietnam War in the Words of the Men and Women Who Fought There.* New York: Berkley, 1981.

Barron, Graham. "The Wild Child." Review of *L'Enfant Sauvage* [The Wild Child], directed by François Truffaut. Apollo Movieguide Review, www.apolloguide.com/mov_fullrev.asp?CID=3314&Specific=4055.

Barry Lyndon. DVD. Directed by Stanley Kubrick, 1975. Burbank, Calif.: Warner Bros. Home Video, 2001.

Baxter, John. *Stanley Kubrick: A Biography.* London: HarperCollins, 1997.

"Beethoven." www.bbc.co.uk/music/classicaltv/eroica/beethoven/napoleon.shtml.

Beethoven, Ludwig van. "Heiligenstadt Testament." Wikipedia, en.wikipedia.org/wiki/Heiligenstadt_Testament.

———. Ludwig van Beethoven to Franz Wegeler, 1802. In "Ludwig van Beethoven," *Encyclopædia Britannica Online*, 1997, www.swil.ocdsb.edu.on.ca/ModWest/Enlightenment/music/bthoven.html.

"Beetle Bailey." www.kingfeatures.com/features/comics/bbailey/about.htm.

"Beetle Bailey at 50: Still Lazy, Still Funny, Still Going Strong." *Jefferson City News Tribune*, September 6, 2000, www.newstribune.com/archives/.

Benjamin, Walter. *The Origin of German Tragic Drama*. Translated by John Osborne. London: New Left Books, 1977.

Bernstein, Jeremy. "Beyond the Stars." *New Yorker*, April 24, 1965. Reprinted in *Stanley Kubrick: Interviews*, edited by Gene D. Phillips, 17–20. Jackson: University Press of Mississippi, 2001.

Bettelheim, Bruno. *The Uses of Enchantment: The Meaning and Importance of Fairy Tales*. New York: Vintage, Random House, 1989.

Bevan, Edwyn Robert. "Alexander the Great." *Encyclopedia Britannica*. 11th ed., vol. 1. 1910.

The Bhagavad Gita. Translated by Ramanand Prasad. eawc.evansville.edu/anthology/gita.htm.

The Bhagavad-Gita: Krishna's Counsel in Time of War. Translated by Barbara Stoler Miller. New York: Bantam, 1986.

Bingham, Dennis. "The Displaced Auteur: A Reception History of *The Shining*." In *Perspectives on Stanley Kubrick*, edited by Mario Falsetto, 284–306. New York: G. K. Hall, 1996.

"The Biography of a Mouse." www.mickey-mouse.com/themouse.htm.

Birren, Faber. *Color and Human Response*. New York: Van Nostrand Reinhold, 1978.

———. *History of Color in Painting*. New York: Reinhold, 1965.

Bizony, Piers. *2001: Filming the Future*. London: Aurum Press, 2000.

Blakemore, Bill. "The Family of Man." *San Francisco Chronicle*, July 29, 1987.

Bloom, Harold. Review of *The Uses of Enchantment: The Meaning and Importance of Fairy Tales*, by Bruno Bettelheim. *New York Review of Books*, July 15, 1976.

Blume in Love. DVD. Directed by Paul Mazursky, 1973. Burbank, Calif.: Warner Bros. Home Video, 2007.

Bogdanovich, Peter. "What They Say about Stanley Kubrick." *New York Times Magazine*, July 25, 1999.

Bondanello, Peter. *The Cinema of Federico Fellini*. Princeton, N.J.: Princeton University Press, 1992.

Boorman, John. *The Emerald Forest Diary: A Filmmaker's Odyssey*. New York: Farrar, Straus, and Giroux, 1985.

Bulfinch, Thomas. "The Golden Fleece—Medea." In *Bulfinch's Mythology: The Age of Fable or Stories of Gods and Heroes*, chapter 17, 1855. www.sacred-texts.com/cla/bulf/bulf16.htm.

Burgess, Anthony. *A Clockwork Orange*. 1962. Reprint, New York: W. W. Norton, 1987.

———. *A Clockwork Orange: A Play with Music*. London: Century Hutchinson, 1987.

———. *Napoleon Symphony: A Novel in Four Movements*. New York: Alfred A. Knopf, 1972.

———. *You've Had Your Time: The Second Part of the Confessions*. New York: Grove Press, 1991.

Cahill, Tim. "The *Rolling Stone* Interview: Stanley Kubrick." *Rolling Stone*, August 27, 1987. Reprinted in *Stanley Kubrick: Interviews*, edited by Gene D. Phillips, 189–204. Jackson: University Press of Mississippi, 2001.

Campbell, Joseph. *The Hero with a Thousand Faces*. 2nd ed. Princeton, N.J.: Princeton University Press, 1968.

Carroll, Lewis. *Alice's Adventures in Wonderland and Through the Looking Glass*. Introduction by Morton N. Cohen. 1865. Reprint, New York: Bantam, 1981.

"Charlie McCarthy: Welcome to Snerdville." www.snerdville.com/characters.htm.

Chion, Michel. *Kubrick's Cinema Odyssey*. London: British Film Institute, 2001.

———. *Eyes Wide Shut*. London: British Film Institute, 2002.

Ciment, Michel. *Kubrick: The Definitive Edition*. Translated by Gilbert Adair and Robert Bononno. New York: Faber and Faber, 2001.

Cirlot, J. E. *A Dictionary of Symbols*. Translated by Jack Sage. New York: Philosophical Library, 1962.

Clarke, Arthur C. *2001: A Space Odyssey*. 1968. Reprint, New York: New American Library, 2000.

———. *Lost Worlds of 2001*. 1972. Reprint, Boston: Gregg Press, 1979.

Clarke, Roger. "Putting the Knife into Stanley: A Review of *Eyes Wide Open* and *Dream Story*." Review of *Eyes Wide Open: A Memoir of Stanley Kubrick*, by Frederic Raphael, and *Dream Story*, by Arthur Schnitzler. *Independent* (London), August 2, 1999.

A Clockwork Orange. DVD. Directed by Stanley Kubrick, 1971. Burbank, Calif.: Warner Bros. Home Video, 2001.

Cocks, Geoffrey. *The Wolf at the Door: Stanley Kubrick, History, and the Holocaust*. New York: Peter Lang, 2004.

Daniels, Don. "A Skeleton Key to *2001*." *Sight & Sound*, Winter 1970/1971, 28–33.

Drinnon, Richard. *Facing West: The Metaphysics of Indian-Hating and Empire-Building*. New York: New American Library, 1980.

Dr. Strangelove. DVD. Directed by Stanley Kubrick, 1964. Burbank, Calif.: Warner Bros. Home Video, 2001.

Dunan, Marcel, and John Roberts. *Larousse Encyclopedia of Modern History: From 1500 to the Present Day*. New York: Harper & Row, 1964.

Ebert, Roger. Review of *Sabrina*, directed by Sydney Pollack. *Chicago Sun-Times*, December 15, 1995.

Edinger, Edward F. *Ego and Archetype*. Baltimore: Penguin, 1973.

Eisenstein, Sergei M. "Color and Meaning." In *The Film Sense*, edited and translated by Jay Leyda, 113–156. New York: Harcourt Brace, 1947.

———. "On Color." In *S. M. Eisenstein: Selected Works*, vol. 2, edited by Michael Glenny and Richard Taylor, 254–267. Translated by Michael Glenny. London: British Film Institute, 1991.

Eyes Wide Shut. DVD. Directed by Stanley Kubrick, 1999. Burbank, Calif.: Warner Bros. Home Video, 2001.

Falsetto, Mario. *Stanley Kubrick: A Narrative and Stylistic Analysis*. Westport, Conn.: Greenwood Press, 1994.

———, ed. *Perspectives on Stanley Kubrick*. New York: G. K. Hall, 1996.

Feeley, Gregory. "The Masterpiece a Master Couldn't Get Right." *New York Times*, July 18, 1999.

Flanders, Judith. "When Pink Was Far from Rosy." Review of *American Prometheus: The Triumph and Tragedy of J. Robert Oppenheimer*, by Kai Bird and Martin J. Sherwin. *Spectator* (London), January 23, 2008.

Freud, Sigmund. *Beyond the Pleasure Principle*. Edited and translated by James Strachey. 1920. Reprint, New York: W. W. Norton, 1990.

———. *Civilization and Its Discontents*. Edited and translated by James Strachey. 1930. Reprint, New York: W. W. Norton, 1962.

———. *The Future of an Illusion*. Edited by James Strachey. Translated by W. D. Robson-Scott. 1927. Reprint, Garden City, N.Y.: Doubleday, 1961.

———. "Totem and Taboo." In *The Basic Writings of Sigmund Freud*, edited and translated by A. A. Brill, 807–930. 1913. Reprint, New York: Modern Library, 1965.

———. "The Uncanny." In *The Standard Edition of the Complete Psychological Works of Sigmund Freud*, vol. 17, edited by James Strachey, Anna Freud, Alix Strachey, and Alan Tyson, 219–252. Translated by James Strachey. 1919. Reprint, London: Hogarth Press, 1955.

Full Metal Jacket. DVD. Directed by Stanley Kubrick, 1987. Burbank, Calif.: Warner Bros. Home Video, 2001.

Gelmis, Joseph. "The Film Director as Superstar: Stanley Kubrick." In *The Film Director as Superstar*. Garden City, N.Y.: Doubleday, 1970. Reprinted in *Stanley Kubrick: Interviews*, edited by Gene D. Phillips, 80–104. Jackson: University Press of Mississippi, 2001.

George, Christopher T. "The Eroica Riddle: Did Napoleon Remain Beethoven's 'Hero'?" www.napoleonseries.com/articles/misc_art/eroica.cfm.

Gilliatt, Penelope. "Mankind on the Late, Late Show." *Observer* (London), September 6, 1987.

Ginna, Robert Emmett. "The Odyssey Begins." *Horizon*, 1960. Reprint, *Entertainment Weekly*, April 9, 1999, 16–17.

Glesner, Elizabeth Schwarm. "Ludwig van Beethoven—Symphony No. 9, Opus 125, 'Choral.'" Classical Music Pages, w3.rz-berlin.mpg.de/cmp/beethoven_sym9.html.

"Goofy." Official Homepage of the Walt Disney Company, disney.go.com/characters/mickey/html/meet/goofy.html.

The Green Berets. DVD. Directed by John Wayne and Ray Kellogg, 1968. Burbank, Calif.: Warner Bros., 1997.

Grimm, Jacob and Wilhelm. "Hansel and Gretel." In *Children's and Household Tales.* Translated by Edgar Taylor and Marian Edwardes. 1857. www.logicalviewinc .com/hanselandgretel/Story.asp.

———. "Little Snow White." In *Children's and Household Tales.* Translated by D. L. Ashliman. 1857. www.pitt.edu/~dash/type0709.html.

Hall, Calvin S. *A Primer of Freudian Psychology.* New York: New American Library, 1954.

Hammer, Richard. *The Court-Martial of Lt. Calley.* New York: Coward, McCann & Geoghegan, 1971.

Hasford, Gustav. *The Short-Timers.* New York: Bantam, 1979.

Herr, Michael. *Dispatches.* New York: Alfred A. Knopf, 1977.

———. Foreword to *Full Metal Jacket: The Screenplay,* by Stanley Kubrick and Michael Herr. New York: Alfred A. Knopf, 1987.

———. *Kubrick.* New York: Grove Press, 2000.

Hobbs, Katharina Kubrick. E-mail to Kubrick News Group, October 29, 1999. www.alt.movies.Kubrick.com.

Hoffman, E. T. A. "The Nutcracker and the Mouse King." In *The Best Tales of Hoffman,* edited and translated by E. F. Bleiler, 130–182. 1816. Reprint, New York: Dover, 1979.

Hofsess, John. "Mind's Eye: A *Clockwork Orange.*" *Take One,* May/June 1971. Reprinted in *Stanley Kubrick: Interviews,* edited by Gene D. Phillips, 105–107. Jackson: University Press of Mississippi, 2001.

Homer. *The Iliad.* Translated by E. V. Rieu. Baltimore: Penguin, 1951.

———. *The Odyssey.* Translated by E. V. Rieu. Baltimore: Penguin, 1946.

Houston, Penelope. "Kubrick Country." *Saturday Review,* December 25, 1971. Reprinted in *Stanley Kubrick: Interviews,* edited by Gene D. Phillips, 108–115. Jackson: University Press of Mississippi, 2001.

Hughes, David. *The Complete Kubrick.* London: Virgin, 2000.

Jagger, Mick, and Keith Richards. "Paint It, Black." ABKCO Music, 1966, Renewed. www.abkco.com.

James, Nick. "At Home with the Kubricks." *Sight & Sound,* September 1999, 12.

Jameson, Frederick. "Historicism in *The Shining.*" In *Perspectives on Stanley Kubrick,* edited by Mario Falsetto, 243–252. New York: G. K. Hall, 1996.

Jameson, Richard T. "Kubrick's *Shining.*" *Film Comment,* July/August 1980, 28–32.

Johnson, Diane. Interview by Michel Ciment. In *Kubrick: The Definitive Edition,* by Michel Ciment, 293–295. Translated by Gilbert Adair and Robert Bononno. New York: Faber and Faber, 2001.

———. "An Interview with Diane Johnson." Interview by Donald Williams. C. J. Jung page Film Review, www.cgjungpage.org/index2.php?option=content&do _pdf=1&id=490.

———. "Stanley Kubrick (1928–1999)." *New York Review of Books,* April 22, 1999.

Johnson, Joyce. Curator, SAIC Information Services, NASA. "Silver Snoopy Award." www.hq.nasa.gov/osf/sfa/snoopy.html.

Jung, Carl G. "Answer to Job." In *The Portable Jung*, edited by Joseph Campbell, 519–650. Translated by R. F. C. Hull. 1952. Reprint, New York: Viking, 1971.

———. "The Basic Postulates of Analytical Psychology." C. G. Jung page, www.cgjungpage.org/content/view/5/15/1/.

———. "Marriage as a Psychological Relationship." In *The Portable Jung*, edited by Joseph Campbell, 163–177. Translated by R. F. C. Hull. 1925. Reprint, New York: Viking, 1971.

———. "On the Relation of Analytical Psychology to Poetry." In *The Portable Jung*, edited by Joseph Campbell, 301–322. Translated by R. F. C. Hull. 1922. Reprint, New York: Viking, 1971.

———. "The Stages of Life." In *The Portable Jung*, edited by Joseph Campbell, 3–22. Translated by R. F. C. Hull. 1930. Reprint, New York: Viking, 1971.

———. *The Undiscovered Self*. New York: New American Library, 1957.

Jung, Carl G., M.-L. von Franz, Joseph Henderson, Jolande Jacobi, and Aniela Jaffe. *Man and His Symbols*. Garden City, N.Y.: Doubleday, 1964.

Kael, Pauline. Review of *The Shining*. *New Yorker*, June 9, 1980. Reprinted on the Kubrick site, www.visual-memory.co.uk/amk/doc/0050.html.

———. *When the Lights Go Down*. New York: Holt, Rinehart and Winston, 1980.

Kakutani, Michiko. "A Connoisseur of Cool Tries to Raise the Temperature." Review of *Eyes Wide Shut*. *New York Times*, July 18, 1999.

Kandinsky, Wassily. *Concerning the Spiritual in Art*. 1912. Reprint, New York: Dover, 1977.

Kaufmann, Walter. *Nietzsche: Philosopher, Psychologist, Antichrist*. Cleveland and New York: World, 1956.

Kempley, Rita. Review of *Full Metal Jacket*. *Washington Post*, June 26, 1987.

Kidman, Nicole. "Remembering . . . Stanley Kubrick, Kidman . . . on Kubrick." Interview by Paul Joyce, July 12, 1999. Special Features, *Eyes Wide Shut*. DVD. Directed by Stanley Kubrick, 1999. Burbank, Calif.: Warner Bros. Home Video, 2001.

Kieslowski, Krzysztof, and Krzysztof Piesiewicz. *Decalogue: The Ten Commandments*. Foreword by Stanley Kubrick. London: Faber and Faber, 1991.

King, Stephen. *The Shining*. New York: New American Library, 1978.

Kloman, William. "In 2001, Will Love Be a Seven-Letter Word." *New York Times*, April 14, 1968.

Knox, Ellis L. "Alexander the Great." August 19, 1996. history.boisestate.edu/westciv/alexander/03.htm.

Kubrick, Christiane. Interview. *La Stampa* (Turin), March 2, 2001.

———. Interview by Patrick Amory. *Paris Match*, September 9, 1999.

———. *Stanley Kubrick: A Life in Pictures*. Foreword by Steven Spielberg. Boston, New York, London: Little, Brown, 2002.

Kubrick, Stanley. Letter to the Editor. *New York Times*, February 27, 1972.

——. "Napoleon." Unproduced screenplay, September 29, 1969. Quoted in Gene D. Phillips and Rodney Hill, *The Encyclopedia of Stanley Kubrick*, 262. New York: Checkmark Books, 2002.

——. "Words and Movies." *Sight & Sound*, Winter 1961, 14.

——, and Arthur C. Clarke. "2001: A Space Odyssey Screenplay." Unpublished screenplay, 1965. Reprinted on the Kubrick site, www.visual-memory.co.uk/amk/doc/0057.html.

——, and Michael Herr. "Full Metal Jacket: A Screenplay: Based on *The Short-Timers*, by Gustav Hasford." A facsimile of the original, 1985. The Kubrick site, www.visual-memory.co.uk/amk/doc/0065.html.

——, Michael Herr, and Gustav Hasford. *Full Metal Jacket: The Screenplay*. New York: Alfred A. Knopf, 1987.

——, and Frederic Raphael. *Eyes Wide Shut*. New York: Warner Books, 1999.

Kubrick, Vivian. "The Making of *The Shining*." Special Features, *The Shining*. DVD. Directed by Stanley Kubrick, 1980. Burbank, Calif.: Warner Bros. Home Video, 2001.

L'Enfant Sauvage [The Wild Child]. DVD. Directed by François Truffaut. Santa Monica, Calif.: MGM Home Entertainment World Films, 2001.

LoBrutto, Vincent. *Stanley Kubrick: A Biography*. New York: Donald I. Fine, 1997.

Lolita. DVD. Directed by Stanley Kubrick, 1962. Burbank, Calif.: Warner Bros. Home Video, 2001.

"Ludwig van Beethoven." *Encyclopædia Britannica*. 15th ed., 650. 1997.

Magid, Ron. "*Full Metal Jacket*: Cynic's Choice." *American Cinematographer*, September 1987, 74–84.

Mainar, Luis M. García. *Narrative and Stylistic Patterns in the Films of Stanley Kubrick*. Rochester, N.Y.: Camden House, 1999.

Markham, Felix. *Napoleon*. New York: New American Library, 1963.

Maslin, Janet. "Farewell to a Fearless Imagination." *New York Times*, March 14, 1999.

McCorry, Kevin. "The Bugs Bunny/Roadrunner Hour, 1971–72." looney.goldenage cartoons.com/tv/bugstweety/.

McDowell, Malcolm. Interview by Michel Ciment. In *Kubrick: The Definitive Edition*, by Michel Ciment, 285–287. Translated by Gilbert Adair and Robert Bononno. New York: Faber and Faber, 2001.

McGregor, Craig. "Nice Boy from the Bronx." *New York Times*, January 30, 1972.

McLuhan, Marshall. *Understanding Media: The Extensions of Man*. 2nd ed. New York: New American Library, 1964.

Melville, Herman. *Moby-Dick*. Edited by Harrison Hayford and Hershel Parker. 1851. Reprint, New York: W. W. Norton, 1967.

Milsome, Douglas. Interview with Ron Magid. *American Cinematographer*, September 1987, 74–84.

Modine, Matthew. *Full Metal Jacket Diary*. New York: Rugged Land, 2005.

——. "What They Say about Stanley Kubrick." Interview by Peter Bogdanovich. *New York Times Magazine*, July 25, 1999.

Montague, Ashley. *The Nature of Human Aggression*. New York: Oxford University Press, 1967.

Nabokov, Vladimir. *Lolita*. 1955. Reprint, New York: Vintage, 1989.

"Napoleon Bonaparte: Emperor of France, 1769–1821." www.napoleonguide.com/leaders_napoleon.htm.

Naremore, James. *On Kubrick*. London: British Film Institute, 2007.

Nelson, Thomas Allen. *Kubrick: Inside a Film Artist's Maze*. 2nd ed. Bloomington: Indiana University Press, 2000.

Nicholson, Jack. Interview with Michel Ciment. In *Kubrick: The Definitive Edition*, by Michel Ciment, 297–299. Translated by Gilbert Adair and Robert Bononno. New York: Faber and Faber, 2001.

Nordern, Eric. "*Playboy* Interview: Stanley Kubrick." *Playboy*, September 1968. Reprinted in *Stanley Kubrick: Interviews*, edited by Gene D. Phillips, 47–74. Jackson: University Press of Mississippi.

An Officer and a Gentleman. DVD. Directed by Taylor Hackford, 1982. Hollywood, Calif.: Paramount Pictures, 2000.

O'Hagan, Sean. "I Flinch, When I See All These Things Repeated about Stanley the So-Called Crazy Man." *Observer* (London), April 17, 2005.

Ordway, Frederick I., III. "Part B: *2001: A Space Odyssey* in Retrospect." In *Science Fiction and Space Futures: Past and Present*, edited by Eugene M. Emme, 47–105. American Astronautical Society History Series 5. San Diego, Calif.: Univelt, 1982.

O'Sullivan, Charlotte. "Body of Evidence." *Independent* (London), August 27, 1999.

Ovidius Naso, Publius (Ovid). *The Love Books of Ovid*. Book 1: *The Art of Love*. Translated by J. Lewis May. New York: Rarity Press, 1930. Reprinted at www.sacred-texts.com/cla/ovid/lboo/index.htm.

Peckham, Morse. *Man's Rage for Chaos: Biology, Behavior, and the Arts*. New York: Schocken, 1967.

Phillips, Gene D. *The Movie Makers: Artists in an Industry*. Chicago: Nelson-Hall, 1973.

———, ed. *Stanley Kubrick: Interviews*. Jackson: University Press of Mississippi, 2001.

———. "Stop the World: Stanley Kubrick." In *Stanley Kubrick: Interviews*, edited by Gene D. Phillips, 140–158. Jackson: University Press of Mississippi, 2001.

———, and Rodney Hill. *The Encyclopedia of Stanley Kubrick*. New York: Checkmark Books, 2002.

Pizzello, Stephen. "A Sword in the Bed: Cinematographer Larry Smith Helps Stanley Kubrick Craft a Unique Look for *Eyes Wide Shut*, a Dreamlike Coda to the Director's Brilliant Career." *American Cinematographer*, October 1999, 28–38.

Pollack, Sydney. "What Stanley Wanted." Interview by Michael Henry. *Positif*, September 1999, 16–20.

Quiller-Couch, Sir Arthur. *The Sleeping Beauty and Other Fairy Tales*. New York: George H. Doran, 1910.

Radice, Betty. *Who's Who in the Ancient World*. Baltimore: Penguin, 1973.

Rapf, Maurice. "A Talk with Stanley Kubrick about *2001*." *Action*, January/February 1969. Reprinted in *Stanley Kubrick: Interviews*, edited by Gene D. Phillips, 75–79. Jackson: University Press of Mississippi, 2001.

Raphael, Frederic. *Eyes Wide Open: A Memoir of Stanley Kubrick*. New York: Ballantine, 1999.

———. "Onward and Upward with the Arts, 'A Kubrick Odyssey.'" *New Yorker*, June 14, 1999, 40.

Rasmussen, Randy. *Stanley Kubrick: Seven Films Analyzed*. Jefferson, N.C.: McFarland, 2001.

Richter, Dan. *Moonwatcher's Memoir: A Diary of* 2001: A Space Odyssey. New York: Carroll and Graf, 2002.

Rousseau, Jean-Jacques. *Emile*. Translated by Barbara Foxley. London: J. M. Dent & Sons, 1966.

Sabrina. DVD. Directed by Billy Wilder, 1954. Hollywood, Calif.: Paramount Pictures, 2001.

Sabrina. DVD. Directed by Sydney Pollack, 1995. Hollywood, Calif.: Paramount Pictures, 2002.

Salinger, J. D. *The Catcher in the Rye*. New York: Bantam, 1964.

Sands of Iwo Jima. DVD. Directed by Allan Dwan, 1949. Vancouver, British Columbia: Lions Gate Home Entertainment, 1998.

Schnitzler, Arthur. *Dream Story*. Translated by J. M. Q. Davies. 1926. Reprint, London: Penguin Books, 1999.

Schott, Richard. Program Notes for "Symphony No. 9 and *Fidelio* Overture." Cleveland Orchestra, conducted by George Szell. Translated by Diana Loos. Sony Essential Classics, Sony Entertainment, 2002.

Schulz, Charles. *Peanuts*. Official *Peanuts* website, www.unitedmedia.com/comics/peanuts/.

Shakespeare, William. *Hamlet*. Edited by Edward Hubler. 1603. Reprint, New York: New American Library, 1963.

———. *Othello*. Edited by Alvin Kernan. 1604. Reprint, New York: New American Library, 1963.

The Shining. DVD. Directed by Stanley Kubrick, 1980. Burbank, Calif.: Warner Bros. Home Video, 2001.

Siskel, Gene. "Candidly Kubrick." *Chicago Tribune*, June 21, 1987. Reprinted in *Stanley Kubrick: Interviews*, edited by Gene D. Phillips, 177–188. Jackson: University Press of Mississippi.

Skinner, B. F. *Beyond Freedom and Dignity*. New York: Alfred A. Knopf, 1971.

———. "B. F. Skinner: An Autobiography." In *A History of Psychology in Autobiography*, vol. 5, edited by E. G. Boring and G. Lindzey, 387–413. New York: Appleton Century-Crofts, 1967.

Smith, Sir William. *Smaller Classical Dictionary*. Revised by E. H. Blakeney and John Warrington. New York: E. P. Dutton, 1958.

"Snoopy," "Woodstock," "Charlie Brown." Official *Peanuts* website, www.unitedmedia.com/comics/peanuts/.

Southern, Terry. "Notes from the War Room." *Grand Street*, 49. Reprinted on the Kubrick site, www.visual-memory.co.uk/amk/doc/0081.html.

Sperb, Jason. *The Kubrick Façade: Faces and Voices in the Films of Stanley Kubrick.* Lanham, Md.: Scarecrow Press, 2006.

Spielberg, Steven. Foreword to *Stanley Kubrick: A Life in Pictures*, by Christiane Kubrick, 9–10. Boston, New York, London: Little, Brown, 2002.

———. "Remembering . . . Stanley Kubrick . . . Spielberg on Kubrick." Interview by Paul Joyce, July 22, 1999. Special Features, *Eyes Wide Shut*. DVD. Directed by Stanley Kubrick, 1999. Burbank, Calif.: Warner Brothers Home Video, 2001.

Stanislavski, Constantin. *An Actor Prepares.* Translated by Elizabeth Reynolds Hapgood. New York: Theater Arts Books, Robert M. MacGregor, 1952.

Stanley Kubrick: A Life in Pictures. DVD. Directed by Jan Harlan. Burbank, Calif.: Warner Bros. Home Video, 2001.

Strick, Joseph, director, producer, screenwriter. *Interviews with My Lai Veterans.* Los Angeles: Laser Film Corporation, 1970.

Strick, Philip, and Penelope Houston. "Modern Times: An Interview with Stanley Kubrick." *Sight & Sound*, Spring 1972. Reprinted in *Stanley Kubrick: Interviews*, edited by Gene D. Phillips, 126–139. Jackson: University Press of Mississippi, 2001.

Swift, Jonathan. *Gulliver's Travels.* 1726. www.jaffebros.com/lee/gulliver/.

"The Tempestuous Ludwig van Beethoven." BBC website, www.bbc.co.uk/music/classicaltv/eroica/beethoven/napoleon.shtml.

Thackeray, William Makepeace. *The Luck of Barry Lyndon.* Edited by Martin Anisman. 1844. Reprint, New York: New York University Press, 1970.

Tripathi, Salil. "Enraged by Madonna and Nicole." *New Statesman*, September 20, 1999.

Twain, Mark. "The Mysterious Stranger." In *Great Short Works of Mark Twain*, edited by Justin Kaplan, 278–366. 1916. Reprint, New York: Harper & Row, 1967.

2001: A Space Odyssey. DVD. Directed by Stanley Kubrick, 1968. Burbank, Calif.: Warner Bros. Home Video, 2001.

Vogel, John. "Plot Summary for the *Phil Silvers Show* (1955)." Internet Movie Database, www.imdb.com/title/tt0047763/plotsummary.

Vooris, Ryan. "Stanley Kubrick's Napoleon." Film Jerk, www.filmjerk.com/nuke/article116.html.

Wainright, Loudon. "The View from Here: The Strange Case of *Strangelove*." *Life*, March 13, 1964, 15.

Walker, Alexander, Sybil Taylor, and Ulrich Ruchti. *Stanley Kubrick, Director: A Visual Analysis.* New York: W. W. Norton, 1999.

Walker, Mort. "Beetle Bailey." King Features website, About the Characters, www.kingfeatures.com/features/comics/bbailey/about.htm.

Warren, Peter. "I Flinch at Those Stories about Crazy Stanley." *Sunday Express*, July 11, 1999.

Weiss, Peter. *Marat/Sade, or The Persecution and Assassination of Jean-Paul Marat as Performed by the Inmates of the Asylum at Charenton under the Direction of the Marquis de Sade*. Translated by Geoffrey Skelton. Verse adaptation by Adrian Mitchell. New York: Atheneum, 1966.

Yosarian, Chester A. "The United States Army's Green Berets: History Re-evaluated, Corrected, and Respected." 1996. earthllink.net/~ amerwar/.

Young, Colin. "The Hollywood War of Independence." *Film Quarterly* 12, no. 3 (Spring 1959): 4–15. Reprinted in *Stanley Kubrick: Interviews*, edited by Gene D. Phillips, 3–8. Jackson: University Press of Mississippi.

Youngblood, Gene. *Expanded Cinema*. New York: Dutton, 1970.

Zimmer, Gene. "B. F. Skinner, Behavioral Psychologist." www.sntp.net/education/leipzig_connection.htm.

Zimmer, Heinrich. *Myths and Symbols in Indian Art and Civilization*. Edited by Joseph Campbell. Princeton, N.J.: Princeton University Press, 1972.

Zimmerman, Paul D. "Kubrick Tells What Makes *Clockwork Orange* Tick." *Newsweek*, April 1, 1972.

~

Index

~

About the Author

Julian Rice has published essays on Ingmar Bergman, Bernardo Bertolucci, and Martin Scorsese, in addition to major work in Native American literature, including *Black Elk's Story* (1991), *Deer Women and Elk Men* (1992), and *Before the Great Spirit* (1998). Now retired after twenty-five years at Florida Atlantic University, Rice devotes his writing exclusively to film.